Roderick Grierson is a Fellow of the W. E. B. Du Bois Institute for Afro-American Research at Harvard University, and Stuart Munro-Hay has recently been appointed Visiting Professor at the University of Berlin. They first worked together on the exhibition *African Zion*, whose catalogue was published by Yale University Press in 1993. During the course of research for a wide range of publications, they have lived and travelled extensively in Africa and the Middle East. They are both contributors to the *Encarta Africana* and *Encyclopaedia Aethiopica*.

Stuart Munro-Hay has recently prepared a comprehensive guide to historical sites in Ethiopia, while Roderick Grierson has written a biography of Sir Ernest Wallis Budge, the Keeper of Egyptian and Assyrian Antiquities at the British Museum, who translated dozens of Ethiopic books, including *The Glory of Kings*.

The Ark of the Covenant

RODERICK GRIERSON AND
STUART MUNRO-HAY

PHŒNIX

For David Godwin

A PHOENIX PAPERBACK

First published in Great Britain
by Weidenfeld & Nicolson in 1999
This paperback edition published in 2000
by Phoenix,
an imprint of Orion Books Ltd,
Orion House, 5 Upper St Martin's Lane,
London WC2H 9EA

A CIP catalogue record for this book
is available from the British Library.

ISBN: 0 75381 010 7

Printed and bound in Great Britain by
Clays Ltd, St Ives plc

And I shall walk in the paths
of the Ark of the Covenant,
Until I taste the dust of its hiding place,
which is sweeter than honey.
— Yehudah Ben Samuel Halevi
(c. 1075–1141)

Arks now we look for none,
nor signs to part
Egypt from Israel;
all now rests in the heart.
— Sir Fulke Greville
(1554–1628)

Contents

List of Illustrations

LIST OF ILLUSTRATIONS

The Temple Mount in Jerusalem, fifteenth-century woodcut (*British Library*)

View of Jerusalem by David Roberts (*AKG London*)

The Dome of the Rock (*Weidenfeld Archives*)

The interior of the Dome of the Rock (*AKG London/Erich Lessing*)

The Ascent of the Prophet Muhammad (*British Library*)

Muhammad replacing the Black Stone in the Kaba (*Edinburgh University Library*)

The Black Stone (*Rex Features/Kazuyoshi Nomachi*)

Pilgrims in procession around the Kaba (*Rex Features/Kazuyoshi Nomachi*)

Between pages 228 and 229

The bedouin 'Ark of Ishmael' (*Roderick Grierson*)

The *mahmal* (*Middle East Centre, St Anthony's College, Oxford*)

The 'Ark of Ishmael' leading the Ruwala through the desert (*Roderick Grierson*)

Aksumite gold coins (*Bent Juel-Jensen*)

Title page of *Prester John of the Indies* (*Bent Juel-Jensen*)

The Church of St George at Lalibela (*Pamela Taor*)

Moses receiving the Ark of Zion in the form of a *tabot* (*Staatsbibliothek, Berlin*)

The Virgin Mary beside the Temple in Jerusalem (*British Library*)

The Covenant of Mercy (*British Library*)

Moses receiving the Tablet of the Law (*British Library*)

David enters Jerusalem with the Ark carried on the head of a priest (*Staatsbibliothek, Berlin*)

Engraving of a *tabot* (*Stuart Munro-Hay*)

Engraving of the Ethiopian emperor Yohannes IV (*Stuart Munro-Hay*)

The round church of Entoto Maryam above Addis Ababa (*Paul B. Henze*)

The modern Chapel of the Tablet at Aksum (*Paul B. Henze*)

Priests in procession at *Timqat* (*Thomas Pakenham*)

Dabtaras dancing at *Timqat* (*Thomas Pakenham*)

Palestine

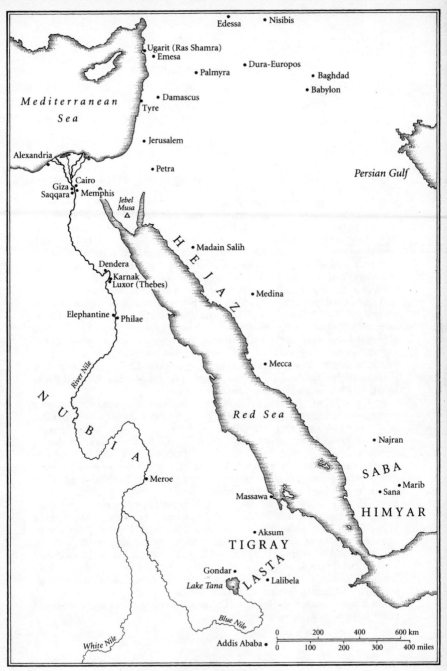

Egypt, Ethiopia and Arabia

Acknowledgements

The great historian Bernard Lewis has recently described his debt to the skill and patience of his editor at Weidenfeld & Nicolson, Benjamin Buchan. The authors of the present volume would like to express a similar gratitude for his sound judgement throughout the various stages of publication, especially for his suggestion that many readers would find a Selected Bibliography more helpful than a mass of annotation to primary or secondary literature. The history of the Ark extends across so many centuries that most specialists will find themselves carried beyond their usual studies at some point, and the story is so extraordinary that we have been encouraged to think of readers without a specialist knowledge who will find it intriguing.

A number of more senior scholars have provided advice or encouragement to one or both of us during the years in which the book was written, especially William McKane, who is now Emeritus Professor of Hebrew and Oriental Languages at the University of St Andrews. Among *ethiopisants*, we are particularly grateful for conversations, correspondence or publications sent to us by Sevir Chernetsov, Stanislaw Chojnacki, Getatchew Haile, Marilyn Heldman, Manfred Kropp, Harold Marcus, Richard Pankhurst, Kay Kaufman Shelemay and Siegbert Uhlig.

At Oxford, Bent Juel-Jenson generously allowed us to consult a number of important manuscripts and early printed books, as well as providing illustrations. We are also grateful that we have been able to include photographs by Paul Henze and Pamela Taor. W.L.G. Randles offered valuable advice on early Portuguese accounts of Ethiopia, and G.S.P. Freeman-Grenville on the history of Jerusalem. At Harvard, Henry Louis Gates Jr, and Karen Dalton took a special interest in the book. Irfan Shahid and T.H. Norris made helpful suggestions about the early history of Arabia. From Sana, Tim Mackintosh-Smith allowed us to benefit from his wide knowledge of Arab historians and local traditions. Throughout the preparation of the book, invaluable assistance was provided by Jerry Begner, John Davis, Carolyn Grierson and Michael Wilson-Smith. We are also indebted to the librarians and curators at the Bodleian Library, British Library, Cambridge University Library, London Library, and the School of Oriental and African Studies, especially to Vrej Nersessian, who has served the Ethiopian collection at the British Library with such dedication.

We have dedicated the book to David Godwin, without whom it could never have been written.

CHAPTER I

The Seventh Seal

In the sixth month of the Year of Creation 7191, the emperor Iyasu rode through the hills of northern Abyssinia toward the holy city of Aksum. Honoured as 'the royal throne of the kings of Zion, the mother of all lands, pride of the entire universe, and jewel of kings', the city was so ancient that no one could remember how or when it had been built. Its priests looked on the great obelisks near the Bath of the Queen of Sheba with suspicion, and thought that demons might have raised them by some sort of magic. Its enemies refused to believe a story that the Lord of the Horns, Alexander the Great, could have laid the first stone, and claimed that Aksum was a mystery to which only God knew the answer. But the emperor and his people were convinced that the city preserved the most sacred relic of the days in which God had brought the Children of Israel into the Promised Land, and it was this that Iyasu was coming to see.

The royal chronicle tells us that the emperor arrived at Aksum on the morning of the first Sunday in the month. The priests and deacons all came to greet him, singing hymns and psalms. With his entourage to accompany him, he rode his horse to the gate of the great church, known as the Gate of the Ark of Zion. Passing through the gate, he entered the sanctuary of the Ark, and there he kissed the Ark and sat on the throne according to the custom of his ancestors. He was arrayed, the chronicle tells us, in robes of a mysterious colour, subtle and delightful to the eye, the glorious vestments that his forefather King David had worn when he led the Ark of Zion to Jerusalem from the house of Obededom.

While Iyasu sat on the throne, the priests brought in the manuscripts that described the achievements of kings and queens who had ruled before him, and they read to him until it was time for them to celebrate the divine liturgy. The emperor then entered the

Holy of Holies, where he received the sacraments of the body and blood of Christ from the priests, and retired to his private chambers for the night.

The devotion that Iyasu displays toward the object that the chronicler calls 'the Ark of Zion', however fervent it may be, cannot prepare the reader for the events of the following morning. The emperor enters the sanctuary for a second time and commands the priests who carry the Ark of Zion to bring it to him. They obey, but the Ark is locked in a chest, and each of its seven seals can be opened only with its own key and in its own way. The keys are brought, and as the priests begin the task of unlocking each of the seals with the key made for it, they start with the first, and the chronicle describes how they open in turn the second, the third, the fourth, the fifth and the sixth. When they come to the seventh, however, they struggle, but in vain. The seal cannot be opened.

There seems to be nothing they can do, and so they bring the chest to the emperor with the seventh seal still in place. When they stand before him, the seal opens by itself. Everyone who sees it unlocked is astonished, and the chronicle insists that the miracle has occurred through the will of the God of the Ark of Zion, who resides above the Ark, because He knows that the emperor is pure in spirit and devoted to the Orthodox faith. As God Himself said in the Holy Scripture: 'If you have faith as a grain of mustard seed, you will say to this mountain, "Raise yourself", and it will raise itself, and if you say to this sycamore tree, "Uproot yourself, and plant yourself in the sea", it will happen just as you have said.'

The God of the Ark of Zion therefore allows the king to live, even though he looks at the Ark and speaks to it directly, as the scribe Esdras had once looked at it and spoken to it. The Ark even speaks to Iyasu in return, offering advice and granting him wisdom and wise counsel, teaching him how to govern the earth and inherit the celestial world of eternal life. Iyasu then places his soul and his body in the care of the Ark, that it might keep him from any evil, and he bids it farewell.

At the main door of the church, the emperor confirms the ancient privileges of the Ark and restores to it all the lands that have been stolen from it. After dispensing justice among the people of the region, he then spends three days hunting elephants.

Even by the exotic standards of the Christian Orient, the events seem astonishing. The chronicler refers to King David bringing the Ark of Zion from the house of Obededom, an event recorded in the Second Book of Samuel, so it is clearly the Ark of the Covenant that he described as talking to an Ethiopian emperor and owning property in his empire. Yet, however fanciful the encounter between Iyasu and the Ark may appear, the chronicler reports that something similar occurred two years later. In the sixth month of 7193, the emperor again made his way toward Aksum, for his coronation. Riding in full ceremony, he entered the city and approached the sanctuary of the Ark with the head of the church and the head of the great monastery of Debra Libanos, 'the Mountain of Lebanon'. There he was received by all the priests of the city and by the Daughters of Zion, with drums and harps, as royal custom decreed, with flutes, shouts of joy and the singing of hymns. The emperor spent the entire day within the sanctuary, talking to the priests about the Ark, which the chronicle assures us had passed through the centuries from the time of his ancestor Ebna Hakim, the son of King Solomon and the Queen of Sheba, until his own reign.

As if these two encounters with the Ark were not sufficiently fantastic, the chronicle reports that in the fifth month of the following year, the emperor consecrated another Ark for the Church of the Holy Trinity. Mounted on a horse and carrying a long spear, he follows this Ark to the church, accompanied by all the dignitaries and elders, the clergy, the head of the church and the abbot of Debra Libanos, with the sound of flutes, drums, jubilation, psalms and hymns. When they arrive at the entrance to the church, the emperor dismounts and carries the Ark on his head into the church. The author of the chronicle was there to witness the procession, and he records the words that he sang himself to glorify the Ark – a song based on the king sharing the name Iyasu not only with Jesus, but also with Joshua, the servant of Moses.

> When Joshua received you, O Ark of the Covenant, from the
>   hands of Moses,
> To bring the people of Sem into the land of Canaan, the
>   heritage of Sem,
> He left with you from Seir,

and the sea withdrew before your majesty when it saw you,
The mountains leapt like lambs before you,
O glorious Ark!
Because my time is short and my days are few,
How could I wait before I spoke of your glory? And what
   could I say?
Does the vintage not reach the harvest?
O Ark of the Law of God, O Ark of the Law of God,
In your days, days of peace and of love,
O Ark of the Law of God, O Ark of the Law of God!

These events are described in a historical chronicle, in the midst of detailed accounts of the battles and administrative burdens faced by the emperor during his reign. They have not been taken from an apocalypse or a mystical treatise, and there is no indication that the emperor had seen a vision or been carried into some sort of ecstasy. The chronicler seems to intend his words to be read as statements of fact. And yet the reign of Iyasu the Great did not occur in a past so remote that we might expect to find its records incomprehensible. The Year of Creation 7191, as it was reckoned in Ethiopia, is AD 1691, and while Iyasu spoke to the Ark, Louis XIV ruled France and its colonies from Versailles. Peter the Great had been crowned in Moscow the year before, and William of Orange had just ensured that Protestants would sit on the throne of the United Kingdom by defeating James II at the Battle of the Boyne. In London, the Royal Society had received its charter almost thirty years earlier, and Isaac Newton had already published the *Principia Mathematica*, on whose foundation modern dynamics and mechanics would be based. Even in New England, where religious dissenters had been seeking refuge from the demands of an established Anglican Church, Harvard University was over fifty years old.

Iyasu did not live in isolation from the rise of the modern world in Europe and its possessions. He is known to have exchanged letters with Louis XIV and to have been treated by the French physician Charles Jacques Poncet. But if he belonged himself to a modern world, why would his chronicler describe him as talking to an object that most Christians and Jews believed had vanished from the Temple in Jerusalem over 2,000 years before, and how could he be involved in making another? Not only does he talk to the Ark, but the Ark talks to him in return, and the chronicler is careful to emphasize that the emperor escapes death in its presence only by the purity of his Orthodox faith. The Ark was obviously an object that he believed to be both real and dangerous.

To anyone who is not familiar with Ethiopia, the story is likely to seem very odd, as well as simply impossible: that a miraculous Ark of the Covenant should be preserved in Africa by Christian kings who claimed descent from ancient Israelites, and whose priests possessed the power to copy it in accordance with a Christian rather than a Jewish ritual. But to Ethiopians, or to those who know something about Ethiopia, it may not seem as extraordinary as perhaps it should. The story of the Ark of Zion has been regarded as the national epic of Ethiopia, but there is a great deal about their devotion to the Ark that remains mysterious even to Ethiopians. Those of us who live in Europe or the Americas have often forgotten how intensely our own societies have been fascinated by the Ark of the Covenant, and by the Temple that the Bible tells us King Solomon built for it in Jerusalem almost 3,000 years ago. While Iyasu spoke to the Ark, the architects of Louis XIV were designing a new chapel at Versailles, and their model seems to have been the Temple itself.

Today, from the hill of Mai Qoho one can look out over Aksum, past the field of stelae erected by pagan kings before Ezana placed the Cross of Christ on his coins in the fourth century AD. In the hours after dawn, the smoke of kitchen fires begins to rise over the city, while small boys with flocks of goats set out for pasture or for market. Camels and donkeys ignore the horns of passing lorries, and as the dust settles behind them, one can hear the gossip and laughter of girls in white shamas who walk along the road that leads past the cathedral and the sanctuary of the Ark. In the midst of the noise of the life of men and women, of children and animals, almost hidden by branches of eucalyptus growing beside the cathedral of Mary of Zion, which Iyasu would have known when he was emperor, the sanctuary preserves the symbol of an eternity that has watched generations rise and fall.

Every year, the arrival of the Ark of Zion is still celebrated at Aksum in the month of Hedar, and the great festival is commemorated in each of the other twelve months of the Ethiopian calendar. Priests and deacons chant hymns and psalms, as they did when they greeted Iyasu, and when they walked with him to Debra Berhan. Foreign Christians who have seen the rituals have remarked on feeling as if they had entered the pages of the Old Testament. Jewish visitors have written that they felt as if they were seeing a lost world, vanished in centuries of persecution – an impression that has seemed all the more poignant in the years following the slaughter of so many Jews in Europe. Each seems to have felt as if they stood in the presence of an Ethiopian faith that allowed them to recover a fellowship that existed before Paul of Tarsus took the Gospel to the Gentiles, which many Jews and many Christians regret as the opening of a wound that is yet to heal. As a distinguished rabbi and professor at the Hebrew Union College wrote some thirty years ago:

> A Jew named Saul,
> Later called Paul,
> Came and spoiled it all.

The joy and the excitement at seeing the hallowed rituals of Aksum conceal a bitter irony. Here, where Jews and Christians might imagine themselves to be most united in their shared inheritance, the division between them is even more marked. The story of the Ark is not just a revelation of a higher wisdom or a greater love, a vision of the healing presence of God; it is a history of conquest and defeat, of power on earth, of desperate struggles to occupy land on which to live, and to control the holy places where God once spoke to men, and might do so again. It is a saga of kingship and power, of the right to proclaim authority in the image of God. Even Iyasu I, who spoke to the Ark in the sanctuary at Aksum, was murdered for his throne, and by his own son. Across thousands of years, there has been argument, suspicion and hatred between those who would claim for themselves or for their people the legacy of the covenant that God made with Abraham – the heritage and the title of True Israel.

This seems to have been in the nature of the Ark even at the beginning. The ancient Hebrew scriptures record blood as well as mystery – a mystery of blood, in fact. From the Bible we learn that the great danger of the Ark was that it could bring death as well as life. The same was true in Ethiopia, whose greatest emperors set out to conquer and rule in the name of Solomon and the kings of Israel, struggling to maintain the purity of their faith against enemies who threatened their borders, and rivals who kept an older devotion to the spirits of nature, or opposed the ambitions of the throne by proclaiming their own visions of Israel.

To begin to understand the mystery enacted at Aksum, during the reign of Iyasu and even today, we must return to the origin of the Ark of the Covenant. This is not a simple matter. In both the Ethiopian and the biblical accounts, the Ark appears from beyond the horizon of history. In the Bible, we are told that it was revealed in earlier days, when God appeared among men in quite a different way. Even the great prophets of Judah never saw God as Moses had seen him, and the Ark is already an ancient and mysterious relic by the time the biblical account of it was written. In Arabia, the Ark appears in tales from the Days of Ignorance, while in Ethiopia its arrival is part of an epic in which the Queen of Sheba conceives a child by King Solomon. After their son has become a young man, the Ark accompanies him of its own will back to Africa – an adventure belonging to a primal and mythic age that almost never touches the Ethiopian history we know from other records. It appears not only from long ago, but from far away as well. It reaches the Promised Land after wandering in the wilderness for forty years, a shrine from an old nomadic life brought to the holy city of Jerusalem, and it crosses deserts and seas to reach Mecca and Aksum.

The story that we read in the Hebrew Bible was meant to be inspiring; it is tantalizing as well. We have inherited a text that was given its final form centuries after the events it describes, and it seems to proclaim a religion in which there is only one God, one true place of worship and one Ark. Duplication would shatter the unity of God, it seems. It would mean idolatry and wickedness. Yet there are traces of earlier cults that contradict this simple clarity. There seem to be rivals to the Ark, or alternatives to it. There are different descriptions of the Ark and its behaviour, and there are suggestions that there may have been several of them.

7

There even seem to be doubts about the authenticity of the Tablets of the Law that Moses placed in the Ark.

At its creation, the Ark and the Law it contained are presented as a complete break with Egyptian idolatry, its worship of animal gods and its cult of the dead. Israel is holy and pure, while the polluted religion of Egypt is an obscenity. The Ark is a proof that Israel is a Chosen People, and it records a covenant with God enforced by sacrifice and execution. But the story in the Bible and the testimony of the later Jewish scholars who struggled to understand it may be more ambiguous and more surprising. They seem to stray into areas that a strict reading would see as pagan, and the Ark itself may be part of this. Throughout the story, we find a tension between the history in which the God of Israel brings his people out of Egypt and into the Promised Land, and a more cosmic vision of the pattern of the seasons, of water and fertility, in which the older gods do not seem to have been forgotten. Should we see these as contradicting each other, and try to choose between them? Or does the presence of both in the final version of the Bible mean that we should see them as somehow true at the same time?

The Ethiopian epic that describes the arrival of the Ark has also been recited as a narrow and exclusive covenant, but we shall see that there may be other ways to read this story as well. It may simply proclaim the right of one people to rule over others, but it could also be an inspiring tale in which hostility and mistrust are overcome, and in which blacks and whites unite to produce a new people on whom God looks with special favour.

The Ethiopian traditions resemble the Bible in their mystery, their ambiguity and their contradictions. We shall see that they too speak of more than one Ark, and of rivals or alternatives to it. As in the Bible, there is often silence when we would expect the Ark to appear in the chronicles of the Ethiopian kings. Sometimes, it seems to have been forgotten, or perhaps to have been lost, and yet across the centuries of Ethiopian history its importance would also be difficult to exaggerate.

Symbols of the Ark still stand in churches and synagogues throughout the world, especially the altars on which the Christian sacraments are consecrated and the Holy Arks that contain the scrolls of the Torah. But even outside these sacred places, we remain fascinated by the memory of the Ark and the possibility that it survived. In recent years, the fascination seems to have become even more widespread and intense. The script for the film *Raiders of the Lost Ark* imagined a race between a Harvard archaeologist and a Nazi expedition to discover the Ark in Egypt, and it attracted immense audiences with a story that drew heavily on ancient mythology. The book that Graham Hancock wrote about the Ark in Ethiopia sold in huge numbers and became the basis of a series of highly successful descriptions of lost ancient wisdom. Websites on the Internet are filled with accounts of excavations at Qumran or even on the Temple Mount, where enthusiasts have claimed to locate the Ark itself or the vessels that were buried with it. At least one of them has been described as the model for Indiana Jones, the hero of the script that George Lucas wrote for *Raiders of the Lost Ark*, while others have begun to be photographed in the sort of leather jacket and brimmed hat that Harrison Ford wore for the role. As in the ancient texts, myth and history often appear to be part of the same story.

In our own attempt to follow the history of the Ark, we shall look at the ancient sources from which the biblical narrative seems to have been drawn, and at the different accounts of the Ark that have been preserved alongside each other. The Bible describes how the Ark led the people of Israel into the Promised Land, and how David found it after years of neglect and brought it to Jerusalem. When Solomon built a Temple for it, it became part of a royal cult in which the house of David ruled as anointed kings in the holy city of Zion, but were denounced by the prophets for their belief that it guaranteed the presence of God. As the armies of Babylon destroyed the Temple, the Ark seems to have disappeared, leaving the following generations to wonder if it had been captured, or destroyed, or carried to safety. Arab historians even reported that it was brought to Arabia, and sacred stones that mark the covenant between God and man are still venerated in Mecca. We shall read the ancient accounts of a crusade led to Arabia by the Christian king of Ethiopia before the birth of the Prophet Muhammad, and ask if the Ethiopian epic of the Ark could have been written in the years that followed his victory. We shall examine the first reports of the Ark in Ethiopia during the Middle Ages, and the rise of a royal house that claimed descent from King Solomon and installed a cult of the Ark as the Virgin Mary. Along with the earliest accounts of the Ark by European travellers, we shall hear traditions preserved at Aksum today and compare them with the fascination that the Ark and the Temple have aroused in the West.

This is not only a search for what happened to the Ark, but a search for what can be believed about it. Robert Runcie, who was Archbishop of Canterbury for many years, recently remarked that the truth is not the same as the absence of ambiguity. With the Ark, the truth seems to lie precisely in ambiguity. The Ark crosses the boundary between myth and history, the desert and the city, Israel and Canaan, life and death, heaven and earth. This is not only the mystery of the Ark, but the reason for its creation. It can exist in two worlds at the same time.

What are we hoping to find as we begin to search for it? What should it look like, and why should it matter? In even the most austere accounts of it, the Ark is the moral heart of the universe, containing the Law given by God. In more mystical or cosmic visions of it, the Ark is the navel of the earth, a microcosm or universe in miniature. It is a door to a higher world, an assurance of the presence of the divine. It is the mandate of heaven, granting kings the power to rule as if they were sons of God. Even its dimensions were thought to reveal the secrets of creation and the end of time. After it disappeared, at least five different explanations were offered: the Ark had become irrelevant so that its loss meant nothing; it was hidden in the earth and would be recovered; it survived in a heavenly Jerusalem; it had been transformed into a chariot of fire; it was preserved in a New Israel. We shall consider all of these. But as we have begun in Ethiopia, we shall consider especially the last.

The Bible has been studied continuously for thousands of years. Almost every possible interpretation of each verse seems to have been explored, and reasonable but quite contradictory statements can be based on them. It may seem ironic, but the more the biblical account of the Ark is exposed to critical inquiry, the less extravagant the Ethiopian claim begins to seem. The contrast is not simply between biblical history and outlandish African legend. The Ethiopian version is not only intelligible; it may also be credible.

CHAPTER 2

The Mountain of God

The greatest king of the ancient world, the Bible tells us, had been humiliated by a god he did not know and whose ways he could not understand. In Egypt, the pharaoh ruled like a god himself, and he had forbidden the Children of Israel to leave the land in which they worked for him in bondage. But a series of plagues had broken his will, and the prophet Moses led the Israelites across the Red Sea. The waters parted to let them pass, and then overwhelmed the chariots that the pharaoh sent in pursuit. Now Moses and the people who followed him were making their way across the wilderness, guided by a pillar of fire and cloud and fed by manna from heaven. Despite the signs and miracles that accompanied them, the people were discouraged, convinced that Moses had led them out of Egypt only to die.

On the third new moon after their escape from slavery, they came into the wilderness of Sinai and made their camp before a mountain. The voice of God, which had spoken to Moses for so many years, now spoke again, announcing a covenant with a people he had chosen for himself.

> You have seen what I did to the Egyptians, and how I brought you to myself on the wings of eagles. Now therefore, if you obey my voice and keep my covenant, you will be my own possession among all peoples; for all the earth is mine. You will be to me a kingdom of priests, a holy nation.

When Moses repeated these words to the Israelites, they agreed that they would obey whatever commandments God might have for them. God then told Moses to purify the people and wait for three days. If they approached the mountain before this time had passed, they would die. Finally, on the morning of the third day, a trumpet blew with such force that the people were terrified. It was time for Moses to lead them out of the camp and introduce them to their God.

As they walked toward the mountain of Sinai, the people could not actually see it. God had descended upon it in fire and covered it in smoke. When Moses spoke to him, God answered in a peal of thunder and summoned the prophet to the top of the mountain. There God told him to consecrate the mountain itself and to forbid the people to approach any closer, otherwise a divine power would be unleashed against them. God then spoke directly to the people of Israel. 'I am the Lord your God,' he told them, 'who brought you out of the land of Egypt, out of the house of bondage.' Now that he had delivered them, he offered the terms of his covenant – the Ten Commandments that they would need to obey as a holy nation consecrated to the one true God.

After Moses had built an altar and offered sacrifices, God spoke to him again, commanding him to climb the mountain to receive tablets of stone on which the Law and the commandments had been written. Moses did so, and the Bible tells us that as the glory of God settled on the mountain, a cloud covered it for six days. On the seventh day, God spoke to Moses from within the cloud. The people who were standing beneath the mountain could see a fire raging on the summit, but Moses entered the cloud and remained there for forty days and forty nights.

In the conversation that God held with Moses on the mountain, he issued precise and detailed instructions in which he explained how the people of Israel were to construct an extraordinary object: a box or chest, which we know in English as an 'ark', after the Latin *arca*.

They shall make an ark of acacia wood; two cubits and a half shall be its length, a cubit and a half its breadth, and a cubit and a half its height. And you shall overlay it with pure gold, within and without you shall overlay it, and you shall make upon it a moulding of gold round about. And you shall cast four rings of gold for it and put them on its four feet, two rings on the one side of it, and two rings on the other side of it. You shall make poles of acacia wood, and overlay them with gold. And you shall put the poles into the rings on the sides of the ark, to carry the ark by them. The poles shall remain in the rings of the ark; they shall not be taken from it. And you shall put into the ark the testimony which I shall give you. Then you shall make a cover of pure gold; two cubits and a half shall be its length, and a cubit and a half its breadth. And you shall make two cherubim of gold; of hammered gold shall you make them, on the two ends of the cover. Make one cherub on the one end, and one cherub on the other end; of one piece with the cover shall you make the cherubim on its two ends. The cherubim shall spread out their wings above, over-shadowing the cover with their wings, their faces to one another; toward the cover shall the faces of the cherubim be. And you shall put the cover on the top of the ark; and in the ark you shall put the testimony that I shall give you. There I will meet with you, and from above the cover, from between the two cherubim that are upon the ark of the testimony, I will speak with you of all that I will give you in commandment for the people of Israel.

As a holy mountain on which God revealed his commandments to Moses, where the religion of the Israelites and their role as the Chosen People of God began, Sinai was obviously a place of immense importance. Yet there is no history of Jewish devotion to the site. It was never a goal of pilgrimage, and the Bible contains no indication that it was ever part of Israelite cult. The fire and cloud from which God appears on Sinai remain the signs of his presence, but the mountain itself survives as little more than a memory of the wanderings in the wilderness. When God chooses a holy mountain, it is Zion rather than Sinai. It is Zion that he will defend, and it is to Zion that the peoples of the world will gather, and from which blessings will flow. The Bible does not really tell us where the mountain can be found, and although Christians begin to venerate the Jebel Musa, the Mountain of Moses, they seem to do this only in the fourth century.

Moses would already have been an old man when he climbed to the top of the mountain, and anyone who has tried to follow his path along the 3,000 'Steps of Repentance' carved in the rock of the Jebel Musa will be astonished at his strength. It still takes three hours for someone half the age the prophet would have been, and there were no steps in the rock until the monks built them.

For centuries, Christian pilgrims have been coming to the moun-tain in the hope of learning something of the miraculous way in which God spoke to man. The world they enter is harsh and barren, and it seems unlikely that any of them stood on the summit filled with a reassuring sense of their own place in creation. Sinai is not the easiest place to enjoy a vision of the unity of life, a revelation of its bounty, of the harmony of the seasons or the joy of the harvest. It is a world that seems dead and empty.

Above the rock, the sky is possessed of a brilliant intensity and clarity. Across the Gulf of Aqaba, the coast of Arabia can be seen, and above that, nothing. At dawn and sunset, the heavens seem to be filled with fire, but at other times of the day they can appear as an absolute and impenetrable veil between man and a celestial realm, not only beyond his touch, but even beyond his imagining. If any truth were delivered from this higher world, one imagines, it would not emerge from human hopes or human efforts. It would be a revelation such as Moses received from powers outside his understanding.

The rocks of Sinai do not possess the calm serenity of a distant snow-covered peak such as Ararat, the holy mountain of the Armenians. Here the ancient granite has been ravaged by wind and rain. It has become twisted and lumpen – a world made not for flesh and blood, but for demons, perhaps, for spirits of the wilderness that might have troubled the meditations of the saints who lived among them, summoned along with the shadows that pass across the crevices and fissures at the end of the day.

The Path of Repentance leads through a cleft in the rock towards the summit, from which the pilgrims who came here looked out at the expanse of rock and sky. In earlier centuries, a monk would have waited for them along at the Gates of Confession, to listen to their sins and grant them absolution, allowing them to walk the final steps cleansed of human wickedness and ready to present themselves to God in a humble imitation of the great prophet.

Finding the right mountain might seem simple enough, but the identification does not appear to have been made until the fourth century, when the Christian historian Eusebius of Caesarea wrote that God had appeared to Moses in the southern part of the peninsula. Helena, the mother of the emperor Constantine, decided that a sanctuary should be built to mark the site, and we know that a wealthy nun named Egeria came to Sinai as a pilgrim a few years later. In her account of the journey, she wrote that the Jebel

Musa was believed to be the mountain on which the revelation had occurred. In modern times, at least a dozen different mountains have been proposed. Some are in Sinai, and some in northern Arabia, and if we only knew where the revelation had occurred, we might be able to speak with more confidence of the God to whom the mountain was sacred and the nature of the objects he told his prophet to make. Should we be looking for the Ark among the processional barques of Egypt, the chests of Tammuz, the carts of the Phoenicians or the sacred stones and tent shrines of the Arabs?

Whichever mountain it might have been, the Ark of the Covenant was not the only thing that God told Moses to build. He provided further instructions, in no less detail, for a tent and all the furnishings that would accompany the tent. Moses was to make a table, a lampstand, an altar for incense, a laver and an altar for burnt offerings. He was to provide holy garments for his brother Aaron and the priests, and prepare oil for anointing and incense. God gave him precise regulations about how the Israelites should use each of these holy things, and it is clear from the story in Exodus that they were perilous even to those who were meant to handle them. They were volatile and filled with a power that could be contained only with elaborate precautions.

It took some time to convey such complicated instructions, and after Moses had been on the mountain for forty days and nights, the people began to suspect that he had disappeared. They were keen to follow an inspiring leader, and ready enough in promising to do whatever he said they should do, but the Bible depicts them as easily discouraged, and once again they became frightened that they would be lost in the wilderness. They asked Aaron, the elder brother of Moses, to make images of gods that could lead them to safety, and when Moses returned and saw the people of Israel dancing around the image of a calf, he was horrified. Breaking the Tablets of the Law that God had given to him, he destroyed the idol that the people had been worshipping and called the sons of Levi to him. The Levites declared their loyalty to God, and together they slaughtered about 3,000 of the Israelites. When the killing was finished, Moses announced to the survivors that they had committed an enormous crime in defiance of the commandments that God had given them. He then climbed the mountain of Sinai once again, to see if the wrath of God might be turned aside.

He succeeded. Although God was angry enough to send a plague upon the Israelites, he did not destroy them. Instead, he instructed Moses to fulfil the promise that he had made to the patriarchs Abraham, Isaac and Jacob, by leading their descendants into a land flowing with milk and honey. After another forty days and forty nights spent on the mountain of Sinai, Moses returned with another two tablets of stone, on which the commandments were written. Now, we are told, the Israelites were frightened of him. He had been changed by his encounter with God. The Hebrew text is notoriously difficult to understand, but it seems to speak of horns, or perhaps rays of light. The prophet had become a mysterious figure, no longer like other men, and for the rest of his life he would lead the tribes of Israel through the wilderness with his face hidden by a veil or a mask.

Moses then began the work of collecting gold, silver and bronze, linen and acacia wood, leather, oil, spices and incense, onyx and all the other costly items required to build the Ark and the other ritual objects in accordance with the commandment of God. When the Ark was ready, Moses put the Tablets of the Law inside it. Placing the poles in the rings and the cover on the top, he brought the Ark into the tent that God had told the people of Israel to make. After all the instructions had been obeyed, a cloud covered the tent, and the glory of the Lord filled it. While the people of Israel travelled through the wilderness toward the Promised Land, they marched when the cloud rose from the tent, and remained in camp when it did not. During the day, the cloud was over the tent; and during the night, the Israelites could see that a fire burned within it.

This is the account of the creation of the Ark of the Covenant that most Jews or Christians would recognize. It was a box containing the Tablets on which the hand of God had written the Ten Commandments, and it led the people of Israel into the Promised Land. This is the Ark that Joshua carried seven times around the walls of Jericho, which brought them tumbling down, and the Ark that the sons of Eli carried against the Philistines – a sign of the Presence of God whose capture brought such disaster to its enemies that they sent it back filled with peace offerings. It is the Ark that David brought into his new capital Jerusalem, and the Ark for which his son, Solomon, constructed a magnificent temple.

The power ascribed to this object, which could cause the walls of a city to collapse and afflict its enemies with disease, was immense. It brought death to anyone who touched it outside the ritual revealed to Moses. Although it was the glory of the splendid Temple erected by Solomon, it was hidden from anyone except the high priest. Even the high priest could approach it on only one day of the year, and only if he blinded himself with a cloud of incense to protect himself from its power. After centuries in which almost no one saw it, the Ark seems to have vanished in circumstances about which the Hebrew Bible has almost nothing to say, either before or during the destruction of the Temple by the armies of Babylon. The Temple was built again, but an Ark was never, it seems, placed within the inner sanctuary. Yet outside the Bible, hope remained that the Ark had been saved from the fire as the Temple burned, that it had been carried into the deserts of Arabia, or across the Red Sea to Ethiopia.

The search for the lost Ark of the Covenant is often imagined as a romantic adventure, but it is not so much a quest for hidden treasure as a struggle to understand a book. If the search ever becomes archaeological, it will still depend on the way in which the book is understood. The primary evidence for the Ark is confined to the Hebrew Bible, a text with which we are very familiar, but of which we remain profoundly ignorant. Even after decades of study, most scholars will admit that they feel no closer to answering some of the most fundamental questions about it. Its significance is almost impossible to exaggerate. The entire Christian religion has been described, quite accurately, as a unique interpretation of the Old Testament. And yet, we do not really know who wrote most of it, or when, or why. Although we often forget the fact, the Bible was not written as the Bible. The canon was not fixed until the first century AD, and the collection as we have it represents only a fraction of the literature that must once have been written in classical Hebrew. The Bible itself refers to a number of books that we no longer possess.

Although the first five books of the Bible have traditionally been ascribed to Moses, the voice that speaks to us in them is an anonymous narrator writing in the third person. It is not the voice of Moses, which we might have expected, and it is not the voice of God. Both the prophet and the Lord he serves are presented as characters in the drama and do not speak to us directly.

The people that this voice addresses are Israelites who live in Palestine after the creation of the monarchy, but before the Babylonians destroy the Temple in 587 BC and carry them into Exile. This does not mean that the books were completed before the Exile. Much of the material they contain would have been written before then, but the evidence of the earliest translations and the fragments found among the Dead Sea Scrolls reveals the extent to which the material was still fluid during the first century AD.

The books comprise a history of the world that is both much more ambitious and much more confined than we might expect. It begins as a history of the entire universe, which God creates from nothing, and then limits itself to the history of one man and his family, the patriarch Abraham, who is portrayed as the ancestor of Israel. Even more surprising is the fact that the greater part of the history is devoted to a single incident: the revelation of God to Moses on Mount Sinai. It is during this revelation that the Ark is introduced. When it disappears from the history is much more difficult to say; because in some ways it seems to vanish immediately. Along with the Ark, God reveals the law that the Children of Israel will obey as his Chosen People, but this law contains no mention of the Ark. If it really is meant to be the Presence of God on earth, it is strange that the Ark should not be included as the focus of cultic and communal life for the Chosen People. When the Israelites wander in the wilderness of Sinai and finally begin the Conquest of the Promised Land, the Ark leads them into battle and destroys their enemies with its terrible power. Yet despite its essential role in battle, it is never mentioned in the Deuteronomic laws of war. After Joshua has led the tribes of Israel into the Promised Land, he assembles them at Shechem and recites the history of their journeys from beyond the Euphrates and down into Egypt and back again. He makes them swear a covenant before a great stone as a witness, but he never mentions the Ark, even though he is said to have marched with it around the walls of Jericho. Now, when the entire people of Israel proclaim a covenant, it seems as if the Ark of the Covenant has no role to play.

The Ark seems to have the mysterious quality of being the most important object in the universe, the actual Presence of God living among the Chosen People, and yet remaining hidden or forgotten at precisely the moments when one would expect it to dominate the history of Israel. The passages in the Bible that describe it have been a source of fascination and bewilderment to generations of priests and rabbis, scholars, doctors and professors, who have laboured to understand them. Even in translation, it can be difficult to reconcile what appear to be contradictory statements made about the Ark in the various books of the Bible, and yet when most of us think of the Ark, this is often what we do, conflating several different passages by removing them from quite separate narratives. The most famous account of building the Ark appears in the Second Book of Moses, which we usually call by the Greek name *Exodos*, but there is another version in the Book of Deuteronomy which is quite different. Beyond this, the Hebrew text on which the translations are ultimately based contains words used to describe the Ark, the Tabernacle or the Temple that are obscure or unique, at whose meaning the translators were forced to guess. And even if these problems could be solved, a greater mystery would still remain. Why had the Ark and the Tabernacle been built, and what was their place and their purpose in the history of the universe that God had created? The Bible often tells us far less than we might hope to know, and the attempts to supply the missing pieces by Palestinian rabbis, Arabian antiquarians, Ethiopian chroniclers and dozens of other scholars or mystics are often no less difficult for us to understand. The earliest depictions of the Ark add to the sense of confusion. They often differ from each other, and bear no relation to the descriptions given in the Hebrew Bible. On the walls of the synagogue at Dura in Syria, the Ark was painted as if it were the Holy Ark that contained the scrolls of the Torah in the synagogue, a motif that seems to begin with coins struck in the second century AD during the revolt that Bar Kokhba led against Rome.

One of the earliest attempts to explain the Ark that has survived outside the Bible itself was written in the first century AD by the Jewish philosopher Philo, whose primary concern was not with its fate, but with how it could still be used as a key to mystical enlightenment. Philo had been born into a wealthy and influential family in Alexandria some twenty years before the birth of Christ. His brother is known to have been one of the richest men in the

Roman empire, said to have donated the gold and silver plates that covered the nine gates of the Temple in Jerusalem. Despite the distractions of political responsibility, Philo himself spent most of his life attempting to resolve the differences between Judaism and the Greek philosophy cultivated in the great Egyptian metropolis – a city built by a Greek conqueror whose people included a million Jews. Having adopted a pagan view of salvation, in which the spirit would escape the bonds of the flesh and return to God, he believed that the mission of Judaism would be fulfilled when men could ascend into ever higher participation in the Being of God, radiating from a supreme and inaccessible One.

Philo believed that the Ark of the Covenant was the very essence of everything sacred in the Jewish religion, the abode of the Presence of God. Indeed, it was nothing less than the key to the mystery of creation, and it revealed the secret of how God had made the universe. He was convinced that the God who had spoken to the Hebrew patriarchs was the same as the Absolute of the Greek philosophers, a single and unique Being completely independent of the world. Like the sun, this Being sends out a stream of light that makes created life possible, and the secrets of the emanations that pass between it and the created world could be discovered in the seven parts of the Ark: the Ark itself, the Law that was written on the Tablets of Moses, the mercy seat that covered the Ark, the two cherubim that adorned the mercy seat, the voice that spoke to Moses from the Ark, and the Presence who spoke through the voice.

When Philo attempts to explain the promise that God made to Moses, that he would speak to the prophet 'from above the mercy seat between the cherubim', he writes:

> We must go over these individually, beginning at the top, if we would understand what they symbolize, for they are symbolic. There is the box of the Ark, and the laws treasured within it, and upon it the mercy seat. Upon the mercy seat are the cherubim, as they are called in Chaldean, and above and between is the voice, the Word, and still above this is the One who speaks. Now if any one could really understand the natures of these things, it seems to me that he would be possessed by the most divinely formed beauty and would be able to renounce every other thing that is desired.

Each part of the Ark, Philo believed, should be seen as a mystical symbol. The Presence who spoke to Moses is the highest God, and from him all the lower manifestations of the created world emerge. The Word that Moses heard is the first of these emanations. The seventh and last emanation is the actual box of the Ark, which Philo saw as the Conceptual World. This contained the Platonic forms that provided the patterns for every created object.

Hidden within the innermost sanctuary, the Ark was the true symbol of the nature of God revealed to humanity, and because it displayed the successive emanation of each power, it offered a mystical way to retrace the process and return to God.

> The purest and most prophetic mind receives knowledge and under- standing of Being not from Being Himself, for the mind is not great enough to compass His magnitude, but from His primary and guardian Powers. One must be content with the fact that beams are borne from these into the soul, so that one may be able to perceive the Older and Brighter by means of the secondary illumination.

As well as being a symbol of the nature of Deity, the Ark was also a revelation of the nature of humanity, of its need for salvation. It offered a way by which men and women could escape from matter by rising into an immaterial realm. This way remained open, and although the Ark was believed to have been lost or hidden for centuries by the time that Philo was writing, he still speaks of it as if it were present.

Wherever it might be, the Ark was part of a living mystical process. It was a very demanding sort of mysticism, however, following a stream of light from the immaterial world. For those who were unable to walk along such an arduous path, there was also a Lower Mystery, which was focused on the Tabernacle in which the Ark was placed and which involved the sensible world.

In this 'Mystery of Aaron', as Philo calls it, after the brother of Moses who served as the first high priest, the candidate for mystical enlightenment stands in reverence in the outer court, and faces the Tabernacle. The five outer pillars of the Tabernacle correspond to the five senses and connect the mind with the outer world of matter. Philo again employs an elaborate symbolism. The altar of incense represents the gratitude of the earth. The seven-branched candlestick stands at the south and represents the heavens, specifically the sun, the moon and the five planets. The table stands at the north and symbolizes the nourishing and fertilizing power of the north wind. The inner courts represent the first stage of spiritual progress, at which the material world as a whole is experienced. The altar of incense represents earth and water, the table and its burdens symbolize air, and the candlestick is heavenly fire, the source of light. The curtains also signify the four elements.

When Aaron entered the Tabernacle as high priest, Philo tells us, his priestly regalia was 'a likeness and symbolism of the cosmos'. The robe that Aaron wore symbolized the four elements. It was the colour of hyacinth, to represent air, which is naturally black. On his shoulders were two large emeralds, which Philo describes as the two celestial hemispheres. Six names were engraved on each stone, to symbolize the six signs of the zodiac in each hemisphere. The mantle extended from the symbols of heaven on the shoulders to the border of tassels shaped like pomegranates, flowers and bells. The flowers represented earth, the tassels symbolized water, and the bells were the harmony between them. By wearing these robes, the priest placed himself in harmony with the universe. He became a model of the cosmos, and when he entered the Tabernacle to worship, the entire universe worshipped with him.

In his account of the mystery of Aaron, Philo seems to have brought into the Jewish cult elements from the rites of the Egyptian goddess Isis. Her priests were also dressed in vestments of various colours, displaying the power of the goddess over the material world, over night and day, dark and light, fire and water, life and death, the beginning and the end. While the pagan mysteries might seem to be totally alien by the standards of Jewish orthodoxy, they were evidently not to an Alexandrian Jew like Philo, and similar passages can be found in the Greek Bible itself. The Wisdom of Solomon was written by another Alexandrian Jew in the first century BC, and it describes a high priest who offers prayer and incense. On his robe, the entire world is depicted, and the history of the patriarchs is engraved upon four rows of stones.

Elaborate cosmic visions of the Ark and the Tabernacle appear in other ancient sources, including the Jewish historian Flavius Josephus, who – born some fifty years after Philo – was a priest at the Temple in Jerusalem. He explains the meaning of the cult in terms of the zodiac and the planets, the arch of heaven, the power of thunder and lightning, and the splendour of the sun, all reflected in the elements from which the shrine was constructed. Before long, Christians had begun to add their own elaborate symbolism, describing the Ark as Christ or his mother. They introduced another element as well, finding symbols of Christian virtues in the precious metals and jewels. Gold was faith, while silver was the word of the Gospel, and bronze was patience. Throughout the Middle Ages, the Ark was seen as containing mystical signs of the humility, the suffering and the glory of Christ, while the colours in the Tabernacle signified hope and the love of heaven.

From an early period, there was also a keen interest in the exact details of the Ark and the Tabernacle, how the corners were constructed, how the bars were arranged, and what the shape of the sockets might be. Even Christian scholars who were fascinated by allegory and symbolism began to consult the illustrations of Temple vessels provided in Hebrew biblical manuscripts. Although the main purpose of the illustrations had been to preserve a sense of the glory of God in the Temple, in the hope that it might be built again at some point in the future, they also served to arouse an even greater curiosity about the precise nature and depiction of the Tabernacle and its furnishings, including the Ark. The search for the literal meaning of the Hebrew text would not prove easy, however. It is one of the ironies of biblical scholarship that pursuing a simple and less elaborate truth has seemed to make it more difficult to understand the legacy of ancient Israel. Under the harsh light of historical inquiry, the ancient truth may seem to shatter or dissolve. Scholars intent on recovering the plain meaning of the sacred text may find it less than plain after all, and the single Ark of which the Hebrew scriptures seem to speak may originally have been something quite different. If we were looking in Ethiopia for the Ark that we think is described in the Bible, what should we be hoping to find?

CHAPTER 3

Ancestral Voices

The death of Moses was the stumbling block. Following Jewish tradition, the Christian writers of the New Testament referred to the first five books of the Hebrew Bible as 'The Books of Moses'. Yet in Deuteronomy, the last of these five books, the great prophet describes his own death and the weeks of mourning that followed his burial in an unknown grave.

> So Moses the servant of the Lord died there in the land of Moab, according to the word of the Lord, and he buried him in the valley in the land of Moab opposite Beth-peor; but no man knows the place of his burial to this day. Moses was a hundred and twenty years old when he died; his eye was not dim, nor his natural force abated. And the people of Israel wept for Moses in the plains of Moab thirty days; then the days of weeping and mourning for Moses were ended.

It would seem difficult to explain how Moses could have written these words. Nevertheless, Philo and Josephus both believed that he had written the five Books of Moses in their entirety, including the account of his own death and burial. The rabbis who compiled the Talmud were slightly more sceptical, and suggested that the final passage might have been written by Joshua, the servant of Moses who succeeded him as leader of the Israelites.

In the twelfth century, more than a thousand years after Philo and Josephus, the Jewish philosopher Moses Maimonides still retained a traditional view of the Books of Moses, claiming that 'the entire Torah in our hands was given to our master Moses'. In other words, he believed that the books had been dictated by God to the prophet. Despite his confidence, one of the most learned biblical scholars of the Jewish community in Spain, where Maimonides lived, had already noticed that the Book of Genesis contained a curious phrase: 'The Canaanites were then in the land'. Abraham ibn Ezra maintained that these words would not make any sense unless they had been written at a time when the Canaanites were no longer in the land. They must therefore have been written many years after the death of Moses and been added to the text of Genesis.

Critical comment about the biblical text required a certain discretion, and Abraham himself sneered at the court physician Isaac ibn Yashush for making a similar suggestion on the basis of the list of Edomite kings in Genesis. It could also be dangerous. The religious authorities of the day thought it quite reasonable to impose orthodoxy by force. While the occasional critical voice survives from the fourteenth and fifteenth centuries, it was during the Reformation that the pace of scholarship began to accelerate. The German reformer Andreas Carlstadt agreed with the earlier claims that Moses would not have written the account of his own death, but he went on to remark that the style of this passage was no different from those that came before it. The obvious conclusion was that, if one could not have been written by Moses, neither could the others. He was followed by Andreas van Maes, Isaac de la Peyrère and Richard Simon, all of whom had noticed that the text contained repetitions and contradictions, which suggested that a single prophet would not have written it all. Their books were banned, and de la Peyrère, who was a Calvinist, was arrested by Catholic authorities and forced to become Catholic himself. But despite the hostility of religious authorities, it began to become obvious that the easiest solution to the problem would be to postulate a later author or editor who compiled the text using several different sources.

Anyone attempting to understand the Ark of the Covenant will soon encounter discrepancies of the sort that these scholars had observed. In Exodus, the skilled craftsman Bezalel constructs the Ark. He is a man, we are told, who is filled 'with the Spirit of God, with ability and intelligence, with knowledge and all crafts-manship, to devise artistic designs, to work in gold, silver, and bronze, in cutting stones for setting, and in carving wood, for work in every craft'. With a team of assistants beside him, the Ark he constructs is elaborate, covered in gold, decorated with a moulding of gold around it, and equipped with rings cast of gold so that it can be carried. In Deuteronomy, however, Moses himself makes a simple ark of acacia wood. There is no reference to gold or to a decorative moulding, and there is no mention of an elaborate cover with the figures of two winged cherubim. Which of these is the correct description? Why would both be included? Could they both be accurate?

There are even greater difficulties in understanding the account of the making of the Tabernacle in which the Ark was placed. After the notorious incident of the Golden Calf, we read a description of the tent being pitched outside the camp:

> Now Moses used to take the tent and pitch it outside the camp, far off from the camp; and he called it the Tent of Meeting. And every one who sought the Lord would go out to the Tent of Meeting, which was outside the camp. Whenever Moses went to the tent, all the people rose up, and every man stood at his tent door, and looked after Moses, until he had gone into the tent.

At this point, however, the Tabernacle has not actually been made, and it will not be made for another three chapters. Is it possible that there could have been two different tents, one of which was already in existence? Both names seem to be used for the same tent, however, at least in some passages. The sequence of the narrative appears to be confused, as if the story had been assembled on the basis of more than one document.

While it may have seemed to be a dramatic departure from traditional assumptions about the role of Moses, and would certainly have an immense impact on the way we understand the Ark of the Covenant, the suggestion that the biblical narrative was compiled from different documents should not have been surprising. The Bible itself refers to documentary sources that no longer survive. After recounting the life of King Solomon, for example, the First Book of Kings refers to 'The Book of the Acts of Solomon'. It goes on to mention 'The Book of the Acts of the Kings of Israel' and 'The Book of the Acts of the Kings of Judah', which were evidently chronicles of the two states that emerged after Solomon died. Even in the Pentateuch itself, the Book of Numbers refers to 'The Book of the Wars of the Lord', while the Book of Joshua and the Second Book of Samuel both mention

'The Book of the Upright'. It is almost certain that more sources than these were available when the Bible was compiled, even though there is no explicit mention of them now. In the Greek version known as the Septuagint, after the seventy translators who were said to have prepared it at Alexandria two or three centuries before the birth of Christ, the First Book of Kings refers to 'The Book of the Song', a document no longer mentioned in the Hebrew text we possess today. It is obviously impossible to guess how many more of these sources there might have been, and often very difficult to detect which source provided the information recorded in the text.

In the seventeenth century, the philosophers Thomas Hobbes and Baruch Spinoza both emphasized the urgent task of disentangling the parts from which the narrative had been constructed. The suggestion was still thought to be deeply subversive, and Spinoza was condemned by both Catholics and Protestants, having already been excommunicated by the Sephardi Jews of Amsterdam. Nevertheless, a serious attempt was made in 1711 by Henning Witter, who was a pastor at Hildesheim, and again four decades later by Jean Astruc, private physician to Louis XV and professor of medicine at Paris. Both men were intrigued by an observation that will have an obvious impact on the way in which we understand the titles applied to the Ark. Different words for 'God' appear at different places in the Hebrew text: the plural form *elohim*, which English versions usually translate as 'God', and the sacred and ineffable name *YHWH*, which used to be translated as 'the Lord' on the basis of the Hebrew vowels that accompany the four letters, but is now often rendered as 'Yahweh'. The question they asked was whether the choice of name reflected the preference of different sources.

It was this curiosity about the different forms of divine name that led to the theory that is now the basis of most research into the first books of the Bible. It was largely described by Heinrich Ewald at beginning of nineteenth century, although its most famous exponent was his student, Julius Wellhausen. The dating of the sources has been the subject of prolonged debate and is still far from settled. This might seem to be a strong argument against the theory, but its advantage is that it supplies a simple way to explain a large number of contradictions in the text. Ancient and medieval scholars had to explain each of these individually.

The two earliest sources are the 'Jahwist', named after its use of the divine name *YHWH* and believed to be a southern tradition, and the 'Elohist', which preferred *elohim* and was produced in the north. The Elohist is suspicious of the Aaronid priesthood, and keen to support the status of the Levites. Both of these sources seem to have been written before the Assyrian invasion of 722 BC, and the Priestly Code seems to have been written as a reply to them by the Aaronid priests during the time of the reforming king Hezekiah, between 715 and 687 BC. It reflects the interests and concerns of the Aaronid priesthood, and relegates the Levites to clergy of the second rank, who perform tasks such as carrying the Ark of the Covenant. The Deuteronomist seems to have written as a reply to the Aaronid Priestly Code by the priests of Shiloh, during the years that followed the reforming king Josiah and the destruction of Jerusalem by the Babylonians. He not only wrote Deuteronomy, but also produced the six books of the Former Prophets, in which we read of the history of the Ark, the building of the Temple and its destruction by the Babylonians. An alternative version of this history is provided by the two books of Chronicles. Like the Priestly Code, they see the Levites as secondary priests beneath the Aaronids and show a great interest in priestly duties, sacrifices, sacred places and objects.

The details of the documentary theory are still debated, and there has been considerable disagreement over the priority of the Priestly Code and Deuteronomy. There are sound scholars who refuse to have anything to do with the theory, and no less learned and clever scholars who take an even more sceptical view, regarding the entire Bible as a late invention whose authors record almost no reliable information about the history of Israel. As we attempt to understand the story of the Ark in Ethiopia, the important point for us is that we find quite different descriptions, which seem to have been written by authors with quite different interests. In the Bible as it has been transmitted to us, these different accounts all seem to be regarded as true and accurate. This may suggest that the Bible is not the best guide to what we might expect to find in Ethiopia, in terms of either the appearance of the Ark or the way in which it behaves. The biblical descriptions are too different to be helpful. But as we shall see, there is other evidence as well to suggest that more than one Ark existed, and the differences between the descriptions suggest that quite different sorts of object could still be regarded as the real Ark.

Even though we refer by convention to 'the Ark of the Covenant', and the title does appear in the Old Testament on forty occasions, other forms are used more often in the Hebrew text itself. There are over twice as many occurrences of 'Ark' with a divine name, such as 'Ark of God' or 'Ark of the Lord', and while 'Ark of the Covenant' is a favourite of Deuteronomy, it never appears in the Priestly Code, which prefers 'Ark of the Testimony'. The early rabbis, the Fathers of the Christian Church, and medieval commentators of both religions tended to understand the Ark as if the various traditions about it in the Hebrew Bible were all true at the same time and all spoke of a single Ark of the Covenant. Modern scholars, however, have been intrigued by the contrast between three different views of the Ark, which they attribute to three different sources. The question that is not always asked is whether these accounts are supposed to describe the same Ark from three different perspectives, or to provide evidence for three different types of Ark. If one were hoping to discover what the Ethiopian emperor might have seen in the great church at Aksum so many centuries after the events described in the Hebrew Bible, it would be essential to understand as clearly as possible what the biblical authors were trying to tell us.

The Priestly Code offers the most detailed account, and the Priestly Ark is described in more elaborate terms than in the other traditions. This is the version that most Jews or Christians who read the Bible would immediately recognize as the basis of their assumptions about the appearance of the Ark – an elaborate gold object with fantastic decoration. The Ark of the Priestly Code was built not by the prophet Moses, but by a skilled craftsman named Bezalel. As we have seen from the account in the Book of Exodus, this Ark was constructed of acacia wood, overlaid both inside and outside with pure gold, and surrounded by a gold rim. Two poles to carry it were inserted into gold rings on the side of the Ark and were never to be removed. It was provided with an elaborate gold lid, which was called the *kapporet*. Although the origin of the word is obscure, it seems to be related to Akkadian and Arabic words that indicate a way of atoning for sin by covering, and is usually translated in English as 'mercy seat'. Upon this *kapporet* were two golden cherubim, with their wings outspread so that God could be enthroned between them, and it is from between these cherubim that he will speak to Moses.

In Deuteronomy, however, Moses rather than Bezalel builds a simple wooden Ark. Gold is never mentioned. The sole purpose of the Ark, according to the text, is to contain the Tablets of the Law.

> At that time the Lord said to me, 'Hew two tables of stone like the first, and come up to me on the mountain, and make an Ark of wood. And I will write on the tables the words that were on the first tables which you broke, and you shall put them in the Ark.' So I made an Ark of acacia wood, and hewed two tables of stone like the first, and went up the mountain with the two tables in my hand.

The supernatural power of the Ark described in the Priestly Code seems to be of no concern to the Deuteronomist. The Ark is not itself the Presence of God, or a throne for God, or a place for God to speak to the prophet. No mysterious force strikes people dead. It is a box to store the Tablets of the Law, and it is the tablets and the covenant they represent that are important to Deuteronomy. This does not necessarily diminish its status, the covenant between God and Israel being of supreme importance to the Deuteronomist, and it does not change it absolutely. The Priestly Ark does contain the 'testimony' after all, and this clearly refers to the Tablets of the Law. In Deuteronomy, however, the Ark seems to exist for this purpose and no other. It is therefore a much more circumscribed idea of the Ark than one finds in the Priestly Code.

While the earlier sources are assumed to have been edited by the Deuteronomist, and the result placed in the framework provided by the Priestly Code, an old epic tradition can still be seen that envisages the Ark primarily as a divine palladium to bring victory to the Children of Israel. This Ark appears in the Jahwist, but not in the Elohist, which seems to envisage a tent as the central shrine at which God appears to man. It never mentions the Ark. We do not have a separate account of the construction or the appearance of the Ark from the Jahwist, but its behaviour is different from the descriptions in the Priestly or Deuteronomist accounts. As they march into battle, God is with the Israelites as they carry the Ark, which displays a more obviously supernatural power than the Ark of Deuteronomy, and yet it is not surrounded by the cultic prohibitions of the Priestly Ark. It can be seen, and it can be approached. If the Priestly Code provides the most memorable account of the construction of the Ark, the Jahwist provides some of the most dramatic events in the entire Bible, including the destruction of the walls of Jericho. As a rule, most of us imagine an Ark that takes elements from all three accounts: it is built by Moses as it is in Deuteronomy, but it has the elaborate appearance of the Ark in the Priestly Code, and it performs the great feats of the Conquest.

When the hero Joshua assembles his people to enter the Promised Land, the narrative describes how they gathered at the banks of the River Jordan and prepared to follow the Ark of the Covenant. This is the beginning of the Conquest, and the biblical account of it has always been of immense significance for the history of Judaism. A substantial portion of the Book of Joshua is devoted to only two events: the crossing of the Jordan and the capture of the city of Jericho. Their significance is not merely theological, of course. Even today, Israeli politicians often claim that the existence of the Jewish state depends on the promises that God made to Moses and then fulfilled under the leadership of Joshua.

To anyone coming out of the plains of Moab, even if they had not been wandering in the wilderness for forty years, the sight of the Jordan Valley and the city of Jericho would seem a vision of milk and honey. The river is often little more than a stream, but the rich silt that it carries from Galilee down to the Dead Sea has produced a land of such beauty that the Bible compared it to 'the garden of God'. The tamarisks and poplars that grew among the palms beside the river were so dense that they were known as 'the jungle of the Jordan'. Lions and wild boar lived among them, and even under the Muslim caliphs, the fields around Jericho were chosen for the pleasures of the hunt and for the cool water and mild air of its oasis.

Jericho itself is perhaps the oldest walled city on earth. As the earliest fortifications were built 10,000 years ago, the city would have been over 6,000 years old by the time that Joshua and the

Ark could have crossed the Jordan from the wilderness. The walls would already have fallen and been raised again on many occasions, as invading armies followed the roads that led through Jericho and stopped to plunder the city itself, but only the miraculous destruction brought by the Ark continues to be told across the centuries. The 'Pilgrim of Bordeaux' who visited the Holy Land in the fourth century wrote that the city remained utterly destroyed except for the house of Rahab the harlot, who hid the first Israelites who came to spy on the city. As one looks at the great mound of earth known as the Tell el-Sultan, which rises above the roofs of the small houses of Jericho and the palms that surround the oasis, it is difficult to believe that even this single house could have survived fifteen centuries between the departure of the Ark and the arrival of the pilgrim.

The excavation trenches cut by several generations of archaeologists who worked at Jericho can still be seen on the Tell, and those that remain open allow one the sensation of peering at a time machine. Not only hundreds but thousands of years pass before the eyes as one stares into the cut. Cities rose and fell, and dozens of walls must have come tumbling down by one means or another. The difficulty has been that while there was no shortage of tumbling walls, none of them seems to have tumbled at anything like the right time for Joshua and the Ark of the Covenant. Even for archaeologists who had little time for miracles, this was discomforting. Only by moving the supposed Conquest further and further away from the supposed date could the archaeological evidence be made to fit with the Bible, and eventually it became obvious that this would not do. The implications of the failure of archaeology to confirm the biblical record became inescapable at Jericho.

Perhaps, it has been suggested, the Conquest was really a more gradual and peaceful settlement than we might assume from the Bible. Yet even this rather minimal way of retaining the biblical account had its problems, as it was not easy for archaeologists to distinguish between supposedly Canaanite and supposedly Israelite sites. In fact, given that the Bible tells us that only part of Israel went down to Egypt, part of Israel must have remained, and the difficulty in distinguishing between the people living in Canaan and the people arriving in Canaan is so far almost impossible to resolve. It reappears at later points in the story as well, and although it is one of the great themes of the Bible, it raises questions that are never really answered. Who actually are the Israelites, and why are they not the Canaanites? And more important, if the Conquest had really been a peaceful settlement, why would such a disturbing and genocidal view of it have to be invented at some later point?

When the time came to cross the Jordan, the Bible tells us that Joshua rose early in the morning and set out from Shittim with all the people of Israel. After reaching the river, they camped there for three days before they actually made their attempt to cross it. At the end of the three days, the officers went through the camp and told the people that when they saw the Ark of the Covenant carried by the Levites, they should follow it at a distance of about 2,000 cubits. They were not to approach it. Joshua told the people to sanctify themselves. Tomorrow, he said, the Lord would perform miracles among them. Then he told the priests to pick up the Ark of the Covenant and march before the people.

God then spoke to Joshua and told him that he would begin to exalt him in the sight of all Israel, so that they would know that just as God had been with Moses, now he was with Joshua. Then he told him that the priests who carried the Ark of the Covenant should march into the Jordan and stand there.

Joshua delivered the command of God to the people and made an astonishing prediction to them. The Ark of the Covenant of the Lord of all the earth was about to pass before them into the Jordan. When the soles of the feet of the priests who carried the Ark stood in the waters of the river, it would simply cease to flow. God had performed a miracle at the Red Sea when Moses led the Children of Israel out of bondage in Egypt, and he would perform another miracle as Joshua led them into the Promised Land. This is exactly what happened, the Bible tells us. As soon as the priests who carried the Ark stepped into the river, the stream was interrupted:

> the waters coming down from above stood and rose up in a heap far off, at Adam, the city that is beside Zarethan, and those flowing down toward the sea of the plain, the Salt Sea, were wholly cut off; and the people passed over opposite Jericho. And while all Israel were passing

over on dry ground, the priests who bore the Ark of the Covenant of the Lord stood on dry ground in the midst of the Jordan, until all the nation finished passing over the Jordan.

Once they were safely across, 40,000 men armed for battle having passed before the Ark of the Covenant, Joshua and the tribes of Israel assembled on the plains of Jericho. This is the first city that the Israelites would attempt to conquer in the Promised Land, and God spoke to Joshua, telling him that he has given the city of Jericho into his hands. He ordered him to march around the city for six days, and assured him that when the Israelites blew on the shofar, the trumpet made from ram's horn, the walls of the city would fall down.

Calling them to him, Joshua told the priests to pick up the Ark of the Covenant. Seven priests would carry seven trumpets of ram's horn before the Ark while the people of Israel marched around the city. Joshua gave strict instructions that the people were not to shout or even utter a single word. The priests blew their horns, but the people marched in silence. They marched with the Ark around the city once, and then returned to their camp.

On the second day, they marched around the city again with the Ark and the trumpets, and they marched every day for a week. On the seventh day, the Israelites rose at dawn to march around the city, and on the seventh circuit Joshua told the people to shout because God had delivered the city to them.

So the people shouted, and the trumpets were blown. As soon as the people heard the sound of the trumpet, the people raised a great shout, and the wall fell down flat, so that the people went up into the city, every man straight before him, and they took the city. Then they utterly destroyed the city, both men and women, young and old, oxen, sheep, and asses, with the edge of the sword.

Although the victory of Jericho is perhaps the most famous adventure of the Ark of the Covenant, for anyone hoping to follow the path of the Ark the most intriguing part of the story happens after the city has fallen. Despite the miracle that God had performed, the people are no more obedient to his commandments than they were when Moses led them in the wilderness. Even

34

though the entire city had been marked by God for destruction, some of the Israelites stole things for themselves, provoking the anger of the Lord against them. In fact, God was so annoyed that he allowed his Chosen People to be defeated in the next battle, as a way of teaching them a lesson. Even Joshua began to despair.

> Then Joshua rent his clothes, and fell to the earth upon his face before the Ark of the Lord until the evening, he and the elders of Israel; and they put dust upon their heads. And Joshua said, 'Alas, O Lord God, why have you brought this people over the Jordan at all, to give us into the hands of the Amorites, to destroy us?'

In their prayers before the Ark, it is remarkable that neither Joshua nor the elders behave in a way that would be safe if they were in the presence of the Priestly Ark. There is no attempt to adhere to the strict regulations that governed any approach to the Ark. Joshua and the elders are in its presence, even though they are not priests or Levites. The tribes are not on the march, but the Ark does not seem to have been placed in the inner sanctum of the Tabernacle. If it has been placed there, and the narrator has simply not thought it necessary to inform the readers, Joshua and the elders should never have entered. By Priestly standards, something would be very wrong. This is either a very different conception of the Ark, or it is a different Ark.

During its adventures at Jericho, the Ark does not appear to be kept in the Tabernacle or any other kind of tent. On the other hand, the northern tradition of the Elohist refers to a sacred tent that does not contain an Ark. These are both difficult to reconcile with the most detailed account of the Ark, which hides it within the elaborate tent of the Tabernacle. Are the Tabernacle and the tent shrine mentioned by the Elohist the same? Just as we need to ask about the Ark itself, we also need to know if these descriptions refer to different things.

The descriptions of the Elohist tent suggest that they do. While the Israelites are in the wilderness, they have begun to suspect that Moses has led them into a desert to die. They long for the fish they ate when they lived beside the Nile, for the cucumbers, melons, leeks, onions and garlic that grew in the fertile soil of Egypt. They are weary of eating the manna that God had provided to sustain them in the wilderness, and they want meat instead. For his part, Moses is thoroughly exhausted, and he asks God to kill him so that he does not have to listen any longer to the constant demands and complaining of the Israelites.

In reply, God tells Moses to gather seventy of the elders of Israel, and to bring them to the Tent of Meeting. The elders will help him to bear the burden of leading a querulous people. Moses then tells the Israelites that they will eat meat on the following day. In fact, because they have refused to trust in God, they will eat meat until they are sick of it, until it comes out of their nostrils and they grow to hate it.

Gathering the seventy elders, Moses places them around the Tent. While they are standing there, God comes down in a cloud and speaks to them, giving each of them some of the spirit that he had placed upon Moses. When the spirit rests on them, they begin to prophesy.

Perhaps the most intriguing part of the encounter between God and the elders is that two men are said to have remained in the camp, while all the others went out to the tent. As we shall learn, the Tabernacle was placed in the middle of the camp. This must be another tent.

Earlier in the narrative, before the revelation of the Ark and the Tabernacle at Sinai, we are told explicitly that Moses used to pitch a tent outside the camp – far away from it, in fact. We are told that everyone who wished to find God would go out to this tent, which was outside the camp. In other words, not only is the tent not in the camp as the Tabernacle should be, its use is also not confined to the priests. We are even told that Joshua, the servant of Moses, was in the tent with his master, and we know that Joshua was not a priest.

We are also told that God appeared in a cloud outside the tent, and spoke to Moses at the door of the tent. Moses evidently waited in the tent for a revelation that would appear outside the tent. As we shall see, the Tabernacle was intended to operate in quite a different way. In fact, much of the Priestly narrative concerning the Tabernacle seems to be written to explain how the authority of the prophet Moses was transferred to his brother Aaron and the priests who were descended from him. With the Tabernacle, prophecy becomes liturgy.

Whatever we think of the order of the narrative, and the Book of Exodus does indicate that this tent existed before the Tabernacle and the Ark were made, this Tent would appear to be a different shrine and even a different sort of shrine. The confusion arises from the fact that the Priestly Code combines the Tent and the Tabernacle, and uses both names, occasionally at the same time.

If we are searching for the Ark, we will not find it in the ancient Tent of Meeting. The authors of the Priestly Code, however, assure us that the Ark is to be found in the Priestly Tabernacle. If this is not the same tent, is it the same Ark?

CHAPTER 4

The Ark and the Priests

In 1712, Herman Witsius remarked that, even though God had created the entire universe in six days, he needed forty to instruct Moses about the Tabernacle. The Bible could describe the structure of the world in a single chapter, but the Tabernacle required six.

Witsius was not joking. For a modern reader, the account of the Tabernacle is perhaps the most perplexing of all passages in the Hebrew Bible. Even if the Ark of the Covenant were placed in its innermost chamber, it is not always easy to understand why the details of how to build a very complicated tent should be a matter of spiritual significance. It would be even more difficult to understand if the description were imaginary, and if a tent had never been built according to the instructions that were written and copied so carefully across so many centuries. Yet the Priestly Ark cannot be understood without it. Unlike the Jahwist Ark that led the Israelites into battle, and the Ark of Deuteronomy that held the Tablets of the Law, the Priestly Ark is part of an elaborate cultic system. In fact, it occasionally seems as if the Tabernacle rather than the Ark is the most important element.

The English word 'tabernacle' is adopted from the Latin translation of the Old Testament. It is related to 'tavern', and it usually refers to a hut or a tent. The Hebrew word is *mishkan*, which is taken from the verb 'to dwell', and after centuries of rabbinic speculation about the ways in which God has moved among his people, it can be difficult for us now to read the word *mishkan* without thinking of its close relative *shekinah*, 'the Presence of God'. But the Priestly Code was not written with the mysticism of later centuries in mind. It is a priestly document, and its main concern is the proper management of a sacrificial cult. This was a matter of immense consequence. The priests were convinced that, unless every precaution were taken to prevent disaster, their failure to protect the fragility of human life against the infinite force that had created the universe would lead to death on an almost unimaginable scale. This awesome responsibility was entrusted to the tribe of Levi and to the family of Aaron. Outside the Priestly Code, any Levite male was believed to be eligible for the priesthood, but in the descriptions of the Tabernacle, the Levites are clergy of a lower status. Only the family of Aaron are anointed to be priests. While the Levites are responsible for dismantling the Tabernacle when the Israelites move the camp, and for transporting it and assembling it again, the most sacred objects in the sanctuary must be covered by the Aaronid priests before the Levites are allowed to enter. They must never see the holy things, especially the Ark of the Covenant.

According to the descriptions in Exodus, the Tabernacle is constructed as a heavy frame of acacia wood, covered by several types of curtain made of different fibres and woven in different techniques, and then by a tent of goat wool. Thousands of years after the biblical account was written, it can be difficult for us to understand the description of the Tabernacle. Some of the words are now obscure. The covering required skins of *tehasim*, for example. This has been translated as 'badger' or 'dolphin'. It has also been connected with an Akkadian word meaning 'sheepskin' and an Egyptian word meaning 'to stretch or treat leather'. At least for the moment, we do not know what it means. Even when we recognize the materials involved, it can be difficult to understand how the Tabernacle was constructed. The frame was clearly built of acacia wood, but scholars have puzzled over the way in which the beams were attached to one another. Do they stand flush against each other or do they overlap, and can their combined measurements be made to correspond to the dimensions of the entire structure? Even if the materials and the instructions can be followed, we may not always see the point. Why should rings made of a precious metal such as gold simply be hidden?

Beyond this, however, the greatest problem for most modern readers, especially Protestant Christians who often have a limited interest in any sort of ritual, is the fact that the authors of these passages found the Tabernacle so fascinating. They wrote a description of it that even the greatest Jewish authorities have described as 'wearisome', then repeated the complete set of instructions, and still felt it necessary to repeat the list of ritual objects on several further occasions. For the later rabbis, of course, each item possessed a special meaning, and their account of the Tabernacle is decidedly more lively. The wood for the frame apparently came from Paradise, Adam having carried it with him when he and Eve were expelled. It passed through the generations to the patriarch Abraham, who gave it as a legacy to Isaac, and Isaac left it to Joseph. When Joseph went down into Egypt, he took the acacia wood with him, and when God delivered them from their bondage, they carried the wood into the wilderness. The frame was held together by a beam taken from the tree that Abraham planted at Beersheba in the Book of Genesis. While Moses led the Chosen People across the Red Sea, the tree was cut down by angels and thrown into the water, allowing the Israelites to carry it with them as they marched toward Sinai. It was 70 cubits in length, and possessed miraculous powers, bending when the Tabernacle was erected, but straightening as soon as it was dismantled.

The authors of the Priestly Code, who are usually assumed to have written the description of the Tabernacle, would have been explaining the divine institution of a sacrificial cult to which they had dedicated their lives. While this may explain some of its obsessive concern with detail, it is not simply a matter of pride in a job well done. The cult ensured the safety of the Children of Israel, but beyond that, it was essential for the order and harmony of the entire universe. For the priests, precise observance would be a matter of supreme importance, and the reason is given in the account of the revelation at Sinai: the Tabernacle was built according to a pattern that exists in heaven. However much Philo and Josephus may have written in terms of Platonic allegory, or even Egyptian mysticism, their view of the cult would be very near to that of the Priestly authors in this sense. The Tabernacle was a sacramental demonstration of a cosmic reality. It was a revelation in material form of divine truth. It was also, as we shall see, a sort of technology for managing a highly volatile and dangerous power. If a thoroughly professional approach were not maintained, this power would prove fatal not only to those who had been authorized to work with it, but everyone else as well.

Even if professional matters can seem dull to the layman, priestly circles were quite capable of seeing their vocation in dramatic or even romantic terms. The author of the Wisdom of Ben Sirach, seems to have been close to the priests of Jerusalem during the second century BC, and when he describes the high priest emerging in a cloud of incense from the inner sanctuary where the Ark of the Covenant would once have stood, it is difficult not to be impressed.

> Like the morning star among the clouds,
> like the moon when it is full;
> like the sun shining upon the Temple of the Most High,
> and like the rainbow gleaming in glorious clouds;
> like roses in the days of the first fruits,
> like lilies by a spring of water,
> like a green shoot on Lebanon on a summer day;
> like fire and incense in the censer,
> like a vessel of hammered gold
> adorned with all kinds of precious stones;
> like an olive tree putting forth its fruit,
> and like a cypress towering in the clouds.
> When he put on his glorious robe
> and clothed himself with superb perfection
> and went up to the holy altar,
> he made the court of the sanctuary glorious.

What sort of a system were the authors actually describing in Exodus and Leviticus, however? There is the obvious question of whether such an elaborate shrine could have been moved through the desert, but it is even more difficult to believe that a structure of the size, complexity and cost described by the Priestly source could have been produced by tribes wandering in the wilderness of Sinai and left to their own devices. This is particularly obvious in the descriptions of the intricate vestments and ritual objects.

And gold leaf was hammered out and cut into threads to work into the blue and the purple and scarlet stuff, and into the fine twined linen, in skilled design ... The onyx stones were prepared, enclosed in settings of gold filigree and engraved like the engravings of a signet, according to the names of the sons of Israel.

The authors do not present the construction of the Tabernacle as a miraculous event. The craftsmen may be inspired by the Spirit of God, but God does not send the materials down from heaven. The tribes simply gather up their possessions so that sufficient amounts of acacia wood, embroidered fabric and precious metal can be applied to the task.

The Priestly source was written by liturgists, rather than by historians, as we might understand the term now, and it is difficult not to believe that they are describing the Tabernacle in the terms of their own day. In other words, they were writing at a time when a Temple at Jerusalem, with elaborate decoration and complex ritual, had actually been built, and they were describing an earlier version of this house of God in what they believed to be the appropriate terms. There is no doubt that Jewish artists in the ancient world adopted the same approach, depicting the Ark of the Covenant as if it were the Holy Ark of the synagogue, or Philistines as if they were Persians. Many of us are uncomfortable taking the same view of religious writing, as if it might undermine the truth of the biblical narrative, but the choice is not simply between a text that was written as a record of contemporary events, which is therefore completely trustworthy, and some sort of pious fraud. The more that we understand about the development of the books in the biblical canon, including the evidence that was discovered among the Dead Sea Scrolls at Wadi Qumran over fifty years ago, suggests a continual process of growth extending well into the first century AD, and this is not the only occasion on which the heroic past may have been described in terms of a later day.

The question is of real importance if we attempt to decide what the emperor Iyasu might have seen when he summoned the Ark into his presence at Aksum, and what the earlier reports of the Ark in Ethiopia might have been describing. Are the descriptions that the Priestly source gives of the Ark and the Tabernacle accurate accounts of objects made at Sinai? If they are not accounts of objects made at Sinai, are they nevertheless accurate accounts of objects that were made for the cult at some later date? Is the Priestly description the criterion by which we should judge the account given by the chronicler of Iyasu, or any of the other witnesses in Ethiopia? By asking the question, are we committing a fundamental error in treating a liturgical text as if it were history, expecting it to provide information of a type that was of little interest to those who compiled it?

Even if the Priestly source has adopted an elevated tone to describe an institution of immense significance for the cult, there may be some doubt about what is actually being described. Is the Tabernacle a depiction of the Temple itself, its proportions reduced to make its passage through the wilderness seem more credible? A century ago, this was the consensus among those who followed the great German scholar Julius Wellhausen, but although the dimensions of the Tabernacle are provided in immense detail, they do not correspond precisely to the proportions of the Temple. If the Priestly source were describing a later shrine, could this be the tent that David pitched when he brought the Ark to Jerusalem, or perhaps the tabernacle at Shiloh, after the Conquest of the Promised Land? The latter, of course, is said to be the Tabernacle itself, erected as a kind of central shrine for the tribes of Israel, but perhaps there could have been a later and more elaborate version. Still, the descriptions of both the tent of David and the shrine at Shiloh are so brief that they offer no more than a way of claiming that the account of the Tabernacle is historical in some sense, even if no evidence is available. Despite the impressive reputations of the scholars who have advocated one or other of these tents, we simply have no way of assessing their validity. Without any evidence, they remain tantalizing and ultimately of little help.

If scholars who assume that such an elaborate structure could not have been built in the wilderness are keen to identify it with a tent mentioned elsewhere, one of the reasons is simply the amount of detail that the Bible provides. They believe that it would have been perverse and eccentric to describe the intricacies of a structure that never existed. The Book of Ezekiel, however, provides an account of a Temple seen by the prophet during a vision, and even though the Temple does not have physical form when the prophet sees it, and was never built in the manner he describes, the account contains precise detail of the sort that we read in the account of the Tabernacle. However strange it may seem to modern scholars, it would not necessarily have seemed odd to the authors of the Priestly Code:

Its side rooms, its jambs, and its vestibule were of the same size as the others; and there were windows round about in it and in its vestibules; its length was fifty cubits, and its breadth twenty-five cubits. Its vestibule faced the outer court, and it had palm trees on its jambs, one on either side; and its stairway had eight steps.

This degree of detail extends over four chapters of the Book of Ezekiel, and with the additional chapters about sacrifices, feasts and various sorts of ritual, it rivals the elaboration of the Tabernacle.

The Ugaritic texts found at Ras Shamra and written during the second millennium BC mention a *mishkan* or tabernacle built for the gods. As these texts are demonstrably ancient, they have been thought to provide evidence for the antiquity or historicity of the biblical Tabernacle. But they are literary evidence of Ugaritic mythology, not archaeological evidence of a Tabernacle similar to the elaborate structure described in Exodus. However fascinating the similarities may be, and they do raise profound questions about the exclusive nature of Israelite institutions and the extent of their insulation from the peoples among whom the Israelites lived, they lead us no closer to the question of whether an Israelite Tabernacle was built according to the biblical instructions.

From an early date, biblical manuscripts and printed books often included diagrams or plans of the Tabernacle and its furniture as well as of the Temple. Without some sort of guide, it can be difficult for anyone reading the Book of Exodus to imagine the structure that its authors were attempting to explain, and especially during the rise of Protestant scholarship after the Reformation, some of the most meticulous and exhaustive research was applied to these reconstructions. If the Tabernacle was the embodiment of a divine plan and if it replicated the structure of the universe in some way, it was obviously a matter of great importance to understand exactly how it was supposed to have been built.

Despite the obscurities and complexities of the Hebrew text, a careful reading of the passages from Exodus indicates a logical and coherent vision of the structure. It comprises three different types of material: furniture, fabrics and beams. The frame of the Tabernacle is made of beams placed in rows on the north, west, and south, but not on the east. The three walls are covered by ten lower curtains and eleven outer curtains, over which the tent of goat wool and a leather covering made of sheepskin and the mysterious *tehasim* is placed. The interior is divided into two parts, an inner sanctum and an outer sanctum, which are separated by a veil known as the *paroket*.

The Ark of the Covenant is placed in the inner sanctum, which has the form of a cube whose length, breadth and height are all 10 cubits. Three items of furniture are placed in the outer sanctum. The table stands by the northern wall, the lampstand is placed by the southern wall, and the altar of incense stands between them, opposite the Ark. An outer veil is hung across the entrance to the Tabernacle.

The court around the Tabernacle is marked by hangings stretched over pillars. There is no exact statement about where in the court the Tabernacle should stand, but the outer altar stands in front of it, and between the altar and the Tabernacle is the laver, filled with water for the priests to wash their hands and feet in preparation for their sacred offices.

The Ark of the Covenant is often imagined as a uniquely hazardous device, liable to bring death on everyone who approached it regardless of whether their intentions were innocent or malign. In fact, it seems to be only one part of a system by which the immensity of divine power could be controlled through ritual means. Every aspect of the Tabernacle was involved, and sudden death was a constant danger.

The technique for containing this power involves the application of holy oil, and precise instructions are given about its preparation. The furniture of the Tabernacle is anointed with the oil. Aaron and his sons are also anointed with it, and the anointing confers the same degree of holiness on them as on the furniture, protecting them from death when they touch it. The priests and their vestments have been placed in the same state of sanctity as the furniture, and an equilibrium has been established. As a result of this, anyone who is not a priest is forbidden to come into contact with a priest while he is anointed or serving near the furniture.

According to the Priestly Code, the Ark was always covered. It was kept in darkness, in the inner sanctum of the Tabernacle. No one could touch it or see it, and anyone who did would die. Even the high priest would place a cloud of incense around it on the

Day of Atonement, when he performed the annual sacrifice that God had commanded.

> Aaron shall present the bull as a sin offering for himself, and shall make atonement for himself and for his house; he shall kill the bull as a sin offering for himself. And he shall take a censer full of coals of fire from the altar before the Lord, and two handfuls of sweet incense beaten small; and he shall bring it within the veil and put incense on the fire before the Lord, that the cloud of incense may cover the mercy seat which is upon the testimony, lest he die.

When the Ark was moved, great care was taken to avoid anyone approaching it or seeing it. Precise regulations described how Aaron and his sons were to enter the Tabernacle and take down the veil of the screen and cover the Ark with it. They would then place a covering of goatskin over it, and spread a cloth of blue over the goatskin. Only then could the Levites move it.

The full force of contagious holiness is reduced while the Tabernacle and its furniture are being moved, but while it stands in camp, the Levites are entrusted with the task of standing guard. To ensure that no one approaches the Tabernacle, they position themselves around the perimeter, while the priests remain at the gate of the court to prevent anyone entering.

For many of us who read the description of the Tabernacle now, the idea of contagious holiness can be deeply disturbing. No value seems to be placed on the intentions of anyone who violates its prohibitions. Whether one might have been planning good or evil is of no consequence; death will result in either case. It is even more alarming that, once the power of holiness is released, it can spread from someone who provokes it to strike down someone else who is innocent of any violation. Moses warns the priests that, if they perform the rites of mourning when the oil of anointing is upon them, not only will they die themselves, but the wrath of God will also be aroused against the entire people. Perhaps we are right to find this unsettling. As we shall see, the rabbis were also uncomfortable about the ways in which it seemed to operate, and applied themselves to finding the mercy of God hidden behind the words of the Bible. There is also a paradox involved in this extreme form of holiness, which may be as unsettling to modern logic as it is to modern morality. The holiness is so extreme that it produces the pollution of death. The theory of holiness even imagined some forms of pollution involving corpses that could be removed only by substances that were themselves polluting. They purified the defiled, but defiled the pure.

When it was finally completed, 'the glory of the Lord filled the Tabernacle', and it began to display a miraculous power. God had instructed Moses to erect it on the first day of the first month, and to put the Ark of the Covenant inside it, and then hide the Ark behind the veil. We are told that the Tabernacle was covered by cloud during the day and by fire at night – the signs that had appeared on Mount Sinai when God revealed himself to Moses. The miraculous display would suggest that the Tabernacle was a smaller and portable version of the holy mountain.

While the inauguration of the Tabernacle was a day of rejoicing for the Israelites, in later Jewish accounts the angels were often jealous of any favours that God might show to the race of men and were now desperately unhappy that the Tabernacle had been made. Once the Presence of God went down from heaven to dwell in the Tabernacle, they feared that they would soon be abandoned in the celestial realm. God tried to assure them that his true home would remain with them, far above the world of mortal men, but they were satisfied only when he allowed them to build a Tabernacle in heaven that was identical to the Tabernacle on earth. The story is intriguing because it seems to reverse the dependence of the Tabernacle on a heavenly pattern. Here, it is the earthly Tabernacle that serves as a model for the celestial Tabernacle.

Once the Israelites had erected the Tabernacle, the rabbis tell us that peace returned to the earth. Through the Tabernacle, God destroyed the power of the demons and announced to the Children of Israel that hatred and anger had once existed between him and his children, but that now there would be only love, friendship and peace. As Moses led the Israelites through the wilderness, however, it was largely hatred and anger that they showed him.

As they made their way towards the Promised Land, according to the biblical account, the mysterious cloud and fire continued to appear, guiding the Chosen People through the wilderness. Later traditions claim that the pillar of cloud stood immediately over the Ark of the Covenant itself, and that two Hebrew letters could be seen within the cloud – the letters by which God had created the world. During the day, the pillar of cloud shone with the light of the sun, and at night it shone with the light of the moon, so that the Israelites could tell whether it was day or night even though they were surrounded by clouds. Throughout the day, the two letters would fly over the tribes of Israel, except on the Sabbath, when they would hover in the air without moving. If God wished the people of Israel to move their camp, the cloud over the Ark that contained the two letters would set out before the people and they would follow it, while wind blew from all sides with the fragrance of frankincense and myrrh.

Even though the power of God was constantly being revealed in the most obvious way, the people of Israel seemed to be incapable of remembering that he was actually with them. In fact, Moses himself does not always display the fortitude and sound judgement that might be expected of him. Some of this may be due to different sources that reflect the interests of factions among the priesthood. As the text stands, the characters seem to be drawn with an acute awareness of human frailty, whether this is due to the combination of contradictory sources or the insight of an original author.

The point has occasionally been made that the Israelites had not recovered from the dreadful experience of living as slaves in Egypt for generations – a degradation that would have robbed them of the maturity, confidence and perseverance necessary for such an arduous undertaking. Perhaps the years spent in the wilderness were necessary to raise a new generation that would have the courage and perseverance to fight for the Promised Land. But this would seem to rob the account of its clear insight into the human heart. While it might seem anachronistic to apply the letters written by Paul of Tarsus to the struggles of the Israelites in the wilderness, even those of us born in freedom are often slaves to our own fear and weakness.

Even the presence of the Ark of the Covenant seems to have given the Israelites only a temporary courage, at least according to later Jewish tradition. Whenever they moved from camp, Moses would tell them to follow the instructions of the Presence of God within the Ark, but they would not believe that the Presence was really there unless Moses spoke the words, 'Rise up, Lord, and let your enemies be scattered; and let them that hate you flee before you.' When the words were spoken, the Ark would begin to move, and this would be taken as proof that the Presence was still with them. Still more dramatic was the custom of the Ark to fly into the air when it had decided that the Israelites should break camp, rushing ahead of the tribes until it found a site for them, even though it might take them three days to reach it.

In the Book of Leviticus, Moses embarks on a lengthy ritual to inaugurate the office of the priests who would serve the Ark and the Tabernacle. Following the commandments of God, he washes Aaron and his sons and then anoints them. He dresses them in vestments and anoints the vestments, and then he anoints the Tabernacle itself and the furniture. Despite the elaborate ritual to ensure their safety as they undertake the awesome responsibilities of holiness, two sons of Aaron decide to make an offering of incense that has not been stipulated by God. As they are said to offer this 'before the Lord' and are struck down 'from the Presence of the Lord', it would seem that they were attempting to make the offering to the Ark of the Covenant.

> Now Nadab and Abihu, the sons of Aaron, each took his censer, and put fire in it, and laid incense on it, and offered unholy fire before the Lord, such as he had not commanded them. And fire came forth from the Presence of the Lord and devoured them, and they died before the Lord. Then Moses said to Aaron, 'This is what the Lord has said, "I will show myself holy among those who are near me, and before all the people I will be glorified."' And Aaron held his peace.

The story is a clear statement of priestly interests and convictions. Cultic ritual, especially concerning the Ark, must be obeyed in all its particulars. Failure to do so will mean death.

In the later Jewish tradition, Aaron does not hold his peace quite so quickly. The rabbis were clearly anxious to depict God as more merciful than the austere account in the Bible might suggest. When Aaron hears that his sons are dead, he complains to God that all the tribes of Israel saw God at the Red Sea and again at Sinai without any harm coming to them. God himself had instructed his sons to serve in the Tabernacle – a place that laymen could not enter and remain alive. All they wanted to do was behold his strength and his might, and they died for it. God tells Moses to pass a message to his brother Aaron that it was actually through kindness that the two young men had died. He had decreed that anyone who entered the Tabernacle without having been commanded to do so would suffer from leprosy. Surely Aaron would not have wanted his sons, who had been ordained to serve in the Tabernacle itself, to be banished beyond the camp of the Israelites because of the dreadful disease. When he hears the reason for their death, Aaron agrees that it was better for them not to have survived.

As Moses struggles to lead the Israelites through the wilderness, threats and even death by earthquake and plague seem to produce faith and obedience for only a little while. God eventually decides that one more miracle will bring his Chosen People to their senses. At the Tabernacle again, God speaks to Moses and tells him that each of the tribes of Israel should write its name on a rod and that they should all be deposited in the Tabernacle 'before the testimony': in other words, before the Ark of the Covenant. All the elders of Israel do so, and the name 'Aaron' is written on the rod of the house of Levi. The next morning, the rod of Aaron has produced buds, blossoms and ripe almonds. As the people of Israel are all able to see that something unique has happened to the rod of Aaron, that all the other rods are still dry and lifeless, God tells Moses to put it next to the Ark of the Covenant as evidence of the miraculous power of God: 'that you may make an end of their murmurings against me, lest they die'. Even if the Israelites are lacking in faith and obedience, they are now thoroughly terrified of the Tabernacle. They cry out to Moses that everyone who comes near the Tabernacle of the Lord seems to be killed, and they ask if they are all going to die in the wilderness.

Despite the frustrations of leading the Israelites toward the Promised Land, Moses is not diminished in body or mind by the time he is 120 years old. Every man has his allotted time, however, and at the end of the Pentateuch, the Book of Deuteronomy records that God summons Moses and Joshua to the Tent of Meeting, in order that Joshua can be appointed as successor. A pillar of cloud appears, and God speaks to them, announcing to Moses that he is about to sleep with his fathers, and urging Joshua to be of good courage, for he will bring the Children of Israel into the Promised Land.

Before his death, Moses gives 'the Book of the Law' to the sons of Levi, who carry the Ark of the Covenant, and tells them to read it every seven years at the Feast of Tabernacles, and to keep it beside the Ark. His exasperation with the Israelites does not seem to have been dimmed by the great age he has reached. He warns the Levites that the book will be placed next to the Ark for a specific purpose. It will be a witness against them. He knows how rebellious and stubborn they are, and if they have rebelled against God while Moses has been alive, how much more will they rebel after he has died.

This passage has been seen as the only occasion on which the Ark of the Covenant seems to be placed in a tent by a source other than the Priestly Code, but even here, this is only by implication. Moses tells the Levites who carry the Ark to put the Book of the Law 'beside the Ark of the Covenant of the Lord your God'. His instructions are not to place the book inside the Ark, and this suggests that the Ark must have been covered in some way. It is difficult to imagine that the Book of the Law would have been left in the open. Some of the rabbis solved the problem by assuming that the book really had been placed inside the Ark. This was not the only addition to the Ark. As we shall see, the number of relics placed inside it seems to grow as the centuries pass.

After Moses has died and Joshua has led the Israelites into the Promised Land, what is the fate of the Tabernacle? It is erected at Shiloh and is described as the only legitimate place of sacrifice, the only centre for the religion of Israel during the time of the judges Eli and Samuel. Compared to the emphasis placed upon it while Israel wandered in the wilderness, however, it seems almost to have been forgotten.

The Ark and the Tabernacle are separated when the sons of Eli take the Ark into battle against the Philistines and it is captured. Even though the Ark is recovered and placed in the house of Abinadab at Gibeah, the Tabernacle remains at Shiloh. The fate of Shiloh is never mentioned in the historical books, and although the prophet Jeremiah refers to its destruction on three occasions, he never speaks of the Tabernacle.

According to the First Book of Chronicles, the Tabernacle was located at the 'high place' of Gibeon. When David brings the Ark to Jerusalem and places it in a new tent, he sends Zadok the priest to Gibeon, to perform sacrifices at the Tabernacle in accordance with the regulations given in the Book of Leviticus.

In the accounts provided by the Chronicler and by the First Book of Kings, when Solomon dedicated the Temple in Jerusalem, the priests and the Levites 'brought up the Ark of the Lord, the Tent of Meeting, and all the holy vessels that were in the Tent'. After the repairs to the Temple and the renewal of worship by the Judaean king Hezekiah in the eighth century BC, there is no further mention of the Tabernacle in the historical books.

Josephus confirms that the Tabernacle was brought up to the Temple, but he has no more to say than the Hebrew Bible about where it might have been placed. One possibility is that it was reunited with the Ark of the Covenant and placed beneath the wings of the great statues of the cherubim that Solomon commissioned for the Holy of Holies. Josephus remarks that the outspread wings of these cherubim looked like a tent, and it has been suggested that a similar image is used by the Psalmist.

I will dwell in your tent forever!
I will be safe under the shelter of your wings!

O Lord, who will live in your tent?
Who will dwell on your holy hill?

If these verses refer to the wings of cherubim, the Tabernacle and the Temple Mount, the phrase 'under the shelter of your wings' may suggest the vast wings of the statues spread across the Tabernacle. The allusions are far from offering direct evidence, however, and although the dimensions of the Tabernacle correspond to the space beneath the cherubim, the rabbis whose opinions are recorded in the Talmud did not believe that the Tabernacle had been brought into the sanctuary. They thought it had been installed in the crypt beneath the Temple.

The Hebrew Bible seems to preserve more information about the fate of the Tabernacle than the fate of the Ark, but there are still only two passages, and neither of them occurs in historical narrative. In Psalm 74, a single verse would suggest that the Tabernacle had been burnt when the Babylonians destroyed the Temple, if the phrase '*mishkan* of your name' were understood as referring to the Tabernacle itself rather than alluding in a more general way to the Temple as the place where God dwells.

> They set your sanctuary on fire;
> to the ground they desecrated the Tabernacle of your name.

In the Lamentations of Jeremiah, the word 'meeting' is sometimes claimed to be an abbreviation for 'the Tent of Meeting'.

> And he has dealt violently with his pavilion as with a garden,
> He destroyed his [tent of] meeting.
> The Lord has caused holiday and sabbath to be forgotten in Zion,
> And he has spurned in his angry indignation king and priest.

If the expressions of grief in the Psalms and Lamentations cannot be relied upon as hard evidence about the fate of the Tabernacle, we must turn to the ancient traditions preserved outside the biblical canon, where the fate of the Temple and the holy objects placed within it attracted both the learned and the imaginative. This was not a matter of idle speculation or merely academic interest. Their fate was believed to be part of the key to the future of the world, of the deliverance of Jews from oppression, or of the New Covenant that Christians were convinced had made obsolete any Temple built by the hands of men. Even if they rejected the Temple itself – and we shall see that both the first Christian martyr and the last book in the Christian Bible leave little room for doubt – the Tabernacle would continue to be indispensable, whatever its fate might have been on earth. And just as the Ark never quite disappears, we shall see that the name of the Tabernacle was remembered at the holiest shrine of Mecca and among the poets and magicians of Aksum.

CHAPTER 5

King and Covenant

The last of the judges of Israel was sleeping near the Ark of the Covenant when God spoke to him. Samuel was still a boy, serving under an elderly priest named Eli in the sanctuary at Shiloh, and the First Book of Samuel describes his bewilderment. Hearing someone call his name, he ran to his master and said, 'You called me, so here I am!' But Eli told him that he had not called, and suggested that the boy go back to sleep. Samuel obeyed, but again he heard his name, and again he ran to Eli. 'Here I am,' he said. 'You called me.' The priest still insisted that he had not called, and he told Samuel to lie down, but when it happened a third time, he realized that the boy must have been hearing the voice of God. Eli told him to lie down again, but if he heard the voice, he should answer with the words, 'Speak, your servant is listening.' God does speak a fourth time, warning Samuel that he is about to destroy the house of Eli because of the wickedness of his two sons, Hophni and Phinehas. Eli insists on hearing what God has said, and when he learns that his lineage will be obliterated, he bows before the will of the Lord. His sons may have committed blasphemy, but their father remains an obedient servant until the end.

This revelation introduces what is often called the 'Ark Narrative': the chapters of the First Book of Samuel that describe how the Philistines captured the Ark and then suffered plague and pestilence until they returned it. The Narrative continues in the Second Book of Samuel when David recovers the Ark from Kiryath-yearim and brings it to his new capital Jerusalem. Although the Ark brought victory in battle to the Israelites as they wandered in the wilderness and fought their enemies during the Conquest, there was one famous exception. When the sons of Eli carried the Ark against the Philistines, the disaster that overwhelmed them may have been reported to explain the disappearance of the Elide priesthood, but it also raises a difficult question. If the Ark had been lost, was this because it was power-less? Was God unable to determine the fate of his house on earth? Was he no longer able to defend and guide his people? This would seem to have been especially troubling at one period in particular, and the suggestion has been made that the narrative might have been written after the destruction of the Temple when the Ark had been lost. It would have been written to assure the faithful that God had not abandoned them.

It is not entirely clear where the Ark had been before its arrival at Shiloh. We are told that the Tabernacle had been erected there, and this has suggested that Shiloh might have been the central sanctuary for the tribes of Israel in the years before they demanded a king. The shrine at Shiloh is also described with the word generally used for the Temple at Jerusalem (*heikal*), and it is not clear whether the structure was thought to have remained unaltered. The Ark seems to have followed a less direct route. It was placed at Gilgal after it crossed the Jordan. Then, if the phrase 'the angel of the Lord' refers to the Ark, it was moved to a place called Bochim, which we cannot identify, but which may have been near Bethel. The Ark then seems to have been at Bethel itself, and after Bethel at Shiloh, until the Philistines captured it. The Bible tells us nothing about a central sanctuary, however. There also seem have been shrines such as Shechem, at which important festivals were celebrated even though neither the Ark nor the Tabernacle was there.

The Ark is taken from Shiloh during a campaign against the Philistines, who had invaded Canaan from the north. The Israelites had not been able to defeat them, so the elders decided that the Ark should be brought into battle. The power of God, who lives between the cherubim on the Ark, would surely be able to secure victory. The sons of Eli therefore carry the Ark from Shiloh, and when the Philistines hear a great shout of joy from the Israelite camp, they realize that the God of their enemies has arrived. Although they understand it to be a serious threat – this was the God, after all, who had caused such havoc in Egypt – their fear causes them to fight with desperation, to avoid being enslaved by the Israelites. They fight with such ferocity that they win the battle. Not only that, they capture the Ark and kill the sons of Eli.

One of the tribe of Benjamin hurries to Shiloh with the terrible news, his clothes torn and earth on his head as signs of mourning and distress. Eli is sitting beside the road, old and blind, and desperately worried about the fate of the Ark. When news of the catastrophe is announced in the city, there is a cry of despair, and Eli asks what is happening. The messenger finds him sitting in his chair, and tells him that the Ark has been captured and that his two sons have been killed. As soon as he learns the fate of the Ark, he falls from his chair and dies.

If the capture of the Ark seemed a disaster for Israel, trouble was only just beginning for the Philistines. They carried the Ark to Ashdod and brought it into the temple of their god Dagon. When they entered the temple on the following morning, they saw that the image of Dagon had fallen on its face before the Ark. They raised the statue again, but by the next morning it had fallen over again, and now its head and hands were cut away from the body.

If the Ark can destroy the statue of Dagon so easily, the Philistines realize, it is too dangerous to be kept among them. They decide to send it to their neighbours in the Philistine city of Gath, but here too the Ark brings disaster. The men of Gath, both young and old, are terrified of the Ark and develop dreadful tumours. It is obvious that the Ark cannot remain in Gath either, so the men of the town decide to pass it along to their neighbours at Ekron. By this time, however, its reputation has gone before it. As soon as the people of Ekron see the Ark coming toward them, the cry goes up that the Ark of the God of Israel has arrived to kill them all.

After seven months, the Philistines decide to send the Ark back to its own place, so that it does not destroy them. This is no easy matter. Such a step might only provoke the Ark to inflict even worse damage. To avoid making a serious mistake, the Philistines summon their own priests and diviners and ask what they should do with the Ark. Their wise men agree that the best course would be to send it back, but they insist that it must not be sent back empty. It should be accompanied by a guilt offering as a form of appeasement: five golden tumours and five golden mice to represent the plagues that the Ark had brought upon the Philistines. Even so, it could be difficult to anticipate the intentions of the God of the Israelites, a deity who seemed to take offence rather quickly, so they propose an experiment to ensure that they are doing what the Ark wishes them to do.

They find a new cart and two milk cows that had never been yoked. They yoke the cows to the cart, but take their calves away from them, and then they place the Ark in the cart, along with a box containing the golden figures that will serve as an offering to the God of the Israelites. If the cows take the Ark away from them, despite their never having been yoked, and despite their calves remaining with the Philistines, everyone will know that the disease and suffering had been imposed by the will of God. If the Ark returns to its own land, to Beth-shemesh, it will be obvious that the Ark had caused all the trouble. If not, then the disasters would be shown to be simply the result of chance, rather than the hostility of God.

The Philistines follow the advice of their wise men, and the cows walk straight along the road to Beth-shemesh, while the lords of the Philistines watch from a distance to see what might happen. When they see the Ark of the Covenant approach, the people of Beth-shemesh are in their fields for the harvest. They are delighted that it should have returned, and when the cattle and the cart stop in the field, they sacrifice the cows as a burnt offering to God, using the wood of the cart to build a fire. The Levites take the Ark and set it beside a great stone, which serves as the altar. Having seen all this, the Philistine lords return to Ekron to tell their people that they are now free from the perils of the Ark. It has returned to Israel without incident.

Even when it is among the people of Israel once more, the danger of the Ark has not diminished. Seventy of the men of Beth-shemesh die because they look inside the Ark, and the people become so terrified of it that they send a message to their neighbours at Kiryath-yearim, asking them to come and remove it. Unlike everyone else, it seems, the men of Kiryath-yearim are not alarmed at the idea of the Ark living among them. They bring it to the house of Abinadab, and consecrate his son Eleazar 'to have charge of the Ark of the Lord'.

After such an extraordinary adventure, one might have expected the Ark to go on to perform even more astonishing miracles, to humiliate the enemies of Israel and to confirm the presence of God among his Chosen People. Instead, it simply disappears. There seems to be almost complete silence until David comes to Kiryath-yearim and brings the Ark to Jerusalem. According to the account of this given in the Psalms, the Ark was not easy to find. It had more or less been forgotten. This is not the first time that a curious silence seems to descend over the Ark, and it will not be the last. It has even been suggested that the Ark had been lost, and that David made another.

Although his master had died, Samuel grew to become a great prophet and judge among the people of Israel. At the end of his life, apparently because his own sons were taking bribes and perverting the course of justice, the people of Israel asked him to anoint a king to govern them, 'like all the nations'. The prophet is obviously disturbed by the request and consults God about it. He is told that it involves no rejection of Samuel as a judge, only a rejection of God as king. The Children of Israel have simply decided that they want a man to rule them rather than God himself. He tells the prophet to answer their request, to give them a king, but to warn them of what it will mean.

The warning that Samuel delivers is a catalogue of the vast expense of a royal court, with its bureaucracy and its military, and the burden that its maintenance will impose on the people of Israel. The king, he tells them, will take their menservants and maidservants, and the best of their cattle and asses, and put them to work for himself. He will take a tenth of their flocks, and they will be his slaves. Eventually, they will cry out to God because of the king that they chose for themselves; but God will not answer them.

Beyond the burden of supporting a king and his court, the demand for a king 'like all the nations' would have meant a crisis of identity, at least for the editors of the Bible. It would have threatened to undermine the unique status of Israel as they saw it. Kingship was an old institution among the peoples of the Near East. It possessed a religious mythology and a place in a cosmic system that the Bible often presents as an abomination in the eyes of God.

In the mythology of the ancient Near East, there was a war between the god of life, creation and order, and the forces of chaos and destruction. In the struggle between these two powers, the god of order is victorious over chaos and builds a palace in which he will live and celebrate his victory. In the Ugaritic tablets discovered seventy years ago at Ras Shamra, in Syria, the hero was the storm god Baal, who fought against the Sea. In the Babylonian tablets deciphered during the nineteenth century, the god Marduk defeated Tiamat, the dragon of the Deep. The battle between the gods was a constant process, often following the ebb and flow of the seasons. Within this struggle between order and chaos, the king was believed to be the son of the god; his maintenance of justice was part of the divine order and contributed to it. He was a guardian of the stability of the cosmos and an actor in the divine drama. By adopting the institution of kingship from their neighbours, the Israelites would be swept into an alien mythology. They could become a nation like all the rest, but they would be nothing more.

Although Samuel first anointed Saul, from the tribe of Benjamin, God began to regret the choice because Saul 'has turned back from me, and has not performed my commandments'. In particular, God seems to have been angry because Saul had mercy on the Amalekites after defeating them in battle, and did not completely destroy them and all their animals and possessions. Samuel is upset that Saul has become a disappointment, but God tells him that he has already chosen a replacement. 'How long will you grieve over Saul?' he asks. 'Fill your horn with oil, and go; I will send you to Jesse the Bethlehemite, for I have provided for myself a king among his sons.'

Samuel becomes anxious that Saul might realize he is acting against him, but God suggests that he invite Jesse and his sons to participate in the sacrifice of a heifer. This will give him a pretext to visit the family, and to anoint the son whom God has chosen as king. He is warned, however, that 'the Lord sees not as man sees; man looks on the outward appearance, but the Lord looks on the heart'. After inspecting seven of the sons, Samuel notices that God has said nothing to him, and he asks Jesse if there are any more. Jesse tells him that his youngest son is guarding the sheep, and Samuel asks him to fetch the boy. When the boy arrives, God finally speaks to Samuel, telling him that this is the one he should anoint. As Samuel takes the horn of oil and anoints David in the presence of his brothers, the spirit of the Lord descends upon him.

If the spirit of the Lord is now with David, it departs from Saul. In its place, an evil spirit arrives to torment him. When David is brought to play the harp before his master, in the hope that music might calm him, the rejected king meets the boy who will replace him. David becomes his armour bearer and musician, and the rest of the First Book of Samuel is devoted to describing the decline of Saul and the growing power of David. After Saul is killed in battle, David is anointed king by the men of Judah at Hebron, and sets about unifying the tribes of the north and the south. Once he succeeds, he is anointed a third time, as king of all Israel. With the tribes of Israel united behind him, David captures the ancient Jebusite capital of Jerusalem, 'the stronghold of Zion, that is, the city of David'. From this great fortress, he begins the task of subduing the Philistines.

The narrative now returns to the question of the Ark, and devotes two chapters to an account of how David brought the Ark from Kiryath-yearim to Jerusalem. It was not carried, but placed in a cart drawn by oxen, just as the Philistines had done when they returned it after pestilence afflicted their people and the statue of their god Dagon had been shattered. On the road to Jerusalem, David and all the house of Israel rejoice before the Ark, dancing and singing, playing harps and tambourines. They are obeying none of the requirements of the Priestly Ark, it seems, but no harm comes to them until they reach the threshing floor of Nacon. Here, the oxen that are yoked to the cart stumble. When Uzzah, the brother of the consecrated guardian, reaches out to steady the Ark, he dies immediately. Not surprisingly, David 'was afraid of the Lord that day'. Even if this does not seem to be the Priestly Ark, it can still destroy anyone who touches it unwittingly, regardless of his intention.

Uncertain if he should bring the Ark inside the walls of Jerusalem after such an alarming portent, and anxious to determine what the will of God might be, David leaves the Ark at the house of Obededom the Gittite. For the next three months, Obededom and his family prosper in the most spectacular manner, and the later rabbis describe how the women were blessed with a miraculous fecundity, bestowed on them by the proximity of God who created every living thing. It seems that danger has been averted; the presence of the Ark will mean life for Israel rather than death.

David decides that it is safe to bring the Ark up to the city. He slaughters animals in sacrifice, and the people sing, blow horns and dance with joy. But at this point, the narrative describes something odd. The joy at the arrival of the Ark was not universal. 'As the Ark of the Lord came into the city of David,' we are told, 'Michal the daughter of Saul looked out of the window, and saw King David leaping and dancing before the Lord; and she despised him in her heart.'

For the moment, David is occupied with installing the Ark in the tent that he pitched for it, and making burnt offerings and peace offerings before it. When he returns to his wife, however, her contempt for his behaviour is undiminished: 'How the king of Israel honoured himself today, uncovering himself today before the eyes of his servants' maids, as one of the common men exposes himself without shame!' David is said to reply that his joy was in the Lord, who chose him above Saul, her father, and the narrative adds that Michal was barren until the day of her death, presumably because of her contempt for the enthusiasm that David displayed before the Ark of the Covenant. She was the last of the house of Saul.

The dance that David performs is unlike anything mentioned in the Hebrew Bible. Was it simply an expression of exuberance? Why should Michal have regarded it as such an embarrassment? A description of the natural world dancing in ecstasy after the power of God has been revealed appears in Psalm 114. Three demonstrations of divine power over nature are mentioned in the Psalm: the parting of the waters of the Red Sea during the Exodus, the interruption of the Jordan when the Levites carry the Ark into the Land of Canaan, and the waters that burst from the rock in the wilderness of Zin when Moses strikes it with his rod.

> When Israel went forth from Egypt,
> the house of Jacob from a people of strange language,
> Judah became his sanctuary,
> Israel his dominion.
>
> The sea looked and fled,
> Jordan turned back.
> The mountains skipped like rams,
> the hills like lambs.

What ails you, O sea, that you flee?
O Jordan, that you turn back?
O mountains, that you skip like rams?
O hills, like lambs?

Tremble, O earth, at the presence of the Lord,
at the presence of the God of Jacob,
who turns the rock into a pool of water,
the flint into a spring of water.

The Psalm is reminiscent of the Ugaritic myth of Baal, where a vigorous and passionate dance of joy follows the victory of the storm god. Is it possible that David and his companions are dancing before the victorious Ark to imitate the dance of nature at the victory of God?

Why should Michal find this so repellent? The charge that David has behaved in a vulgar way in front of the servants, and his later difficulty in confining his attentions to his own wives, have led to the suggestion that Michal is denouncing him for sexual impropriety. This seems a lesser charge than cultic impropriety, unless, of course, the two could be combined. Does Michal see her husband as having been polluted through some abominable Canaanite ritual, an orgiastic frenzy in which the celebrants abandon themselves to the rites of fertility, instead of good clean Yahwistic convention? Is the matter made even worse by the fact that David is not of pure Israelite descent, the blood of Moab and Canaan flowing through his veins as a tainted legacy of Ruth and Tamar?

The purity of Israel is a fault line running through the Hebrew Bible, and the political agenda that David was pursuing when he brought the Ark to Jerusalem may seem clear enough in general terms, but the details are now difficult to follow. Would a cult in which the great shrine of the tribes of Israel began to be venerated in terms of the mythology of the surrounding peoples serve to unite his kingdom? Is this the point of the ideology of Zion, the ancient Jebusite city now proclaimed to be the seat of the God of Israel, and glorified in Psalms that seem so similar to the epics of Baal discovered at Ras Shamra? And is this the reason that David will take the extraordinary step of appointing two high priests to serve before the Ark in Jerusalem? One is Israelite, but could the other, Zadok the priest, be the last of the Jebusite priesthood and bring with his appointment the loyalty of a people born outside Israel?

Once the Ark has arrived at Jerusalem, David proposes to build a house for it. 'See now,' he complains to the prophet Nathan, 'I dwell in a house of cedar, but the Ark of God dwells in a tent.' Nathan assures the king that God will allow him to proceed, that God is with him in what he proposes to do. During the night, however, the word of God speaks to the prophet, asking if the Israelites are about to build him a house. He reminds Nathan that he has not lived in a house since he brought his Chosen People out of Egypt, but has been moving about in a tent. If the Ark had been in a tent for so many years, and God has never asked for a house of cedar, why should he want one now?

The voice of God then recites the events of David's life, and in a passage of immense importance for the history of Judaism and Christianity, he inverts the proposal that David has made, announcing what has become known as the Davidic Covenant. David will not build a house for God; God will build a house for David.

> I took you from the pasture, from following the sheep, that you should be prince over my people Israel; and I have been with you wherever you went, and have cut off all your enemies from before you; and I will make for you a great name, like the name of the great ones of the earth ... Moreover the Lord declares to you that the Lord will make you a house. When your days are fulfilled and you lie down with your fathers, I will raise up your offspring after you, who shall come forth from your body, and I will establish his kingdom. He shall build a house for my name, and I will establish the throne of his kingdom for ever. I will be his father, and he shall be my son. When he commits iniquity, I will chasten him with the rod of men, with the stripes of the sons of men; but I will not take my steadfast love from him, as I took it from Saul, whom I put away from before you. And your house and your kingdom shall be made sure for ever before me; your throne shall be established for ever.

The Covenant of David is unlike the earlier covenants that God had made with the people of Israel. It is a covenant with a single family, and it seems that it will endure regardless of the failings of that family. The 'Court History' on which the account of David is thought to be based speaks of his faults with a candour that can be highly critical, and which may reflect sources that were hostile to the pretensions of the dynasty. As it stands, however, the text seems to deliver a clear message: God has chosen David and his line; his steadfast love for them will endure.

The Chronicler provides a less nuanced account of David, drawing attention to his splendid achievements and ignoring his faults. In the Second Book of Chronicles, he also provides another reason for David not being allowed to build the Temple. The king remarks that he intended to build a house of rest for the Ark of the Covenant of the Lord, and for the footstool of God. He even made preparations for building, but God told him that he could not build a house for the divine name. David was a warrior and had shed blood.

This seems very odd, however, given that the Ark has been a palladium in war, and that David had been fighting as the anointed of God. It would be perverse if his victories were to disqualify him from building the Temple. And even if the bloodshed had been a crime, the covenant speaks of God standing by the Davidic house regardless of any failings. Is the problem not that something was wrong with David, but that something was wrong with the Temple?

The problem would seem to be that the Temple was not an ancient Israelite institution, but belonged to the world 'of the other nations'. When Solomon does eventually build a Temple, he relies on foreign craftsmen, and the description of his Temple would seem to be very similar to what we know of temples among neighbouring peoples. The issue is not so much the plan or the construction of the Temple, although these are important, as the descriptions of the cosmic arena in which it functions. These are closely tied with role of the king and the status of Zion as the holy mountain of God.

The cosmic nature of Israelite kingship is especially obvious in Psalm 89, which proclaims the covenant with David, the victory of God in heaven, and his rule over the waters of chaos. David is anointed to rule not only over man, but over nature as well, and God has set the hand of his anointed king on the waters of the sea and the rivers. His lineage and his throne will endure for ever, as long as the sun and the moon. The house of David is therefore confirmed as part of the natural order of Creation. God has created life through his victory over the waters of chaos and over Rahab, the monster that inhabits them. While the victory was achieved by God, his king is depicted as sharing in it.

This triumph over the forces of the Deep appears throughout the Psalms, where the crossing of the Red Sea during the Exodus is often seen in terms of the cosmic battle with chaos. When the waters of the Deep see God, they are terrified. In the midst of a storm, God opens a way through the sea with his lightning and his thunder, and Moses and Aaron lead the children of Israel as shepherds lead their flock.

The same vision of cosmic war appears in the later prophecies included in the book of Isaiah. The prophet proclaims the Exodus from Egypt as a victory of God over the Great Deep, where the monster Rahab lives among the waters of the sea. 'Was it not you who dismembered Rahab and pierced the dragon?' he asks of God. 'Was it not you who dried up the sea, the water of the great deep, who made the depths of the sea a way for the redeemed to cross over?' As in the Psalms, the power of God over the monsters of chaos is an essential part of the belief that Zion will endure. After he describes the deliverance of Israel at the Red Sea in terms of the ancient myth, the prophet ties the myth to his hope in Zion: 'And the ransomed of the Lord shall return, and come to Zion with singing.'

The name 'Zion' will become inseparable from the later history of the Ark of the Covenant. We know almost nothing of its origin, however. It referred to the ancient Jebusite fortification captured by David, who is said to have changed its name from 'the stronghold of Zion' to 'the City of David'. At first, it probably referred to a ridge in the south-eastern part of Jerusalem, but once the Temple had been built, the hill on which it stood came to be known as Mount Zion. From this, the name was applied to Jerusalem itself, the city in which the Temple stood, and by extension, it came to refer to the people of Israel as a whole. In later centuries, it would be adopted by Christians who regarded themselves as the New Israel, and in Ethiopia a fascination with Zion would lie at the heart of an imperial cult of the Virgin Mary as the New Ark of the Covenant.

One of the more mysterious remarks about Zion appears in Psalm 48: 'His holy mountain, beautiful in elevation is the joy of all the earth; Mount Zion, in the north, the city of the great King.' The problem is that Zion is not 'in the north'. The Hebrew word is actually *zaphon*, and in the Ugaritic texts discovered at Ras Shamra, Zaphon is the holy mountain of Baal. It is a mountain north of Ugarit, and therefore north of Jerusalem as well. However unorthodox it might seem, the Psalmist has identified the holy mountain of God and the abiding symbol of Jewish identity with a pagan sanctuary and a pagan mythology.

It is difficult to know when this borrowing began. While it is possible that the vision of Zion incorporates an ancient Jebusite cult, the Book of Genesis tells us that the god of Jerusalem was named *El Elyon*. The Canaanite high god El has no connection with the mountain of Zaphon, or with the victory of the storm god over the waters of chaos. If the biblical traditions about Zion are based on myths associated with Baal rather than El, they would seem to be a later invention to enhance the prestige of the king by offering him a role in the victory of God over chaos. The appointment of Zadok as priest may reflect a political manoeuvre no less subtle than the manipulation of an ancient Jebusite cult, but it would seem to be connected with the unification of northern and southern factions within Israel.

The choice of Zion became one of the favourite themes of the great cultic hymns. Zion is the holy mountain of God. He has elected to live there, and the Ark and the Temple now stand there. The classic proclamation in which the Davidic Covenant, the choice of Zion and the Presence of God in the Ark of the Covenant are inextricably bound together is Psalm 132. It describes the oath that David swears to build a house for the Ark. He finds the Ark at Kiryath-yearim, and God and his Ark set out for their new home. For his part, God swears an oath that the sons of David will sit for ever on the throne of Israel. God has chosen Zion as his eternal house. The people of Zion will be blessed, their priests will be clothed in salvation, and the enemies of the king will be humiliated.

The promise contained a danger, however. If the people of Israel and their kings believe that God will never desert Zion under any circumstances, if they believe that the Covenant of David has replaced the moral demands made in the covenant revealed at Mount Sinai, would they continue to behave in the manner that God expected of his Chosen People? The great prophets wrestled with this dilemma: would trust in God lead to complacency, and then to destruction? Isaiah even considered the appalling prospect that God was deliberately leading his people toward disaster; that his prophecies were intended to close their eyes and their ears so that escape became impossible. In the end, the fears of the prophets seemed to be confirmed by the loss of the Temple and the disappearance of the Ark when the Babylonians occupied Jerusalem. In the Ethiopian epic about the Ark, there is little doubt. The people of Israel had behaved with such wickedness that the Ark itself decided to leave Jerusalem and find a new home in Africa.

Although disaster came upon the Temple, heaven and earth had been united while it stood, and those who dreamed of its restoration believed that the blessings it provided would return to Israel and to the world. Yet there were also those who saw it as a terrible mistake from the beginning. It belonged to the idolatrous cults of the nations and meant that Israel was now abandoning the Promised Land and walking back to Egypt. There were claims that the Temple was built with demonic assistance, and it is true that the cost of it destroyed the kingdom of Israel. Solomon might have raised the Temple to place his kingdom on a sure foundation, but his dream died with him.

It is often claimed that the Ethiopians are devoted to the Temple just as they are to the Ark, but we shall see that this is not true. And while it has also been claimed that the Ethiopian epic repeats the confident assertions of the Davidic Covenant, the pages of curses that will fall upon the New Israel if it displays the disobedience of the Old show that this is mistaken. In Ethiopia, as in the pages of the Old Testament, an imperial cult in which the Ark plays a central role is denounced as a rejection of the true faith.

CHAPTER 6
The Gates of Eden

At the end of time, as the dead awake from the grave, they will look across the Valley of Kidron to the Noble Sanctuary, where the Temple of Solomon once stood. Within the Temple, the Ark of the Covenant and the Presence of God had lived among the Chosen People, but for almost 2,000 years, no trace of them has been seen in the Holy City. On the Temple Mount today, the most beautiful shrine of Late Antiquity marks the triumph of another Chosen People, the lineage of Ishmael, whose prophet ascended to heaven from the Rock on which Solomon had placed the Ark.

Even today, among the tombs on the Mount of Olives, the vision of the Old City is perhaps the most enchanting and the most troubling that one could see. While Athens has been called a city of the mind, Jerusalem has been a city of the spirit – a spirit torn between the demands of earth and heaven. It stands as a witness not only to inspiration, but also to torment – to the collision of truths that we have been unable to reconcile. 'Ten measures of suffering', according to a Jewish proverb, 'were sent by God upon the world, and nine of them fell on Jerusalem.' By the tenth century, the Arab geographer al-Muqaddasi described the city as 'a golden basin full of scorpions'.

The Old City appears much as the Scottish painter David Roberts would have seen it 160 years ago, when the six monumental volumes of his *Holy Land, Egypt and Nubia* brought a vivid record of the biblical world to readers who could afford the subscription price. The hills beyond the city walls may now be covered with apartment blocks built of concrete, but Roberts had preferred an imaginary Jerusalem long before they were placed there, ignoring whatever he thought might spoil the charm of his picture. In averting their eyes from what they choose not to see in Jerusalem, modern pilgrims follow a hallowed custom.

The air of Judaea is still clear, however, and the sun is still brilliant, and we can gaze upon the same walls that Roberts sketched when he sat among the tombs on the Mount of Olives. The walls were built by the greatest of the Ottoman sultans, Suleiman the Magnificent, but they seem to have risen by their own power from the limestone ridge on which his masons laid the foundations. We can admire the domes among the trees, and the arcades of graceful arches from which Muslim tradition tells us that scales will be hung to weigh the souls of the dead on the Day of Judgement.

For the past thirteen centuries, the Temple Mount and indeed the prospect of all Jerusalem have been dominated by the Dome of the Rock. It is often known as the Mosque of Omar, but it is not a mosque and it was not built by the caliph Umar. It is a shrine, and although it is one of the holiest sites in the Islamic world, the Abbasid caliph Abd al-Malik commissioned it in the shape of a Byzantine church. On the ruins of the ancient Temple of the Jews, a sinuous calligraphy whose letters adorn the dome with words revealed to Muhammad by God himself now proclaims the victory and the perfection of the truths given to the last of the prophets.

As the sun rises behind the Mount of Olives, the golden dome of the shrine appears to reflect the brilliance of a celestial realm, and the Armenian tiles that cover the octagonal walls in the colours of heaven reveal the perfect geometry of a harmonious creation. The prospect seems to be an ideal garden, a sanctuary in the midst of a fallen world, and even though much of it displays the skill of Christian artisans working for a Muslim master, their achievements recall the aspirations of the ancient Israelites. According to the Book of Kings, the First Temple was decorated with trees and flowers, in the image of the Garden of Eden, and later traditions maintained that when the Ark was carried into the sanctuary on the order of Solomon, the wood and the stone were brought to life.

Walking into the Old City through the immense arch of the Damascus Gate, which Suleiman the Magnificent built in 1538, the modern pilgrim can pass through the Arab Quarter toward the Haram al-Sharif, the Noble Sanctuary with the Dome of the Rock. Despite the collapse of Ottoman power almost four centuries after Suleiman first sat on his throne in Constantinople, despite the withdrawal of the British Mandate that replaced the Turks when General Allenby entered the Old City as a conquering hero in 1917, and despite the birth of the Jewish state declared twenty years later, some things seem to have changed little since earlier generations followed the same route. Elders whose heads and shoulders are wrapped in kaffiyeh drink coffee as the smoke from Turkish tobacco in their nargileh drifts along the pavement. Mounds of oranges, melons, cucumbers and aubergines have been carefully piled by the fruit merchants in front of their shops. The fragrance of cardamon, cloves and cumin lingers among the shelves of the spice sellers, while trays of sweetmeats filled with pistachios, almonds and rosewater tempt the passerby from the window of the pastahane. Through the narrow lanes and the awnings of the shops, light and shadow play across the ancient stone, as boys with trays of bread fresh from the oven of the bakery deliver it to restaurants and shops nearby.

However much the eye of the visitor can find delight in the recollections of an earlier world, the Old City is not a happy place. Ottoman governors used to devote such energies as they possessed to keeping peace between squabbling Christians. Now, Palestinians of both Christian and Muslim belief, as well as the Greeks and Armenians who have lived in the Old City for centuries, find themselves a stumbling block to Jewish ambitions over Jerusalem as a whole. After the horrors of modern Europe, the creation of the Jewish state as a refuge and homeland was a wonderful thing, and yet the place of communities that have lived in Jerusalem longer than anyone can now remember, and for whom the city is no less holy, has not been resolved. The weight of the immense sanctity and the centuries of joy and sorrow that the city has witnessed, and caused, can seem impossible to bear even for the few minutes it takes a pilgrim to walk toward the site where the Temple built for the Ark once stood.

Near the Western Wall of the Temple Mount, the narrow streets of the Old City suddenly open on to a vast and empty plaza. Here the Moroccan Quarter stood until 10 June 1967. The day after Israeli troops had brought Jerusalem under Jewish control during the Six Day War, the entire quarter was destroyed, even the twelfth-century shrine of Sheikh Aid, in a dramatic move that might have been taken from the biblical account of Joshua and the conquest of Canaan. Israelis had been denied access to the wall since the Jewish state was founded. Now they would not only have access, but they would have access enough for thousands of faithful who would hope to gather by the wall to mark the loss of the Temple destroyed first by the armies of Nebuchadnezzar in 587 BC, and then by the Romans in AD 70.

The Western Wall was often known as the 'Wailing Wall' to European visitors who saw Jews grieving over the loss of the Temple. After the French novelist Pierre Loti had passed through Jerusalem, he described the scenes he had witnessed there.

Against the wall of the Temple, against the last debris of its past splendour are the lamentations of Jeremiah which they all repeat ... 'Because of the Temple which is destroyed,' cries the rabbi. 'We sit alone and weep!' replies the crowd. 'Because of our walls which are fallen,' 'We sit alone and we weep!' 'Because of our majesty which has passed, because of our great men who are no longer alive,' 'We sit alone and we weep!'

Christian pilgrims in the Middle Ages had seen the same despair. Lamenting that Zion had become a wilderness, and Jerusalem a desolation, Jews would tear their clothes as they approached the city, and tear them again when they reached the Temple Mount itself. According to the rabbis, their clothes should be torn until the heart was laid bare, and then never sewn again.

The grief was not simply a matter of personal loss. Even if the laments were uttered by Jews, they were not laments for Jews alone. The Temple and its sacrifices had given peace and order to the world. The waters that flowed from beneath its foundations had brought fertility and prosperity. The Rock on which the Temple was built was believed to be the foundation stone of the universe itself. Beneath the Temple were the waters of the great abyss that had burst forth and flooded the earth in the days of Noah. The loss of the Temple was a disaster of cosmic proportions, like the expulsion of Adam and Eve from Paradise.

In the Bible, the story of the Temple begins with the accession of

King Solomon. His father David, the beloved of God, was growing old, and as his death approached, he assured Bathsheba that Solomon would inherit the throne. According to the First Book of Kings, the succession was by no means straightforward. Adonijah, whose mother was Haggith, attempted to set himself up as king even while his father was alive, but Zadok the priest opposed him, along with Nathan the prophet and the 'mighty men' of David. Nathan warned Bathsheba that Adonijah was ambitious, and advised her that she would be able to save herself and her son only if she faced David and reminded him of the oath that he had sworn to her. Even though he was not the eldest son, David had promised that Solomon would become king when he died.

Solomon was therefore taken to Gihon, riding on a mule belonging to his father, and when they arrived, Zadok the priest anointed the young man with 'the horn of oil from the tent'. The account is difficult to understand. We are never told why Gihon should be chosen as the site for the anointing, and it is hard to imagine why the holy oil needed to prepare a king to rule over Israel should be placed in a tent at Gihon, which we otherwise know as a spring outside the walls of Jerusalem. Could this have been the tent that David erected when he brought the Ark of the Covenant to his new capital? Could the Tabernacle itself have been at Gihon? The site is never mentioned as a sanctuary, however, and it seems to have nothing to do with the Ark or the Tabernacle. In an attempt to solve the puzzle, scholars have suggested that the name might simply be a corruption for Gibeon, where the Tabernacle was kept after the Ark had come to Jerusalem, and where God would later appear to Solomon in a dream. This is little more than a guess, however, and the mystery remains.

Once Solomon was anointed, his inheritance seemed to be secure. He ascended the throne after David 'slept with his fathers', but even though he had promised his elder brother that he would not be harmed, it was not long before Adonijah drew attention to himself and hastened his own death. He approached Bathsheba and asked her to intercede with Solomon on his behalf, hoping that a concubine who had served David in his final years might become his own wife. Solomon assumed that the request would lead to more provocative and more perilous demands, and he ordered an immediate execution. While he spared the priest Abiathar, even though he was known to have supported Adonijah in his earlier attempts to become king, he nevertheless banished him to an estate outside Jerusalem, explaining the reason why he escaped death. 'Go to Anathoth,' he told the priest, 'to your estate, for you deserve to die; but I will not put you to death because you carried the Ark of the Lord God before David my father, and because you shared in all his affliction.' The departure of Abiathar would mean that the dual priesthood established by David passed into the hands of Zadok. The priests of Shiloh would now be isolated and unhappy. Even when Solomon died and the north and south became separate kingdoms, they were not invited to serve at the great shrines. The legacy of their bitterness may be found in the traditions that denounce Solomon as an idolator, and that try to undermine their rivals and even the cult of the Ark itself.

Shortly after Solomon becomes king, God appears to him in a dream while he sleeps at Gibeon. When God asks what he should give him, Solomon replies that the kingdom of David had been entrusted to him even though he was only a child. He did not even know how to go out or come in. He therefore asks God to give him 'an understanding mind', so that he can distinguish between good and evil, and use his knowledge to govern the Chosen People. When he hears the request, God is delighted and tells Solomon that, because he has asked for wisdom and not for long life or riches or for the lives of his enemies, he will grant his wish. Solomon will have a wise and discerning mind, so that none like him will ever have been before and none like him will ever arise again. Even more, he will give Solomon the things that he had not asked to receive, both riches and honour, so that no other king will be compared to him as long as he lives.

Solomon awakes and, realizing that he has been dreaming of God, he returns to Jerusalem. Standing before the Ark of the Covenant, he makes burnt offerings and peace offerings, and then provides a feast for all his servants. God then gives Solomon wisdom and understanding beyond measure, like the sand on the seashore. His wisdom surpasses the wisdom of all the people of the East, and all the wisdom of Egypt. He becomes wiser than any other man.

The fame of Solomon and his great wisdom now spread through all the nations. He is said to have uttered 3,000 proverbs and over

1,000 songs. His wisdom became so vast that it extended beyond the knowledge of men into the world of nature. The First Book of Kings claims that 'he spoke of trees, from the cedar that is in Lebanon to the hyssop that grows out of the wall; he spoke also of beasts, and of birds, and of reptiles, and of fish'. This was taken to mean that Solomon not only spoke of the animals, but also spoke to them; he knew their language and could discover their secrets. His power over nature grew so great that he was said to control the spirits of the air. When the Aramaic homilies of the *Targum Sheni* to Esther were composed during the seventh or eighth century AD, Solomon's powers over the natural and the supernatural world were made explicit. He rules over the wild beasts, we are told, over the birds of the heaven, and over the creeping beasts of the earth. He even rules over the devils and the spirits of the night, and he understands the languages that all these creatures use. After all, it is written that 'he talked with the trees'.

The power that Solomon gained over devils and spirits of the dark meant that his name was used in spells and incantations. In later Jewish, Christian and Muslim tradition, he became a great magician and sorcerer, and ever more elaborate ways were sought to extol his brilliance. As recently as the eighteenth century, the Baal Shem Tov, the most illustrious of Jewish mystics and the founder of the Hasidim in eastern Europe, was said to have been given a mysterious book found in a cave by Rabbi Adam. It was filled with a sacred light, and in letters of black fire it revealed celestial mysteries hidden even from the angels. God had revealed these to Adam while he was still in Paradise, and in his mercy allowed the father of the human race to retain the book after the Fall. It passed down the line of the Patriarchs and was buried with Joseph in Egypt. It was retrieved along with his body, and carried through the wilderness beside the Ark of the Covenant on the journey to the Promised Land. The book contained the secret knowledge that Solomon had used to erect the Temple, and although it was thought to have been lost when the Temple was destroyed, God had commanded the angel Hadarniel to conceal it in a cave, allowing only men with pure souls to see it in later generations. The Baal Shem Tov, 'Master of the Good Name', was one of these, and although he lived only two centuries ago, the story is known to have been told as early as the third or fourth century when the *Book of Mysteries* was written in Palestine.

The claim that Solomon raised the Temple with demonic assistance is made in great detail by the *Testament of Solomon*, which seems to be a Christian version written in Egypt at some point between the first and the third centuries. In response to his prayers, the archangel Michael gives a ring to Solomon, set with a precious stone on which a seal has been engraved. The angel announces that it is a gift from God, and that by using the ring Solomon will be able to imprison every demon in the universe and command them to build Jerusalem for him. His encounters with the demons and the tasks they perform for him are described in great detail, the point of the story being that, as Solomon grew older, he began to follow the gods of his foreign wives, until the spirit of God departed from him and the demons treated him with contempt.

The origin of the legends about Solomon and his wisdom are often thought to lie in the demands for a more sophisticated form of government, and it is true that in the Hebrew Bible itself 'wisdom' is a subtle and complex theme that can be practical as well as mystical, including lists of maxims to help readers lead better lives in terms that one suspects the prophets would have thought irrelevant or simply nauseating: 'a rich man's wealth is his strong city; the poverty of the poor is their ruin', or 'a son who gathers in summer is prudent, but a son who sleeps in harvest brings shame'. Some of them seem to preserve career advice from a professional elite: 'Without counsel plans go wrong, but with many advisers they succeed.'

If the empire established by his father was far larger than the tribal alliances of earlier generations, it would have been difficult for Solomon to govern it without the bureaucracy that Samuel warned the Children of Israel would accompany kingship. Neighbouring empires in Egypt and Mesopotamia employed scribes to manage their civil service, and the biblical books attributed to Solomon reveal not just a knowledge of these traditions of right conduct, but an actual dependence upon them. Just over a century ago, substantial portions of the Proverbs of Solomon were revealed to be Egyptian when Ernest Wallis Budge returned from his first mission to Egypt with a papyrus containing the *Teachings of Amenemope* – a treatise of scribal wisdom known to have been written in the latter half of the Twenty-first Dynasty.

Nevertheless, aside from the record preserved in the Hebrew Bible, we know very little of the empire ruled by Solomon or his father. It is presented as a vast territory in which the kings of Israel ruled over many different peoples, but it is not easy to imagine space for this among the great powers of the day, and so far little record of it has been found in the inscriptions of neighbouring empires or excavations by archaeologists. But even if their dominion had been praised in extravagant terms by later writers who looked back on it as a golden age, an ambitious ruler in the ancient Near East would certainly have required a Temple, an outward and visible sign of the mandate of heaven in his capital. Whether or not Solomon would have needed a large and sophisticated civil service, he would have needed to establish the legitimacy of his reign in his own eyes and those of his subjects by the sort of statement understood throughout the ancient Near East. The description that we are given in the First Book of Kings describes a Temple similar to those we know from other regions in the area, including those that have been excavated elsewhere in Syria and Palestine. Although the Bible is usually anxious to emphasize the unique nature of Israelite religion, this should not be surprising. The Second Book of Chronicles is quite clear about the extent to which foreign workmen were involved in the construction of the building, one of the first steps that Solomon took being a request to the neighbouring king of Tyre for men and material.

The huge number of workers required for such an enormous undertaking meant that Solomon relied upon forced labour. Apparently he compiled a census, a step that might seem to require the sort of skilled bureaucracy associated with professional wisdom, and assigned tasks to both Israelites and foreigners living within his borders. Some 70,000 men carried burdens, 80,000 worked in the quarries and 3,600 served as overseers. Teams of men were sent to the Lebanon to work alongside the Sidonians, hewing wood and stone. The prophecy of Samuel, it seems, was being fulfilled, and the cost of demanding a king was being confirmed to the people of Israel. Solomon himself would pay a heavy price for building his Temple, and his heirs an even heavier price. To meet the debts that he owed the king of Tyre, Solomon was forced to yield twenty cities in Galilee, and even this did not seem to be enough. After his death, one of the captains of the forced labour would lead a rebellion that would shatter the empire into two separate kingdoms, leaving the lineage of Solomon with only a portion of land that he and his father had once controlled.

The start of work is announced in the First Book of Kings with a formal chronology: 'in the four hundred and eightieth year after the people of Israel came out of the land of Egypt, in the fourth year that Solomon reigned over Israel, in the month of Ziv, which is the second month, he began to build the house of the Lord'. We are then told the dimensions of the Temple, the materials from which it was built, and the various types of furniture and ritual objects that were made for it. The obscurity of a number of the Hebrew terms and our ignorance of the methods that ancient Near Eastern masons and carpenters might have used means that it is often impossible for us now to understand exactly what the author intended to say. The standard translations read by anyone who does not know Hebrew are reliable enough, but the translators will inevitably have been forced to guess in a number of places. This is not simply a modern problem. Even by the third century BC, the translators of the Septuagint found some passages of the Hebrew text to be quite incomprehensible.

The Temple is described in the First Book of Kings, and then in the Second Book of Chronicles, with a few variations. The basic ground plan of the Temple was a rectangle, 100 cubits long and 50 cubits wide. In the custom of many of the temples found in Palestine and Syria, its inner sacred space was divided into three separate areas. At Jerusalem, each of these was 20 cubits wide. The height of the central area was 30 cubits, although the innermost sanctuary was only 20 cubits high. The biblical narrative offers no explanation for the difference.

In the cubical space of the innermost sanctuary known as the *debir*, there were two enormous cherubim, carved from olivewood and covered with gold. The wingspan of each cherub was 10 cubits, and each was 10 cubits in height. Their wings were stretched to protect the most holy object in the Temple, and indeed the most holy object in the world, the Ark of the Covenant. Here, according to the words spoken by Solomon in the biblical account, 'the Lord has said that he would dwell in thick darkness'.

After explaining the structure and decoration of the Temple itself, the account goes on to describe the two pillars of bronze named Jachin and Boaz, which stood by the entrance, and the other furniture for the Temple. There was a molten sea, ten stands of bronze, ten lavers of bronze, as well as pots, shovels and basins. There was also a golden altar, a golden table for the bread of the Presence, and ten lampstands of pure gold. There were flowers, lamps and tongs of gold, cups, snuffers, basins, dishes for incense, and firepans of pure gold. Sockets of gold were made for the doors of the inner sanctuary, where the Ark was hidden, and for the doors of the nave.

Along with the difficulty of understanding Hebrew technical terms and ancient methods of construction, anyone who has attempted to reconstruct the plan of the Temple has been frustrated by the lack of any corroboration from ancient witnesses. The descriptions that have survived, such as the lengthy account by Josephus, describe the Second Temple with the elaborate additions made by Herod the Great in the first century AD. They do not describe the Temple of Solomon. There has been an additional problem. In the Book of Ezekiel, six chapters are devoted to a detailed vision of the Temple, ostensibly written while the Temple of Solomon was still standing. It is not the same temple described in the books of Kings and Chronicles, however, and in the belief that a divinely inspired prophet must have described the Temple without error, elaborate attempts to correlate the two descriptions were undertaken by some of the most gifted and learned Jewish and Christian commentators. Muslim scholars, as we shall see, had their own solution.

Beyond the quest to determine the plan and structure of the Temple, it was not always easy to understand the details of the rituals performed in it. For many Christian readers, the biblical narratives might seem to be describing a superior kind of cathedral, in which immense wealth and consummate skill have been dedicated to constructing a sanctuary where the mystery of God could be celebrated in the most exalted of surroundings. But the Temple was an ancient vision of the cosmos, not a modern vision, and its workings were far removed from the conventions of modern sensibility. The primary purpose of the Temple was sacrifice, and this was performed on a scale that meant that the courts of the Temple resembled not so much a cathedral as a vast slaughter house.

Even the greatest of medieval Jewish scholars, Moses Maimonides, found the idea of sacrifice appalling, and in his *Guide of the Perplexed*, he claimed that it had been instituted as a necessary evil, to wean the Israelites from paganism. At an early stage in their history, they simply could not have grasped the idea of a religion without sacrifice. His complaints did not pass without comment, however, and Nahmanides, an eminent biblical scholar and kabbalist who lived in Catalonia several decades later, claimed that Maimonides was arguing against the Bible itself, which stated beyond any doubt that sacrifice had been divinely ordained as the most noble form of serving God.

Details of sacrifice are given in the Pentateuch, especially the Book of Leviticus, as well as in the Mishnah tractate *Tamid*. The precise regulations are complex, and as they clearly evolved over time, they are occasionally contradictory. Nevertheless, there are clear distinctions between burnt offerings, in which the sacrificed animal was burnt whole on the altar; sin and guilt offerings, in which the fat was burned on the altar and the meat was given to the priests; and peace offerings, in which the fat was burned on the altar and the meat was given to the worshipper for a joyful sacrificial feast. Public sacrifices required the burnt offering of a year-old ram every day at dawn and dusk. There were also supplements for the Sabbath and for the great festivals. Two rams were offered at each of the Sabbath sacrifices, while during the seven days of Passover, two bullocks, a ram and seven lambs were offered, along with a male goat as a sin offering. The most extensive public sacrifices were made during the Feast of Tabernacles. On the first day, thirteen bullocks, two rams and fourteen lambs were sacrificed, and this continued throughout the festival, the number of bullocks being reduced by one on each of the subsequent days. Even these public festivals accounted for only a small number of the animals slaughtered. They were far exceeded by sacrifices offered on behalf of individuals, and ancient sources confirm that these were so numerous that, during the great festivals, thousands of priests served in the Temple but were barely able to cope with the numbers of animals required.

The animals were slaughtered and skinned, the carcass was divided and the entrails were washed, and the blood was poured or splashed on the altar. All this occurred within the Temple court.

Most people in modern Europe, even though they eat the flesh of animals or wear leather made from their skins, are no longer accustomed to the realities of slaughter. We find it difficult to imagine the circumstances of animal sacrifice on this scale, and if we could, we would be horrified. We would also find it difficult to regard this as a spiritual matter, even if we admitted that slaughter might be a necessary fact of life. And yet, our own sensitivities or hypocrisies should not lead us to dismiss an ancient institution as barbaric. The Temple was not so much a diagram of the universe, which it is often said to be, as a kind of working model – a universe in miniature that contained the constant exchange between life and death. It was certainly regarded as such by the rabbis of later centuries.

The Bible itself has almost nothing to say about the role of the Ark in any of this sacrifice. From the account of the ritual for the Day of Atonement given in the Book of Leviticus as part of the service in the Tabernacle, we know that the high priest would enter the Holy of Holies to sprinkle blood on the cover of the Ark, and that he would place a cloud of incense between himself and the Ark to avoid injury from its power. It is generally assumed that the same ritual would have been performed in the Temple itself, once Solomon had ordered the Ark to be installed. The Mishnah tractate *Yoma*, which is devoted to questions about the Day of Atonement, describes the way in which the incense was brought into the Holy of Holies to ensure the survival of the high priest, and it speaks explicity of the terrifying nature of the ritual.

They brought out to him the ladle and the fire-pan and he took his two hands full of incense and put it in the ladle, which was large according to his largeness, or small according to his smallness; and such was the prescribed measure of the ladle. He took the fire-pan in his right hand and the ladle in his left. He went through the Sanctuary until he came to the space between the two curtains separating the Sanctuary from the Holy of Holies. And there was a cubit's space between them. Rabbi Jose says: Only one curtain was there, for it is written, *And the veil shall divide for you between the holy place and the most holy.* The outer curtain was looped up on the south side and the inner one on the north side. He went along between them until he reached the north side; when he reached the north he turned round to the south and went on with the curtain on his left hand until he reached the Ark. When he reached the Ark he put the fire-pan between the two poles. He heaped up the incense on the coals and the whole place became filled with smoke. He came out by the way he went in, and in the outer space he prayed a short prayer. But he did not prolong his prayer lest he put Israel in terror.

The same tractate also describes the way in which the priest would sprinkle the blood, after it had been stirred to prevent it coagulating.

He took the blood from him that was stirring it and entered again into the place where he had entered and stood on the place whereon he had stood, and sprinkled the blood once upwards and seven times downwards, not as though he had intended to sprinkle upwards or downwards but as though he were wielding a whip. And thus he used to count: One, one and one, one and two, one and three, one and four, one and five, one and six, one and seven. He came out and put it on the golden stand in the Sanctuary.

If we are disturbed by the idea of animal sacrifice, we are almost as uncomfortable at the thought of eroticism as part of the cult. The excitement and embarrassment with which the Song of Solomon has been read throughout the centuries is a direct result of the suspicion that it does not really belong in the Bible, and yet the rabbis were often much happier with the thought than we have been. They describe the Holy of Holies in which the Ark was kept as a bridal chamber. Solomon himself was believed to have written the Song of Songs, and to explain one of its verses the *Tanhuma* on Numbers makes an allusion to the Temple: 'Behold his bed, which is Solomon's: And why was the sanctuary compared to a bed? Because just as this bed serves fertility and reproduction, everything that was in the sanctuary was fertile and reproduced.'

When the Ark was brought into the sanctuary, carved trees and flowers burst into life, and the trees of gold that Solomon placed in the Temple grew heavy with fruit. The cedar that the king of Tyre sent to Solomon for the building of the Temple apparently realized that the Life of the World had been brought into the sanctuary and became green once again, while the poles that were used to carry the Ark of the Covenant began to grow when it was placed in the Holy of Holies. Eventually they grew so long that they reached the curtain covering the entrance, and as they continued to grow, the curtain began to swell like the breasts of a woman. This occurred when the Ark and the cherubim were placed in the Holy of Holies, and as the poles came to life, the cherubim began to spread their wings, covering the Ark and hovering over the sanctuary.

Some rabbis believed that the cherubim were the most important part of the sanctuary, their significance for the Temple rivalling or even surpassing the Ark of the Covenant itself. It was upon the cherubim, as well as upon the Ark that the Presence of God rested. They were also believed to represent the union between God and his Chosen People, and the rabbis often spoke in explicitly erotic terms about the nature of this union. Whenever the people of Israel came up to Jerusalem for the great festival, we are told, the curtain would be removed for them and the cherubim shown to them. The bodies of the cherubim were intertwined with one another, and the people would be told that God loved Israel as a man and a woman loved each other. As long as the people of Israel were obedient to the will of God, the faces of the cherubim apparently turned toward each other like those of two people embracing, to indicate the love that God felt toward Israel. When the people of Israel disobeyed the will of God, however, the cherubim looked away from each other and turned their faces toward the wall.

The greatest of the kabbalistic texts, the *Zohar* or 'Book of Splendour', gives a description of the Temple as a bridal chamber for God and the symbol of Israel known as the Matrona. Since the destruction of the Temple, the Matrona has descended every night to the site on which the Temple stood, and entered the place where the Ark had once been hidden. When she sees that her house and her bed have been ruined, she wanders in distraction, looking at the place where the cherubim had stood and weeping bitterly. She recalls that the Lord of the World would come to her as a husband and fulfil all her desires. She remembers how she would come to her bed in joy, and how the cherubim would come out to meet her, beating their wings in welcome. She asks how the Ark of the Covenant that stood in the sanctuary could have been forgotten. From the sanctuary, the entire world was nourished, and light and blessing were given to everyone. She looked for her husband, but he was no longer there. She remembered that this was the hour at which her husband used to come to her, and that she would hear the sound of the bells on his feet while he was still far away. All her maidens would offer praise to the Holy One, and then retire each to her own room, leaving them alone to embrace each other in love. She calls out to her husband, asking where he has gone. Does he not remember how he held his left arm beneath her head and his right arm around her body, swearing that he would never stop loving her, and saying, 'If I forget you, O Jerusalem, let my right hand forget ...'

According to the medieval *Midrash Rabbah*, 'the court surrounds the Temple just as the sea surrounds the world', and even as early as the second century AD, the Talmudic sage Rabbi Pinhas ben Yair provided an elaborate account of Creation in which he refers to the Tabernacle at first, and then describes the pillars of the Temple as if the Tabernacle and the Temple were identical. The Tabernacle, we are told, was made to correspond to the Creation of the world, and the two cherubim over the Ark of the Covenant were made to correspond to the two holy names of God. The sanctuary in which the Ark was placed was made to correspond to the highest heaven, the outer sanctuary was made to correspond to the earth, and the court was made to correspond to the sea. The eleven hangings of the Tabernacle were made to correspond to the highest heaven. The table was made to correspond to the earth. The two shewbreads were arranged to correspond to the fruit of the earth, in two rows of six that corresponded to the months of summer and winter. The laver was made to correspond to the sea and the candlestick was made to correspond to the lights of heaven. The pillar named Jachin corresponded to the verse 'it shall be established (*yikkon*) for ever as the moon', because the moon determined the feasts for Israel. The pillar named Boaz corresponded to the sun which comes out in power and in strength: as it is written, 'it rejoices as a strong man to run the course'.

The cherubim that the Bible describes on the cover of the Ark and as statues in the Holy of Holies were winged sphinxes, lions with human heads. The Akkadian word *karibu* or *kurubu* refers to a guardian spirit or intercessor, but although these figures appear in Mesopotamia during the third millennium BC, they are primarily associated with Egypt. They were guardians, and in the Book of Genesis we are told that, after the Fall, God placed cherubim at the east of the Garden of Eden to guard the Tree of Life. In the Temple, not only were two statues of cherubim placed in the Holy of Holies, but the walls of the Temple were covered with them, along with trees and flowers. The Temple, it seems, was intended to be another Garden of Eden.

The Temple was also said to shine with a light from the first day of Creation, which God made before the sun, the moon and the stars. These lights in heaven were created only on the fourth day, and according to Rabbinic tradition, the first ray of light on the first day illuminated the entire world, shining forth from the site on which the Temple was later built. While the Temple was standing, this first light continued to shine, its rays glowing within the Holy of Holies where the Ark of the Covenant was kept. Not only did it illuminate the Temple; the light also shone through the windows to fill the world. For this reason, the windows in the Temple were unlike those anywhere else. Other windows allow light to enter a house, but the windows in the Temple allowed light to escape.

The site from which this light shone upon the world was the first fixed point placed by God in the midst of the waters of chaos, before he built up the earth around it. It was known in Jewish tradition as the 'Stone of Foundation', and it was said to form the floor of the Holy of Holies on which the Ark rested. The Temple, and the Ark within it, stood at the very centre of the earth. Even though the Stone of Foundation was placed above the Abyss, the waters it contained had not disappeared. Rabbinic tradition preserves several accounts of David opening the Abyss and threatening the world with destruction. In the Babylonian Talmud, Rabbi Johanan is recorded as saying that, when David dug perpendicular shafts reaching down under the Temple to the Abyss, the waters rose up and threatened to flood the world as they had in the days of Noah. David asked his companions if anyone knew whether it was lawful to write the name of God on a piece of pottery and then throw it into the Abyss so that the water would subside. No one replied, and David told them that, if anyone knew the answer and kept quiet, he would be killed. Ahitophel then assured him that it was lawful, and David wrote the name of God on a potsherd and threw it into the Abyss. The waters withdrew to a depth of 16,000 cubits, and when David saw that the Abyss was now so far beneath the surface, he realized that it would be difficult to water the earth. He therefore spoke the fifteen Songs of Ascent, and the Abyss climbed 1,000 cubits for each of the songs, and remained 1,000 cubits beneath the surface. The songs that he spoke are Psalms 120–34, each of which begins with the title 'Song of Ascent'.

According to some traditions, the altar in the Temple had been built by Noah after the Flood had subsided. Later Jewish legends claimed that Noah had only restored the altar, and that it had already been used by Adam, Cain and Abel, and then by Abraham, before it was finally placed in the Temple itself.

Although the waters of the Abyss could be dangerous, life could not survive without them, as David understood. The loss of the Temple was to disrupt the fertility and abundance that the earth enjoyed while it stood, but the rabbis maintained that the waters would return in abundance during the Messianic Age. The river that flowed from beneath the Temple would divide into twelve streams – the number of the tribes of Israel. Every field and vineyard that was barren would be irrigated by these waters and would bear fruit. Every kind of fruit tree would grow beside the streams and bear fruit every month, and not only would their fruit provide nourishment, but also their leaves would cure anyone who suffered from any sort of ailment.

The Temple apparently took seven years to construct. This would seem to be a rather short time for the elaborate structure described in the Bible, and it may be a symbolic number chosen to recall the seven days of Creation. When all the preparations had been completed, it was time to fulfil the purpose for which the grand project had been undertaken. Solomon assembled the elders of Israel, the heads of the tribes and the leaders of all the houses in Jerusalem to witness the procession of the Ark and the miracles that accompanied it.

And all the men of Israel assembled to King Solomon at the feast in the month of Ethanim, which is the seventh month. And all the elders of Israel came, and the priests took up the Ark. And they brought up the Ark of the Lord, the Tent of Meeting, and all the holy vessels that were in the Tent; the priests and the Levites brought them up. And King Solomon and all the congregation of Israel, who had assembled before him, were with him before the Ark, sacrificing so many sheep and oxen that they could not be counted or numbered. Then the priests brought the Ark of the Covenant of the Lord to its place, in the inner sanctuary of the house, in the most holy place, underneath the wings of the cherubim. For the cherubim spread out their wings over the place of the Ark, so that the cherubim made a covering above the Ark and its poles. And the poles were so long that the ends of the poles were seen from the holy place before the inner sanctuary; but they could not be seen from outside; and they are there to this day. There was nothing in the Ark except the two tables of stone which Moses put there at Horeb, where the Lord made a covenant with the people of Israel, when they came out of the land of Egypt. And when the priests came out of the holy place, a cloud filled the house of the Lord, so that the priests could not stand to minister because of the cloud; for the glory of the Lord filled the house of the Lord.

The king then addressed the people and told them that God had fulfilled the promise that he had made. Solomon had risen in the place of David, his father, and was sitting on the throne of Israel. He had now built a house for the God of Israel, and he had provided a place for the Ark of the Covenant, in which the demands that God made of the Children of Israel when he brought them out of Egypt were recorded.

Before Solomon built the Temple, God appeared to him at Gibeon, and now he appears again. He confirms the Davidic Covenant, but this time it is conditional. Solomon should know that God has heard his prayer. The house that Solomon has built is consecrated by the presence of God, and his heart will be there for all time. Provided that Solomon conducts himself with integrity and adheres to all the commandments that God has given him, his lineage will be established on the royal throne of Israel for ever, just as God had promised David. However, God also delivers a dreadful warning. If Solomon or his children turn aside from following God and do not keep his commandments, if they ignore the statutes that he has provided for them and worship other gods, then he will cut off Israel from the land that he has given them. The Temple that he has consecrated for his name he will cast out of his sight. It will become a heap of ruins. Everyone who passes by it will be astonished and will hiss. They will ask why God has destroyed it, and then they will say that it was because Israel abandoned the Lord their God who brought their fathers out of the land of Egypt, and worshipped other gods.

Solomon was to do precisely what God had warned him not to do, however. The Bible tells us that he 'loved many foreign women', and among the 700 wives and 300 concubines were women born among the nations that God had commanded the men of Israel to avoid. Solomon showed some scruple at first, installing the daughter of Pharaoh in a separate house and explaining that she would not live in the house of David, 'for the places to which the Ark of the Lord has come are holy'. In the end, however, his resolution began to waver, and he followed the foreign gods whose cults his foreign wives had brought with them. He built altars to unspeakable deities, which the Bible denounces as 'the abomination of Moab' and 'the abomination of the Ammonites'. When he was old, apparently, his wives turned away his heart after other gods. His heart was not true to the Lord his God, as the heart of David his father had been.

God eventually loses patience with Solomon, and announces to him that, since he has decided to behave with such ostentatious disobedience, ignoring the covenant and the statutes that had been given to him, God will now take his kingdom from him and give it to one of his servants. The only restraint that he will show is due to the love he felt for David. He will therefore let Solomon live out his days. The kingdom will be taken after Solomon dies and his son has inherited the throne. Even then, however, God will not take everything. For the sake of David his servant, and for the sake of Jerusalem, the city that God has loved, the line of Solomon will be allowed to keep one of the tribes of Israel as its kingdom.

After Solomon dies, his son Rehoboam becomes king, but the young man fails to listen to his counsellors when the people complain of the heavy burdens that Solomon had placed upon them. He speaks harshly to them and tells them that, while

Solomon had chastised them with whips, he will now chastise them with scorpions. Horrified, the people announce that they now have no portion in the inheritance of David. 'To your tents, O Israel!' they cry. 'Look now to your own house, David.' Jeroboam, who had once commanded forced labour for Solomon and had fled from him into Egypt, becomes king of Israel, and he builds shrines at Bethel and Dan to rival the Temple of Solomon. Rehoboam is left with the house of Judah and the tribe of Benjamin, and although he hopes to recover his kingdom through war, God warns him not to try.

Even while he lived, the Testament of Solomon claims that the collapse of his extraordinary powers was so dramatic that a king who had once commanded the demons of the air was forced to endure their laughter and their contempt. Until then, however, news of his great wisdom and the extraordinary Temple that he had built for the God of Israel spread throughout the kingdoms of the earth, and men came from every people and every king to see him and marvel.

The most romantic of these encounters involved not a man but a woman, and in it lies the source of many different legends that would fascinate Jews, Christians and Muslims. Its heroine was not only a queen; she became a sorceress and a witch as well – a woman of astonishing beauty, who nevertheless bore a dreadful disfigurement. It is also the source of one of the most extraordinary chapters in the history of the Ark, in which the Queen of Sheba is proclaimed to be the founder of an African dynasty that guarded the Ark for thousands of years. The earliest account to survive is preserved in the First Book of Kings.

Now when the Queen of Sheba heard of the fame of Solomon concerning the name of the Lord, she came to test him with hard questions. She came to Jerusalem with a very great retinue, with camels bearing spices, and very much gold, and precious stones; and when she came to Solomon, she told him all that was on her mind. And Solomon answered all her questions; there was nothing hidden from the king which he could not explain to her. And when the Queen of Sheba had seen all the wisdom of Solomon, the house that he had built, the food of his table, the seating of his officials, and the attendance of his servants, their clothing, his cupbearers, and his burnt offerings which he offered at the house of the Lord, there was no more spirit in her.

And she said to the king, 'The report was true which I heard in my own land of your affairs and of your wisdom, but I did not believe the reports until I came and my own eyes had seen it; and behold the half of it was not told me; your wisdom and prosperity surpass the report which I heard. Happy are your wives! Happy are these your servants, who continually stand before you and hear your wisdom! Blessed be the Lord your God, who has delighted in you and set you on the throne of Israel! Because the Lord loved Israel for ever, he has made you king, that you may execute justice and righteousness.' Then she gave the king a hundred and twenty talents of gold, and a very great quantity of spices, and precious stones; never again came such an abundance of spices as these which the Queen of Sheba gave to King Solomon.

The Book of Kings has little to say about the challenges posed by the Queen of Sheba, but later Jewish tradition has provided accounts of these, including one in which Solomon did not hesitate to employ the Ark itself to secure the correct answer. The *Midrash ha-Hefez* claims to be based on the authority of Rabbi Ishmael, a famous scholar of the second century AD, and a similar version is found in the midrash on the Book of Numbers.

She now brought him a group some of whom were circumcised, the others unclean. 'Distinguish between them,' she said. Solomon immediately signalled to the High Priest who opened the Ark of the Covenant. The circumcised bowed down to half their height and at once their faces were lit with the radiance of God. The uncircumcised fell fully prostrate. He then replied, 'Those are the circumcised and those are the unclean.' And she said, 'You are indeed a wise man.'

While almost all the traditions about Solomon testify to his wisdom, he remains a curious sort of hero – a tragic figure undone by his mastery of the secrets of the world and his enthusiasm for the mysteries of women. The Temple he created with his magical power destroyed his kingdom, and in the most ambitious of the traditions about the Queen of Sheba, his love for the woman who came to see the marvellous achievement not only stripped him of his wisdom, but also led to the greatest glory of Israel, the Ark of the Covenant itself, fleeing Jerusalem and embracing another people. They lived across the Red Sea, and their skins are black.

CHAPTER 7

The New Law

Amon was a bad king. The Bible is very sure of this. He worshipped idols and refused to humble himself before God. Eventually his servants killed him, but however wicked he might have been, the people of Judah thought it was even worse for servants to murder anointed kings of the house of David. They killed the servants and put the son of the murdered king on the throne.

Josiah was only eight years old, but even at such a young age it was obvious that he would be a different sort of king than his father. He did what was right in the eyes of the Lord, and he walked in the ways of David. When he was sixteen, the Second Book of Chronicles tells us, he began to seek the God of David, and by the time he was twenty, he was removing the shrines that we know as the 'high places' from the kingdom of Judah and the holy city of Jerusalem. Along with the 'high places', he destroyed pillars dedicated to the Canaanite goddess Asherah, and graven and molten images. These were all abominations in his eyes, and he treated them with violence, grinding them into dust and pouring the remains on the graves of those who had sacrificed to them. He burned the bones of their priests on the altars at which they had served, and then destroyed them.

The violence that Josiah displayed was enough to secure his reputation. The Wisdom of Ben Sirach, often known in the West as Ecclesiasticus and included among the apocrypha of English versions of the Bible, was written in Jerusalem during the first century BC by someone close to the circle of the high priest. 'The memory of Josiah', its author proclaimed, 'is like a blending of incense prepared by the art of the perfumer; it is sweet as honey to every mouth, and like music at a banquet of wine.'

Two years later, after the war against the pernicious cults of the idols had proved a success, the Chronicler tells us that Josiah decided to repair the Temple of Solomon. It had apparently been allowed to decay through what the Chronicler saw as the dreadful idolatry of the previous kings of Judah. In itself, this would have been a programme of immense importance, but it led to a discovery whose implications still determine the way that we read the Bible. The Second Book of Kings places the events in a different and more intriguing order. Josiah does not begin his campaign against the idols until after the discovery in the Temple. It is the discovery that changes everything.

At the beginning of the restoration, Josiah sent several notables to the high priest, so that the necessary funds in the Temple treasury could be released to pay for the workmen, and to allow them to buy quarried stone and timber for beams. While they were bringing out the money that had been deposited in the house of God, the high priest himself, whose name was Hilkiah, found a book. Astonishing as it may seem, this appeared to be the actual 'book of the law of the Lord given through Moses'. Hilkiah gave the book to one of the courtiers, who presented it to Josiah and delivered the news that the high priest had discovered it in the Temple. He then read it aloud before the king, and when Josiah heard it, he tore his clothes in a gesture of anguish and desperation.

The discovery would obviously be of immense significance if it were genuine. But how would the king be able to tell? He decides to send the high priest and the notables to consult a woman named Huldah, the wife of an official in either the Temple or the court, and the only woman mentioned as a prophet in the Books of Kings. 'Go,' he commands them, 'inquire of the Lord for me and for those who are left in Israel and in Judah, concerning the words of the book that has been found; for great is the wrath of the Lord, to do according to all that is written in this book.' The extraordinary implication of his decision is that no one around him, including the high priest himself, was competent to judge the authenticity of a book purporting to contain the laws delivered to Israel by Moses. Something was seriously wrong at the heart of Israelite religion.

Whatever anyone else might have thought, the prophet is in no doubt that the book is genuine, and she speaks the word of God to the delegation in confirmation of this fact. 'Thus says the Lord, the God of Israel,' she tells them, and then she announces that

God will bring evil upon Jerusalem and its people. All the curses written in the book that had been read to Josiah will be fulfilled. The people have turned away and burned incense to other gods, provoking the anger of the God of Israel. Josiah has been penitent, tearing his clothes and weeping. Because of this, he will not see the evil that God is bringing upon the kingdom. He will die before it arrives.

When the words of the prophet are brought to him, Josiah gathers all the elders of Judah and Jerusalem, and goes up to the Temple with them. He summons all the men of Judah and the inhabitants of Jerusalem, the priests and the prophets, and all the people, the small as well as the great. He then reads the book to them while they listen. After he has finished, the king stands by the pillar at the entrance to the Temple, and makes a covenant before God, 'to walk after God and to keep his commandment and his testimonies and his statutes, with all his heart and with all his soul, to perform the words of the covenant that were written in the book'. All the people, we are told, join him in his covenant.

The book found in the Temple is called 'the Book of the Law' or 'the Book of the Covenant', and it reveals to Josiah that a covenant is already in effect. His kingdom is subject to the curses contained in the covenant, even though the king and the people had been ignorant of its terms and conditions. This is the reason why the king begins tearing his clothes as he hears the book read to him, and the reason why he embarks on the destruction of the high places and the sacred pillars. He is attempting to avoid the curses that will be enacted under the covenant with God. The discovery of the ancient book has not been a cause for joy or for antiquarian curiosity. It is absolutely terrifying.

Now that he has read the contents of the book to his people, Josiah sets about cleansing the Temple, the city of Jerusalem and the kingdom of Judah. His actions seem to be driven by the desperation of a man who sees disaster before him. To prove that the covenant with the God of Israel really will be obeyed, he not only destroys all evidence of foreign cult, but destroys it with the most violent and extreme measures he can imagine.

His first step is to command the priests and the Temple officials to bring out all the vessels made for Baal, Asherah and the host of heaven. He burns these outside the city, in the fields of the Kidron, and carries their ashes to Bethel. He brings out the pillar of Asherah and burns it at Kidron, beating it to dust and throwing the dust on the graves of the common people. He then demolishes the houses of the cultic prostitutes that had been built inside the Temple.

He removes the horses that the kings of Judah had dedicated to the sun and placed at the entrance to the Temple, and he burns the chariots of the sun. He pulls down and smashes the altars on the roof of the upper chamber of Ahaz, and the altars that Manasseh had made in the two courts of the Temple, casting the dust into the brook of Kidron.

He dismantles the 'high places' by the gates of Jerusalem, and defiles the shrine to the god Moloch built near the city at Topheth, where children were burnt as sacrifices. He then defiles the 'high places' to the east of Jerusalem that Solomon had built for Ashtoreth, Chemosh and Milcom, which the Bible describes as the abomination of the Sidonians, the abomination of Moab and the abomination of the Ammonites. He shatters the pillars and cuts down the Asherim, filling their places with human bones to defile them.

He orders all the priests out of the cities of Judah, and defiles every 'high place' where they had burned incense between Geba and Bathsheba. He pulls down the altar at Bethel, the 'high place' erected by Jeroboam, breaking it in pieces and crushing the stones to dust. He also burns the Asherah, and defiles the altar by burning bones upon it. He removes the 'high places' in the cities of Samaria that the kings of Israel had made, his fury against idolatry carrying him beyond the boundaries of his own kingdom. He kills all the priests on their altars, and then he defiles the altars by burning human bones on them. He also 'puts away' the mediums and wizards, and the images of household gods, and he eliminates all the idols and all the abominations that he could find in the kingdom of Judah and the city of Jerusalem.

After presenting this frightening catalogue of implacable hostility and ruthless violence, the Bible remarks that before Josiah 'there was no king like him, who turned to the Lord with all his heart and with all his soul and with all his might, according to all the law of Moses; nor did any like him arise after him.'

Once he had purged Jerusalem and Judah, the king restored the observance of the Passover, which apparently had not been kept since the days of the judges. According to the Book of Exodus, the instructions for the ritual had been given by God to Moses when he destroyed the firstborn of Egypt as a means of forcing the pharaoh to set the Israelites free. It involved the sacrifice of a lamb, followed by a meal of unleavened bread eaten in haste, and its purpose was to ensure that the Israelites never forgot the night in which the angel of God passed over their houses when he brought death to the Egyptians.

What Josiah seems to be doing, and it may seem a curious decision for a king to have taken, is limiting the cultic status of kingship. He is reducing the importance of the covenant that God made with David when he brought the Ark of the Covenant to Jerusalem, and placing it below the covenant that God made with Moses when he brought the Israelites out of Egypt. This becomes clear in the Second Book of Chronicles, which provides a much longer account of the restoration of the Passover than the Second Book of Kings.

As part of the preparation for the ritual, after the Passover lamb had been killed on the fourteenth day of the first month, Josiah is said to have appointed the priests to their offices. He then is reported as issuing his remarkable command to the Levites. It is no longer necessary for them to carry the Ark on their shoulders, he tells them. They should put it in the Temple, and then serve God and the people of Israel. They should also observe the Passover, according to the instructions that God had delivered through Moses.

The verse has aroused intense interest, and has been interpreted in a number of ways. The most likely explanation would seem to be that the Levites were used to carrying the Ark in procession. Now they are being told that they no longer have to do so. They are to place the Ark in the sanctuary, and go and serve God and people according to a different view of things – a Mosaic view, in fact. What Josiah seems to be doing is suppressing the ceremonial procession of the Ark.

The Hebrew Bible describes processions that involve the Ark of the Covenant when David brings it up to Jerusalem, and when Solomon installs it in the Temple. On both occasions, the Ark is clearly the focus of the procession, and its progress is accompanied by music. There are singers, tambourines, horns and shouts of joy from the people. Although these two processions are described as individual events, the Psalms suggest a ceremony in which the Ark was carried through the city. It seems that it would have entered the Temple by the eastern gate, while a liturgy was recited that included questions and responses from those waiting in the courtyard and those in the procession itself. 'Who will climb the hill of the Lord?', they ask, 'and who will stand in his holy place?' The answer is that he who has clean hands and a pure heart will climb the hill of the Lord – he who does not lift up his soul to what is false. As the procession approaches the gates, the people call out, 'Lift up your heads, O gates, and be lifted up, O ancient doors, that the King of glory may come in.'

The Psalms are liturgical hymns themselves, however, and aside from the occasional reference to processions entering the sanctuary of the Temple, they offer little explanation of the circumstances in which they were sung. As for the two processions described in the Books of Samuel and Kings, they are not only presented as unique occurrences, but also reported as if they were historical rather than sacramental or cosmological events.

The Hebrew Bible provides no other information about the origin, the frequency or the significance of rituals in which the Ark might have been carried. Assuming that ceremonies of this sort did exist, were they intended to commemorate or recreate the great events of history through which God saved his Chosen People? Or did they reflect the cosmological battle between God and the forces of chaos?

Although history and mythology are often thought to be very different, in this case at least, it may be unwise to separate them. The saving events of the history of Israel are certainly described in cosmological terms in the Bible – a fact that has become increasingly obvious after the discovery of the Ugaritic epics at Tell Ras Shamra in Syria almost seventy years ago. If the triumph of God over the waters of the Red Sea when Moses led the Children of Israel out of bondage in Egypt could be presented as if it were the victory of a storm god over the waters of the Abyss, surely the procession of the Ark of the Covenant could have both historical and mythological significance.

The fascination with a cosmological approach to the Psalms

really began with the Norwegian scholar Sigmund Mowinckel, some sixty years ago. He claimed that the ancient autumn Feast of Tabernacles was originally a New Year Festival, similar to Canaanite and Babylonian New Year celebrations, and he argued that its primary event was the enthronement of God. As in the Babylonian *akitu* festival, Mowinckel believed that the central element of the Israelite New Year Festival was a procession. The Ark of the Covenant would have been carried in this procession to the Temple, where the God of Israel would have been proclaimed king after his defeat of the forces of chaos.

The *akitu* festival, whose name is a complete mystery, had been observed twice a year in Sumeria, but only once a year in Babylon, where it had gradually become identified with the New Year Festival. Dedicated to Marduk, the patron god of Babylon, it was celebrated with great display during the height of Babylonian power in the first millennium BC. The climax of the festival was a procession in which the image of the god was carried to the *akitu* temple, and a detailed account of the festival written in the third century BC describes its dramatic recreation of the victory that the god had won over the waters of chaos, and the prayers and incantations that were recited to him as a means of averting his anger.

Mowinckel was fascinated by the possibility that Psalm 132 might have been the liturgical text of an equivalent festival procession in Jerusalem, in which the Ark of the Covenant was carried to dramatize the victory of the God of Israel just as the image of Marduk was carried in Babylon. The suggestion was thought to be very bold when it was made, but the Psalm certainly seems to describe the Ark being carried in procession to Jerusalem, with priests and worshippers shouting in joy at its arrival. It mentions the Ark by name, and it refers to the fields of Jaar, or Kiryath-yearim, where the Ark had apparently been kept after it returned to Beth-shemesh from the cities of the Philistines. The Psalm clearly refers to enthronement, explaining that God had placed David on his throne in Zion, where God will live for ever, and it speaks in terms of victory as well, the enemies of the king being clothed in shame through the victory of his God.

Remember, O Lord, in David's favour,
all the hardships he endured;
how he swore to the Lord
and vowed to the Mighty One of Jacob,
'I will not enter my house
or get into my bed;
I will not give sleep to my eyes
or slumber to my eyelids,
until I find a place for the Lord,
a dwelling place for the Mighty One of Jacob.'

Lo, we heard of it in Ephrathah,
we found it in the fields of Jaar.
'Let us go to his dwelling place;
let us worship at his footstool!'

Arise, O Lord, and go to your resting place,
you and the Ark of your might.
Let your priests be clothed with righteousness,
and let your saints shout for joy.
For the sake of your servant David,
do not turn away the face of your anointed one.

The Lord swore to David a sure oath
from which he will not turn back:
'One of the sons of your body
I will set on your throne.
If your sons keep my covenant
and my testimonies which I shall teach them,
their sons also for ever
shall sit upon your throne.'

For the Lord has chosen Zion;
he has desired it for his habitation:
'This is my resting place for ever;
here I will dwell, for I have desired it.
I will abundantly bless her provisions;
I will satisfy her poor with bread.

Her priests I will clothe with salvation,
and her saints will shout for joy.
There I will make a horn to sprout for David;
I have prepared a lamp for my anointed.
His enemies I will clothe with shame,
but upon himself his crown will shed its lustre.'

Why would such a procession have seemed so disturbing to Josiah, or to the scribes who compiled the account that appears in Kings and Chronicles? The problem would seem to be the involvement of the Ark in a theory of kingship that owed too much to the cosmological imagination of neighbouring peoples. The Psalm and the procession of the Ark may celebrate the election by God of Zion, but they were fixed in a system of beliefs that extended across the ancient Near East and included the other nations with whom the tribes of Israel seem to have had to share the Promised Land.

For centuries, the book that Hilkiah found in the Temple has been identified with the Book of Deuteronomy, and the Deuteronomist has a simple but effective reply to what he regarded as an unseemly veneration of the Ark. He describes an Ark with a specific function. It is a container for the record of the Law revealed to Moses on Mount Sinai. As the Deuteronomist sees it, the Ark is not a cultic demonstration of the presence of God, and it is not a palladium to secure victory in battle. It is a box to store a legal document, and when it is made, it is described as a simple wooden box very different from the elaborate golden shrine of the Priestly Code.

There are precise indications of this change in direction. While the Book of Numbers explains that the Israelites were defeated in battle with the Canaanites and the Amalekites because the Ark had not accompanied them, Deuteronomy does not mention the Ark, believing the disaster to have occurred because God had not been with the Israelites. The Ark may once have gone before the people to find campsites for them during their wandering in the wilderness, but in Deuteronomy we are told that God goes before the people. Even in the Deuteronomic law of warfare, there is no mention of the Ark. Given that the presence of the Ark had once been the reason why the Israelites could defeat their enemies, its omission is startling. As for the *kapporet* placed on the Ark in the Priestly Code, whose cherubim allow it to serve as a divine throne or chariot, the Deuteronomist never mentions it.

In itself, this part of the Deuteronomist programme may seem rationalist and even modern, but it is only part of the programme. It was initiated because of an ideology that may seem more troubling to us now – a rejection of the idea that Israel should be part of the world in which other peoples live. Israel was not like the nations, it seems. At any rate, it was not meant to be like the nations, and its God demanded a fierce intolerance of foreign practice. It was this ferocity that Josiah displayed in his slaughter and desecration of the 'high places' of Judah and Israel.

Was this really something new, however? Had it not been set out in the Ten Commandments revealed to Moses at Mount Sinai? The lists of prohibitions given in Exodus certainly warns against other gods and against graven images, but other parts of the Bible suggest a world in which such distinctions were not drawn so finely, or at least not in the way that the Deuteronomist would draw them. We read in the Bible of statues of the God of Israel, and the frequent mention of the images of the cherubim on the lid of the Ark and the immense statues in the inner sanctuary of the Temple could hardly be missed. The patriarchs erect pillars to mark sites of special holiness, and even the God who reveals himself to Abraham, the basis of all the revelations to come, is given the name of the Canaanite deity *El Shadday*. The unspeakable name *YHWH* is revealed to Moses only many generations later. None of this is described in the Bible as unusual, let alone as outrageous or offensive to God.

Where or when would the unique nature of Israel have become such a critical issue for those who prepared the literary record that we now read in the Bible? It might have occurred during the Exile in Babylon. There it would have seemed necessary to preserve an Israelite identity as a minority in a strange land. After the Exile, it would have remained a critical issue, and would perhaps become even more urgent. According to the Book of Ezra, those who had been in Babylon and had returned to rebuild the Temple regarded the 'People of the Land' as thoroughly polluted, and rebuffed their offer to assist with the Temple. If Israelites who were attempting to build the Second Temple became engaged in a struggle with the people who had been living in Jerusalem or other parts of the kingdom, enforcing a strict distinction between those who were acceptable to God and those who were not may have seemed an essential part of the strategy.

Even in later centuries, however, it is not always clear if things were really the way they are said to have been. Excavations at Arad, near Beth Sheeva in the southern Negev, have revealed a temple built along the same lines as the Temple of Jerusalem, and it appears to have survived the supposed reform. Perhaps the most peculiar temple belonged to Jewish colonists at Elephantine in Upper Egypt. Excavations have not yet revealed its precise location, but correspondence and other documents in Aramaic have been recovered, and these confirm that it did exist and that its cult was highly irregular, at least by the standards of Josiah or the Deuteronomist. Other gods were worshipped along with *YHWH* at Elephantine, and he evidently had consorts as if he were one of the deities known from the epics of Ras Shamra or the other scriptures in the ancient Near East. Yet when the temple was destroyed in the fifth century BC, the Jews at Elephantine wrote to the Persian governors of Judah and Samaria to ask for assistance in rebuilding it. This is intriguing for two reasons. The fact that they wrote at all suggests that they did not believe that their own cult would be seen as deviant and offensive, and the fact that they wrote to both Judah and Samaria suggests that they did not regard Jerusalem as possessing a unique authority.

The remains of what has been identified as a temple from the second century BC have been excavated at Araq el-Emir in Transjordan. It was evidently built by a member of the Tobiad family, a clan who were prominent in Judah during the third and second centuries BC and who are mentioned by Josephus. As the family were related by marriage to the High Priests of Jerusalem, it is unlikely that they would have been ignorant of the standards of orthodoxy regarded as acceptable, and yet they appear to have built a temple.

Another temple was built at Leontopolis in Egypt by the son of the last Zadokite high priest of Jerusalem, who had been deposed by Antiochus Epiphanes in 175 BC. The son of the high priest would certainly have known about the unique status of Jerusalem, and the events are reported by Josephus, who was a priest himself, without any comment about its irregularity.

Josephus also reports on the Jews in Sardis in Asia Minor, who were allowed by the governors of the city to establish a sacrificial cult during the time of John Hyrcanus II in the middle of the first century BC. According to the orthodoxy of Deuteronomy, a sacrificial cult should have existed only at Jerusalem, and yet Josephus, a priest himself, does not remark on the event as unusual.

The problems of dating and identification should not be underestimated. It can be very difficult to agree on whether excavations have revealed a temple, a palace or even more modest domestic structures, especially given the religious and political circumstances in which Palestinian and Near Eastern archaeology must be practised. Nevertheless, it is not unreasonable to suggest that orthodoxy has been defined more generously than the Deuteronomist might have liked, or than Josiah might have been prepared to tolerate.

If the description of his reform is historically accurate, it may be that Josiah was attempting to assert his independence as the power of Assyria declined. Foreign cults were often imposed as a way of announcing political dependence. While one might imagine the kings of Israel and Judah to have found idols simply irresistible, and the Bible does describe this attraction as a kind of lust, it would seem more likely that they were imposed at the demands of foreign masters. The reformation of the cult at Jerusalem and throughout Judah that Josiah is described as launching would certainly have had political implications, and it would be difficult to imagine him attempting it if he had not believed that it would strengthen his own political hand. Indeed, his raids across the border to destroy 'high places' in the neighbouring kingdom of Israel may have been an attempt to eradicate local centres of power that might have threatened his rule.

Although Josiah is a Deuteronomic hero, the prophet Jeremiah seems to regard him with more detachment. If his reforms were not simply a matter of piety, the prophet may have seen them as acceptable, but as fundamentally a matter of politics rather than devotion. Nevertheless, Jeremiah seems to inhabit a world in which the agenda of Deuteronomy has become a fact. The reform of cultic procession and the role of the Ark would seem to explain the remarks that Jeremiah made about it, even though many scholars have found them perplexing.

> And when you have multiplied and increased in the land, in those days, says the Lord, they shall no more say, 'The Ark of the Covenant of the Lord.' It shall not come to mind, or be remembered, or be missed; it shall not be made again. At that time, Jerusalem shall be called the throne of the Lord, and all the nations shall gather to it, to the presence of the Lord in Jerusalem, and they shall no more stubbornly follow their own evil heart.

One of the leading modern authorities on the Temple and its ritual has assumed that the prophecy was delivered as a way of comforting the people of Jerusalem for the loss of the Ark, which had already occurred. This would seem to be forced. Jeremiah is not speaking of its disappearance, but rather of its irrelevance. Except in the context of the reforms of Josiah, and the agenda of Deuteronomy, this would be very difficult to understand. Why should the presence of God at the centre of the cult in Jerusalem, and the palladium that had guided the Children of Israel through the wilderness and delivered the Promised Land to them through conquest, simply become irrelevant? Someone, it seems, was keen to see it in very different terms, to reduce its status or at least to define it more narrowly.

There is also a fascinating verse in the of Book of Ezekiel, the prophet whose vision of the Temple included no reference to the Ark. The east gate of the Temple that he described would be closed for ever. This is the gate through which processions would have passed, and its irrelevance for the future is made quite explicit.

> Then he brought me back to the outer gate of the sanctuary, which faces east; and it was shut. And he said to me, 'This gate shall remain shut; it shall not be opened, and no one shall enter by it; for the Lord, the God of Israel, has entered by it; therefore it shall remain shut.'

Once God had entered the Temple, it seems, he would no longer leave it and return to it, coming and going as part of a cosmic drama repeated across time.

The reform of Josiah, or the account given of it by the Deuteronomist, was a turning point in the way that the world was understood in Jerusalem. It tried to destroy a system of belief that had existed over centuries, by denouncing any cult outside Jerusalem as illegitimate. For the Deuteronomist, God did not even live in the Temple as he had once done. Only his name could be said to be present, while God himself remained far away in heaven. The sanctuary of the Temple was thought to be a house of prayer, rather than a cultic or sacramental point where heaven and earth could meet. Worship was not just centralized in Jerusalem; it was stripped of its cosmic dimension.

The God of Israel was no longer the sort of God who needed or depended on sacrifice, and the basic assumption of the ritual now seems to have been removed. At an earlier period, all slaughter had been sacrificial, but under Deuteronomy a clear distinction is made between sacrifice and profane slaughter, which is allowed for the first time. The Deuteronomist constantly encourages his readers to share the meat of sacrifice with the poor, and however laudable this might be, it does not seem to have been the primary concern before Deuteronomy was compiled.

The Deuteronomist is filled with a nationalist fervour, and is keen on military speeches. He describes the promise made to Israel that it will be exalted above all the nations of the earth, and that it will rule many nations but will never be ruled by them. He does not seem to accept the limits to the borders of Israel that one finds in the Book of Numbers, where Moses regards the request made by the tribes of Reuben and Dan to live across the Jordan as a sin. Transjordan is now considered to be an integral part of Israel, and the Conquest begins not with the crossing of the Jordan, but with the crossing of the Amon, the border between Moab and Mishor.

This aggressive spirit is certainly applied to the question of the Canaanites, who are said to have lived in the Promised Land when the Conquest began. In the Books of Numbers and Joshua, total destruction is to be adopted as a policy only in specific cases. In Deuteronomy, it is applied to the entire country. The Canaanites are simply to be exterminated.

The account that we are given of the death of Josiah suggests an adherence to this sort of extreme nationalism. He dies in a pointless encounter with the vastly superior forces of Egypt, challenging a pharaoh who insists that there is no need for them to fight, and who is said to have spoken the word of God when he did so. 'What have we to do with each other, king of Judah?' the pharaoh asks him. 'I am not coming against you this day, but against the house with which I am at war; and God has commanded me to make haste. Cease opposing God, who is with me, lest he destroy you.'

Josiah may have been a hero to the Deuteronomist, but the account of his reign can make disturbing reading now. It is not so much that we see him falling short of our own enlightened sensibilities, as that we can see the suffering of the twentieth century reflected in the uncompromising idealism of a reforming king who was ready to embark on a campaign of slaughter and destruction to attain racial and ideological purity. The rabbis who wrote about the Ark and the Temple in later centuries, and whose thoughts on these matters are recorded in the Talmudic literature, embraced and embellished a more cosmic sense of the presence of God in the holy places. After the stern vision of the Deuteronomist, one may feel relieved that only part of his dream of Israel survived in their world.

We have now seen three very different versions of the Ark. A palladium in battle, a throne where God meets man, and a box to house the Law by which Israel should live according to the terms of the covenant that God had made with his people at Mount Sinai. Were these meant to be complementary or even contradictory accounts of the same Ark, or is it possible that they reflect traditions in which more than one Ark was made? The Deuteronomist would certainly have been horrified at the idea of more than one of these objects, convinced as he was that singularity rather than multiplicity was the only way that religion could be acceptable in the eyes of the one true God. Fortunately, the Bible seems to contain a great many things that the Deuteronomist would have found disturbing. More than we might have expected has survived the careful work of later editors, and paradoxically, we may feel inclined to trust the biblical account precisely because of its inconsistency. For the same reason, it may also provide a better guide than we might have expected to the encounter between Iyasu and the Ark at Aksum.

CHAPTER 8

By the Waters of Babylon

With a few words written in cuneiform characters on a small clay tablet, the ancient Babylonian Chronicle records the disaster that came upon the Children of Israel. 'In the seventh year, in the month of Kislev,' we are told, 'the king of Babylon mustered his troops, marched to the land of Hatti, and besieged the city of Judah; on the second day of the month of Adar, he seized the city and captured the king.' The last date corresponds to 16 March 597 BC, and worse was to follow a decade later. Exasperated by political intrigue at Jerusalem, by the attempts of its king and its aristocracy to ally themselves with Egypt and rebel against the authority of their Babylonian masters, Nebuchadnezzar finally destroyed the symbol of Judaean resistance. The sign that God had chosen the House of David and would defend his holy mountain, the proof that Zion would remain inviolable, was in ruins. According to the Second Book of Kings, the house of the Lord was plundered and then burnt, and the Children of Israel were carried away into captivity. Years later, the poet sang of their despair: 'By the waters of Babylon, there we sat down and wept, when we remembered Zion.'

The words of the prophet Isaiah, it seems, had contained a terrible irony. He had warned the people of Jerusalem not to trust in the powers of the world and to have no faith in strategic alliance. Only the God of Israel could deliver the kingdom from the armies of Assyria. In 701 BC, in the face of an Assyrian invasion, Isaiah had prophesied that Jerusalem would be delivered and that God would never allow the enemy to approach the holy city of Zion. When the prophecy proved to be accurate, the people of Judah became convinced that they were safe. The great empires would never threaten them.

Before long, it is true, Assyria was no longer a threat. The

Chaldean general Nabopolassar had rebelled and declared himself king of Babylon, and in alliance with the Medes he destroyed the Assyrian capital in 612 BC. The Medes now established their own kingdom in the eastern part of the empire, while the west became a battleground on which Babylon and Egypt fought for supremacy. Although the Judaean king Jehoiakim became a Babylonian vassal, he was not a willing subject. In 601 BC a Babylonian army had been unable to defeat the Egyptians, and he decided to rebel. He escaped the vengeance of Nebuchadnezzar but only through death. Before the Babylonians could march against him, Jehoiakim was already dead, perhaps the victim of assassins who hoped to secure better terms from their masters. As the Chronicle records, Jerusalem surrendered and the new king Jehoichin, the queen mother, princes and members of the ruling class were carried into exile.

The Babylonians chose another king, but they were disappointed in their hopes that he might prove more obedient and amenable than Jehoiakim. Zedekiah was unable to withstand the patriotic fervour of the aristocracy who remained in the city. Convinced that Zion would remain inviolable, that God would not allow his holy mountain to be defiled, they were plotting to rebel again.

In the midst of this adventure, the prophets of Israel began to speak with increasing urgency. Some insisted that God would indeed stand by Zion, and that the Children of Israel should resist Babylon with the support of the Almighty. But the prophet Jeremiah tried to call the leaders of the nation to their senses. He had chosen a dangerous course. When the prophet Uriah delivered the same message at Kiryath-yearim, the old shrine of the Ark, he was killed. Jeremiah would have to flee for his life, and a book of prophecies read aloud by his servant Baruch at the Temple was confiscated and destroyed.

The prophecies that survive in the Book of Jeremiah reveal a man in torment. He had been born into a priestly family, which may have traced its descent from the priests of the ancient sanctuary at Shiloh, where the Books of the Former Prophets tell us that the Ark of the Covenant had been kept. Jeremiah would therefore have been raised among men whose ancestors once served the Ark, and he remained acutely aware of the fate of the shrine.

The opening words of the Book of Jeremiah describe his call to prophecy in 626 BC, when Josiah was king: 'Now the word of the

Lord came to me saying, "Before I formed you in the womb, I knew you, and before you were born I consecrated you; I appointed you a prophet to the nations." ' At a time of desperate peril, the warning that Jeremiah felt compelled to utter in Jerusalem caused him immense anguish. Haunted by a sense of foreboding, a premonition that the Children of Israel were doomed, he preached what has been described as the funeral oration of his people. He told them that their confidence in the Covenant of David and the election of Zion was utterly misplaced. 'Do not trust in these deceptive words,' he told them. In their hearts they had been assuring themselves, 'This is the temple of the Lord, the temple of the Lord, the temple of the Lord.' Far from guaranteeing the safety of Jerusalem and the Children of Israel, the cult of the Temple was simply irrelevant. When he had brought them out of the land of Egypt, God had never ordered the Israelites to make burnt offerings or sacrifices. He never mentioned them; the Israelites had simply invented them.

Even though the covenant and the promises of God had been true, Jeremiah insisted that the people of Israel had failed to fulfil their obligations in return. The promises of God had therefore become deadly. Just as he had destroyed the shrine of the Ark at Shiloh, God would now destroy Jerusalem and its Temple.

Rather than being an enemy that God would crush when it threatened his people, Jeremiah announced that Babylon was the instrument chosen by God to impose his judgement upon Israel. In a bizarre enactment of his prophecy, the prophet appeared in Jerusalem wearing a yoke around his neck, proclaiming that God himself had placed the yoke of Babylon on the peoples of the earth. They must submit to it, or perish.

In the years to come, he prophesied, the world would be a different place. Once the Children of Israel had returned to their God, the Ark of the Covenant itself would no longer be needed. It would not be remembered or missed, and it would not be made again. Jerusalem itself would be the throne of God.

As Jeremiah had predicted, the Babylonians did march against Jerusalem to enact a final judgement. The captain of the guard, Nebuzaradan, took the city in 587 BC and destroyed the Temple. The Children of Israel, the Bible tells us, began their Exile beside the waters of Babylon.

*

Before they burned the Temple, the Babylonians apparently removed an immense treasure. An inventory of the loot is provided in the Second Book of Kings and repeated as a historical appendix to the prophecies of Jeremiah.

> And the pillars of bronze that were in the house of the Lord, and the stands and the bronze sea that were in the house of the Lord, the Chaldeans broke in pieces, and carried the bronze to Babylon. And they took away the pots, and the shovels, and the snuffers, and the dishes for incense and all the vessels of bronze used in the temple service, the firepans also, and the bowls. What was of gold the captain of the guard took away as gold, and what was of silver, as silver. As for the two pillars, the one sea, and the stands, which Solomon had made for the house of the Lord, the bronze of all these vessels was beyond weight. The height of the one pillar was eighteen cubits, and upon it was a capital of bronze; the height of the capital was three cubits; a network and pomegranates, all of bronze, were upon the capital round about. And the second pillar had the like, with the network.

The Ark does not appear in this list. It is also absent from the inventory of vessels that the scribe Ezra reports as having been returned to Jerusalem 150 years later, after the Persians defeated Babylon. Cyrus evidently brought out the vessels of the house of the Lord that Nebuchadnezzar had carried away from Jerusalem and placed in the house of his gods. Under the supervision of Methredath the treasurer, they were delivered to Shesh-bazzar, the prince of Judah, and included 1,000 basins of gold, 1,000 basins of silver, 29 censers, 30 bowls of gold, 2,410 bowls of silver and 1,000 other vessels. The number of gold and silver vessels was 5,469, all of which Shesh-bazzar is said to have brought to Jerusalem when the exiles returned. Even when the Book of Daniel explains that the Babylonians had taken these vessels from the Temple to dedicate them to their own gods, there is still no mention of the Ark.

Whatever might have happened to the Ark, the rabbis who compiled the Talmud were certain that it never stood in the Second Temple, built after the Persian victory and the return of the exiles to Palestine. There were five matters, they said, in which the

First Temple differed from the Second: the Ark, its cover and the cherubim; the fire; the Presence of God; the Holy Spirit; and the mysterious Urim and Tummim. They believed that when the Ark was hidden, the jar containing the manna, the flask of anointing oil, the staff of Aaron with its petals and almond blossoms, and the chest that the Philistines had sent as a gift to the God of Israel were hidden with it. They believed that all these things had been hidden by Josiah, after he had read the biblical verse predicting that 'the Lord will bring you, and your king whom you shall set over you, unto a nation that you have not known.' The decision to hide the Ark was recorded in the command that Josiah gave to the Levites, that they should put the Ark in the Temple because they no longer needed to carry it upon their shoulders. The rabbis also believed that, if the Ark were carried into exile in Babylon, it could not be restored to its place in the inner sanctuary. For this reason, Josiah commanded the Levites to go and serve the Lord their God and his people Israel.

The Mishnah also records that the high priest in the Second Temple no longer made offerings to the Ark, but made them upon the rock that protruded through floor of the inner sanctuary. It was called the 'Foundation Stone', and it was believed to be the site where Abraham had been ready to offer Isaac, and where King David had seen the destroying angel on the threshing floor of Arawna the Jebusite. It was the place on which the Ark had apparently once stood. The judgement of the rabbis is supported by Josephus, who confirms that the Ark did not stand in the Second Temple, and by the Roman historian Tacitus, who records that when Pompey entered the innermost sanctuary in 63 BC, 133 years before Titus destroyed the Herodian Temple, he found it empty.

Some ancient writers assumed that the Ark had been present in the Temple when the Babylonians entered, and that it was either captured or destroyed. The Second Book of Esdras, also known as the Fourth Book of Ezra, is a Jewish apocalypse written in the last decade of the first century AD, six centuries after the Temple of Solomon was burned by the Babylonians, and several years after the Herodian Temple was destroyed by the Romans. In a vision, the seer meets a woman in mourning, and as he tries to comfort her, he sees her transformed into the Heavenly Jerusalem.

In the course of their conversation, he speaks of the troubles of Zion and the sorrow of the holy city, telling her that the sanctuary has been laid waste, the altar thrown down and the Temple destroyed. Their song has been silenced and their rejoicing is finished. The light of their lampstand has been extinguished, the Ark of the Covenant has been plundered, the holy things have been polluted and the name by which they are called has been profaned.

Even though the apocalypse was written long after the event, other sources support its claim. Two rabbis are known to have believed that the Ark had been taken to Babylon, and a record of their arguing the case is recorded in the commentary to the Mishnah. Rabbi Eliezer and Rabbi Simeon ben Yohai relied on three biblical verses to support their argument: the statement by the Chronicler that Nebuchadnezzar had brought 'the precious vessels of the house of the Lord' to Babylon; the prophecy of Isaiah that 'all that is in your house, and that which your fathers have stored up till this day' would be carried away to Babylon; and the Lamentation of Jeremiah that all the majesty of the daughter of Zion had departed. Their opponent, Rabbi Judah ben Ilai, cited a verse from the First Book of Kings that the poles of the Ark were visible in the Temple 'until this day'. Rabbi Eliezer and Rabbi Simeon raised the objection that the phrase 'until this day' did not mean 'for ever'. This was thought to have undermined the position held by Rabbi Judah, and his argument was regarded as having been refuted.

Despite the vision of the apocalypse and the scriptural arguments of the rabbis, the absence of the Ark from the inventory in the Book of Kings raises the question of whether it really had been in the sanctuary when the Babylonians entered. Is it possible that those who compiled the inventories made no mention of the Ark among the loot carried to Babylon simply because it had been removed from the Temple at an earlier date? Three kings might be candidates for having taken the Ark before Nebuzaradan arrived: an Egyptian pharaoh, a king of the northern state of Israel and Nebuchadnezzar himself.

The First Book of Kings describes an invasion around 926 BC by a pharaoh named 'Shishak', who is obviously Sheshonq I, founder of the Twenty-second Dynasty. In the fifth year of King

Rehoboam, we are told, the pharaoh came to Jerusalem, taking away 'the treasures of the house of the Lord and the treasures of the king's house'. Evidently, he took everything, including all the shields of gold that Solomon had made. The Second Book of Kings describes the victory of Jehoash, king of Israel, over Amaziah, king of Judah, in 785 BC. Jehoash seized all the gold and silver, and all the vessels that were kept 'in the house of the Lord and in the treasuries of the king's house'. Ten chapters later, the same book describes the arrival of Nebuchadnezzar in 597 BC. Jehoiachin the king of Judah surrendered himself to the king of Babylon, along with his mother, his servants, his princes and his palace officials. After the king of Babylon took him prisoner, he removed 'all the treasures of the house of the Lord, and the treasures of the king's house', cutting into pieces 'all the vessels of gold in the temple of the Lord, that Solomon king of Israel had made'.

None of these passages refers to the presence or the removal of the Ark, but the reason for their apparent silence is likely to be that they were not describing objects in the sanctuary of the Temple. The objects whose plunder they report would seem to have been part of the Temple treasure, and this would never have been kept in the inner sanctuary near the Ark. Additional repositories called 'treasures of the house of the Lord' are described in the First Book of Kings: 'And Solomon brought in the things which David his father had dedicated, the silver, the gold, and the vessels, and stored them in the treasuries of the house of the Lord.'

It has also been suggested that the Ark would have been removed in the seventh century, during the reign of Manasseh, the king who succeeded Hezekiah and became a notorious paradigm of evil. The 'sin of Manasseh', as his crimes were called, was believed to be uniquely wicked, although it may have been the result of cultic obligations imposed by foreign masters rather than any unusual enthusiasm for idolatry on the part of Manasseh himself. The authors and editors of the Hebrew Bible display a profound concern for orthodoxy, although they often define it in different ways, and they report that during the reigns of earlier kings, foreign cults had been increasing. Even Solomon had built 'high places' for his foreign wives 'on the mountain east of Jerusalem', and these stood for centuries until they were swept away in the reforming zeal of Josiah. While none of the earlier foreign cults had actually polluted the Temple itself, Manasseh not only worshipped foreign gods, but also built altars for them in the two courts of the Temple, erected 'houses of the male cult prostitutes' and made an idol of a local goddess. This he placed in 'the house of the Lord', which may mean that it stood in the inner sanctuary of the Temple, the most appropriate place for an image in any of the temples throughout the ancient Near East.

According to the Second Book of Kings, Josiah removed the idol and then burned it and beat it to dust. There is no mention of the Ark in this passage, and the silence of the biblical text has been taken as an indication that the Ark was no longer in the inner sanctuary. Yet arguments from silence are usually precarious, especially when we rely on a small number of ancient sources. If Manasseh really had removed the Ark as an act of apostasy, one would have expected it to be cited as the worst of his crimes. If any of his opponents had removed it to avoid pollution while the king was captivated by strange gods, one might also have expected their devotion to have been recorded. Even when Manasseh repents of his crime – and the Second Book of Chronicles does report that he restored 'the altar of the Lord' – there is still no mention of the Ark.

It has also been suggested that one of the prophecies of Jeremiah supports the claim that Manasseh had removed the Ark: the verse in which the prophet predicts that the Ark will not come to mind, or be remembered, or be missed, or ever be made again. The assumption is that the prophecy would not have been delivered if the Ark had still been in existence. In other words, the prophet is apparently saying that, in the good times to come, there will be no more need for the Ark, and that in these happy days its absence will no longer be a cause for grief. It is not at all clear that this is the meaning of the verse, however. Even if it were, it would seem to be contradicted by the report that Josiah, the grandson of Manasseh, had ordered the Levites to put the Ark in the Temple. It may just be possible to understand the actions of Josiah as an indication that the Ark had been carried away by the Levites, and then returned when the reforming king had ensured that there was no longer any risk of pollution. It would seem far more likely that Josiah was in fact proscribing the ceremonial procession of the Ark rather than restoring it to prominence in the cult. Even so, the passage would certainly not allow one to assume that the Ark had been removed during the reign of Manasseh and then lost. If one tried to suggest that the Ark had been lost, and that Josiah was speaking to the Levites about another Ark, an attempt to save the argument in this way would simply undermine it.

Another possibility suggested by the ancient sources is that the Ark survived in the Temple until the Babylonian army laid siege to Jerusalem, and was then saved from destruction at the last moment. There are a number of traditions that refer to the Ark and other equipment of the cult being hidden or buried, either on the Temple Mount or elsewhere. Some of these involve miraculous powers, but others do not.

The Mishnah records that the Tent of Meeting was stored 'beneath the crypts of the Temple', along with all its boards, hooks, bars, pillars and sockets. Other Jewish traditions claimed that the Ark, the altar of incense, the rod of Aaron, the pot of manna and the Tablets of the Law were hidden within a secret compartment under a woodshed on the west side of the Temple, near the site of the Holy of Holies. Apparently, members of the house of Rabbi Gamaliel and of Rabbi Hananiah used to bow at fourteen stations in the Temple rather than the usual thirteen, and the additional bowing was performed in the direction of the woodshed. The families did this because they knew the secret of where the Ark had been hidden. The knowledge was evidently dangerous, and was said to have brought death to at least one priest who discovered it. As he was chopping wood, he noticed that one of the blocks of pavement sounded different from the others when he struck it with his axe. Realizing that something must lie beneath it, he went to tell his friends, but before he had time to reveal the exact spot, his soul was taken from his body. His friends regarded this as proof that the Ark lay hidden beneath the woodshed of the Temple.

A similar tradition describes the death of a priest whose body had been disfigured. As this kept him from serving in the Temple itself, he used to prepare wood for the sacrificial fires in the courtyard. Along with another priest, he was removing the sticks that had been eaten by worms, when his axe slipped out of his hand and fell upon the secret place. Immediately, a flame burst forth and consumed him.

Traditions about the hidden vessels continued to be told during the Middle Ages. The Spanish physician and philosopher Yehudah ha-Levi not only wrote verses about the Ark in Hebrew, but also recorded that the Ark had been hidden on the Temple Mount in his treatise *The Khazar King*, which he completed around 1140. In the Second Temple, he says, stone paving was put in the place of the Ark, hiding it behind a curtain, because the priests knew that the Ark had been buried in that place.

Another Spanish physician and philosopher, Moses Maimonides, was born six years before Yehudah ha-Levi died in 1141. In the eighth book of his *Mishneh Torah*, which became one of the standard works of Jewish law, he discusses the Temple service and considers the fate of the Ark, drawing on the verse from the Second Book of Chronicles that had so intrigued the earlier rabbis. There was a stone by the western wall in the inner sanctuary, Maimonides tells us, on which the Ark rested. In front of it stood the jar of manna and the staff of Aaron. When Solomon built the Temple, he knew that it was destined to be destroyed, so he built secret chambers in which the Ark could be hidden in deep and winding tunnels. Josiah ordered the Levites to place the Ark in the chamber that Solomon had prepared for it, just as the Bible tells us. It would no longer be a burden on their shoulders, and they would now serve God and Israel. Maimonides noted that the staff of Aaron, the jar of manna and the oil for anointing were also hidden with the Ark, and that none of these appeared in the Second Temple.

As Jeremiah had delivered a famous prophecy about the Ark of the Covenant, he may have seemed an obvious choice when Jewish traditions began to display an interest in whether anyone might have saved it. There is a certain irony in this. The most likely reading of the prophecy suggests that Jeremiah regarded the Ark as irrelevant, yet now he is depicted as ensuring its survival for the generations to come. In a series of adventures that become increasingly miraculous, the prophet rescues the Ark by removing it from the Temple and hiding it just as disaster is about to begin.

The first of these occurs in the Second Book of the Maccabees, which was written in Greek sometime before 63 BC and describes the history of the Maccabaean wars. The Hellenistic king of Syria, Antiochus Epiphanes, had hoped to seize the treasure in the Temple, to ease the financial crisis that his empire was facing. Instead, he provoked a reaction more furious than he had encountered at any pagan temple. Deciding to replace Judaism with a more accommodating religion, he introduced his own altars into the inner sanctuary. After he threatened to kill anyone who continued to perform Jewish ritual of any kind, including circumcision, he found himself facing a revolt that has been named after the Jewish hero who won the final victory, Judas Maccabaeus.

The Second Book of the Maccabees, which is part of the Ethiopian as well as the Greek canon, begins with a letter ostensibly written to the Jews of Egypt, reporting that the Temple had been purified from the outrages of the Hellenistic king. After describing the fire on the altar, the writer mentions the role of Jeremiah in the last days of the First Temple. Records had apparently survived that the prophet Jeremiah had ordered those who were being deported to Babylon to take some of the fire from the Temple. He then gave them a copy of the Law, telling them not to forget the commandments of the Lord, and not to be led astray when they saw the gold and silver idols of Babylon. The records also indicate that he gave orders for the Tent and the Ark to be carried to the mountain where Moses had looked upon the Promised Land. When they arrived, Jeremiah found a cave, and after he placed the Tent and the Ark and the altar of incense inside it, he sealed the entrance. Some of those who followed him tried to find the path, but when Jeremiah learned this, he rebuked them and told them that the place would remain unknown until God gathered his people together at the end of the age. He would then reveal these things, and he would display the glory and the cloud that had appeared in the days of Moses, and when Solomon built the Temple.

The report seems to have been written in the belief that the Children of Israel would soon return to Jerusalem, having been delivered from the power of the Gentiles. The author imagines the restored community in a purified Temple, and preserves the story of the hidden vessels as a way of strengthening the hopes of his readers. Solomon had placed the Tabernacle and its furnishings in the Temple when he built it, and even though it had been destroyed,

Jeremiah preserved the Tabernacle, the Ark and the altar of incense. They would all be restored after the return of the tribes to the Temple, and just as the cloud and the glory of God had appeared when Moses first made the Tabernacle and when Solomon brought it to the Temple, so the glory and the cloud would appear again when the hidden treasures were displayed to those who gathered in Jerusalem.

In the Second Book of Baruch, a Jewish apocalypse originally written in Greek but now preserved in Syriac, there is a rather more miraculous account of the Temple vessels being hidden as the Temple is destroyed. Although the author describes the destruction of the First Temple, he was actually writing after the Romans had burned the Second Temple, and he looks toward a future in which Jerusalem and its Temple are finally restored for ever. He does not mention the Ark specifically, but the mercy seat that served as the cover of the Ark is included in the list of sacred things, along with the Tablets of the Law.

The episode begins as the Babylonian army approaches Jerusalem. Baruch, the servant of Jeremiah, is sitting alone beside an oak tree, lamenting the fate of Zion. As he imagines the suffering that the people of Jerusalem will be forced to endure in captivity, a spirit lifts him into the air and carries him above the walls of the city. He sees four angels standing at the four corners of the city, each of them holding a burning torch in his hand. Another angel comes down from heaven and tells them not to destroy the city before he gives the word. He has been sent by God to hide something in the earth. Baruch then sees the angel descend into the inner sanctuary of the Temple and take the veil, the holy ephod, the mercy seat, the two Tablets of the Law, the vestments of the priests, the altar of incense, the forty-eight precious stones with which the priests were clothed, and all the holy vessels of the Tabernacle. The angel then speaks in a loud voice, calling on the earth to hear the word of God and receive the things that the angel will entrust to it. The earth should guard them until the last times, so that strangers will never find them, and it should then restore them at the end of time. God has decided that Jerusalem will be delivered to the enemy, until the time in which it will be restored for ever. The earth then opens its mouth and swallows the holy treasures.

After he had seen this miracle, Baruch heard the angel speak to the four angels who held the torches, telling them to destroy the walls and foundations of the city before the Babylonians could claim that they had overthrown Zion, the fortress of God, by their own power. Then the spirit returned him to the oak tree.

Another version appears in the Fourth Book of Baruch, a Jewish account of the final years of Jeremiah, with some additions by a Christian editor. It is also known as the Rest of the Words of Baruch, or the *Paraleipomena* of Jeremiah, the 'Things Omitted from Jeremiah', and it seems to have been written in Greek during the second century AD. Jeremiah and Baruch climb on to the walls of the city one night as the armies of Babylon prepare to destroy Jerusalem. They hear the sound of trumpets and see angels coming out of heaven with torches in their hands. As the angels stand on the walls of the city, Jeremiah and Baruch begin to weep because they realize that the prophecy of destruction is true. Jeremiah pleads with the angels, begging them not to destroy the city until he can speak to God. The voice of God then calls to the angels, telling them that he will speak to his chosen one, Jeremiah, before the angels set about their work. Jeremiah asks God if he might speak, and when he is given permission, he says that he realizes the city is about to be surrendered to its enemies, and the people carried into exile, but he wants to know what God expects him to do with the holy vessels in the Temple. God tells him to take them and entrust them to the earth, ordering it to listen to the command of the God who made it, who formed it in the waters, and who sealed it with seven seals in the seven ages of time. It should guard the vessels of the Temple until the arrival of 'the beloved one'. Jeremiah and Baruch then enter the sanctuary, and after they have collected the holy vessels, they deliver them to the earth as God has instructed. Immediately, the earth swallows them, and the two men sit down and weep. When the Exile begins, Jeremiah follows the people to Babylon, while Baruch remains in Jerusalem, waiting for the word of God.

A fourth version appears in the Life of Jeremiah, one of a series of stories about the prophets that seem to have been written in Greek by Palestinian Jews during the first century AD, although they are preserved in Christian rather than Jewish manuscripts. Before the capture of the Temple, we are told, Jeremiah takes the

Ark of the Law and everything kept inside it. The Ark disappears into the rock, and Jeremiah tells the people who are with him that God has left Zion and departed into heaven. He will return, and there will be a sign to announce his coming: all the Gentiles will begin to worship a piece of wood. Jeremiah also tells the people that no one is going to be able to bring the Ark out of the rock except Aaron, and that none of the priests or the prophets will be able to open the Tablets in it. Only Moses, the chosen one of God, can do this. At the resurrection, the Ark will be the first to arise from the rock. It will be placed on Mount Sinai, and all the saints will be gathered to it as they wait for the Lord. Jeremiah then writes the name of God with his finger as a seal in the rock. It is like a carving made with iron, and a cloud covers it to prevent anyone discovering the place or reading the name until the end of time. The rock is said to be in the wilderness, where the Ark was first made, between the two mountains on which Moses and Aaron lie buried. At night there is a cloud of fire, just as there had been in the early days, for the glory of God will always be with the Tablets of the Law. As he performs this mystery, Jeremiah becomes a partner with Moses, through the grace of God, and the two prophets are together to this day.

Eupolemos, a Jewish historian who wrote in Greek during the second century BC, also knew of the tradition concerning Jeremiah and the Ark. A brief passage from his work was preserved by the Christian historian Eusebius of Caesarea, in which he discusses the Tabernacle and the Ark, stresses the continuity of the Tabernacle and Temple of Solomon, and mentions the sack of the Temple. When the Babylonians seized Jerusalem, they captured Jonachim the king of the Jews, and took the gold and silver and bronze in the Temple as tribute. They did not take the Ark and the Tablets in the Ark, because Jeremiah had preserved them.

The obvious similarities between these traditions have suggested that one of them might be the source of the others, the Fourth Book of Baruch being dependent on the Second Book of Baruch perhaps, or the Life of Jeremiah on the Second Book of the Maccabees. But there are also differences between the various accounts, and these suggest that direct dependence is unlikely. In the Second Book of Baruch, for example, an angel hides the vessels, but in the other texts it is Jeremiah. In the Second Book of the

Maccabees and the Fourth Book of Baruch, Jeremiah hides the vessels in response to an oracle, but not in the Life of Jeremiah. The gathering of Israel that appears in the other three texts is not mentioned in the Second Book of Baruch. It also seems that reports of the hidden vessels circulated in more ancient documents than we have been able to recover. The author of the Second Book of the Maccabees refers to a version of the story preserved in the Memoirs of Nehemiah, which is not known to survive. He also mentions a document that included a version of the story similar to that in the Epistle of Jeremiah. There is no reason to assume that these are the only books that might have contained accounts of the Ark. At least their titles have been recorded. Many more could have disappeared completely.

According to the Talmud, when Josiah realized that the Temple would be destroyed, he concealed the Ark of the Covenant. Along with it, he hid the vessel filled with manna, the jug containing the sacred oil used by Moses for anointing the implements of the cult, and other holy utensils from the Temple. They will be restored by the prophet Elijah, who was often regarded in later Jewish tradition as a forerunner of the Messiah. Given the famous verse in the Second Book of Chronicles that refers to Josiah and the Ark, it is hardly surprising if traditions were applied to his name as well to Jeremiah. The contrast between king and prophet has been thought to reflect a struggle between later groups who tried to advance the rival claims of anointed kings or charismatic prophets as the true elect of God, but at such a distance and with so little evidence to guide us, it is impossible to be sure.

Some accounts of the hidden vessels do reveal the aims of rival factions, however, and the most obvious of these concerns the Samaritans and their devotion to the sacred mountain Gerizim, a rival to Mount Zion. In his *Jewish Antiquities*, Josephus describes an insurrection that occurred towards the end of the prefecture of Pontius Pilate, about AD 36. While Christians remember Pilate for his place in the Gospel accounts of the Crucifixion, it was the actions he took against the Samaritans in this disturbance that ruined his political career. Josephus reports that a false prophet had told the Samaritans to accompany him to Mount Gerizim, which according to Samaritan tradition is the most sacred of mountains. The prophet assured them that on their arrival he would show them the holy vessels that Moses had buried there. As the Samaritans believed him, they armed themselves and took up positions at a village named Tirathana. An immense crowd prepared to climb the mountain, but before they could do so, Pilate sent a troop of cavalry and heavy infantry to block the road. They killed some of the Samaritans in a pitched battle and put the others to flight. They also captured a large number of prisoners, and Pilate executed the leaders.

The Samaritans are known to have believed that a prophet like Moses would restore the hidden vessels from the Temple, and probably expected the restoration of the Mosaic cult to occur in the incident described. The *Memar Marqah*, an Aramaic text written in the fourth century AD, refers to Mount Gerizim at a time when 'what is hidden there will be revealed'. The appearance of the Tabernacle is thought to signify the return of glory and divine favour, just as its concealment indicates a time of apostasy. The Samaritan tradition may be linked to destruction of their temple on Mount Gerizim in 128 BC by the Hasmonean king and high priest John Hyrcanus, the nephew of Judas Maccabaeus. When the *Memar Marqah* refers to the desecration of the 'tabernacle' and the 'house', it would seem to be speaking of the Samaritan temple: 'My tabernacle they have defiled, my holiness they have profaned ... my house they have destroyed. From the True One they have turned away. My Favour they have concealed.'

If Mount Gerizim is the sacred mountain of the Samaritans, why should Moses have chosen such a site to bury the Temple vessels? At least, why should the Samaritans have claimed that he did? And why would they have believed that the vessels could be recovered in AD 36? A number of ancient writings, including scrolls found in the caves at Qumran, the Alexandrian philosopher Philo and the authors of the New Testament, all refer to a prophet like Moses, who became identified with the Messiah. In the account that Josephus provides of the Samaritan insurrection, the Samaritan prophet at the time was evidently seen as a figure like Moses. By the fourth century, Samaritan literature identifies this prophet like Moses as the *Taheb*, the 'Returning One' or Samaritan Messiah. The *Taheb* will restore true worship on Mount Gerizim, which would involve the restoration of the sacred vessels hidden there. Moses therefore has a role to play in concealing and in revealing the vessels, and the tradition allowed the Samaritans to venerate him as the great and true prophet, in contrast to the rival prophetic or messianic heroes of Judaism and Christianity. It also allowed them to exalt Mount Gerizim as the true place of worship, in contrast to Jerusalem.

This devotion to Mount Gerizim was considered by Jews to be the most vile of all the Samaritan heresies. As a result, the rabbis and the Pseudo-Philo replied with a counter tradition, claiming that the objects hidden on Mount Gerizim were not Temple vessels but idols. Rabbinic hostility to the Samaritan claims is recorded in the midrashic commentary on Genesis, *Bereshit Rabbah*. When Rabbi Ishmael ben Rabbi Jose was going up to Jerusalem to pray, he met a Samaritan. The two men began to quarrel over the question of whether God required worship on Mount Gerizim or in Jerusalem. Rabbi Ishmael told the Samaritan that he was no better than a dog hungry for carrion. The Samaritans all knew that idols were buried on Mount Gerizim because the Bible recorded that Jacob had hidden them there. This was the reason that they venerated the mountain. They were simply idolaters.

While the rabbis and the authors of the apocrypha and pseud-epigrapha believed that the Ark had gone into hiding and would be restored when the Messiah brought a New Age, the ancient symbol of the Presence of God had already undergone an even more dramatic transformation. Far from Jerusalem, among the exiles at Babylon, the third of the great prophets of Israel had received his call: 'In the thirtieth year, in the fourth month, on the fifth day of the month, as I was among the exiles by the river Chebar, the heavens were opened, and I saw visions of God.' The vision that Ezekiel sees is of the throne of God, but whereas Isaiah had seen his vision in the Temple of Solomon, Ezekiel was not even in the holy city, but in a strange and unclean land. Nevertheless, the vision that he sees beside the Chebar takes the form of the revelation at Mount Sinai. God displays himself with all the terror of the storm, in the manner of Baal, the ancient storm god of Ugarit.

As I looked, behold, a stormy wind came out of the north, and a great cloud, with a brightness round about it, and fire flashing forth continually, and in the midst of the fire, as it were of gleaming bronze. And from the midst of it came the likeness of four living creatures.

These creatures have the shape of men, but they also have four wings and four faces: the faces of a man, a lion, an ox and an eagle. As a later passage explains, 'I knew that they were cherubim.' In other words, they are the creatures who support the throne of God, whose statues stood in the sanctuary of the Temple built by Solomon, and whose images appeared on the cover of the Ark. It was between the wings of the cherubim that God promised to meet with Moses.

Ezekiel sees that beside each creature is a wheel: four wheels appearing as wheels within wheels, filled with eyes and containing the spirits of the creatures. Above them, a firmament shines like crystal. Above the firmament, he sees a throne like sapphire, and above the throne, a human form whose brilliance resembles fire and rainbow. The prophet finally falls upon his face when he sees the glory of the Lord, and he hears a voice saying to him, 'Son of man, stand upon your feet, and I will speak with you.' What Ezekiel had seen, it becomes clear in following chapters, is a vision of the throne of God in the inner sanctum of the Temple. He is later taken in his vision to the Temple in Jerusalem, and there he sees the same creatures, the same throne and the same glory of God.

These visions have been of immense importance for the survival of Judaism during the Exile and across the centuries that followed the destruction of the Second Temple by Titus. When the First Temple was destroyed and the people of Israel were scattered, where was the Presence of God? Had the Ark of the Covenant been lost? Was Israel abandoned in its Exile? The visions of Ezekiel reveal the Presence leaving the Temple in Jerusalem before its destruction, the throne of God travelling east with his Chosen People, where he appears to the prophet beside the river at Babylon.

The throne that Ezekiel describes is mysterious and difficult to understand, although some of the other furniture in the Temple had been provided with wheels, and mobile thrones were known in the ancient Near East. The throne of Ezekiel appears only as the Ark is about to vanish and the Temple is about to be destroyed.

It seems that the Ark has abandoned the restrictions of physical location. It has become a chariot that can ascend to heaven, its cherubim still alongside it to support the throne of God. It is no longer eschatological or messianic. It has become mystical.

Over the following centuries, the vision of Ezekiel became one of the foundations of the Jewish mystical path known as *merkabah* or 'chariot', which involved physical as well as mental techniques. The title was first given to discussions of the celestial vision that Ezekiel describes in the first chapter of his prophecies, and was later applied to any description of the higher realms. As the main theme of these writings was an ascent to celestial palaces and a vision of the throne of God, they were also known as *heikhalot*, the Hebrew word for 'temples' or 'palaces'. Some of the books are magical. The ascent was believed to be perilous, and instructions were essential if the mystic was to pass by the angelic guardians and celestial gatekeepers. The books also record hymns sung by celestial choirs, which the mystic might hear as he made his way through the heavens.

The legacy of *merkabah* can be found among the Jewish mystics of Europe, such as Elazar ben Yehudah of Worms, one of the greatest of Ashkenazi hassidim in the Rhineland. The kabbalists of Spain and Provence also relied on *merkabah* terms in their mystical symbolism, which fascinated Christian scholars during the Renaissance and was one of the main incentives for the progress of humanist and Orientalist studies. It seemed to offer a way to recover the secrets of the ancient sages, to inaugurate a New Age of wisdom and harmony. It is also the milieu from which one of most fascinating of Jewish traditions about the Ark emerged.

Many Jews have regarded *merkabah* with intense suspicion. When Gershom Scholem, the greatest modern authority on the subject, suggested that ancient Jewish mysticism was created by the same culture that had produced the classic rabbinic form of Judaism, he provoked indignation as well as confusion. The Jewish sages who produced the Mishnah, it was felt, were rational men. They must have been completely unlike the authors of an irrational and even degenerate literature filled with the worst sorts of superstition: magical spells, fantastic accounts of palaces in heaven, and a bizarre obsession with the names of angels. These elements could only have been due to foreign influences, probably from Islam, and the texts must have been written long after the age of the Talmud and the midrashim.

Scholem confounded his critics by proving that rabbinic discussions of mystical and magical themes could be understood only in relation to the *heikhalot* and *merkabah* texts. Midrashic discussions of the first chapters of Ezekiel used the term 'Work of the Chariot', while Talmudic authorities had been sufficiently interested in the subject to define it as esoteric and to set regulations about how it might be studied. Only two subjects were defined in this way, the Creation and the Chariot, and the Chariot was thought to be the more esoteric. The Mishnah ruled that the account of Creation must not be expounded before two or more persons, while the Chariot must not be expounded before even one person, unless he were an advanced scholar in his own right, who understood 'of his own knowledge'. This prohibition was taken very seriously, and stories were told of those who had died because they disobeyed it.

One of the most fascinating passages that Scholem discussed is found in the Mishnah tractate *Abodah Zarah*, and he was convinced that it offered proof that hymns of the type preserved in the *heikhalot* were known in the third century AD. It concerns the meaning of a verse in the First Book of Samuel, in which the Philistines are sending the Ark of the Covenant back to the Israelites and have placed it in a wagon drawn by cattle: 'And the cattle went straight in the direction of Beth-shemesh.'

Several Talmudic sages explain the Hebrew text by a clever play on words, taking the verb not from the root meaning 'to be straight', but from another root meaning 'to sing'. The cattle were therefore singing a hymn of praise. But what hymn would they have sung? Some rabbis suggested one of the more famous Psalms, or the Song of the Sea, which Miriam had sung at the crossing of the Red Sea during the Exodus: 'I will sing to the Lord, for he has triumphed gloriously ...' But Rabbi Isaac Nappaha, who taught in Palestine during the third century, maintained that the cattle were singing a different song, and that they were singing to the Ark itself:

> Rejoice, rejoice acacia shrine!
> Stretch forth in all your majesty!

Adorned with golden embroidery
Praised in the innermost sanctuary
Resplendent in the finest of ornaments.

Scholem realized that Rabbi Isaac Nappaha had introduced this hymn in imitation of the hymns sung by the cherubim who carry the throne of God in the vision of Ezekiel. These hymns were recorded in *heikhalot*, and Scholem cites a particularly close parallel:

Rejoice, rejoice, throne of glory!
Sing, sing for joy, seat of the Most High!
Exult, exult, precious vessel, so marvellously fashioned!
You will bring joy to the king who sits upon you
as the joy of the bridegroom in his bridechamber.

The words of Ezekiel may have described a chariot throne rather than an Ark, but the mystics seem to have moved without difficulty from one to another. If Ezekiel could imagine a Temple without an Ark, perhaps it might also be possible to imagine an Ark without a Temple? The answer, as we shall see, is that it was possible, but as it moves away from the Temple, the Ark is transformed yet again.

The story of the Ark in Ethiopia is often believed to be part of an ancient Jewish legacy in Africa, but it is not a tradition that has simply stepped from the pages of the Hebrew Bible. The Ethiopian Ark that appears in the earliest account from Egypt, and the Ark that appears in the Ethiopian epic *The Glory of Kings*, are not simply Israelite shrines. They are Christian. They have not only been taken from the inner sanctuary of the Temple, but also been removed from the Temple cult. This has often been forgotten, or overlooked. Most European scholars seem convinced that Ethiopians have been obsessed with the Temple for centuries, and have covered the highlands of the Christian empire with thousands of copies of it. Yet the evidence, as we shall see, suggests a very different conclusion. If anything, the Ethiopians were more interested in the Tabernacle than the Temple. To understand why, we need to look at the varieties of Judaism that appeared in the final decades before the Romans destroyed the Second Temple, one of which became the Christian Church. The Ark is not confined to the Old Testament, after all. It appears in the New Testament as well.

CHAPTER 9

The New Covenants

In the final year of the British Mandate in Palestine, a young Arab named Muhammad al-Dhib was searching for one of his goats among the cliffs near the Dead Sea. When he tossed a stone into a cave, thinking that the animal might have strayed inside, instead of the bleating of his goat he heard pottery breaking. Confused and alarmed at being alone in such a desolate place, he ran away. But he returned with a friend, and when they climbed into the cave, they found several large jars of earthenware, in which scrolls made of skin had been wrapped in linen rags.

The discovery was of little interest to a young goatherd, but he thought that the leather might be of some use, and gathering the seven largest scrolls, he took them to his tent. He kept them for two years, before selling them to an antique dealer in Bethlehem, who sold some of them to the Syrian Orthodox Archbishop, Mar Athanasius Samuel. Three of them were acquired for the new state of Israel by Eleazar Sukenik, a professor at the Hebrew University. The others were bought for the state by his son, Yigael Yadin, after the archbishop had tried to avoid a dispute over ownership between Israel and Jordan by advertising the scrolls in the *Wall Street Journal*.

News of the discoveries caused immense excitement throughout the world, and before long the search was under way for more scrolls. There was also rumour and scandal. Popular reports suggested that the Dead Sea Scrolls, as they were soon called, contained evidence that would undermine the essential beliefs of Christianity. Perhaps they would prove that Jesus was not divine. Perhaps the 'Teacher of Righteousness' who was mentioned in the scrolls was actually Jesus himself, and the 'Wicked Priest' was St Paul. Sensational theories about the scrolls have been offered over the decades, the most startling being an assertion that Jesus was a hallucinogenic mushroom rather than God incarnate and that the scrolls were the secret teachings of a fertility cult. In fact, the discoveries revealed much more of the history of Judaism than the history of Christianity, and after delays in publication that have been called 'the academic scandal *par excellence* of the twentieth century', the process of interpretation is in many ways only just beginning.

Although it was soon suggested that the documents had been written by the Essenes, a sect described by Josephus, Philo and the Latin historian Pliny, the new discoveries revealed a sect very different from anything reported by these historians. The authors of the scrolls were not cultivating a philosophical mysticism, but observing laws of priestly purity. They were expecting divine judgement, and were more keenly aware of the separation between darkness and light than between the mind and the body. Even their name, 'the sons of Zadok', reveals a priestly connection.

For the sectarians who preserved their library in the caves of Wadi Qumran, the destruction of the Temple in Jerusalem had occurred long before AD 70. By rejecting the Temple and its cult, they had begun to live in a world from which Jerusalem was already absent, even while the city was still standing. The sect had been founded by temple priests, who saw themselves as the true priestly line, as the heirs of Zadok. For them, the old Temple had been destroyed in the time of the Maccabees. The cult had been defiled not by Roman soldiers, but by the rise to power of Jewish high priests from a lineage other than their own. The priestly factions that had left their mark on the composition of the Hebrew Bible were still a fault line along which Judaism could fracture.

Before the Exile, the Chosen People had been ruled by kings. After the Exile, they were not. Although the Persians installed a governor of Davidic lineage when the Exiles returned from Babylon, the Davidic monarchy disappeared. Only in the rabbinic age do men who claimed descent from the house of David emerge again as leaders. During the Second Temple, political power was held by priests rather than kings. Under the Maccabees, the priests even assumed the title of king themselves, until they were toppled by Herod the Great, who built the most elaborate Temple of all.

A number of sects had arisen in the second century BC, most of them arguing that the priests were corrupt and that the Temple was polluted. Each presented itself as the true Temple, and its members as the true priests. Only they knew how to serve God according to his commandments. In the meantime, it was the duty of the sect at Qumran to create a substitute for the Temple, until God sent the Messiah in the line of Aaron who would build the Temple once again. They believed that the Presence of God had departed from Jerusalem and now lived with them beside the Dead Sea. The community itself was now a new Temple.

One of the questions that has perplexed anyone who looked for the origins of Christianity among the sectarians at Qumran has been the obvious difference between their devotion to the Law and the decision taken by the early Church that Old Testament law no longer applied under the New Covenant. Even aside from the fact that many Christians have tried to preserve or recover something of the Old Testament law, the Church does seem to have learned an important lesson from the Essenes or from other sectaries like them: the last days have begun and God is now living with his Chosen People as he had once lived in the Temple. Instead of sacrificial animals slaughtered at the Temple, God now requires the offering of a blameless life. When St Paul wrote to the Christians at Corinth in one of the earliest documents preserved in the Christian canon, he told them that the Spirit of God lived among them and that they were the Temple of God. When he wrote to the community at Ephesus, he told them that the cornerstone of this new Temple was Jesus himself, the Christian Messiah. Even a group as distinct from the Church as the Pharisees can be seen as reaching a similar conclusion, although they act upon it in quite a different way. If the Temple is now a community of people, it is essential for the entire community to keep the laws of ritual purity that would earlier have applied only to the priests who served in it. It is this emphasis on ritual purity that explains the importance that the Pharisees and the rabbis who came after them gave to laws relating to food. If the community is to live in a state of ritual purity, every meal must be eaten in a state of ritual purity.

One of the greatest of the Pharisees whose teachings are preserved in the Mishnah, Yohanan ben Zakai, insisted that preserving the Temple was not an end in itself. His predecessors may have taught that the Temple should be everywhere, even in the home, but Yohanan now believed that the altar of the Temple was to be found in the streets and the markets of the world. If the Temple had been destroyed, sacrifice must now consist of compassion. Renunciation and sacrifice of self would allow Jews to build a sacred community.

But where is the Ark of the Covenant in all this? Was the prophecy of Jeremiah correct, and the Ark no longer missed? The Temple Scroll from Qumran, which describes an ideal Temple and the laws of purity required to serve it, is badly mutilated, and there is no mention of the Ark in the passages that we can read with confidence. Nevertheless, the entire document may have been written with the Ark of Covenant firmly in mind. Among the documents discovered at Qumran were passages of a text known as the Damascus Document, which had evidently been written for a festival at which the covenant would be renewed. Among its other stipulations, it prohibits the king from marrying a second wife if his first wife is still alive. It then attempts to explain why David had so many wives in defiance of the prohibition. Apparently, this was because David had not read the Book of the Law that was sealed in the Ark of the Covenant. The Ark had not been opened in Israel from the day of the death of Eleazar and Joshua, and the elders who worshipped Ashtoreth. 'It was hidden and was not revealed until Zadok arose,' the Document claims. David should therefore be excused because he was not aware of a prohibition written in a sealed Book of the Law that had not yet been revealed.

The same restrictions on royal marriage also appear in the Temple Scroll, and while it is often assumed that the Damascus Document is referring to the Book of the Law that began the reform of Josiah after the high priest Hilkiah discovered it in the Temple, the Document mentions Zadok rather than Hilkiah. The Temple Scroll would therefore seem to be a more likely candidate, but then who might Zadok have been? We know that the sectaries called themselves 'the sons of Zadok', and it has been suggested that Zadok could have been the founder of the sect and the author of the Temple Scroll. He presented it as the Book of the Law that would once have been sealed in the Ark of the Covenant.

Within their Renewed Covenant, the Essenes were attempting to penetrate the secrets of heaven. Like the prophet Ezekiel, who saw the cherubim that had once adorned the Ark of the Covenant drawing a chariot of fire, the sectaries consecrated themselves to contemplating the chariot throne and the palaces of heaven. An account survives of one of their visions in which the cherubim bless the image of the chariot throne. When the chariot advances, angels of holiness come and go, and a vision of holy spirits appears between its wheels. Streams of fire and brilliant colours appear among the spirits, as they move with the glory of the marvellous chariot.

More elaborate visions of the chariot were recorded in another book, fragments of which have been found at Qumran. The Book of Enoch had been lost in Europe until the Scottish traveller James Bruce returned from Ethiopia with a manuscript, and when it was published and translated by Richard Laurence almost two centuries ago on the basis of the manuscript that Bruce had acquired, its appearance caused great excitement. Rather like the discovery of the Dead Sea Scrolls, it seemed to open a door into a new and unexpected world of ancient Judaism, describing visions of the cosmos, fire in the heavens, mystical revelations, and angels flying among celestial palaces. The fragments that were found at Qumran proved that at least part of the document was much older than anyone had realized. Dated to the late third or early second century BC, they are believed to constitute the oldest Jewish religious text outside the Bible, written long before the Maccabaean Revolt.

The revelations in the Book of Enoch describe the structure of the universe, and the origin and final judgement on evil. The prophet Enoch, who was seventh in line from Adam, travels through the cosmos, receiving a revelation about the judgement to come and the heavenly realm in which it is already beginning. It promises salvation to the righteous who listen and obey its message. In a vision included in a portion known as the 'Book of the Watchers', there is a description of the celestial palace. The visionary ascends through the realms of heaven and finally looks upon the Throne of God. This is written in the technical language of *merkabah*, and although Gershom Scholem had already demonstrated that this tradition was earlier than other scholars had suspected, the discovery at Qumran has proved that the heavenly ascent and the chariot were older still.

The description of the throne is based on the vision of Ezekiel.

The Church of Mary of Zion from the hill of Mai Qoho at Aksum, with the dome of the modern Chapel of the Tablet visible above the trees.

Left The Church of Mary of Zion at Aksum, in which the emperor Iyasu I spoke to the Ark of the Covenant.

Below The castle of Iyasu I at Gondar, built in 1685.

Above Sacred barques carried in procession by Egyptian priests in the Temple of Amun at Karnak, carved and painted during the reigns of Seti I and Ramesses II, between 1318 and 1237 BC.

The storm god Baal, on a stele found at Ras Shamra and dated to the second millennium BC.

The Ark of the Covenant carved in bas relief at the synagogue of Capernaum in the third century AD. As in the fresco of Dura, the Ark resembles the Holy Ark of the synagogue, placed on a cart and surrounded by a Tabernacle.

Below The Ark of the Covenant being returned to the Israelites after it destroyed the Philistine god Dagon, painted on a wall in the synagogue at Dura during the third century AD. The Ark is depicted in the shape of the Holy Ark in which the scrolls of the Torah were placed in the synagogue.

The Ark of the Covenant with a rainbow above the mercy seat and the two cherubim depicted as living creatures rather than images, from a Hebrew manuscript illuminated by Christian artists from Paris during the late thirteenth century.

Aaron placing the pot of manna and his staff beside the Tablets of the Law in the Ark of the Covenant, following the Epistle to the Hebrews rather than the Old Testament, depicted in enamel by Nicholas of Verdun in the twelfth century.

The idol of the Philistine god Dagon is shattered before the Ark of the Covenant in a fresco painted for the Cathedral of Anagni during the thirteenth century. Despite the descriptions in the Biblical text, the Ark resembles a medieval reliquary.

Below The Philistines return the Ark of the Covenant with a coffer containing offerings to the God of Israel, in a fresco at the Cathedral of Anagni.

The horned figure of Moses supervising the building of the Ark, from the Bible of Guiart Desmoulins produced early in the fourteenth century.

The Ark of the Covenant depicted as an altar in a stained-glass window at St Denis. The image includes the wheels of the cart on which the Ark was taken to Jerusalem, the four creatures from the vision of Ezekiel, which have become symbols of the Evangelists, a crucifix, and Christ himself.

The Ark of the Covenant carried into the Temple as one of the Prefigurations of the Virgin, in a fresco painted at the Chora Monastery in Constantinople during the fourteenth century. The Ark resembles the gabled lid of a sarcophagus.

The Ark of the Covenant carried across the Jordan, from the Abbot Walther Bible produced at Salzburg in the twelfth century. The Ark resembles medieval European depictions of the Temple as the Dome of the Rock.

As Enoch flies through the sky, carried by the wind past the stars of heaven, he approaches a wall of white marble surrounded by tongues of fire. Although he is frightened, he enters the fire and comes upon a great house of white marble. Its floor is made of crystal, and its ceiling reminds him of the stars among which the fiery cherubim live in a heaven of water. The walls of the house are surrounded by fire and its gates are burning. When Enoch enters the house, he sees nothing inside it. Although he is now so terrified that he falls upon his face, he sees a vision in which a door opens before him and a second house appears, even greater than the first. Within it he sees a throne that appears to be made of crystal, its wheels shining like the sun. He hears the voice of the cherubim, and beneath the throne there are streams of living fire. Enoch can barely look at the throne, as the robes of the figure who sits upon it are more brilliant than the sun, with a light that is whiter than snow. Even the angels cannot approach it or look at it. The throne is surrounded by flames, and a great fire stands before it.

Visions of the chariot throne appear again in the Aramaic parts of the Book of Daniel, written after the Second Temple had been desecrated by Antiochus Epiphanes in 167 BC. While the followers of Judas Maccabaeus believed that they could defeat the Hellenistic kings by force of arms, the Book of Daniel represents a mystical and interior solution to the crisis. The author was anxious to convince his readers that the desecration of the Temple and the suppression of Judaism were not merely the whims of an earthly king. Behind the armies of the Hellenistic rulers stood angelic princes locked in combat with God. Cosmic war was obviously beyond human control, but the beast from the sea would be destroyed, and the armies of God would prevail. The realization that war had engulfed the entire universe was meant to be reassuring rather than alarming. The fate of the world lay in the hands of God and the archangel Michael, who commanded the armies of heaven.

Prophetic warnings of the Day of Judgement, and the visions of heavenly thrones reported by Isaiah and Ezekiel seem to be the forerunners of the apocalypse. The prophecies of Jeremiah were also essential, as they describe the fall of Jerusalem and the triumph of Babylon as depending on the unalterable decision of God, rather than being a simple matter of sin and punishment. God controls the universe he made, and for reasons beyond our understanding, he decided that the kings of Babylon would rule for generations. Until their power collapsed, and Israel returned from Exile, no one could alter the events that God had planned. The only way for the Chosen People to survive was to obey the powers that ruled the world, and to wait for the future that God had ordained.

Whether this was the view of Jeremiah himself, or an addition by those who collected and edited his prophecies, is difficult to say, but they were certainly inspiring. When the author of Daniel tried to explain the desecration of the Temple by Antiochus Epiphanes, he turned to the prophecies of Jeremiah, and when the author of the Apocalypse of Baruch tried to explain the destruction of the Second Temple by the Romans, he turned to Jeremiah as well. They repeated the answers that the prophet had given to the mysteries of the world. The nations will rule over Israel until the day arrives that God has set for their destruction. Until then, no one can resist the kings of the earth. When the day comes, no one can save them.

The vision in Daniel recalls the victory of the storm god Baal: the destruction of the monsters in the waters of chaos that was given such prominence in the cult of Zion. It begins with four great beasts rising from a turbulent sea. They are subjected to judgement. One is destroyed, and they are all stripped of their power. In the vision, Daniel sees the pronouncement against them delivered from a throne of fire: 'As I looked, thrones were placed, and one that was ancient of days took his seat; his raiment was white as snow, and the hair of his head like pure wool; his throne was fiery flames, its wheels were burning fire.'

After Enoch and Daniel, the vision of the chariot of fire becomes a favourite theme and appears in a whole series of visionary testimonies. The Apocalypse of Abraham was written some time after the destruction of the Second Temple, and it describes the election of Israel and the covenant with God. Following the Book of Ezekiel, the visionary sees four creatures of fire beneath a flaming throne. Behind the creatures, he sees a chariot with wheels of fire, each filled with eyes, and above the wheels the throne appears again, covered in flame. The Latin Life of Adam and Eve describes a chariot like the wind, with wheels of fire. In the Greek

Apocalypse of Moses, which is closely related to it, God appears in paradise on a chariot of cherubim. The third of the books called by the name of the patriarch Enoch also describes Rabbi Ishmael ascending to heaven and seeing the throne of glory and the wheels of the chariot.

The writers who recorded these visions may have preferred the fiery chariot to the Ark of the Covenant as a throne of God, but the Ark does not disappear entirely. At least one author reported that he had seen them both during his vision of the heavenly realm. The claim is made in the most famous apocalypse of all, at least among Christians. This is the Apocalypse of John, known as the Book of Revelation. It is the last of the books in the Christian canon, and although Christian tradition has attributed it to St John the Divine, who wrote the Fourth Gospel and experienced a series of apocalyptic visions while he was on the island of Patmos, we know little more than that it was written after the persecution of Nero in AD 64. One of the visions is set in the heavenly Temple, during the Feast of Tabernacles, the festival at which the Ark of the Covenant may have been carried in procession. The visionary sees the sevenfold lamp, the altar, the golden incense altar and the Ark of the Covenant itself: 'The Temple of God in heaven was opened, and the Ark of his Covenant was seen within his Temple; and there were flashes of lightning, voices, peals of thunder, an earthquake, and heavy hail.' Once again, the power of God is displayed in the fury of the storm at Sinai, recalling the revelation of the Law, the Ark and the Tabernacle to Moses, as well as the visions of Isaiah and Ezekiel.

The visionary not only sees the Ark, but also describes the chariot throne that appeared to Ezekiel. Lightning and thunder issue from the throne, and before it are seven torches of fire and a sea of glass. Around the throne are four living creatures, with eyes in front and behind. The first is like a lion, the second like an ox, the third has the face of a man, while the fourth is like an eagle in flight. Each has six wings, filled with eyes, and they sing throughout the day and the night: 'Holy, holy, holy is the Lord God Almighty, who was and is and is to come.'

When the Apocalypse of John reaches its climax with a vision of the New Jerusalem, there is a surprising omission. The visionary reports that he sees no Temple in the city. If there had once been a Temple without an Ark, now there is an Ark without a Temple. Instead, the visionary gazes upon the holy city as it descends from heaven and hears a loud voice from the throne saying, 'Behold the Tabernacle of God...'

If the Temple of Solomon was thought by the Jewish sects to have been polluted, in the New Testament one finds an even more extreme position: the Temple was simply wrong from the beginning. When the first Christian martyr meets his death in the Acts of the Apostles, he is supposed to be defending himself against the accusation that he had made blasphemous remarks against both the Temple and the Law of Moses. His defence contains a summary of the dealings of God with the Children of Israel, but the history of salvation that Stephen offers would have convinced anyone who heard it that the charges had been justified. It is hardly surprising if the crowd is driven to a murderous frenzy.

In the desert, he tells them, the Israelites had the Tent of Witness, which God commanded Moses to make according to a divine model. This Tent was brought into the Promised Land, and David was asked to find a Tabernacle for the house of Jacob. But Solomon built a house, even though the Most High does not live in houses. As the Book of Isaiah says, 'Heaven is my throne and earth is the footstool for my feet; what kind of house will you build for me, says the Lord, or what is the place of my rest?'

While Stephen approved of the Tabernacle, he condemned the Temple as a house 'made with hands' – a phrase that Leviticus, Isaiah, Daniel and other books of the Old Testament apply to idols. The Temple, in other words, is an idolatrous invention by man. It is no better than the Golden Calf that the Israelites begged Aaron to make while Moses was talking to God on Mount Sinai. The Tabernacle was something completely different, built according to the divine plan revealed to Moses, and Stephen would see no continuity between it and the Temple. The Tabernacle was holy; the Temple was an abomination.

This hostility to the Temple is so obvious that the question has been asked whether Stephen was in fact Samaritan, or had been influenced by the Samaritan belief that Jerusalem was simply the wrong place to worship God. There is a tradition from the fourteenth century, recorded in Arabic by Abul Fath, that Stephen was Samaritan, but this is late, and there seems to be nothing in the speech that reveals a specifically Samaritan denunciation of Jerusalem and its cult. Hostility to the cult can, of course, be found in the Hebrew Bible itself. Stephen quotes from the later prophecies now included in the Book of Isaiah, and elsewhere the prophet certainly approves of those 'who turn away from all temples and altars, futile buildings of speechless stone, soiled by the blood of living creatures and the offering of animals'. The Temple and its cult, it seems, are nothing more than pagan. Stephen would have agreed.

It is now very difficult for us to reconstruct the various stances that might once have been adopted toward the Temple and its cult, but among the accounts of Jewish-Christian sects in the first century, descriptions survive of the Ebionites, or 'poor men'. They lived to the east of the River Jordan, and their hostility to the Temple was absolute. They looked for a prophet like Moses, and they believed that the role of Jesus was to abolish the Temple and its sacrifices, to cut away the corrupted parts of the Law and return to the true Law of Moses. The Temple had been built simply from royal ambition and not from the will of God. While the Samaritans were also looking for a prophet like Moses, in the absence of any other Samaritan beliefs it may be that Stephen or the author who included such a lengthy speech in the Acts of the Apostles should be placed among or near the Ebionites.

Although Stephen never mentions the Ark of the Covenant when he recites the history of the Chosen People, the Ark appears once more in the New Testament, in the Epistle to the Hebrews. The origin of the Epistle is a mystery, and although it has been attributed to St Paul, the thoughts of its author and the Greek in which he has expressed them are completely unlike any of the Pauline letters. They are also different from the speech attributed to the martyr Stephen. The author argues with some eloquence for the superiority of the New Covenant of Christ over the Old Covenant between God and the Israelites. He sees the Temple and its cult as 'a shadow of the good things to come' and as 'pictures of the True', whereas Stephen simply denounced them as wrong.

The author of the Epistle reminds his readers that under the Old Covenant, the High Priest would have to make atonement every year, according to the regulations set out in the books of Exodus and Leviticus. He would enter the sanctuary, blinding himself with incense so that he would not be killed by the power of the Ark of the Covenant, and sprinkle blood on the *kapporet*.

As the basis for his claim that a New Age has begun, the author of the Epistle provides his own summary of the Levitical cult, during which he contradicts the statements made in the Old Testament about the contents of the Ark. Along with the Tablets of the Law, the Ark contains a golden urn preserving the miraculous food that saved the tribes of Israel as they wandered in the desert, and the rod of Aaron that produced blossoms and ripe almonds when the tribes doubted the wisdom of Moses. The rabbis had usually placed these objects in the secret chamber beneath the Temple, although they too had been inclined to increase the contents of the Ark, adding the broken Tablets, the Book of the Law, the peace offerings of the Philistines, the oil for anointing the priests, and the water for purification. They were not alone in this. The Biblical Antiquities attributed to Philo even added twelve stones engraved by angels with the names of the tribes of Israel. They were placed in the Ark along with the ephod of the high priest, and at the End of Time the light from these stones would replace the sun and the moon. Later Christian writers followed the New Testament, however, and the Ark that appears in the Ethiopian epic owes more to the Epistle of the Hebrews than it does to Exodus or Deuteronomy.

> Now even the first covenant had regulations for worship and an earthly sanctuary. For a Tabernacle was prepared, the outer one, in which were the lampstand and the table and the bread of the Presence; it is called the Holy Place. Behind the second curtain stood a Tabernacle called the Holy of Holies, having the golden altar of incense and the Ark of the Covenant covered on all sides with gold, which contained a golden urn holding the manna, and the rod of Aaron that budded, and the Tables of the Covenant; above it were the cherubim of glory overshadowing the mercy seat. Of these things we cannot now speak in detail.

The ancient cult, according to the author of the Epistle, has been made obsolete by the death of Christ, who appeared as high priest of the New Age. He entered once into the Holy of Holies and obtained the eternal redemption that purifies the conscience. He did this not with a Tabernacle made by human hands in this world, and not with the blood of goats and bulls, but with the celestial Tabernacle and with his own blood. The entry of Christ into this heavenly Tabernacle marks the beginning of the New Age. The Levitical cult and the Mosaic Law are now obsolete; the Second Covenant has been inaugurated. Nowhere in his discussion of either the Old Covenant or the New does the author mention the Temple. His gaze seems to be fixed upon the Tabernacle.

The author lived in a curious time. The belief that the charismatic preacher Yehoshua ben Yosef was the expected Messiah, and that he had risen from the dead after dying in agony on a Cross, had been carried by Paul of Tarsus far beyond the Jewish world in which the preacher had been born. As the mission to the Gentiles began to accelerate, the majority of these who adopted the new faith had little knowledge of the Jewish cult from which it arose. The Epistle to the Hebrews may have been as much a treatise about Hebrews written for Gentiles as it was an explanation of the New Covenant written for Hebrews. This apparent paradox is easy enough to understand, even if the lessons it could teach are often forgotten. Ties to the past are expressed with the greatest force precisely when they are weakest. We shall see this in other times and at other places.

For the moment, however, the Epistle to the Hebrews had preserved the Ark in the Holy of Holies for a New Age, but it did so by placing them both in heaven rather than on earth. The New Covenant evidently had no need of them in physical form, at least for now. In other hands, however, the ancient shrines carried into Canaan from the wilderness survived in their former vigour. Beyond the caravan cities of the Ishmaelites, among the People of the New Covenant who lived across the Red Sea, we shall see the Ark appear on earth again.

CHAPTER 10

The Ark of Saul

The silence about the Ark of the Covenant seems to begin even before it disappears. After it is installed in the Temple, there is remarkably little mention of it aside from the cryptic statement about Josiah ordering the Levites to deposit the Ark in the Temple. It is almost as if the prophecy of Jeremiah had already become true. The Ark would not come to mind. It would not be remembered, and it would not be missed.

Outside the historical books, the Ark is mentioned only twice in the Hebrew Bible. The prophecy of Jeremiah is itself one of these verses. The other appears in Psalm 132, which describes the immense importance of the Ark for the covenant that God would make with King David. Its arrival signifies the choice of Zion as a holy mountain and confirms the Presence of God in the Temple: 'Arise, O Lord, and go to your resting place, you and the Ark of your might.'

But is this all we have? Does the Hebrew Bible have nothing more to tell us about the Ark of the Covenant? If the Presence of God were believed to reside either inside the Ark or somewhere above it, it might be quite reasonable to refer to the Ark by mentioning the deity whose presence it signified rather than the Ark itself. One might expect to find this more readily in the poetic and liturgical language of the Psalms, but it is occasionally true of the historical books as well.

In the Second Book of Samuel, God speaks to the prophet Nathan, and tells him that he has not lived in a house since the day he brought the people of Israel out of Egypt, but has been moving about in a tent. These remarks are made four verses after David has clearly spoken of the Ark: 'See now, I live in a house of cedar, but the Ark of God lives in a tent.' There seems little doubt that, when God says that he has lived in a tent, he means that the Ark has been placed in a tent.

The Book of Leviticus refers to the earlier death of Nadab and Abihu, the sons of Aaron, who had attempted to offer incense to the Ark in defiance of ritual specified by God: 'The Lord spoke to Moses, after the death of the two sons of Aaron, when they drew near before the Lord and died.' They drew near to the Lord, it seems, by approaching the Ark.

In the Second Book of Samuel, after David and his followers have placed the Ark on a cart to bring it up to Jerusalem, the statement that David 'rejoiced before the Lord' would also seem to refer to the Ark:

> And they carried the Ark of God upon a new cart, and brought it out of the house of Abinadab which was on the hill; and Uzzah and Ahio, the sons of Abinadab, were driving the new cart with the Ark of God; and Ahio went before the Ark. And David and all the house of Israel were making merry before the Lord with all their might...

The First Book of Chronicles records that fourteen verses of Psalm 105 were used in the ceremonial procession when David brought the Ark to Jerusalem and placed it in a tent. In the last of these verses, 'the presence of the Lord' would seem to refer to the Ark. Psalm 24 is also believed to have been used when the Ark was carried in procession, and the entrance of the Lord through the gates of the city would seem to mean the entrance of the Ark: 'Lift up your heads, O gates, and be lifted up, O ancient doors, that the King of glory may come in.' If these Psalms really do refer to the Ark, one would want to make the same claim for the verse 'God has gone up with a shout, the Lord with the sound of a trumpet', which appears in Psalm 47, or for the first verse of Psalm 68: 'Let God arise, let his enemies be scattered; let those who hate him flee before him!' The result would be a dramatic increase in the number of times that the Ark appears in the Hebrew text.

Any mention of the Ark or even any allusion to it might be thought to increase our appreciation of its significance, but it is really the passages in the Psalms that can change our understanding of why the Ark might have been made and how it might have been used. They suggest rituals in which the Ark was an essential element, but which are scarcely mentioned elsewhere. Without the testimony of the Psalms, our view of the Ark would have been much more like that of Josiah or the Deuteronomist who described his reform, and yet we would have found it much more difficult to understand why he would have wanted to reform the cult.

Even in the historical books, there are other passages that could transform our understanding of the Ark, if we were sure that we could interpret them correctly. The challenge they present to us is that we must follow the trail of the early scribes and translators, studying whatever clues we might find along the way. Although it is often assumed that a critical attitude to the text of the sacred scriptures is a thoroughly modern achievement – or a thoroughly modern failing, depending on one's point of view – the earliest biblical scholars were often much more daring in their enquiries and much more flexible in the answers they proposed than those who followed them. The text of the Bible became more holy as the centuries passed, not less holy. By examining the traces that the early experts have left in the text, we may reach a surprising conclusion ourselves.

The opening verse of Psalm 68, which has been mentioned above, is remarkably similar to a passage in the Book of Numbers. This is one of the two verses that are known as the 'Song of the Ark', and are often believed to be of immense antiquity: 'And whenever the Ark set out, Moses said, "Rise up, O Lord, and let our enemies be scattered; and let them that hate you flee before you." And when it rested, he said, "Return, O Lord, to the ten thousand thousands of Israel." '

Despite their apparent age, the position in which these verses have been preserved has puzzled scholars for over 2,000 years and led to rabbinical arguments of remarkable ingenuity. Anyone reading the Hebrew text will see a letter whose shape resembles a square bracket placed at the beginning and the end of these verses. It is one of only two passages in the Bible where this unusual symbol appears, and the oldest Jewish authorities to discuss it claim that the text had been corrupted at an early stage of transmission: 'These two verses are marked at the beginning and at the end to show that this is not their proper place.'

Rabbi Yehudah ha-Nasi, who is believed to have edited the Mishnah, displays the conviction of later times that the sacred text could not have been dislocated in any way. To preserve the text as it stands, he made the astonishing claim that the brackets placed before and after the verses indicate that by themselves these verses constituted separate books of Moses. The consequence of this statement would be a Pentateuch that consisted not of five books, but of seven.

The Talmud records both the earlier and the later explanations, and cites a famous verse from the Book of Proverbs as proof that the Law actually did comprise seven books: 'Wisdom has built her house, she has set up her seven pillars.' However resourceful Rabbi Yehudah may have been, his argument did not convince his own father-in-law, who insisted that the symbols indicated some kind of dislocation. He claimed that 'in future this passage will be removed from here and be written in its proper place'. At the time, unfortunately, no one knew what that place might be, or at what point in the story the 'Song of the Ark' might have been sung.

The kabbalists who compiled the *Zohar* in the thirteenth century were less concerned with recovering the original order of the text or preserving the received version against clever criticism. They were interested in the mystical properties of the two verses, and they record Rabbi Eleazar and Rabbi Simeon engaged in a discussion about the purpose of the two symbols that appear at the beginning and the end of the passage. While they continued to argue over the details of what earlier rabbis had said, they agreed that the symbols represented the Presence of God. Rabbi Eleazar said that, when the Ark would set out before the Children of Israel to look for a new camp, the Presence would hover over it, but would keep its face turned towards the people. When the Ark stopped, the Presence would turn its face back to the Ark. This explained the direction in which the brackets appeared in the text. Rabbi Simeon agreed with him, but claimed that the Presence of God would be able to look both on the Ark and on the Children of Israel, until the disobedience of the people forced it to look away.

Another corruption that attracted the attentions of rabbis and textual critics occurred in the First Book of Samuel, and its implications for the history of the Ark of the Covenant are difficult to exaggerate. Whatever solution may be thought to offer the most credible and the most complete explanation, something very unusual has obviously occurred. Our decision about a single word in this one verse could transform our understanding of the Ark.

The verse appears in a passage where Saul is leading a campaign against the Philistines. Most English versions translate the Hebrew as: 'And Saul said to Ahijah, "Bring the Ark of God." Because the Ark of God was at that time with the Children of Israel.' But this is only an attempt to make sense of a text that has obviously been corrupted. As it has been passed down to us, the Hebrew contains 'and' rather than 'with': 'And Saul said to Ahijah, "Bring the Ark of God." Because the Ark of God was at that time and the Children of Israel.'

Translators must try to make sense of the text they are translating, but the Hebrew cannot be understood in a way that would support the usual English rendering. The problem is that it cannot really be understood. Even if the second sentence in the verse has been inserted by a scribe, the phrase 'because the Ark of God was at that time' requires a predicate to complete the sentence. Something has been lost, or the Hebrew has been corrupted in some other way.

With textual problems of this sort, the usual first step would be to look at the earliest translations of the Bible, which were made before the Massoretic Text itself was produced, and which are certainly earlier than the majority of the Hebrew manuscripts that have survived. They may depend on earlier and more original forms of the Hebrew than appear in the Hebrew manuscripts themselves. In this particular case, it may be possible to restore at least part of the Hebrew on the basis of the Greek text of the Septuagint, but we also find a startling difference: 'And Saul said to Ahijah, "Bring the ephod." Because he carried the ephod at that time before Israel.'

Where the Hebrew speaks of the Ark, the Greek mentions an 'ephod'. This is usually understood to be part of the elaborate vestment of the high priest. Which of the two words is correct? It seems very unlikely that any Hebrew scribe would have written 'Ark of God' in place of 'ephod', because it creates enormous problems for the accepted understanding of the Ark. At the time Saul was speaking, the Ark had been housed at Kiryath-yearim. If it was also with Saul and his troops as they campaigned against the Philistines, there must have been more than one of them.

On the other hand, there would have been considerable incentive for a Greek translator or scribe to alter 'Ark of God' to 'ephod'. It would not only remove the difficulty about the number of Arks, but also make the verse agree with other passages in the First Book of Samuel that refer to the ephod. The most likely solution would therefore seem to be that the verse did originally refer to the Ark of God, and that the presence of the Ark at Kiryath-yearim means that there was more than one Ark.

The difficulty with this conclusion was spotted by Jewish commentators in earlier centuries. Isaac Abravanel, who was a biblical scholar as well as treasurer to King Alfonso V of Portugal in the latter years of the fifteenth century, suggested that the Ark of God demanded by Saul in the First Book of Samuel was not the Ark that contained the Tablets of the Law, which he admits was at Kiryath-yearim. Instead, he argued, it might have been a movable box for the ephod containing objects used in divination. Abravanel proposed the same solution for the Ark mentioned by Uriah the Hittite in the Second Book of Samuel, when he refuses to accept the invitation of David that he visit his wife Bathsheba. David had learned that Bathsheba was pregnant with his own child, and he had hoped to disguise his adultery by persuading her husband to visit her, but Uriah insists that, while the Ark and the men of Israel were in the field for battle, he should not be making love to his wife. This conversation occurred at a time when the Ark was known to have been deposited in the tent that David pitched for it at Jerusalem. The army was camped at Rabbath Ammon.

While the modern scholar most interested in the verse was dismissive of Abravanel, the suggestion is more interesting than he seems to have realized. If it were correct, then it would admit the possibility that there were a number of different objects called 'Ark of God', and this in itself would force us to abandon the conventional view.

In fact, Jewish tradition contains a number of fascinating accounts of additional Arks. When the Babylonian Talmud discusses the verse in Exodus 'And Moses took the bones of Joseph with him', it records a rabbinic discussion about the fate of the body of the patriarch Joseph and the procession of two Arks through the wilderness, one containing death and the other the Presence of God.

The rabbis were anxious to know how Moses could have known where Joseph was buried. They reported a tradition that Serah, the daughter of Asher, was still living despite having been born when Joseph was alive. When Moses went to her and asked if she knew where Joseph was buried, she told him that the Egyptians had made a metal coffin for him, which they sank into the Nile, in order that the waters might be blessed by its presence. The Egyptian magicians and sorcerers had also told the pharaoh that the Israelites would never leave Egypt if they could not find it.

Moses went to the bank of the Nile and called out to Joseph, telling him that the time in which the Holy One swore to redeem Israel had come, along with the time of the oath that Israel had sworn to Joseph. The Presence is waiting for you, he told him. Israel is waiting for you. If Joseph did not show himself now, Israel would be released from the oath that it had sworn. Immediately, the coffin of Joseph began to rise from the depths as if it were no heavier than a reed, and Moses took it.

Another version was offered by Rabbi Nathan, who claimed that Joseph was buried in the royal sepulchres. Moses went and stood by these sepulchres, announcing to Joseph that the time for the oaths to be fulfilled had arrived. If he did not show himself, Israel would be released from its oath. As soon as he spoke, the coffin of Joseph began to shake. Moses took it and carried it with him.

During all the years that the people of Israel were in the wilderness, the Ark in which Joseph had been buried and the Ark of the Covenant moved side by side. When anyone asked about the meaning of the two Arks, they were told that one was the coffin of a man, and one was the Ark of the Presence of God. If they questioned whether a corpse should move side by side with the Presence of God, they were told that the corpse in one Ark had fulfilled all that was written in the other.

Much earlier than Abravanel, the Jerusalem Talmud records that Rabbi Yehudah ben Laqish had also suggested that there was more than one Ark. One of them contained the Tablets of the Law, and the other contained the fragments of the Tablets that Moses had shattered after he had seen the Children of Israel worshipping the Golden Calf beside the mountain of Sinai. Rabbi Yehudah ben Laqish is reported as saying that two Arks travelled with the

Israelites in the wilderness: one in which the Tablets of the Law were deposited, and one in which the fragments of the first Tablets were deposited. The Ark with the Tablets deposited was kept in the Tent of Meeting, about which it was written that neither Moses nor the Ark of the Covenant of the Lord moved from the midst of the camp. The Ark with the fragments deposited was carried in and out of the camp, and it was mentioned on two occasions.

Other rabbis claimed that there was only one Ark, and that it went out of the camp only once, in the days of Eli, when it was captured. They cited the biblical verse that described the Philistines seeing the Ark for the first time: 'Woe unto us! Who will deliver us from these mighty gods?'

Biblical evidence could also be found to support Rabbi Yehudah ben Laqish: 'And Saul said to Ahijah, "Bring the divine Ark." ' This should mean that there was an Ark at Kiryath-yearim, although his opponents claimed that Saul was referring to the ephod, the golden breastplate of the high priest.

A second verse was thought to support Rabbi Yehudah ben Laqish: 'The Ark and Israel and Judah are living in tents.' If the Ark was already in Jerusalem, how could it have been in the field with the armies of David at the same time? The opponents of Rabbi Yehudah argued that the Temple had not yet been built when Uriah was speaking to the king. Although the Ark had been brought to Jerusalem, it would still have been in a tent. This would mean that the verse did not assume the existence of more than one Ark.

In the eyes of some modern scholars, Rabbi Yehudah ben Laqish did not go far enough. They believed that the Ark was not a single object, and that Arks existed at every sanctuary in Palestine that possessed a priesthood. In this view, the theory of a single Ark is a 'Deuteronomistic conceit', an imposition of a later view of orthodoxy on an ancient text. One God should have only one shrine, in other words.

If the Ark brought to Saul in the First Book of Samuel is a different Ark from that deposited at Kiryath-yearim, and if the Ark said by Uriah the Hittite to be encamped with the army at the siege of Rabbath Ammon was perhaps another, is it possible that the 'ephod' with which Abiathar accompanied David on his wanderings was a third? Could there have been others in the sanctuary of Nob, or with Micah and the Danites, or with Gideon? To answer this question, we need to understand what the ephod mentioned in the First Book of Samuel might have been, and why Saul might have called for it.

Instructions to prepare the ephod are given in Exodus as part of the equipment of the Tabernacle, and they are repeated more or less exactly when it is actually made:

> And they shall make the ephod of gold, of blue and purple and scarlet stuff, and of fine twined linen, skilfully worked. It shall have two shoulder-pieces attached to its two edges, that it may be joined together. And the skilfully woven band upon it, to gird it on, shall be of the same workmanship and materials, of gold, blue and purple and scarlet stuff, and fine twined linen. And you shall take two onyx stones, and engrave on them the names of the sons of Israel, six of their names on the one stone, and the names of the remaining six on the other stone, in the order of their birth. As a jeweller engraves signets, so shall you engrave the two stones with the names of the sons of Israel; you shall enclose them in settings of gold filigree. And you shall set the two stones upon the shoulder-pieces of the ephod, as stones of remembrance for the sons of Israel; and Aaron shall bear their names before the Lord upon his shoulders for remembrance.

It seems certain that the ephod is an elaborate vestment to be worn by Aaron as high priest. Elsewhere, however, the word seems to refer to quite different things. There is the type of linen ephod worn by Samuel and then by David, which is obviously unlike the heavy ritual vestment worn by the high priest. There is also something that is not a garment at all. It seems to be an object of some sort that was worshipped or used for divination.

When Gideon makes one of these, the description in the Book of Judges indicates that it required 1,700 shekels of gold and a great deal of other unspecified precious metal as well. It would seem to be a more substantial object than the vestment described in Exodus. The Book of Judges also states that Micah made an ephod and placed it in a shrine, which is not the usual way of employing a new article of clothing.

On more than one occasion in the First Book of Samuel, David calls for an ephod to be brought to him when he learns that Saul is plotting against him, and uses it to ask the advice of God. This object does not seem to have been worn. It was carried, and only by priests.

There have been various attempts to make sense of the different meanings. Perhaps, it has been suggested, the ceremonial apron was so heavily decorated with gold embroidery that it 'could stand of itself'. Perhaps the word 'ephod' was also used to describe an idol dressed in the apron. Perhaps the ephod was initially the idol, and the name was then applied to the garment in which the idol was clothed, and finally applied to the loincloth of the ministrant. Perhaps it was not an idol or a loincloth, but a bag for sacred lots to be used in divination. Perhaps it was primarily an instrument of divination, which might be either a costly idol or a sacerdotal vestment. None of these is convincing.

One possible explanation is that the supposedly solid ephod, whenever it is mentioned in the Hebrew Bible, represents the use of the word by the Jewish scribes for another word whose implications could have threatened the orthodoxy of later times. While this may be thought a drastic solution, there is a verse where it seems to be precisely what the scribes have done. A substitution of this sort is the most reasonable explanation for the discrepancy between the Hebrew and the Greek that we have seen in the First Book of Samuel.

This conclusion was presented at length and with considerable vigour over eighty years ago. It has not been generally accepted, but it has never been successfully refuted either, and it continues to find advocates among scholars who have studied the narrative in the Books of Samuel from several different perspectives.

In fact, it may not matter if the claims about a single verse in the First Book of Samuel are accepted. Whether or not 'ephod' was actually substituted for 'Ark' in the Hebrew text, it remains clear that the ephod is remarkably similar to the Ark. It seems to appear in the text when the Ark disappears, and to disappear when the Ark reappears. It never appears at the same time as the Ark. Later in the First Book of Samuel, it is mentioned as a priestly privilege, but it was not included in the earlier lists of these privileges. The Ark, which had been mentioned as a priestly privilege, is not mentioned here. The ephod seems to have been carried and used in battle, and to be in the possession of the priesthood at Shiloh. The same is true of the Ark. In fact, there seems to be nothing about the ephod that could not be applied to the Ark. Even if 'ephod' has not been written in place of 'Ark' in the First Book of Samuel, it would seem to be an object so like the Ark that the assumption of the singularity of the Ark would have to be placed in doubt. If this is admitted, an entirely different history of the Ark begins to emerge.

If there were more than one Ark, would it increase the chances that one of them survived into more recent history, even to the present day? There have been suggestions that other Arks were made, but only as replacements. Is it really likely, according to this view, that the Philistines would have returned the Ark that they had captured in battle, despite the statements in the Bible that they did? Would it not have been more likely for David to have brought a new Ark to Jerusalem, rather than finding the ancient Ark preserved but almost forgotten at Kiryath-yearim? Was the Ark deposited in the Temple at the command of Josiah the plain box described in Deuteronomy, and was this a later and simpler version for a new and more austere age, in contrast to the elaborate Ark of the Priests? The questions are not in themselves unreasonable, and if we are tempted to ask whether these would have been real Arks, it may be helpful to remember that the Second Temple was still the Temple even if it was a replacement for the Temple of Solomon. The famous prophecy of Jeremiah predicts that an Ark would not be made after the Exile, but he does not seem to be saying that the Ark would never be made again because it would have been impossible to do so.

Even aside from the question of a series of Arks, if more than one Ark existed at the same time, which one of them would have been the real Ark? Here too, the ancient view may be rather different from our own. The Ark is said to have been made according to a plan in heaven. It is therefore an earthly copy of an immaterial original. Would only one copy be original, and the others false or inauthentic if they were ever made? We know that the first set of Tablets was shattered. Another set was made, and the rabbis were fascinated by the idea that another Ark might have been made for them. Was the second set of Tablets less real than the first?

Could an Ark have survived in Ethiopia, but be another Ark and not the Ark of the Covenant? Would it be just as real? As we shall see, given the way in which the Ethiopians discuss the matter, the answer is likely to be that it would. And given that we have two descriptions in the Hebrew Bible of what is supposedly the real Ark of the Covenant, it is not immediately obvious whether we should be hoping to find an elaborate gold Ark or a simple wooden Ark. At some point, of course, questions have to be asked about whether a wooden box could survive for so many centuries even if it had been covered in gold. As we shall see, such a box could certainly have survived in an Egyptian tomb. But outside the dessicated air of the tomb, especially if the Ark were carried into battle and through the wilderness, it would seem quite unlikely.

The stone tablets that the Ark was built to contain could have survived, however. In fact, in another holy city, we know that sacred stones of great antiquity have survived. The shrine has been replaced several times, although the replacements are not thought to be any less real. The holy city is Mecca, and we need to know more of the ancient Arab shrine before we consider what the Ethiopians claim they possess at Aksum. It is important to remember that the description of the Ark in the chronicle of Iyasu does not correspond to anything that we found in the Hebrew Bible. And we shall see that it does not agree with the earliest description of the Ark in Ethiopia. We shall also see that Ethiopians themselves have believed that David made a new Ark at Kiryath-yearim, but that it was still authentic. It may be that by looking carefully at the descriptions of the Ark in the Bible, and by finding more than one, we have not increased the likelihood of an authentic Ark surviving in Ethiopia as much as we have increased the likelihood of believing that what survives in Ethiopia is authentic.

CHAPTER 11

The Ark of Abraham

Dressed in robes of white, thousands of the faithful kneel in circles around an immense black cube. Its proportions are those of the sanctuary in which the Ark of the Covenant once stood in the Temple of Solomon, and it too contains an ancient and venerated stone that descended from the sky on a sacred mountain and shone with a brilliant light. The Kaba, as the cube is known in Arabic, is the centre of the universe to over a billion Muslims. Their faith requires them to turn toward it as they pray five times a day, wherever they might be, and on the tenth day of the lunar month of pilgrimage known as *Dhu 'l-Hijja*, Muslim pilgrims walk around the Kaba like stars travelling about the Pole. For this is what the Kaba has been said to be: the point on which the pole of the seven worlds and the seven heavens is planted, the highest point on earth and the nearest to God.

The immense sanctity of the Kaba for so many people throughout the world is the consequence of a revelation that began almost fourteen centuries ago, when the angel Gabriel spoke to a merchant at Mecca on the Night of Power, summoning him to a new life as the prophet of God. 'Recite,' the angel told him, 'in the name of the Lord who created man.'

Muhammad was called to be the last and the greatest of the messengers of God, the 'Seal of the Prophets' according to the Quran, the apostle who brought the revelations granted on earth to a glorious completion. His childhood had been spent as a poor orphan, and even though he had married the widow of a wealthy merchant, the years before the revelation of his mission had been difficult for him. He had begun to spend his days wandering among the rocks and searching for God, and he was asleep on Mount Hira when Gabriel spoke to him at last. But if the way was not yet clear to Muhammad himself, Islamic tradition assures us that animals and birds had begun to see the signs of his calling. Even the stones and trees would cry out to him, 'Peace unto you, Apostle of God!' Holy men could see it as well. For some years, Jewish rabbis, Christian monks and Arab magicians had all been predicting the arrival of a prophet in Arabia, and while Muhammad was travelling with one of the Meccan caravans, a monk recognized that his body bore the signs that marked him out as a prophet.

The verses that the angel now revealed to Muhammad, and that came to be preserved in the Quran, were written on a tablet in heaven. It was from these sacred writings that the revelations to earlier prophets such as Moses had been taken. Muhammad had not been sent to establish a new religion. God was losing patience because the earlier revelations had not been obeyed, and the teachings of the prophets had been corrupted. Now Muhammad had come to announce the impending Day of Judgement to a people who had never been sent a prophet to warn them, and to Jews and Christians as well. They should abandon their idolatry, and return to the true faith revealed by prophets over the centuries. Above all, they must recognize the absolute unity of God. 'There is no God but God,' begins the confession of Islamic faith, and idolatry was the most appalling denial of this fundamental truth.

Even if Muhammad had not intended to create a new religion, the response of the Jews and Christians would have forced him to do so. His arrival created the most intense crisis for the Christian states in particular. If Christ had brought the final and perfect revelation, the incarnation of God himself, why should another prophet have been sent? The conclusion seemed inescapable: Muhammad was a false prophet, perhaps the antichrist himself described in the Revelation of St John. Yet the armies of Islam defeated the greatest powers of the ancient world, including Rome, whose Christian emperors ruled from Constantinople like the shadow of God on earth. For some reason, it seemed, God must have sent the scourge from the desert.

The events of the following centuries never answered the old question. Even when the Muslim advance was checked at the beginning of the modern age, and when European military technology placed most of the Islamic world under the control of

Christian powers, a fundamental mystery remained. If God sent Muhammad as a prophet, not only was the Christian message suspect, but it was suspect for betraying the ancient faith revealed to Abraham and the Israelite prophets who had come after him. In particular, Christians had denied the claim of God to be unique, and had defied his insistence that they should renounce the worship of images. These were two of the commandments that had been delivered to Moses at Mount Sinai, written in stone on the Tablets within the Ark of the Covenant. In effect, the prophets of Israel had returned to denounce Christian idolatry, and now they had an army.

For Jews themselves, the implications were scarcely more encouraging. They knew that Ishmael, the eldest son of the patriarch Abraham with whom God made his covenant, had been driven from the presence of his father. His mother was the concubine Hagar, and even though Abraham and Sarah were man and wife, Sarah was jealous of Hagar because she had borne a son. Now, inspired by an Ishmaelite prophet, the descendants of Hagar had appeared from the desert to claim their inheritance.

This prophet, Muhammad, was indeed 'the prophet like Moses' predicted in the Book of Deuteronomy, announcing an absolute faith in One God and leading his people toward a Promised Land. If this seems a startling way to describe the birth of Islam, it is largely because our sense of what it means to be Jewish or Christian or Muslim has been changed so dramatically, especially by the history of Jewish persecution in Europe, and by the founding of the state of Israel fifty years ago. In the century before Muhammad was born, there were Jewish cities in Arabia, there were Jewish armies, and there were Jewish princes who would use these armies to fight for the Jewish faith. The Jewish poet Samaual ibn Adiyah, who was the son of a Jewish priest and was remembered as a paradigm of honour and courage, wrote in the sixth century: 'We are men of the sword, and when we draw it, we exterminate our enemies.'

That so much of this Jewish history has been forgotten may be the result of it contradicting so absolutely the rabbinic and Talmudic assumptions of what it meant to be a Jew. It did not fit their particular vision of Judaism as a moral example. It was a history in which Jews not only were victims of oppression, but were able to inflict it themselves. Yet Rabbi Akiba, whose disciples provided the basis of the Mishnah, is known to have travelled into Arabia. Not only was he the greatest of rabbis and the most famous of martyrs, he also proclaimed the Jewish warrior Bar Kokhba as the messiah. Judaism was much richer and more diverse, it seems, than we can ever know, and so much has been forgotten that the history of Jews in Arabia can scarcely be recovered. Our ignorance of Arabian Judaism means that the origins of Islam are all the more mysterious.

When Muhammad heard the voice of the angel Gabriel, he might have seemed to anyone who saw him to be a Jewish mystic. He wrapped himself in a mantle, he recited prophecies, he brought a message from heaven, and he even travelled to heaven himself. Early Muslim sources contain reports of these mystics, including a young Jewish boy named Ibn Sayyad about whom prophetic and messianic claims were made. In his mystical contemplation, the boy apparently saw the throne of God surrounded by water and accompanied by the Living Creatures from the book of Ezekiel, the cherubim who carried the throne and had been depicted on the Ark of the Covenant and in the Temple of Solomon. Ibn Sayyad induced his vision by wrapping himself in a cloak and murmuring incantations in Hebrew – techniques that can be identified with the 'Descent of the Chariot', the mystical path that was based on the vision of Ezekiel. The adepts who were led into the seven heavens by the prophet Enoch returned to earth convinced that they had actually visited the highest realm and were now messengers from God. In this sense, the claim of Ibn Sayyad that he was an apostle of God was not as exotic or as presumptuous as it might appear.

Certainly Muhammad seems to have been venerated as a prophet like Moses. The fast of Ramadan, which he imposed on his followers, was seen as a solemn festival associated with Moses and the Day of Atonement. During the seventh century, any Muslim who was interested in the origin of his faith could have learned from Jews living in Arabia that they believed the Day of Atonement to commemorate the day on which Moses completed his second sojourn of forty days on Mount Sinai and then descended with the new Tablets of the Law. Muslims also saw Ramadan as a recollection of the Exodus, a physical deliverance of the Jews that corresponded to the spiritual deliverance of the Day of Atonement.

When had Jews arrived in Arabia? One answer is provided by Sozomenos, a Christian historian in the fifth century who was born near Gaza and had a good knowledge of the lands to the east and the south. He describes the Arabs as descendants of Ishmael, the son of the patriarch Abraham by his concubine Hagar. They had been in Arabia since Hagar and Ishmael had been driven from the house of Abraham. They had inherited the faith of Abraham, according to whose precepts the Hebrews had lived before Moses. As they were living in the midst of pagans, their faith had been corrupted, but Sozomenos knew of a group of Arabs who eventually came into contact with the Hebrews. By learning from them, the Arabs were able to return to the true faith of the Israelite patriarch.

We know from the New Testament that Paul of Tarsus spent three years in Arabia. In the following generation, we know that Rabbi Akiba travelled to Arabia when he recruited men for the revolt of Bar Kokhba against Rome. Who would have been there to receive these visitors? The Syriac *Book of the Himyarites* describes 'Jewish priests' from Tiberias in the caravan city of Najran during the sixth century. This is often thought to be a mistake for 'rabbi', or to be propaganda intended to turn the court of the Roman emperor Justin against the Jews, but there do seem to have been Jewish priests in Arabia. Islamic traditions assert that the Banu Quarayza and the Banu Nadir, two of the major Jewish tribes in Medina, were priests and descendants of Aaron, and they were known as *al-kahinan*, 'the priests'. In fact, there seem to have been towns in Arabia inhabited exclusively by priests many centuries after the destruction of the Temple, as the elaborate laws of priestly purity could be kept more easily in separate communities. Some Midrashim refer expressly to the flight of priests into Arabia, and there is a Talmudic story that 80,000 children who were descendants of priests fled to 'the Ishmaelites' after the destruction of the Temple.

Is it possible that the accounts of the Ark of the Covenant having been carried to safety when the Temple was destroyed might be related to this escape into Arabia? There is evidence that at least some Muslim historians believed that the Ark had reached Arabia, and indeed the difficulty that Arabia presents for the story of the

Ark is a confusing array of evidence as well as a shortage of hard fact.

We do know that the early followers of Muhammad were by no means ignorant of Jewish tradition. Abu Hurayah was one of the Companions of the Prophet, and while he may have been illiterate, he had a wide knowledge of the Torah. He was not alone in this. Ibn Abbas was known as 'the Ocean of Commentary' and 'the Rabbi of the Community' because of his detailed knowledge of Jewish, Christian and Muslim tradition. The Prophet himself and two of his caliphs, Abu Bakr and Umar, are said to have made several visits to Jewish scholars in Medina, and Zayd ibn Thabit, who served as secretary to the Prophet, is said to have learnt Hebrew at a Jewish school. Alongside their pursuit of Jewish learning, Jewish converts such as Ubayy ibn Kab and Kab al-Ahbar brought a great many traditions with them when they embraced Islam, which were clearly based on rabbinic teaching.

The Arab historian Ibn Jurayj, who died in AD 767, had been born in Mecca and he knew the holy city well. His account of the Kaba is fascinating, because he tells us that it was originally an *arish*. This is an Arabic word used for the Tabernacle that the Israelites built in the wilderness after God revealed himself to Moses on Mount Sinai, and his choice of word seems to imply that the Kaba was originally conceived and built with a similar intention. This should not be surprising. After the revelation to Muhammad, the Tabernacle of Moses apparently served as the model for the Mosque of the Prophet in Medina as well, and as we shall see, there is no shortage of traditions comparing or even combining the Kaba with the Temple of Solomon. These beliefs do not seem to have been limited to Muslims. Abdallah ibn Salam, a prominent Jew in Medina, evidently regarded the Kaba as the 'House of Abraham', and according to Ibn Hisham, he was not the only Jew who referred to it in this way.

The view that the Kaba was the sacred 'House of Abraham' may be traced back to the Book of Jubilees, where Abraham tells Jacob that the house he has built for himself will be named the house of Abraham for ever. He built the house to bear his name, and it is given to Jacob and to his seed for ever 'because Jacob will build his house and establish his name before God forever'. We are told that Jacob decides to build the sanctuary at Beth El, but an angel appears to him in a vision, showing him seven tablets that contain the history of the generations to come. The angel tells him that Beth El is not the chosen place, and that the true site has not yet been revealed. The messianic idea of building the 'House of Abraham' described in the Book of Jubilees or other similar accounts could easily have been known in Arabia. Although the book was lost in most of the Christian world, it still survives in Ethiopia as part of the Old Testament canon.

This is not the only Muslim tradition about the origin of the Kaba. It is said to be the navel of the earth and to have existed before the universe was created. It was built by Adam, the first man, or perhaps by the patriarch Abraham. In the days of Adam, apparently, the Kaba was a tent. Mamar ibn Rashid, who died in AD 770, reported that in the Days of Ignorance before Islam, the Kaba was built with loose stones and without clay. It was so low that young goats could leap into it. It had no roof, and coverings of cloth were simply laid over it.

Only a few years before the first revelation to Muhammad, the ancient *arish* had been given a more solid and permanent structure. This was built by the Quraysh, the tribe who controlled the sanctuary at the time, and to one of whose minor families Muhammad himself belonged. According to tradition, a ship from Byzantium was carrying marble, timber and iron needed to restore a church in Ethiopia, when it was wrecked on the Arabian coast. As well as using materials intended for a church, Ibn Hajar also reports that the Quraysh wanted to follow the pattern of a church. Apparently, a Christian craftsman named Pachomius built the roof and decorated the Kaba with images of the prophets, including Abraham, Mary and Jesus. After he established Muslim rule in the city, Muhammad allowed the portraits of Jesus and Mary to remain in the Kaba, and they did so until the fire that destroyed them in the twelfth century.

The Kaba that stands in Mecca today is built according to the proportions of the inner sanctuary of the Temple of Solomon, and when they describe the sanctity of Mecca and the Kaba, Muslims often applied to them the exalted status of Jerusalem and the Temple. Al-Azraki records that Aisha, the wife of the Prophet, declared that in no place had she seen heaven closer to earth than in Mecca, and Kisai records a tradition that the position of the

Pole Star proves the Kaba to be the highest point on earth, fixed beneath the centre of heaven. While Jewish tradition maintained that the Temple Mount had not been covered by the Flood, and the Samaritans believed that their own holy mountain Gerizim had remained above the waves, Muslims in turn asserted that the Flood had not threatened the Kaba. Although the waters surrounded it, the Kaba stood above them, reaching to heaven.

Just as Zion had been created before the rest of the world, so al-Azraki claimed that forty years before God created the heavens and earth, the Kaba was a dry spot floating on the water. From this point, the entire world had spread. There was also a tradition that the Kaba was created as many as 2,000 years before the rest of the world. Adam was believed to have been created there.

The Quran speaks of seven heavens, and of seven earths as well. Every earth and every heaven has a navel represented by a sanctuary, and the axis of the universe runs through each of these. In both Jewish and Muslim traditions, the divine throne is exactly above the seventh heaven, as the pole of the universe.

When the message that Muhammad delivered to the people of Mecca met with concerted resistance, he left for the Jewish city of Yathrib, usually known as Medina. Here he attempted to unite Muslims and Jews into a new community. As part of his plan, the Prophet instructed his followers to adopt the Jewish custom of praying toward Jerusalem, but when his alliance with the Jewish tribes collapsed, God revealed to him that his prayers should be directed to the Kaba at Mecca. The Quran itself describes the change in direction, but offers little elaboration: 'The foolish of the people will say: What has turned them from the direction that they formerly observed? Say: Unto God belong the East and the West. He guides whom He will to a straight path.'

The usual explanation of these verses is found in the commentary of al-Tabari, who tells us that the Prophet of God was given the choice of turning his face in whatever direction he wished. Apparently, he chose the Holy House in Jerusalem in order that the People of the Book would be conciliated. Everyone prayed toward Jerusalem for sixteen months, but all the while, the Prophet kept turning his face to the heavens until God turned him toward the Kaba.

Al-Tabari also reported that the Jews of Medina were naturally pleased when God commanded Muhammad to face Jerusalem. He did so for more than ten months, but he always loved the direction of Abraham. When he prayed to God, he turned his face to the heavens. The Jews became suspicious and asked why he should have abandoned the direction in which they had been praying. This was the reason that God revealed the verse 'Say, to God belongs the East and the West...'

The Jews apparently insisted that Muhammad should continue to face Jerusalem if he was truly intent on following the religion of Abraham. From their point of view, Jerusalem was the true centre of the religion of Abraham, and not Mecca. The direction of prayer became a matter of bitter dispute, and this may have been the cause as much as the result of their being described in such a similar way. Although it may seem absurd from a logical or historical perspective, in symbolic terms they are often identical. Just as the Tabernacle and the Temple of the Israelites had been built to house the sacred stones placed in the Ark of the Covenant, so there were sacred stones at the Kaba as well. In fact, the prayers of the faithful may have been directed toward the stones rather than the Kaba itself.

The historian al-Fakihi reported that, long before the revelation of the Quran, the tribe of Quraysh had discovered two stones on the summit of the sacred mountain Abu Qubays. This was a site of immense holiness where in the Days of Ignorance they used to pray for rain. The stones were brighter and more beautiful than any others that the Quraysh had seen. One was yellow and the other was white. The Quraysh were convinced that such stones could not be found in their own country, or in any other country as far as they knew. They must have descended from heaven. The yellow stone, which the Quraysh used to name 'al-Safir', was eventually lost. They kept the white stone until they built the Kaba, and then placed the stone within it. This became known as the Black Stone and can still be seen in Mecca today. The brilliance of both stones had apparently been due to their celestial origin, but it was lost when they became stained with the blood of sacrifice.

Another sacred stone transferred to the Kaba when it was built by the Quraysh was known as the *maqam Ibrahim*, 'the Station of Abraham', because Abraham was believed to have stood on it as he built the Kaba. The Station of Abraham is mentioned twice in the Quran, and its name seems to be taken from a verse in the Book of Genesis: 'Abraham rose early and went to the place where he had stood in the presence of the Lord.'

A tradition recorded on the authority of Wahb ibn Munabbih, who died in 728, claims that both the Black Stone and the Station of Abraham were sapphires that descended from heaven and were placed by God upon al-Safa, a sacred foothill of Abu Qubays. God later took away their brilliance and set them in their present place. Both stones were thought to be divine and were venerated because they shone in such an extraordinary way.

When the Quraysh decided to rebuild the Kaba, many people in Mecca objected to their demolishing such a sacred edifice. Those who were digging reached what al-Azraqi described as 'the Abrahamic foundations'. As they were trying to remove them, lightning struck and an earthquake shook the city. The stones were left where they were, but soon a remarkable discovery was made, an inscription in Syriac that could not be read until the Quraysh found a Jew to translate it. 'I am God the Lord of Bakka,' it proclaimed. 'I created it on the day that I created heaven and earth and formed the sun and the moon, and I surrounded it with seven pious angels. It will stand while its two mountains stand, a blessing to its people with milk and water.'

In the tenth century, the Meccan historian al-Fakihi was able to see the Station of Abraham when it was being repaired. It had become cracked and the parts were pinned together. He noticed a variety of lines and geometric shapes on the stone, and an inscription in Hebrew or Himyari. After he copied the inscription, he tried to find scholars who could translate it. Abu Zakariyya al-Maghribi, an expert in Egyptian hieroglyphics, finally succeeded. 'I am God, there is no god except Me,' it announced, 'a king who is unattainable.' There was a final word, 'Isbaut', which he claimed was equivalent to the Arabic *al-Samad*, 'the Eternal'. Al-Fakihi records another tradition, on the authority of Ibn Abbas, and it offers a different translation of the inscription on the Station of Abraham: 'This is the House of God. He put it on the quadrangles of His throne, its sustenance will come from this and that, its people will be the first to suspend its sanctity.'

During the tenth century, Arabia was plunged into turmoil when Ismaili Shiites known as the Qarmatians attacked caravans along the pilgrim road called *Darb Zubayda*. By 902, they were on the outskirts of Damascus, and they harassed Iraqi pilgrim caravans for most of the next five years. Then they were quiet for almost twenty years, but in 925 the caravan from Baghdad failed to reach Mecca. Pilgrims no longer dared to leave the capital, and finally a catastrophe occurred. The Qarmatians entered Mecca itself.

Their leader, Abu Tahir, seized the treasury in the Kaba and removed the Black Stone. According to the Ottoman historian Qutb al-Din, he returned to his own land of Hajar, carrying the Black Stone with him in the hope that he could divert the pilgrimage from Mecca to a mosque that he called 'the Refuge'. The Black Stone remained in the mosque for more than twenty years, while in Mecca people put their hands on the place where it had been and kissed it.

Qutb al-Din regarded the capture of the Black Stone as one of the greatest disasters ever to occur and the most severe test of the Islamic faith. God finally destroyed the Qarmatians, he tells us, and Abu Tahir was afflicted with a gangrenous sore, his flesh was eaten away by worms, and he died a terrible death. In the end, the Qarmatians despaired of diverting the pilgrimage to Hajar. They returned the Black Stone to Mecca.

In the eleventh century, Ibn Jubayr had an opportunity to inspect the Station of Abraham when he made his pilgrimage from Granada. He reported that it was 'covered with silver, about three spans high and two spans wide'. It was also easy to see the footprints of the patriarch, who had stood on the stone when he built the Kaba. Along with this, Ibn Jubayr recorded an even more fascinating custom. He tells us that the stone was lifted out of a box and displayed to the people. It was usually kept in the Kaba, and after it was displayed, the stone and the box were returned to the Kaba. The clear meaning of his remarks is astonishing. Here we have a sacred stone that was believed to have come down from heaven to a sacred mountain. It was inscribed with words spoken by God, it shone with an unearthly light, and it was kept in a box that was stored in a sanctuary whose proportions are those of the inner sanctuary of the Temple in which the Ark of the Covenant was kept. It may be even more astonishing that the stone has survived throughout the intervening centuries and can be seen in Mecca today.

There is even another similarity between the Ark and the sacred stones of Mecca. As part of the tradition that the Kaba was built by Adam, it is said that God gave Adam both the Black Stone and the Station of Abraham. When he made a covenant with man, the document on which the covenant was recorded passed into the Black Stone, where it will remain until the Day of Judgement. This would mean that, in addition to being a sacred stone that descended from heaven on a sacred mountain, the Black Stone contains a covenant between God and man and was deposited in a sanctuary whose proportions are those of the sanctuary in which the Ark of the Covenant had been kept. And like the Station of Abraham, the Black Stone can still be seen in Mecca.

We do not know if the Black Stone or the Station of Abraham was part of the Kaba from the beginning. Sacred stones may have been brought to Mecca by the early tribes that settled there, and may have been incorporated into the structure of the Kaba. Similar stones were apparently placed on the walls of temples at Madain Salih and elsewhere, when nomadic tribes decided to establish permanent sanctuaries. Greek and Latin geographers and historians, as well as later Muslim authorities, report that stones were venerated throughout Arabia before Islam by the Nabateans of Petra, by the priestly Arabs of Emesa in Syria, and among nomads who carried stones enclosed in portable shrines when they went to battle. The high priest of Emesa, Elagabalus, even took the black stone of his god from the temple and carried it to Rome when he became emperor.

Ibn al-Kalbi, who wrote a history of idols, regards the veneration of stones as a degenerate form of the rituals of the Kaba. Arabs were passionately fond of worshipping idols, he tells us. Some of them had temples around which they based their worship, while others chose idols to which they offered their adoration. Anyone who could not afford to build a temple for himself would erect a stone in front of the Kaba or in front of some other shrine, and then walk around it in the same way that he would walk around the Kaba. The Arabs called these stones *ansab*, but whenever the stones resembled a living creature they called them *asnam* and *awthan*. Whenever a traveller stopped somewhere, he would choose four stones, pick out the best of them to worship as his god, and use the other three as supports for his cooking pot. When he departed, he would leave the stones behind and then do the same at the other stops in his journey.

Despite the pagan associations of these sacred stones, Muslim tradition has made the claim that Mecca is the true Zion – a claim that is closely connected to the Black Stone. The 'precious cornerstone' mentioned by Isaiah is thought to refer to it, and Ibn Qutayba seems to have been the first to understand it in this way. He adds the Muslim explanation of the name Zion as 'the House of God' and alters the final words of the prophecy so that it speaks of 'a stone in a precious corner'. Ibn Qayyam al-Djawziyya provides an even more explicitly Islamic account. He claims 'that Zion according to the People of the Book is Mecca, and the Black Stone that kings and commoners kiss was assigned exclusively to the Prophet Muhammad and his People'.

Muslim scholars quoted other prophecies of Isaiah that referred to the precious stones. Al-Qarafi connects the verses with the rebuilding of the Kaba by the Abbasid caliph al-Mahdi, and claims that it is impossible to think that the verse referred to Jerusalem. The city never became a centre of idolatry, as Mecca did during the Days of Ignorance, and it never became a peaceful shelter for pilgrims, as Mecca had become since the rise of Islam.

Ali ibn Rabban also claimed that the vision of Ezekiel referred to Mecca rather than Jerusalem. At the end of his book, Ezekiel tells us that God showed him a house. The prophet describes its pillars, halls, courtyards and doors, and an angel tells him to remember all these things and to think about them. But since the description of this house is very lengthy, Ali ibn Rabban noticed that most people dismissed it as unintelligible or ambiguous. Nevertheless, he believes, it is obvious that the description of the house that God described through the prophet Ezekiel applies to Mecca. It contains elements that were not part of the Second Temple built after the Jews returned from exile in Babylon. If anyone disagrees, he suggests that they compare the description in Ezekiel with what is known of the Temple. If they can harmonize the two, Ali ibn Rabban will accept their opinion. If they cannot, they should accept his.

According to the great historian and Quranic scholar al-Tabari, when the Jurhum controlled the Kaba they actually buried the Black Stone and other holy objects in the well of Zamzam. Apparently they threw the cornerstone of the Kaba and two golden gazelles into the well, and then filled it up to conceal its exact location from their rivals, the Khuzaa and the Quraysh. The treasure remained hidden until Abd al-Muttalib, the grandfather of the Prophet, was commanded in a dream to dig up the well and was given instructions about how to find it. In Islamic tradition, the well of Zamzam was often confused with the pit beneath the Kaba, known as 'the Well of the Kaba' and believed to be the navel of the earth. The tradition is not only reminiscent of Jewish and Samaritan accounts of the burying of the sacred vessels from the Temple in Jerusalem; it is also similar to Islamic reports that the Jurhum buried the Ark of the Covenant itself, and these are perhaps the most intriguing passages in the entire history of the Ark.

In his *Kitab al-Tijan*, the historian Wahb ibn Munabbi tells us that, after the death of David and Solomon, the Children of Israel still marched with the Ark. When war broke out, the Israelites who carried the Ark threw away its shafts, but the angels held the Ark above David until he defeated the giants. The Children of Israel continued to march with the Ark until the time of al-Harith ibn Mudad al-Jurhumi, after the death of Ismail the prophet and after the death of his son and heir, Nabt ibn Qaydar ibn Ismail. When they marched to Mecca, the king of the city and the surrounding area was al-Harith ibn Mudad al-Jurhumi. He went forth against the Israelites with 100,000 men, and the Amalekites with 100,000, and they fought them fiercely. The Children of Israel and their allies were defeated. They threw aside the Ark, and the Jurhumites and the Amalekites took it and brought it to one of the dung heaps of Mecca. They dug a pit and buried it, and although Hamaysa ibn Nabd ibn Qaydar ibn Ismail and al-Harith ibn Mudad al-Jurhumi tried to prevent them, they paid no attention. Hamaysa told them that the scrolls of the Psalms were in it, along with the Sakinah, the Presence of God. A terrible plague came upon them as punishment, and because there seemed to be no escape, al-Harith ibn Mudad went to the dung heap and removed the Ark by night. Hamaysa took it and kept it, and his heirs inherited it until the time of Jesus, the son of Mary.

A similar account is given by al-Hamdani, who wrote on South Arabian history and antiquities in the seventh century AD. He describes how a cave that sheltered the necropolis of the kings of Jurhum was discovered near Mecca, in a place called the Olive Grove. The cave had been explored by Iyad ibn Nazar ibn Maadd ibn Adnan, who loaded his camels with jewels and riches from the tombs. As he could take only one load, he sealed the entrance of the cave and left it as he found it. Many years later, Abdullah ibn Judan the Qurayshite discovered the cave, just before the revelation of Islam.

Apparently, Abdullah ibn Judan was very wealthy and very generous, especially to pilgrims in Mecca. When he was asked about the source of his wealth, he described how he had led a raid in which he captured a hundred camels. The owner complained to the Quraysh, telling them that someone from their tribe had stolen a hundred camels, and threatening that as long as the Quraysh did nothing about it, they would not be allowed to attend the great fair of Ukaz. As the Quraysh were merchants, they could not afford to lose such an important market, and they conspired to have Abdullah ibn Judan killed. When he learned of the plot, he fled to the Olive Grove with the Quraysh in pursuit. Looking for some place to hide, he finally found a gap between two rocks that was wide enough to permit a thin man to slip through. As he entered, dragging his provision bag behind him, the earth around the rocks began to slide. Deciding that it was better to die in the tunnel than at the hands of his own tribe, he continued to run through the tunnel until he reached a chamber in which jewels, emeralds, silver and gold were stored. There were also four biers, on each of which he saw the body of a man with a marble tablet inscribed in Himyarite characters on his head. Reading the first tablet, he discovered that the body had been al-Harith ibn Mudad al-Jurhumi, whose people had captured the Ark of the Covenant when the Israelites marched to Mecca. This was the Ark that God had mentioned in the Quran. Then the Jurhumites, Adnan, Tasm, Jadis, the Amalekites and all the Arabs had marched against the Children of Israel, driving them back to Jerusalem and capturing the Ark.

Abdullah ibn Judan remained in the cave for five days, surviving on his provisions and drinking the water he carried with him. Eventually, the Quraysh abandoned all hope of finding him, and he crept out of the rocks under cover of darkness, taking the tablets as well as the treasure, in case the Quraysh were not prepared to believe his story. Although he paid the owner of the camels, the Quraysh were suspicious of his new wealth until he described the cave and showed them the tablets as proof. They sent him back to the cave with the father of Khadijah, the wife of the Prophet, and the father of Aminah, the mother of the Prophet. In their company, he carried the tablets into the cave and returned everything to its place, rolling a huge stone over the entrance to prevent the sepulchre being desecrated by vandals.

Al-Hamdani described the way in which the Jurhumites acquired the Ark on the basis of details provided by Wahb ibn Munabbih. When they captured the Ark, the Jurhumites and their Arabian allies were not interested in it, and simply buried it in a dunghill. They were warned against this by al-Harith ibn Mudad al-Jurhumi and by the prophet Ismail ibn Alhamaysa, but they buried it anyway. Because of this, God destroyed the Jurhumites and all the inhabitants of Mecca. No one survived except a few people who had not wanted to bury the Ark. There were only about forty of them, while over 200,000 died. Al-Harith ibn Mudad was distraught at the loss of his people and roamed the earth for 300 years until he was blind. He appointed Ismail ibn Alhamaysa to rule over the remnant of his people, and ordered him to recover the Ark from the dunghill and to keep it. Ismail did as he was told.

The Quran itself refers to the Ark of the Covenant in the Second Surah, known as 'The Cow', and this is the passage to which al-Hamdani referred.

> And their prophet said to them, 'Behold, the sign of his kingdom is that the Ark will come to you, within which is the Presence from your Lord, and a remnant of that which the house of Moses and the house of Aaron left behind, the angels carrying it. Behold, in this will be a sign for you if you are believers.'

The Ark of the Covenant became the subject of legend among the Arabs as it did among the Jews. According to al-Thalabi, God sent it down from Paradise with Adam when he fell. In it, cut from a ruby, were figures of all the prophets for the ages to come, especially of Muhammad and his first four caliphs. And just as there were disagreements among the Jews, so there were disagreements among Muslim authorities as to where the Ark might be. Ibn Abbas, the cousin of the Prophet, claimed that the Ark and the rod of Moses were lying in the Lake of Tiberias and would be brought forth on the last day, but others simply assumed that they had been lost when the Temple was destroyed.

The Ark also became a central element in the bitter arguments between Muslims, Jews and Christians about the accuracy with which their sacred books had been transmitted. If Muslims claimed to be returning to the original revelation of the prophets after the earlier teachings had been corrupted, the subject was obviously critical in deciding which of the three religions was authentic and should be believed. From the beginning, Muslims were keenly aware of the need to establish the authenticity of any prophetic tradition. Usually they did this by supplying several unbroken chains of transmission for the Quran or for the *hadith*, the sayings attributed to the Prophet. As quickly as they could, they established ways of determining the reliability of the individual authorities involved, and they saw this as the only way of distinguishing authentic teachings of the Prophet.

When they looked closely at the biblical texts of both the Old and the New Testaments, they were astonished that there were no reliable chains of transmission, and that neither Jews nor Christians seemed very anxious to establish them. In contrast, Muslim scholars not only stressed the unbroken transmission of their own Quran, some of them also claimed that any belief in the Torah or the Gospel was dependent upon the Quran. Its authority could provide proof of their divine origin and corroborate much of their teaching.

One of these scholars, Ibn Hazm, had realized that the Aaronid high priests had only a single copy of the Pentateuch in the Temple in Jerusalem. The Israelites would visit the Temple only three times a year, and most of them never entered it. This was the custom for at least four centuries, during which time corrupted Levite priests might easily have altered the holy text. In claiming this, he accepted the rabbinic tradition that one authoritative copy of the Pentateuch was always deposited in the archives of the Temple to provide a standard by which forgeries could be detected, and he used this tradition to undermine Jewish claims to possess a reliable scripture. Ibn Hazm now accused Ezra the Scribe of having deliberately corrupted this biblical text in the absence of adequate controls over its transmission.

A century later, after Samaual al-Maghribi converted from Judaism to Islam, he claimed to supply the missing motive for the corruption. As a priest, Ezra hated the royal house of David. He wanted to discredit the Davidic dynasty and secure victory for the priestly families who competed against it for power. To do this, he added tales of sexual intrigue to the biblical genealogies. 'I swear to God,' wrote Samaual, 'that Ezra achieved his purpose, for in the Second Commonwealth which they had in Jerusalem, it was not the house of David that reigned, but the house of Aaron.'

Samaual also claimed that the history of the Jews was full of invasions and wars that devastated Palestine, and that under such conditions the transmission of their holy text must have suffered. As a result, some parts of their history may even have been lost entirely. The Jews were also known to have lapsed into idolatry and to have killed their own prophets. Given all this, it would have been very difficult for the ancient text to have survived intact.

Despite the tradition that God instructed Muhammad to change the direction of prayer away from Jerusalem, Muslim interest in the city where the Ark and the Temple once stood remained intense. It was known as 'the Holy House' or 'the City of the Holy House'. By the tenth century, this was being abbreviated to 'the Holy', the name by which Jerusalem is known in Arabic today. Christian sources confirm that the Muslim commanders were fascinated by the site of the Temple when they captured Jerusalem. In his chronicle for the year AD 635, Theophanes reports that the caliph Umar led an expedition to Palestine, where the Holy City had been besieged for two years. In the end, the city surrendered to him, after the patriarch Sophronius had negotiated a treaty. Umar then entered the Holy City in garments of camel hair, all soiled and torn. Making a show of piety as a cloak for his diabolical hypocrisy, Theophanes tells us, Umar demanded to be taken to the site of the Temple built by Solomon. This he converted into what Theophanes calls 'an oratory for blasphemy and impiety'. When Sophronius saw it, he exclaimed, 'This is the Abomination of Desolation spoken of by Daniel the Prophet, and now it stands in the Holy Place.' Then he began to weep.

Even though Theophanes was obviously writing from a Christian perspective, Muslim sources agree with him in confirming that Umar was keenly interested in the site of the Temple. As soon as Umar had finished writing the treaty that allowed him to enter the Holy City, he asked Sophronius to take him to the sanctuary of David. When the patriarch agreed to do so, Umar set out with 4,000 of his troops, all of them wearing swords. A crowd of Arabs who had come up to the Holy City followed him, while the patriarch walked at the head of the procession. Sophronius took everyone to the church called the 'Dung Heap' and announced that this was the sanctuary of David. Umar looked at it and then told the patriarch that he was lying. The Prophet had described the sanctuary of David, and the church did not resemble his description. Then the patriarch took them to the Church of Zion and again told them that this was the sanctuary of David. Again the caliph told him that he was lying. Finally the patriarch led them to the Noble Sanctuary of the Holy City and stood by the gate later called 'the Gate of Muhammad'.

At that time there was dung all around the Noble Sanctuary. It had settled on the steps of the gate so that it spilled out into the street where the gate opened, and so much was piled on the steps that it almost reached the top of the gateway. The patriarch told Umar that they could not go on any further except by crawling on their hands and knees. He then began to crawl, and everyone crawled after him, until he had brought them out in the court of the Noble Sanctuary.

This fascination with the site of the Temple was in marked contrast with what seems to have been Byzantine indifference. The Rock on which the Ark of the Covenant had once been placed and the area around it were deserted and covered with filth. According to Muslim tradition, the Christians neglected the site and never tried to build a church on it because Christ had prophesied that no stone would be left upon another, that everything would be destroyed. When they reached the Noble Sanctuary, the patriarch Sophronius held Umar ibn al-Khattab by the hand as he stood over the filth. Umar took off his cloak and, filling it with dirt, he threw it into the Valley of Gehenna. As soon as the Muslims saw the caliph carrying filth with his own hands, they all began to use their cloaks and shields and anything else they could find until the entire site was cleaned and the Rock was revealed. Then they said that they should build a sanctuary with the Rock at its centre, but Umar disagreed and said that they should build a sanctuary and place the Rock at the end. A mosque was then built at the southern edge of the Herodian Temple platform. In the seventh century, however, another building was erected. It was placed over the Rock, to enshrine it, and is known as *Qubbat al-Sakhra*, 'The Dome of the Rock'.

Between the destruction of the Temple in AD 70 and the decision of the Muslim conquerors to build on the Temple Mount, we know almost nothing about what had occurred there. Christians evidently had their own holy places in Jerusalem, and they do not seem to have been concerned with the Temple. The Bordeaux pilgrim records that there was 'a pierced stone where the Jews came and which they anoint every year', where 'they groan and tear their garments and then depart'. The biblical scholar Jerome had seen this ritual, which was performed on the ninth day of the month of Ab, the anniversary of the destruction of the Temple and the only day on which Jews were allowed into Jerusalem by the Christian authorities.

We know that Bar Kokhba had moved some of the debris in order to build his own sanctuary after AD 132, but his rebellion against Rome had been crushed. There was another attempt at restoring the Temple in AD 362, with the encouragement of the emperor Julian the Apostate, who was notorious for his hatred of Christianity. The Persians also gave permission in 614, and then revoked it in 617. The ground was cleared, but nothing more was done.

After the Roman emperor Heraclius defeated the Persians in 627, he returned in triumph to Jerusalem with the remains of the True Cross that had been discovered in the fourth century by Helena, the mother of the emperor Constantine. Did he regard the Jewish attempt to reclaim the Temple Mount as a threat to true religion, and did it bring an abrupt end to centuries of Christian indifference? When the Samaritans had attempted to reclaim Mount Gerizim in 484, the emperor Zeno had responded to this act of defiance against the true faith by building a church on top of the sacred mountain. Could Heraclius have responded to the Jewish attempt to reclaim the Temple Mount in the same way? One of the mysteries of the Temple Mount is the construction of the Golden Gate, which seems pointless unless something had been built on the Mount, or had been planned.

The church that Zeno built on Mount Gerizim was an octagon with an ambulatory, enshrining a relic of the rock of Golgotha. Whether or not Heraclius had planned something similar for the Temple Mount, and had then been interrupted by the arrival of the armies of Islam, remains little more than a tantalizing possibility. But the Dome of the Rock is unlike any other building in the Islamic world, and it is almost identical to the octagon churches with ambulatories built by Christian architects at the time.

Muslim fascination with Jerusalem and the Rock is often thought to be based on the Night Journey described in a famous passage of the Quran: 'Praise be to Him who caused His servant to journey by night from the haram shrine to the distant shrine, whose environs we have blessed, to show him some of our signs.' The servant would seem to be Muhammad and the haram shrine is clearly the sanctuary at Mecca, but what is the 'distant shrine'? Muslim tradition maintains that this is Jerusalem, but the tradition does not seem to be recorded before the end of the seventh century, when Muslims were building their own shrine on the Temple Mount.

Jerusalem has also been claimed as the site from which Muhammad ascended to heaven, during the *mihraj* or 'Ascent' that is said to be mentioned in two Surahs of the Quran. The Night Journey and the Ascent are often confused or conflated. The mysterious *buraq* on which the Prophet rode is borrowed from the Night Journey and introduced into traditions about the Ascent. In early accounts, the Ascent had been made on a splendid ladder, similar to that mentioned in the Ethiopic Book of Jubilees and called by an almost identical name. And even though the Ascent is described in the Quran as a vision, the Night Journey involves the Prophet travelling in his body, and eventually this is said of the Ascent as well.

If the claim that Jerusalem is 'the distant shrine' began to be made after the decision was taken to build the Dome of the Rock, why was the decision taken? Muslim historians debated the issue at length. Al-Yaqubi believed that the caliph Abd al-Malik was hoping to divert the annual pilgrimage from Mecca to Jerusalem. As he was facing revolt in Mecca, the Dome would be his substitute for the Kaba. Apparently, Abd al-Malik forbade the people of Syria to make the pilgrimage because his rival Abdullah ibn Zubayr often arrested them during the pilgrimage and forced them to transfer their allegiance. When the people complained that pilgrimage was a commandment of God, the caliph answered that the Prophet had described how men would journey to only three mosques: Mecca, Medina and Jerusalem. Jerusalem could serve in place of Mecca, and the Rock on which the Prophet set his foot when he ascended into heaven could serve for the Kaba. Abd al-Malik then built a dome above the Rock and hung it with curtains of brocade. The people began the custom of walking around the Rock, just as they had walked around the Kaba, and the custom continued throughout the Umayyad dynasty.

Although this is usually regarded as polemic against the Umayyads, the Christian pilgrim Arculf claims that Muawiyya actually had been crowned in Jerusalem. There are also remains of a large palace at the southern edge of Temple Platform. It had direct access to the Temple Mount and seems to have been built during the Umayyad dynasty. Was the Dome of the Rock built by Abd al-Malik as part of a plan to rule the Islamic world from Jerusalem? Was it intended to proclaim that Islam had replaced the Byzantine empire and become heir to the ancient Judaic covenant, as well as the New Covenant of the Christians? It was certainly a public expression of Islamic sanctity, surpassing in magnificence and beauty any Christian rival.

According to al-Muqaddasi, the Dome was an Islamic reply to the Christian Church of the Holy Sepulchre, as well as an affirmation of the ancient biblical claims to the sanctity of the site of the Temple, the Gate of Heaven and the foundation of the earth. It was not originally built to commemorate the Night Journey described in the Quran, even though this became the traditional interpretation. One day when Abd al-Malik was speaking to his uncle, he remarked that the caliph al-Walid should not have spent so much money on the mosque at Damascus. He should have spent the money on building roads or caravansaries, or restoring mosques that had been occupied by Christians. But the Christians still possessed so many beautiful churches, including the Holy Sepulchre and the churches of Lydda and Edessa. The caliph therefore built a mosque that would surpass these churches, something unique, a wonder to the world. Having observed the magnificent Dome of the Sepulchre, he was anxious that its beauty might undermine the faith of Muslims. This was the reason that he built the Dome of the Rock.

Even if the Dome of the Rock was not built because Muslims believed that Muhammad had made the Night Journey to Jerusalem or had made his Ascent to heaven from the Rock on which the Ark had stood, it did not take long for these assumptions to be made. Even today, there are marks and signs on the Temple Mount that are believed to have been left by the Prophet and the miraculous steed that carried him. But if the Dome had been built for reasons that were political as much as religious, this would not seem to represent a departure from the ambitions of Solomon himself, and as we shall see, within a few centuries Christian pilgrims to Jerusalem had begun to believe that the Dome of the Rock actually was the Temple of Solomon. The belief was held despite the fact that the octagonal shape of the Dome is completely unlike any of the descriptions of the Temple given in the Bible or the ancient Jewish histories. Descriptions of the Dome may even have played a central role in the transmission of Judaic themes to Ethiopia, when Ethiopian traditions about the Ark of the Covenant were given their most elaborate form, although this has never been noticed by even the most enthusiastic proponents of an ancient Judaic legacy across the Red Sea.

In the years before the Dome was built, Muslim fascination with Jerusalem can be seen in the debate over the direction of prayer. The antiquity of the debate is confirmed by the fact that the earliest mosques were not aligned with Mecca, and in fact the direction of prayer may not have been altered until rather later than Muslim tradition assumes. Ultimately, it seems, the need to choose between Jerusalem and Mecca may become less pressing. On the Day of Judgement, Muslim tradition tells us, the Kaba will fly from Mecca to Jerusalem and will appear at the Temple Mount as a bride. The prediction reveals something not only of the enduring Muslim devotion to Jerusalem, but also of the way in which ancient loyalties survive across the centuries. They change, and yet they retain their original form as well. They may be destroyed, they may be rebuilt, but somehow they remain the same.

Does the Arab fascination with Jerusalem and its Temple provide a key to unlock the mystery of the Ark that is said to be preserved across the Red Sea in Ethiopia? Could the Arabian Zion explain how one might believe in the African Zion as well? If the Black Stone and the Station of Abraham are sacred stones like the Tablets of Moses – stones that came from the sky, contained a covenant and were kept in a wooden ark – what could all this tell us about the Ark in Aksum that the emperor Iyasu engaged in conversation? Does it tell us anything about what he might have seen when the priests placed the great relic before him? Certainly a stone that was venerated in the sixth century AD is quite able to survive into the seventeenth century, and for many centuries beyond that. The stones at Mecca have achieved nothing less, it seems. Even beyond this, Arab historians tell us that the Ark of the Covenant itself was brought to Arabia and passed into the hands of the Jurhum, the tribe who controlled the Kaba in Mecca. It is intriguing that Mecca was not the only place in Arabia to possess a Kaba. There was a Kaba in the caravan city of Najran as well, and it was also controlled by the Jurhum. Jewish priests from Tiberias had reached Najran, and as we shall see, it became the site of massacre by a Jewish prince, who was killed when the king of Aksum launched a crusade against him in retaliation for the outrage. The prince, we know, swore oaths by the Ark. Before we turn south to Najran and Himyar, however, there are other memories of the Ark and the Tabernacle that have survived into modern times in northern Arabia, and have fascinated the travellers who saw them and scholars who heard of them.

CHAPTER 12

The Arks of Ishmael

Almost seventy years ago, the Austrian adventurer Carl Raswan returned to the bedouin with whom he had ridden in northern Arabia before the Great War. The account of his years among the Ruala is one of the classics of romantic travel in the East, but it also provided the basis of one of the most fascinating investigations into the Ark of the Covenant. If the prophet Ezekiel had seen a vision by the waters of Babylon, Raswan claimed to have witnessed with his own eyes the Ark of Ishmael in the Arabian desert, and to have ridden with it into battle.

He describes the gathering of the Ruala as they set out for new pastures, desperate to secure fodder and water for their animals. The Ruala would have to cross the lands of their enemies, and if they failed, they would die. The tribe and its herds had swollen to a size unseen for generations, and an entire people seemed to be in movement. Raswan knew that this was not the ordinary migration of spring or autumn, and he imagined it as a historic tribal crusade that occurred only once in a century.

His account of the migration depicts hundreds of thousands of camels swarming across the desert, their long necks rising and falling rhythmically, flowing over the wilderness as if they were driven by some invisible force within the ground. Like locusts, he thought them, looting the pasture that lay before their hungry mouths, leaving a naked and trampled earth, and a veil of dust that hung in the still air for hours after they passed.

At the head of the tribe, Raswan saw a camel that carried 'a singular structure adorned with hundreds of small tufts of black ostrich feathers and barbaric decorations'. A large framework of acacia wood was balanced and secured on a saddle. This was the *markab*, or 'ship', also known as *abu duhur*, 'Father of the Ages', which Raswan called the Ark of Ishmael. He describes it as the altar before which the tribes had made their offerings over the centuries. There was only one Ark in all Arabia, he believed. Throughout history, it had moved from tribe to tribe, as one conquered the other. The Ruala had held it for nearly 150 years when Raswan rode with them. It had become the symbol of their unity and their emblem of war. They claimed that it had been moved by the spirit of God at critical moments in their history, especially in battles that might decide the fate of the tribe. It revealed the time and place at which they should face their enemy and begin to fight. Now, as they marched to new pasture, they expected to see the presence of God revealed again from the ancient shrine on the back of the camel.

At the critical point in their search for new land, Raswan saw the Ark employed as a palladium – a standard to lead the tribe into battle. He was making his way through a noisy crowd of people and animals, the voices of women and children mingling with the grunts of laden camels, when he noticed a group of women on foot waving their head-cloths and chanting in high voices. They were escorting a young woman who walked quietly in their midst. Her face was radiant and serene, and her eyes were grave and devout. Of all the Ruala maidens, she had been chosen to ride in the *markab*.

Once they reached the camel that bore the Ark, a tall powerful animal led by a slave, the young woman ran beside it for a while. The chanting and waving of the women rose to a joyous frenzy, and suddenly she broke away from her retinue. Grasping the shoulder-girth, she climbed nimbly on to the back of the camel and into the *markab*. In one of the corners there was a seat with a footrest, and she sat on it, enthroned, as Raswan thought, like a desert queen above her people. Then she untied the cloth about her head and her glorious hair fell over her shoulders. She gave a sign, and the women who had been walking beside the camels climbed into their litters.

From the midst of the tribe, Raswan heard the sound of shots fired in jubilation, and soon there were men galloping forward from all directions. Together they raced toward the *markab*, and above the thunder of hoofs, they began to chant as they pressed around their queen. The maiden in the acacia shrine was now transfigured in an ecstasy of joy. Putting both her hands to her throat, she tore open her dress and broke into jubilant song. Her breasts were now bare, and she stood high above the Ark, holding a bunch of white ostrich plumes. Raswan describes her as looking like a goddess, the bravest and most beautiful maiden of her great tribe. She called to the young men and inspired them with a passion for war. She told them to remember the heroes of the tribe who once had chained themselves to this Ark with the iron shackles of their mares, so that they could not leave it, but stood beside it and defended it with their lives.

Although the tribe would be facing disaster, and their search for pastures had become desperate, Raswan felt that a festive spirit had begun to enliven the whole people. 'It was a festal day, for the Ruala had a queen again – a virgin in the sacred ark; and under her symbolic leadership they pressed forward to their destiny.'

Raswan was both intrigued and excited by what he had witnessed, and he attempted to provide a history of the shrine – an account of the origin and meaning of a tradition he believed to be so like the Ark of the Covenant. He claimed that the Ark of Ishmael, as he called it, meant safety and power to the tribe that held it, while its loss would mean disaster. Without it, the tribe would be scattered. He had been told that the Ruala had held their Ark for almost 150 years, and that it had been the possession of the Amarat before them. According to Ruala tradition, the tribe was in alliance at the time with the Wuld Ali, who were at war with the Amarat. One of the Ruala, whose name was Jidua ibn Mudabir, was visiting the Wuld Ali, and he took part in the campaign. At the height of the decisive battle, Jidua apparently charged the horsemen who guarded the *markab* and the Amarat girl enthroned in it. He cut his way through, and with a single blow of the sword he severed one of the legs of the camel that bore the emblem of the tribe, bringing it to the ground. Appalled by the collapse of their sacred Ark, the Amarat fled in terror. Jidua had won a great victory by himself.

The Wuld Ali searched the battlefield for him, and found him lying dead. He had been killed in an ambush by a foot soldier. Beside him lay the Amarat girl who had ridden in the *markab*. Her name was Jamila, and she had stabbed herself to avoid the shame of defeat. Among the Wuld Ali, a legend was passed down that Jidua and Jamila had been lovers. Their lifeless bodies had been found together beneath the *markab*, Jamila still gripping the hilt of her dagger. Her other hand clasped the hand of the hero.

After the famous victory, the sheikh of the Wuld Ali presented both the *markab* and the sword of Jidua to the Ruala. The hero had been a Ruali, and he had overthrown the shrine and won the day. Since then, the sacred emblem rode with the Ruala in all their victories, a symbol of their pre-eminence among the bedouin of Arabia.

Raswan was not the only European to ride with the Ruala in the early years of the century, or to report on the *markab*. Alois Musil even claimed to share the distinction of having been blood brother to Nuri Shaalan, a chief renowned throughout the tribes for having killed seventy people with his own hand. Apparently, most of his brothers were included in this figure, although he never counted Turks, convinced that they were less than human. In his own account of the Ruala, Musil reported that they called the *markab* by the name *abu zhur*, which meant 'father of time'. This was because it passed from generation to generation throughout the ages, and because it would survive for ever. Anyone who possessed the *markab* became prince of the tribe, and everyone else would follow him in battle. Each year a white camel was sacrificed to it, and its blood was sprinkled on the corner posts. God was believed to reside in it, and to reveal the direction the tribe should follow on their travels through the desert. The ostrich feathers might tremble, even if there was no wind, or the *markab* would bow to the right, indicating the will of God. When the camel that carried the shrine began to move, the entire tribe would follow it, and if it stopped, they pitched their tents. If they were threatened by a powerful enemy, they would follow it into battle. But if the fighting were nothing more than a minor raid or skirmish, they would not employ it.

Almost sixty years ago, the American scholar Julian Morgenstern quoted at length from these reports, and remarked that the similarity between the *markab* and the Ark of the Covenant was 'almost startling'. Both possessed the power of selecting the road they wished to take, both led their people through the desert and determined their camps at night, both granted oracles, both led their people into battle, especially decisive battles that could mean life or death for the tribe, and both gave victory over the enemy. Above all, God was thought to reside in both of them, if not permanently, then at least on the occasions when their people had need of divine assistance.

Morgenstern prepared a compendious account of such reports. He began with one of the greatest Oriental travellers, the Swiss explorer Johann Burckhardt, who studied Arabic at Cambridge in 1808, and then mastered the language at Aleppo in the hope of reaching Timbuktu. He often wandered with the bedouin of northern Arabia, especially with the Aneyzeh, and a century before either Raswan or Musil he reported the existence of the *markab*. He even claimed to have spoken to men who had seen the Ruali hero Jidua, whom he calls Gedoua, and whose sword Raswan reported seeing so many years later.

The heroism of Gedoua is recorded in hundreds of poems, Burckhardt wrote, and his feats in arms have been recited by many witnesses. He was famous for having slain thirty of his enemies in one battle. He had never been put to flight. The booty that he had captured was immense, but his friends grew rich from his generosity while he lived in poverty. In the end, he sacrificed his life to valour. A war had begun in 1790 between the Ibn Fadhel and Ibn Esmeyr tribes, with most of the Aneyzeh joining on one side or the other. After many small engagements, the two sheikhs met near Mezerib, a town on the pilgrim road, some 50 miles from Damascus. Each of them had about 5,000 horsemen, and each had decided that a full battle would end the war. The armies were drawn up in sight of each other, and some slight skirmishing had commenced, when Gedoua decided to offer his life for the glory of his tribe. He rode up to the Ibn Esmeyr, under whose banner he was fighting, removed his coat of mail, and approaching the chief, kissed his beard to announce that he devoted his life to him. With only his sabre, he rode his mare furiously against the enemy. Everyone knew of his courage and waited to see if he would live or die. His strength soon opened a way through the ranks of the enemy. Reaching their *markab*, which was carried at the centre of their troops, he felled the camel that bore it by cutting its leg. He then turned his horse, and he had already reached the open space between the two armies when he was killed by a shot from a foot soldier. Seeing the *markab* fall, his friends rushed with a loud cheer upon their enemies and routed them. Whenever the *markab* has

Woodcuts published in 1481, showing two different reconstructions of the Ark of the Covenant and the cherubim according to Jewish and Catholic scholars.

Illustration of the Temple Vessels, placed at the beginning of a manuscript of the Hebrew Bible produced in northern Spain during the fourteenth century.

A reconstruction of the Tabernacle and its court, surrounded by the tribes of Israel, engraved to illustrate the polyglot Bible published by La Fèvre de la Boderie in 1569.

A classical reconstruction of the Temple of Solomon, engraved to illustrate an English Bible printed in Cambridge in 1660.

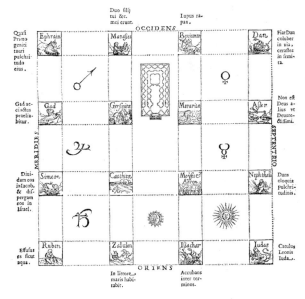

The tribes of Israel camped around the Tabernacle with the corresponding signs of the Zodiac, from the *Explanationes in Ezechielem* published by Villalpando in 1605.

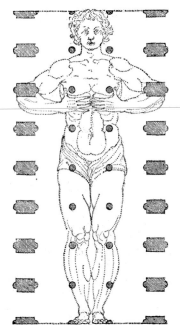

A plan of the Temple and the cosmological man, from the *Explanationes in Ezechielem* of Villalpando.

Below Woodcut of the Temple Mount in Jerusalem, with the Dome of the Rock labelled as 'The Temple of Solomon', published at Mainz in 1486.

CIVITAS·IHERVSALEM

Above View from the Mount of Olives toward the Valley of Kidron and the Dome of the Rock, engraved by Louis Haghe after a sketch by David Roberts, and published in 1842.

The Dome of the Rock, built on the Temple Mount in AD 691 by the Umayyad caliph Abd al-Malik.

The interior of the Dome of the Rock, including the rock on which the Ark of the Covenant is believed to have stood in the Temple of Solomon.

The Prophet Muhammad carried through heaven by the miraculous Burak, from a Persian manuscript of the fifteenth century.

Above The Prophet Muhammad replacing the Black Stone in the Kaba, from the universal history of Rashid al-Din produced at Tabriz in 1314.

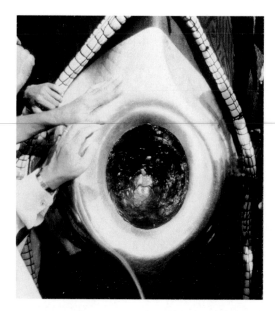

The Black Stone, visible through the brocade covering of the Kaba.

Below Pilgrims in procession around the Kaba at Mecca, believed by some Muslim commentators to symbolize the passage of the stars around the Pole.

fallen, Burckhardt reported, the battle is believed to be lost by the party to whom it belonged.

When he describes the *markab*, it is obvious that Burckhardt has seen the same shrine, or the same type of shrine, but there seem to be differences in detail. He tells us that when some of the Aneyzeh chiefs went to war, they carried a 'battle banner', which is displayed only in critical and decisive actions, where its fall or its loss is regarded as a sign of defeat. There are two sorts of standard, he believes. One is called *markab*, which means 'ship', and is built of two stands of wood about six or seven feet high. They are placed opposite each other on the back of a camel, so that there is no more than a hand's width separating them at the top, but still room at the bottom for a person to sit between them on a saddle. The upper part of the standard is covered with black ostrich feathers. The other sort is called *otfe* and consists of two boards along the sides, forming an oblong square about five feet high. Like the *markab*, it is ornamented with ostrich feathers. In battle, all the horsemen would assemble around the standard, and the main effort of each party was directed against the *markab* or *otfe* of the enemy. If one was captured, it was carried in triumph to the tent of the victorious sheikh.

Morgenstern quotes at great length from virtually every account of these shrines that he can find, noting agreements and disagreements between them about the details of what they had seen or what the tribes had told them. He is concerned to discover if there was only one *markab*, or if several tribes possessed them. He was searching for evidence about whether the *otfe* was identical to the *markab*, or only related to it. A more profound theological question that might have implications for the history of the Ark of the Covenant was whether Abu Zhur had originally been the name of the tribal deity and, after the tribe embraced Islam, had been assimilated to Allah. Perhaps most important of all, he was hoping to determine the origin and the age of the shrine.

At least one reliable witness, he decides, identifies the *markab* with the *otfe*. They are the same sort of shrine, and originally each of the tribes may well have possessed one. Only the Ruala, the greatest of the bedouin tribes, still preserved the custom. The question of Abu Zhur was probably beyond recovery, while the origin of the *markab* required that Morgenstern look for other shrines in the world of Islam.

In 1867, Charles Doughty set out from Damascus with a caravan of pilgrims bound for Mecca. He was hoping to reach the ruins of Madain Salih, despite the opposition of the Turkish authorities. It was one of seven great cities that had grown rich, according to Muslim legend, with the trade that passed along the Incense Road from Arabia Felix. Even the great Burckhardt had never seen it, and Doughty was keen to surpass him. When he wrote an account of his travels, he adopted a peculiar archaic style that displayed what he called 'the old manly English, full of pith and stomach'. His tales of the pilgrim caravan, of the slaves who carried charcoal to light the pipes of the hajjis, of a white cock that travelled with the Persian pilgrims, and of dogs that walked beside the caravan 2,000 miles from Damascus to Mecca and back remain an astonishing testimony to his fortitude and his eccentricity. T. E. Lawrence, who acquired fame and notoriety himself as 'Lawrence of Arabia', called it 'a book not like other books, but something particular, a bible of its kind'.

As a Christian, Doughty was not permitted to stay with the caravan until it reached Mecca, but his route to Madain Salih would take him west in any case. Of his time with the caravan, he wrote that he sometimes saw, heaving and rolling above all heads of men and cattle in the midst of the caravan, the naked frame and posts of the sacred *mahmal*. It resembled a bedstead, he thought, and was made after the fashion of the camel-litter used by bedouin women. On high days it was covered with a glorious pall of green velvet, the colour of the Prophet Muhammad, and the four posts were crowned with ornaments of silver that caught the light. Doughty was told that the litter was the standard of the *haj*, and that it followed an ancient Arabian custom still preserved among the bedouin. At any great battle of tribes, a beautiful girl chosen from among the daughters of the sheikh would inspire her people in the presence of their enemies, inflaming the hearts of the young men to leap toward death or victory.

Along with the confession of faith, prayers, fasting and alms, the pilgrimage to Mecca is one of the five pillars of Islam. Even before the angel Gabriel began to dictate the word of God to the Prophet Muhammad, however, the pilgrimage had been a custom among the Arabs of the Hejaz. It may have taken place every autumn, like the Feast of Tabernacles described in the Hebrew Bible, which itself is sometimes given the name *hag*. When the Prophet established a lunar calendar, the month of the pilgrimage known as *Dhu 'l-Hijja* began to move through the year. In the heat of summer, the journey could prove arduous, and the Prophet himself is said to have remarked that the pilgrimage was a kind of punishment.

There was further danger: the threat of raids from the tribes through whose lands the pilgrim caravans would need to pass. If the pilgrims submitted, they usually escaped with their lives, but the depredations of the tribes were often intolerable. There seemed to be two solutions. The authorities at Mecca tried to buy off the tribal chiefs, by paying them a fee known as a *surra*, and the caravans travelled under such heavy guard that they were virtually armed expeditions.

The greatest of the caravans set out from Damascus, Baghdad, Cairo and the Yemen. When they arrived at Mecca, the first camel to enter the city would be carrying the *mahmal* described by Doughty, a decorated litter, empty except for a copy of the Quran. It was met with great joy.

It is no longer seen, however. In 1808, it was suppressed by the followers of the reformer Muhammad ibn Abd al-Wahhab, who opposed all innovations made after the first three centuries of Islam. As Burckhardt observed, the Wahhabi regarded the *mahmal* as 'a vain pomp, of idolatrous origin, and contrary to the spirit of true religion'. As there was no tradition of its having existed under the four orthodox caliphs, or during the Umayyad or the Abbasid dynasties, they regarded the *mahmal* as pagan. With more recent witnesses describing two flute players in the cortège of the *mahmal* at Mecca, in defiance of the Islamic prohibition of flutes in religious ritual, it is hardly surprising that the Wahhabi would have been horrified. Even though the *mahmal* was restored, it was interrupted again a century later because of a dispute with the Egyptian government when the Hashemite sharif Husain ruled the Hejaz. After Husain had been driven from power by Ibn Saud, the founder of the Saudi state and an adherent of Wahhabi reform, the objections were repeated. Ibn Saud also regarded the military escorts as an affront to his own rule. When the dispute became violent in 1926, he had to intervene personally. A compromise was reached: the music that had once accompanied the *mahmal* was abandoned as pagan, and the litter was sent to Mecca again in 1929. It did not last, however.

In earlier centuries, Muslim princes had struggled to ensure that the magnificence of their own *mahmal* would surpass that of any rival. The contest reflected the political ambitions of the princes, and their hopes of being recognized as patrons of the sharifs who ruled in Mecca. The *Chronicle of Mecca* records a *mahmal* sent from Iraq in 1322, covered in gold, pearls and precious jewels, although the power and wealth of the Mamluk sultans in Egypt meant that the most lavish splendour was usually seen on the *mahmal* from Cairo. It seems that the rivalry often led to fighting between the factions that represented the various princes, and in these battles the *mahmal* itself was employed as a standard.

The custom was associated with the Ark of the Covenant by the first Europeans who claimed to have seen it. One traveller reported in the sixteenth century that the Quran was carried from Cairo to Mecca 'in a little chest made of pure legmane wood in likenesse of the ark of the old testament'.

Maundrel described in more detail the *mahmal* he saw at Damascus in 1699, as it was about to leave for the *haj*. It was a large pavilion of black silk, borne by a huge camel, and adorned on every side with gold fringes that reached to the ground. Under the pavilion, the Quran was placed with great solemnity, along with a new rich carpet, which the sultan sent every year to Mecca as a covering for the tomb of the Prophet. The old carpet was carried home when the caravan returned, and was believed to be a treasure beyond price. For the rest of its life, the camel that carried the *mahmal* was exempt from bearing any burden.

Just over a century later, Burckhardt described the Egyptian *mahmal* and offered an explanation of its origin. He believed that the custom had arisen from the battle standards of the bedouins, the *markab* and *otfe*, which resembled the *mahmal* in being high wooden frames placed upon camels. He insisted that it did not contain a copy of the Quran, however, only a book of prayers.

As with the *markab* and the *otfe*, even careful observers seem to differ in the details they recall. After years of living in Egypt to gather information for his famous Arabic lexicon, William Lane published *An Account of the Manners and Customs of the Modern Egyptians*. He not only described the *mahmal*, in terms that suggest he had read Burckhardt, but also attempted to explain its origin.

It was a square skeleton-frame of wood, he tells us, with a top shaped like a pyramid. It had a covering of black brocade, richly worked with inscriptions and ornamental embroidery in gold, in some parts upon a ground of green or red silk. There was a fringe of silk along the edge, with tassels and silver balls. The covering, it seems, was not always decorated in the same way, but on every one that Lane had seen, there was a view of the mosque at Mecca, worked in gold, and above it was the monogram of the sultan. The *mahmal* contained nothing, except for copies of the Quran. One had been written as a scroll, and the other in the form of a little book. Both were enclosed in cases of gilt silver attached to the top of the *mahmal*. The camel that carried the *mahmal* was chosen for its beauty and its strength, and for the remainder of its life it was never required to work again.

Lane had been told that Baybars, the sultan of Egypt, had been the first to send a *mahmal* with the caravan of pilgrims to Mecca, around AH 670 (AD 1272). The more general assumption was that the custom had begun a few years before his accession to the throne. A beautiful Turkish female slave became the favourite wife of the sultan al-Salah Najm al-Din. On the death of his son, and in the absence of any other heir, she caused herself to be acknowledged as ruler of Egypt. She performed the pilgrimage in a magnificent covered litter borne by a camel, and for several years after this her empty litter was sent with the caravan 'merely for the sake of state'. The sultans who succeeded her retained the custom of sending a litter with each pilgrim caravan as an emblem of royalty, and the rulers of other countries followed them. Eventually, the Wahhabi prohibited the *mahmal* as 'an object of vain pomp'.

If the information that Lane provides about the origins of the *mahmal* is correct, it means that the institution is over 700 years old. If this date is accepted, however, it means that the custom had become very significant very quickly. Records at Mecca confirm that the arrival of the *mahmal* from Iraq was an important event by 1320. The *mahmal* from the Yemen was noted in 1380, and was probably not the first to arrive from the south. Its origins may therefore be earlier than we know, and whatever the earliest date for the *mahmal* itself, there is certainly evidence for older shrines in Arabia to which the *markab* and the *mahmal* both seem to be related.

The Battle of the Camel was fought near Basra on 4 December 656. Ali ibn Abi Talib, the cousin of the Prophet Muhammad and the husband of his daughter Fatima, was facing a coalition that refused to accept his claim to succeed the murdered Uthman as caliph of the Prophet. Among them was Aisha, 'the Mother of the Faithful', who had been the favourite wife of the Prophet. Aisha had regarded Ali as a mortal enemy for years. He had urged Muhammad to repudiate her when a young man rescued her after she had been left behind by a caravan on the road to Medina, and accusations had been made that her virtue was now compromised. She was still only eighteen years old when the Prophet died, and she remained determined to oppose Ali.

Their meeting in the Battle of the Camel was described by the Arab historian al-Tabari, who reports that Aisha took her place in a litter mounted upon a sturdy camel. The litter was closed on all sides and protected with armour. Within it, Aisha carried a copy of the Quran, and in contrast to earlier custom, there were no women in attendance. Once inside the litter, however, she bared her breasts, even though she remained concealed in obedience to the Islamic view of modesty. Hidden from the gaze of the troops, she advanced into the thick of the battle. The bridle of her camel was held by one warrior after another, as the enemy slaughtered them in a desperate bid to capture the camel and the litter. At the critical point of the battle, it seemed as if her warriors might turn and run, but Aisha gave orders that the camel should be led into the very heart of the battle, where the greatest danger lay. Her warriors rallied about the litter, but they could not check the advance of the enemy. Even so, their opponents could not capture the camel or drive it from the battlefield. Ali therefore ordered his men to hamstring the animal, and in this they succeeded. The camel sank to the ground and brought the litter and

Aisha down with it. The Battle of the Camel was over, and Ali had won.

Within the litter, the person of Aisha was inviolable. Ali gave her to her brother Muhammad, the son of Abu Bakr, still hidden inside the litter. Although the Arabic text does not mention the incident, the Persian translation records that when Muhammad put his arm between the curtains of the litter, his hand touched the naked breast of his sister, who was greatly distressed.

The Arabic scribes may have thought this detail too shocking to include, but their account of the battle nevertheless confirms that the litter in which Aisha rode was red in colour. This was the traditional colour of the tents used as shrines in the centuries before Islam, and Muhammad himself had denounced it as the colour of Satan.

An earlier incident recorded by al-Tabari also involves Aisha and what appears to have been a similar shrine. A girl named Selma, the daughter of Malik of the Banu Ghatafan, had been captured in a raid by Muhammad. Aisha had freed her and converted her to Islam, and she was permitted to return to her own people, with the aim of converting her parents. After the death of Muhammad, she led an insurrection to exact blood revenge for her brother, who had been killed during a raid on Medina. When Khalid ibn Walid marched against her, Selma faced him on the battlefield. In the midst of her followers, she was seated in a litter and mounted on a camel. As soon as Khalid saw her, he shouted to his men, 'Unless this camel is overthrown and the woman killed, we cannot win!' Even though he offered the reward of a hundred camels, none of his warriors dared to try. Finally Khalid himself gathered a few men about him, and charged toward the camel. After killing a hundred warriors who were guarding it, he finally stood close enough to hamstring the animal. As it fell, Selma was thrown from her litter. Khalid killed her and won the battle.

Al-Tabari tells us almost nothing about the litter in which Selma sat as she rode into battle on her camel, but the statement that Aisha rode in a red litter even though the Prophet had spoken against the colour, and the report in the Persian text that she had disrobed, suggest a strong relationship with the ancient shrine known as the *kubbe*.

The *kubbe* was a tent made of red leather, with a domed top. It was smaller than an ordinary tent, small enough to be mounted on a camel. Red leather was a sign of its antiquity, as the bedouin had once lived in tents of red leather themselves. Even after they began to live in tents woven from black goat hair, they retained the ancient red leather for the *kubbe*, and the custom was preserved among people who lived in Mecca and other cities as well.

The sacred images of an Arab tribe were regularly housed in a *kubbe*, and they were carried into battle in a sacred procession. However, it was never carried on raids, but only into decisive battles. The sight of it would inspire warriors to great deeds of heroism, but its capture would be disastrous.

The *kubbe* was usually attended by two women, mounted on camels. They followed it in procession, playing on the tambourine and the flute. Even in battle, the women still rode with it. When the fighting became most fierce or when there was danger of defeat, the women would let their hair fly loose, bare their breasts or remove their clothing entirely. Although many of the reports of the *markab* were written in modest terms, this was obviously similar to the modern custom among the bedouin.

In times of need, the *kubbe* could provide guidance. If the tribe were forced to find new pasture, especially if its route involved unusual danger, the guardian of the *kubbe* would consult it and communicate the oracle to the people.

According to tradition, the images within the *kubbe* represented female rather than male deities. The young woman in the *markab*, the tent that Raswan and Musil believed to resemble the Ark of the Covenant in such a dramatic way, would therefore have stood in the place once occupied by the goddesses of the Time of Ignorance.

One of the most famous appearances of a *kubbe* occurred at the Battle of Uhud. Abu Sufyan, the leader of the Quraysh at Mecca, was looking for revenge when he took the field against the Prophet Muhammad in AD 624. Muslim raiders had been attacking Meccan caravans, and at the Battle of Badr they had overcome superior Meccan forces – a sign in Muslim eyes that the power of God was with them. The Battle of Uhud was fought beside a hill near Medina, and Abu Sufyan was accompanied by his gods. Images of the two goddesses al-Lat and al-Uzza entered the battle in their *kubbe*, and he cried out to the Companions of the Prophet, 'Uzza is with us! With you, there is no Uzza!'

Muhammad himself employed a *kubbe* of red leather, both in battle and on the march, but while the *kubbe* of his enemies contained idols of pagan goddesses, Muhammad was accompanied by the *kubbatu 'l-Islam*, the 'kubbe of Islam'. Unlike the *kubbe* of the Jahiliyya, the Days of Ignorance before the Quran had been revealed, it was empty. The sacred stones of al-Lat and al-Uzza had been removed.

The decision to remove them was not necessarily as obvious as it now seems. One of the most controversial events in the life of the Prophet concerns the 'Satanic Verses' which once appeared in the Quran after verse 19 of Surah 53, known as 'The Star'. They were originally proclaimed in the precinct of the Kaba at Mecca, and Muhammad is said to have been hoping for a revelation that would encourage the merchants of the city to embrace Islam when the verses came to him:

> Have you considered al-Lat and al-Uzza
> and Manat, the third, the other?
> These are the intermediaries exalted,
> whose intercession is to be hoped for.
> Such as they do not forget.

Later, the Prophet received an emended revelation and realized that these verses could not have come from God. The Quran now contains the abrogation:

> They are nothing but names that you yourselves
> have named, and your fathers; God has
> sent down no authority concerning them.

The first version had referred to intercession by the local deities whose images had accompanied Abu Sufyan in their *kubbe*. The story of the Satanic Verses and their abrogation is assumed to be historically accurate, as it is difficult to imagine any Muslim inventing such a story about the Prophet. Surah 22, known as 'The Pilgrimage,' is thought to refer to the incident:

We have not sent any Messenger
or Prophet before you, but that Satan
cast into his thoughts, when he was imagining;
but God abrogates what Satan casts – surely God is All-knowing,
   All-wise

If the abrogation of the Satanic Verses made it impossible for the ancient goddesses of the Days of Ignorance to be venerated as angelic beings who might intercede with God, the presence of Aisha in her litter at the Battle of the Camel seems to be an echo of the female images that had been removed from the *kubbe*. The presence of the Quran is an obvious statement that the revealed word of God is the most powerful evidence of divine power in the world, far greater than any idol.

The *kubbe* was also brought into battle by the caliphs of the Prophet. Just as his father had employed one when he fought Muhammad at the Battle of Uhud, Muawiyya, the founder of the Umayyad dynasty, brought a *kubbe* to the Battle of Siffin when he faced Ali ibn Abi Talib. The *kubbe* that he erected by his tent was empty – the *kubbe* of Islam.

Other shrines have been recorded, and at least one of them was explicitly compared to the Ark of the Covenant. Five years after Hussein, the second son of Ali, was martyred at Karbala in AD 680, al-Muktar ibn Ubaid Allah went to Kufa to avenge him. He took a throne and told his troops that it contained a mystery, being for them exactly what the Ark had been for the Children of Israel. When he sent the army to attack Ubaid Allah ibn Zayad, he went out with his throne on a mule which carried it into battle.

Beyond the literature of Islam and the Days of Ignorance, little evidence survives of the *kubbe*, but there are three fascinating images from Roman Arabia. First, two goddesses appear in a litter on a camel, with evidence of red paint, and a canopy or tent visible above the figures. Could the tent be a *kubbe*, and could the figures be al-Lat and al-Uzza?

A second image also depicts two figures within a litter on a camel. Their breasts are exposed, and one is playing flute while the other beats a drum. Could these be the women who accompanied the *kubbe*, and the *mahmal* as well?

There is also a bas-relief from Palmyra, in which a low structure like a tent sits on the back of a camel. There are traces of red paint, and once again the image seems to depict a *kubbe*. The camel is being led in a ritual procession, with three female figures behind it. Other figures with arms upraised stand before it, in a gesture of homage to the *kubbe* and the image that would have been placed within it.

All these images are from the Roman period, probably the second or third century AD. All have come from Syria or Palmyra, which were in close contact with other parts of Arabia due to the caravan trade, and which the earliest records describe as the source of the images used at Mecca and among the neighbouring tribes.

Morgenstern gathered his evidence and published his assessment of it almost sixty years ago. When he was writing, the foundation of the state of Israel was still several years away, and the great oil reserves of Arabia had not yet been exploited. The accounts that he cites of European travellers in the Orient, and his own interests in the possibility of close similarities between the institutions of ancient Israel and the desert nomads of Arabia, are all part of a lost world. Orientalists were once fascinated by this, but no longer, it seems.

The article that Morgenstern published is still cited, but it is rarely discussed. The most detailed criticism of it appeared over fifteen years later, and was written in Hebrew by one of the leading authorities on the Temple and the Tabernacle, Menahem Haran, who taught at the Hebrew University of Jerusalem. His article too is often cited and rarely discussed, perhaps because it was written in Hebrew and never translated. It is nevertheless immensely interesting.

By 1959, when it was published, the search for similarities between Jews and Arabs seems to have become more problematic, even for scholars who were concerned to pursue a disinterested vision of the past. Similarities no longer seemed to suggest that Jews should have a right to live in Palestine because they were heirs to an ancient biblical heritage. With the foundation of the state of Israel, that much was regarded as obvious. Instead, discovering bedouin parallels to the Bible might raise the possibility that Israelis should adopt a different attitude to the Arabs who were living in Palestine before the arrival of so many refugees from the horrors of Europe. The question that appears throughout the ancient texts had reappeared in modern politics: Who were the Israelites, and why were they different from their neighbours? Its impact on Christian scholars may have been even more marked than upon their Jewish colleagues, and the Orientalist vision of interpreting the Old Testament on the basis of Arabic etymologies and scenes from the camel market at Gaza began to seem a quaint memory from the vanished world of the Ottoman Empire or the British Mandate.

Haran simply denies that any similarity could exist between the Arab shrines and the Ark of the Covenant, and noting the absence of early archaeological evidence, he decides that any apparent similarity would simply be coincidental. After insisting on clear distinctions, he simply dismisses the accounts of the *otfe* as containing differences in detail, and therefore being 'not sufficiently clarified' to be discussed. The precision that could be so valuable in his discussions of biblical texts works against him here. It is hardly surprising that members of the tribes to whom Raswan or Musil spoke might give different answers to questions asked about the *otfe* or *markab*. The same problem is likely to occur any time that scholars attempt to pin down an oral tradition. Different people may say different things. He does make a valuable contribution, however, by repeating a point that had been made several decades earlier. Why should the Arab tent shrines be compared to the Ark of the Covenant? As tents, surely they would resemble the Tabernacle or, more precisely, the Tabernacle of the Priestly source?

This sort of precision may contain another problem, however. Given the fluid nature of religious symbols, the sharp distinctions that Haran prefers may frustrate or prevent a real understanding of them. As portable shrines, the Arab traditions could be similar to both Ark and Tabernacle. We have already seen that the Ark and the Tabernacle may have been separate but parallel institutions that were brought together when the biblical sources were edited, and Haran himself has claimed that the Ark and its Mercy Seat were originally separate elements that were combined at some later point. The question is of real importance if we are trying to understand what Iyasu might have encountered in the Church of

Mary of Zion at Aksum. As we shall see, Ethiopia is filled with portable shrines that are described as identical to the great relic, and we have read that Iyasu was involved in making at least one of these himself. A great deal will depend on how we understand the claim that the Ark itself survives in the midst of these thousands of shrines. Haran regards Morgenstern as proposing a single institution, and he rejects the possibility that such an institution could have existed, or could be known to have existed, given the expanse of time. But Morgenstern does not appear to be claiming that the Ark of the Covenant is the same thing as the *otfe*, or the *mahmal*, or the *kubbe*. He is claiming that it is the same sort of thing, and this is a very different sort of assertion.

It is unfortunate that neither Morgenstern nor Haran discussed the relation of the shrines to the Black Stone or the Station of Abraham. Originally, it seems, these were sacred stones placed in the Kaba before the revelation of the Quran. They may have been identical to the sorts of sacred stones carried in the *kubbe*. In many ways, they become Arks, and yet there are separate but related traditions about the Ark of the Covenant itself. In the Hebrew Bible, we have seen evidence of different forms of the Ark of the Covenant, of more than one Ark, and of other shrines that were employed in the way that the Ark was employed. And we have seen a different sort of Ark – the chariot throne – that begins to replace the Ark of the Covenant, but eventually appears alongside it in the Greek New Testament. With all this in mind, the number of shrines we encounter in Arabia is fascinating, but not unexpected. We find a history of the Ark of the Covenant itself, we find sacred stones in the Kaba that resemble the Ark in many ways, and we find other types of shrine that seem to be related to them. In neither Israel nor Arabia do we encounter a single great relic surrounded by silence. Instead, we find a rich and fertile matrix of symbols, from which new forms emerge and combine with each other, all of them attempts to provide a visible answer to questions that for centuries proved so tantalizing for the human mind, or at least for the human spirit: What lies beyond the world of men? Is there a point at which heaven touches earth? Does God display himself within the world that he created?

In Ethiopia, what has been called the Great Tradition, the founding epic of the Christian empire, tells us that the Ark of the

Covenant arrived through the mission of a woman who herself became a complex and ambiguous symbol of both good and evil. Her wisdom and her piety impressed Solomon himself, and she is often confused with Queen Candace, whose eunuch brought the Christian faith to Ethiopia according to the Acts of the Apostles. Yet she also appears among the demons of the Red Sea as the first wife of Adam, made by God before Eve and expelled from Paradise even before the Fall.

CHAPTER 13

Queen of the South

The fame of Solomon and his wisdom spread to Arabia and Egypt, and throughout the Hellenistic world. Like Alexander the Great, he became one of the legendary heroes of antiquity. With his magical powers, he could speak to birds and animals, and command the spirits of the air, and yet through his love of women this power slipped from his grasp. Everything that he had once possessed stood as a warning for those on whom God has bestowed exceptional gifts, a reminder of the frailty of the human heart when it turns away from the God who made it. Yet despite the loss of his magic, his reputation as a sorcerer grew through the ages. Wizardry is often thought to involve supping with the devil, or at least with demons of some sort, but his fate may be preferable to that of the Queen of Sheba. We meet her as a symbol of wisdom and piety, but she becomes a demon herself.

In the gospels according to Mathew and Luke, the meeting of Solomon and the Queen of Sheba is recalled by Christ himself, who warns the Jews that on the Day of Judgement, the Queen of the South will testify against them. She had come from the ends of the earth to hear the wisdom of Solomon, but now that a greater wisdom has appeared among them, they have turned away.

The most elaborate account of the meeting between Solomon and the Queen of Sheba, and of the child who was born from their union, brings the Queen and her descendants into the history of the Ark. Because she desires to learn the wisdom of Solomon, a new dynasty arises in Ethiopia, the king of Israel sinks into idolatry without the presence of God to guide him, and the Ark of the Covenant moves by its own miraculous power to Africa.

This version appears in *The Glory of Kings*, which is often described as the Ethiopian national epic – an enigmatic work about which almost nothing was known in Europe until the Scottish traveller James Bruce returned from Ethiopia and presented two manuscripts to the Bodleian Library in Oxford. The book introduces the Queen of the South by repeating the words of Christ that describe her rising up to condemn the Jews on the Day of Judgement. We are then told of her beauty and intelligence, her great wealth in gold, silver, slaves and merchants, and her high character, 'such that she braved the burning sun and desperate thirst to travel from the ends of the earth to hear the wisdom of Solomon'.

The queen was named Makeda, and she had apparently learned of Solomon's great wisdom from the merchant Tamrin. He possessed as many as 73 ships and 520 camels, and had been summoned to Jerusalem when Solomon was building the Temple. Messages had been sent to all the merchants of the east, west, north and south, so that Solomon might furnish the Temple with the finest things that the world could offer. He wrote to Tamrin along with the others, telling him to bring whatever he wished from the country of Arabia, sapphires, red gold, and the black wood that could not be eaten by worms.

When he arrived in Jerusalem with his caravan, Tamrin was greatly impressed by the wealth of Israel. Gold was as common as bronze, and silver as lead. God had obviously given Solomon glory and riches and wisdom and grace in abundance, and Tamrin had never seen anyone like him.

Once he had returned to his own country, Tamrin told his queen in great detail about the noble bearing of the Israelite king, his sound judgement, gracious manner and keen intellect. He was building a marvellous temple and learning all the secrets of the craftsmen and artisans who worked for him. Tamrin described the feasts that Solomon gave for his people, and the justice in his kingdom, where no man stole from his neighbour. Makeda was filled with wonder, weeping tears of joy to hear of such a splendid country. Finally, she decided to see it for herself.

She had become convinced that wisdom was better than gold or silver, that nothing under the heavens could be compared to it. It was sweeter than honey and made the heart rejoice more than wine. It was light to the eyes, a shield for the breast and a helmet for the head. It could make the ears hear and the heart understand. No kingdom could stand without it. For all these reasons, she decided, she would have to follow the footprints of wisdom, believing that if she should find it, wisdom would protect her for ever.

When she prepared to set out for Jerusalem, her servants loaded 797 camels, along with mules and asses too numerous to count. With confidence in God, she embarked on the long and hazardous journey and was received with great honour when she arrived. Solomon invited her to live in the palace near his own rooms, and sent her food and wine, the finest honey, and musicians to play and sing to her. She was astonished at his grace and his eloquence.

As Tamrin had told her, the king was occupied with building a temple, and she saw him teaching his workers how to measure and weigh, how to use the hammer, the drill and the chisel. Everything was done at his command, and Makeda could see the skill that God had given to him when he asked for wisdom rather than riches or the death of his enemy.

The queen told Solomon how much she admired him, that she looked on him as a lamp in the darkness, as the moon in the mist, as the Morning Star in the sky, as the glory of the dawn and the rising sun. Solomon replied that he possessed only what God had given to him, but that she had wisdom in herself. What is more, she had acquired her wisdom even though she did not know the God of Israel. He was merely a slave of this God, building a sanctuary for his Lady, the Ark of the Law of God, the holy and heavenly Zion. While they were talking, he pointed to one of his workers and remarked that he himself was no better than the man in ragged clothing who stood before them, sweat pouring from his face as he carried a stone and a skin of water. Men are nothing but dust and ashes, he told the queen. There is no point to human life if we do not show love and kindness towards each other.

Makeda was delighted with his words and longed to hear more. She tells Solomon that some of her people worship images of gold and silver, of stone or wood. She herself worships the sun, but she has heard that Israel knows a God whom she has never known, and that he has sent an Ark from heaven along with a Tablet revealing the divine commandments written by the hand of Moses the prophet. She has even heard that this God comes down from heaven to speak to Solomon.

It is all true, the king assures her. The God who created the entire universe, the heavens and the earth, and everything that lives in them, who has made both angels and men, has given an Ark to the Children of Israel, which was formed before the entire universe. When she hears this, Makeda announces that she will no longer worship the sun, but will serve the God who actually made the sun, the God of Israel. And from this moment, the Ark of the God of Israel will be her Lady.

In the following days, the queen visited Solomon to hear more of his wisdom, and he visited her to answer the questions that she put to him. After six months, she told him that however much she wished to remain in Jerusalem, where wisdom could be found in such abundance, her own people would need her to return.

When he heard that she was about to leave him, Solomon began to wonder. She was very beautiful. Perhaps God would allow him to have a child by her. The Bible reports that Solomon was a lover of women, that he had 400 queens and 600 concubines. *The Glory of Kings* is adamant that this was not because he was addicted to fornication, but because he was wise, and because God had said to Abraham that he would make his descendants as numerous as the stars of heaven or the sands of the sea. Solomon also knew that his children would inherit the kingdoms that had belonged to idolaters, and would destroy the worship of idols.

With all this on his mind, he sent a message to Makeda inviting her to dine with him in his tent, so that she could learn how the righteous ate. This was evidently an important part of the wisdom by which a wise king rules his country. She accepted the invitation, and Solomon ordered the most lavish preparations. When she arrived, she was amazed at the carpets, the marbles and the precious stones, and delighted by the aromatic powders that were burned, and the oil of myrrh and cassia and the frankincense that had been scattered about. Solomon also added generous amounts of pepper and vinegar to the food and drink that he gave her, 'with wise intent', we are told. At the end of the banquet, he invited her to spend the night with him, and she asked him to swear that he would not take her virginity by force. He agreed, as long as she would swear to take nothing from him. She laughed at the suggestion. Her kingdom was as rich as his. What could she possibly want to take from him? She had come to Jerusalem in search of wisdom and nothing more.

Solomon has laid his trap carefully, however, and he tells one of his servants to place a bowl of water in the room. In the middle of the night, the queen awakes and is tormented by thirst. Her mouth is dry, and when she moves her lips she can feel no moisture on them. She sees the water, looks at Solomon and assumes that he is asleep. In fact, he is only waiting to catch her. As she walks quietly across the floor and lifts up the bowl, Solomon seizes her by the hand before she can drink. 'Why have you broken your oath?' he asks her. She replies by asking him if the oath could be broken simply by drinking water. He then asks if she can think of anything under heaven more precious than water. At this point, she realizes that she has been caught, and when she releases him from his part of the bargain, he allows her to drink the water. Once her thirst has been satisfied, the king satisfies his own desire.

In the middle of the night, however, Solomon begins to feel uneasy. He dreams of a brilliant sun that comes down from heaven and shines with a great light over Israel. After it has shone for some time, it flies away to Ethiopia and shines with even greater brilliance, remaining there for ever. In his dream, Solomon waits to see if the sun will return, but it never does. While he is waiting, an even stronger light comes down from the country of Judah, but the Israelites refuse to walk in the light of this sun, and they hate it. They try to extinguish it, and succeed in casting darkness over the world, placing the sun in a tomb and setting guards over it. Yet the sun arises when they do not expect it, and brings light to the entire world, especially to Ethiopia and Rome. It simply ignores Israel.

After seeing the vision, Solomon awakes with a sense of foreboding, but he continues to marvel at the queen, at her beauty and her strength, and at the fact that she had remained a virgin even though she had already ruled for six years. He gives her wonderful gifts, and loads 6,000 camels and wagons, a vessel that could sail over the sea, and another that could sail through the air, which he had made with the wisdom that God had given him.

Makeda was delighted with her gifts, and the king sent her on her way with great joy and ceremony. He gave her a ring and told her that, if she had a son, the ring would be a sign to him that Solomon was his father. He then told her of the dream and suggested that Ethiopia might be blessed through her. God would know. Finally, he told her to depart in peace.

The queen gave birth to a son nine months and five days after she left Jerusalem. She named him Bayna-Lehkem, 'the son of the wise man', and when she had completed the days of her purification, she entered her own country with pomp and ceremony. She gave lavish gifts to her people, and she ruled them with wisdom.

When her son was twelve years old, he asked his friends if they knew who his father might be. They mentioned the name of Solomon, king of Israel, and when he heard it, he went to his mother, asking for permission to visit him. Makeda tried to discourage the boy and managed to keep him beside her for another ten years, until he had learned the arts of war, horsemanship, hunting and everything else that young men did. He then told her that it was time for him to go to his father, but by the will of God, the Lord of Israel, he would return to her.

When she heard this, the queen told Tamrin the merchant to prepare for a journey, to guide the prince on the long road to Jerusalem. Tamrin arranged everything that they would need, and Makeda gave the ring of Solomon to her son, so that his father would remember her and the covenant she had made to worship the God of Israel.

Once Solomon finally sees the young man, he thinks him even more handsome than he had been at that age himself – the image of his father David, in fact. 'Behold,' he cries out, 'my father David has renewed his youth and has risen from the dead.' Bayna-Lehkem presents the ring to Solomon and reminds him of the conversation he held with Makeda before she left Jerusalem to return to Ethiopia. He then asks that a portion of the fringe on the covering of the Ark of the Law be given to him, as his mother had requested it at the time. For his part, Tamrin asks Solomon to anoint Bayna-Lehkem to rule in Ethiopia, telling the king that even though he had been anxious about taking the young man on such a perilous journey, he trusted in the holy heavenly Zion, the Ark of the Law of God, that Solomon would not withhold his wisdom from his son.

In fact, Solomon is so fond of his son that he tries to persuade him to remain with him in Jerusalem, where he can visit the House of God and the Ark of the Law, but Bayna-Lehkem replies that he has come to Jerusalem only to hear the famous wisdom of Solomon. He will leave without sorrow if he is allowed to take part of the fringe that adorns the covering of the Ark. He and his mother will worship it in Ethiopia, for the queen has freed her country from idolatry and has brought her people to Zion, the Ark of the Law of God.

When Solomon persists, his son reminds him that the king has a son already, Rehoboam, who is legitimate. The Queen of Sheba had never been married to Solomon, after all. Solomon argues that he himself was not the legitimate son of David, and that Rehoboam is not the firstborn son, even if his mother was married. Despite his father urging him, however, Bayna-Lehkem has given his oath to his mother that he will return, and he believes that the Ark of the God of Israel will bless him wherever he goes. Having failed to persuade his son to stay with him, Solomon gathers his courtiers, his officers and the elders of his kingdom. He asks them to give their firstborn sons to accompany his own son to Ethiopia, to help him rule there, and they agree.

The king and his priests now prepare to anoint the young man for kingship. The people of Jerusalem fill the air with the sound of flutes and pipes, of harps and drums, and they shout with joy. Bayna-Lehkem is brought into the inner sanctuary of the Temple, where he takes hold of the horns of the altar. He is anointed and given the name David, after his grandfather.

After David is anointed, Zadok the priest instructs him in the ways of God, and warns him of the dreadful punishment that awaits him if he fails to obey the divine commandments. The land will be cursed, along with the cattle, all the herds and the flocks of sheep, even the children of his own body. Famine and pestilence will come upon his kingdom. The heavens will turn to brass and the earth to iron. The rain will be black, and dust will fall from heaven. He will be defeated by his enemies in battle. He will die and be eaten by vultures. He will be afflicted with leprosy and plagues. The list of dreadful calamities continues for pages.

Zadok then recites the blessings that will come upon him if he obeys, and there are pages of them to rival the curses. The fruit of his land will be blessed, the fountains of his waters, the fruit that he has planted, his cattle and sheep and granaries. The blessing of the heavens will be upon him and he will rule over nations and not be ruled himself. He will have victory in war, honour will rise up like cedar and like the Morning Star, and the brilliance of his glory will be before all the nations of the earth. God will be with him always, and his majesty will terrify everyone else. In case any confusion remains about what God expects, Zadok describes the Ten Commandments.

While there is great joy at David having been anointed king, the young men who have been ordered to accompany him to Ethiopia are unhappy at leaving their families and the country of their birth. Above all, they are distressed by the thought that they will be leaving the Lady Zion. In the end, they decide that this would be simply unbearable, and Azarias, the son of Zadok the priest, suggests that they make a covenant. He asks them to promise not to tell anyone else what he is about to say. When they agree, he proposes that they take the Lady Zion with them to Ethiopia. What is more, he says that he has a plan. They should each provide ten didrachmas and hire a carpenter to make planks for a wooden box the size of the Ark of Zion. If he seems suspicious, Azarias will tell him that he is making a raft. When the planks have been made, they will place them in the inner sanctuary of the Temple and cover them with the draperies of Zion. Then they will hide Zion in a hole in the ground until they are ready to leave Jerusalem.

During the night, the Angel of the Lord appears to Azarias to offer his help. He tells him that he should ask David to speak to Solomon, on the pretext of making a sacrifice to the Lady Zion before he leaves Jerusalem. Solomon will obviously agree, and David should then suggest that Azarias offer the sacrifice. As the son of the high priest, he knows about such things. Once he has entered the sanctuary, Azarias will be able to remove the Ark.

Awaking from the dream, Azarias is filled with joy and tells his companions about the plan the angel has given him. They follow his instructions, and the angel appears in the Temple to be of further assistance, standing over Azarias like a pillar of light. He opens the doors of the sanctuary and tells Azarias that he will have no difficulty in carrying the Ark with his three companions. The reason is that the Ark itself has decided to leave Jerusalem.

When they are ready to set out for Ethiopia, Solomon blesses his son and tells him that the Ark of Zion will be his guide, unaware that his words will be fulfilled quite literally. The young men have placed the Ark on a wagon and hidden it under some dirty clothes. Once all the wagons have been loaded, the masters of the caravan arise, and as the horns begin to blow to announce their departure, the people of the city are seized with a strange excitement. The old men begin to wail, children cry out and young women weep when they think that the sons of the great families of Israel are departing. But this is not the real reason, we are told. Even though the people do not know why, they are overcome with sorrow. The animals too are in distress, the dogs howling and the asses screaming. Everyone is in tears.

Solomon is dismayed to hear their anguish. He is trembling himself, and his tears fall on the ground as he cries out that he is lost. His glory is gone and the crown of his splendour has fallen. His son has left him. The majesty of his city has been taken away. From this moment his glory has passed away and his kingdom has been carried off to a strange people who do not know God, just as the prophet said, 'The people who have not looked for me have found me.' From now on, the Law and wisdom and understanding will be given to them. His father had prophesied that Ethiopia would bow before God, and that Ethiopia would stretch out her hands to God, who would receive her with honour, and that the people of Ethiopia, who were born without the Law, would be given it. They would speak of Zion as their mother, because of a man who would be born. Will this man, Solomon wonders, be the son that he has begotten with the Queen of Sheba?

Solomon then tells Zadok to take a new covering into the inner sanctuary, and to give the covering from the Ark to David. Although David is delighted, Azarias tells him that if he is pleased with the covering, he will be much more pleased with the Ark itself.

The travellers load their wagons and set off, with the archangel Michael leading them. He spreads his wings and tells them to march through the sea as if they are standing on dry land. When they walk on the land, he cuts a path for them, holding his wings above them like a cloud to hide them from the great heat of the sun. He makes their wagons fly through the air, along with the animals and the men, and they travel in the wagons like ships on the sea when the wind blows, like a bat through the air or an eagle when his body glides above the wind. When they arrive in Egypt, they realize that in a single day they have come as far as a man could march in thirteen days. No one is tired, hungry or thirsty, not even the animals.

David did not seem to have noticed that anything unusual was happening until the young men of Israel took him aside and asked if he could keep a secret. When he promised that he could, they described how the sun had come down from heaven and was given to Israel on Mount Sinai. Now, God has chosen David to be the servant of the holy and heavenly Zion, the Ark of the Law of God. It will guide him for ever, and his descendants after him, provided that he keeps the commandment and performs the will of God. He will not be able to return the Ark to Jerusalem, even if he wants to. The Ark goes of its own free will wherever it wishes, and it cannot be taken if it has not chosen to go. The Ark, they say, is their Lady, their Mother and their salvation, their fortress and their place of refuge, their glory and the haven of their safety, to all who trust in it.

When David realizes that the Ark of the Covenant has come with them from Jerusalem, he is overcome. He takes three breaths and asks God if he has remembered the castaways in his mercy, the people that he had rejected. He asks if he will see the holy Zion, which is in heaven, and wonders how he could repay God for all the good things that he has done. Then he jumps and skips like a lamb or a kid that has been fed on the milk of its mother, just as his grandfather David had danced before the Ark of the Law of God. He beats the ground with his feet, shouting in his delight and calling out to the Ark.

Behold Zion, behold salvation, behold the one who rejoices, behold the splendour like the sun, behold the one adorned with praise, behold the one who is decorated like a bride, not with the robes of a passing glory, but the one who is decorated with the glory and praise that come from God, whom men should look upon with desire and not abandon, whom men should desire above all things and should not reject ... you are the habitation of the God of heaven.

The Ethiopians then play their flutes, blow their horns and beat their drums, until the Nile itself is astonished at the sound. The idols of Egypt, which were made in the shapes of men and dogs and cats fall down, the obelisks collapse, and the images of birds in gold and silver fall over and break. Zion shone like the sun, we are told, and they were dismayed at its majesty.

The travellers went on their way early in the morning, singing songs to Zion. Once again, they were all lifted into the air, and they passed before the people of Egypt like shadows. The Egyptians worshipped them, for they saw Zion moving in the heavens like the sun.

When Moses crossed the Red Sea with the Children of Israel, the Ark of the Law of God had not been revealed. The waters simply stood to one side, allowing Israel to pass. Now, however, the Ark of Zion crossed over as all the people sang with their harps and flutes. The waves leapt in joy and the roaring of the water mingled with the music of the instruments. As they passed Mount Sinai, the angels there sang the praises of Zion.

In Jerusalem, meanwhile, Zadok the priest came to see Solomon and found him quite miserable. The king described the dream that he had seen during the night when he was sleeping with the Queen of Sheba, a vision in which a sun shone over Israel. He told Zadok that the sun departed for Ethiopia and that another sun came down from heaven to Judah, even more brilliant than the first. When the Israelites ignored it, the sun departed to bring light to Rome and Ethiopia, and to anyone who believed in it.

Zadok is appalled that the king had not told him of the dream before. He now suspects that the young men have carried Zion away with them. Solomon for his part is astonished that Zadok had not looked to see if the Ark was in the Temple when he changed the covering. Zadok rushes to the Temple and opens the sanctuary. He finds the boards that Azarias had left in place of the Ark, and collapses as if he were dead. When he is revived, his cries of despair can be heard in the palace. Solomon immediately sends his soldiers to pursue the young men, ordering them to bring his son to Jerusalem along with the Ark and to kill everyone else.

The horsemen ride ahead of the troops as far as Egypt, and learn that the Ethiopians passed through the air with the Ark nine days earlier. Solomon then meets an ambassador who had been sent to him by the pharaoh, and who tells him how the idols of Egypt had been destroyed. When the Egyptians asked their priests to explain what had happened to the idols, the priests told them that the Ark of the God of Israel, which came down from heaven, was travelling with the Ethiopians and would now live with them for ever. The ambassador is astonished that Solomon should have given such a thing away – the Ark that had delivered Israel from its enemies, and contained the spirit of prophecy, the Ark that used to speak to the Israelites, and in which the God of heaven used to live.

Solomon wept bitterly, tormented by the realization that the Israelites had been frivolous. They had not listened to their priests and never thought of repentance. Their lives had become polluted. Because of their wickedness and immorality, their thieving, oppression and fornication, their envy, fraud and drunkenness, and all their other sins, God had taken away the Ark of the Covenant.

The Spirit of Prophecy now answers Solomon, and asks why he is feeling so sorry for himself. Everything that has happened has been the will of God. Zion has been given not to a stranger, but to the firstborn son of Solomon himself, who will sit upon the throne of David his father. Solomon will still build the Temple. It will be his glory and it will be the foundation of his reign. Provided that he refrains from serving other gods, he will be loved by the God of Israel just as his father David had been.

After he listens to the words of consolation, Solomon returns to Jerusalem, and with the elders of the city he weeps in the Temple. Together they decide to disguise the loss of the Ark. They replace the boards that Azarias had left in the sanctuary, nail them together, cover them with gold, decorate them as our Lady Zion had been decorated, and place the Book of the Law inside this new Ark. Without the Ark of Zion to guide him, however, Solomon begins to lose his wisdom. Through his excessive love of women, he is seduced into following the foreign gods of the foreign wives he marries.

David, however, arrives in the city of his mother, and as he looks in the sky he sees the heavenly Zion shining like the sun. When Makeda sees it as well, she gives thanks to God, clapping her hands and dancing with joy. All of Ethiopia, man and beast, rejoices with her. The hearts of the people shine when they see Zion, the Ark of the Law of God. Throwing their idols away, they worship the Creator, the God who had made them, and in the sight of the heavenly Zion, they renounce fornication and choose to live in purity.

The Ark of Zion is placed in the fortress of Dabra Makeda, with 300 guards wielding swords over the pavilion of Zion. The queen provides 300 men, while David sends 700 more, and she makes her nobles swear an oath, promising that no woman will ever rule again as queen in Ethiopia. Only the male line of David, the son of King Solomon of Israel, will sit on the throne.

Makeda gives the kingdom to David, telling Elmeyas and Azarias to protect him, to teach him the path of the kingdom of God and the honour of the Lady Zion. She tells her son that his confidence should be in God and in Zion, in the Ark of the Law of God. Azarias replies that the queen possesses great wisdom, the only person to rival her being her son. Later he says that even Solomon is no match for her wisdom, for she has drawn the Ark of the Law of God from Israel to Ethiopia.

Azarias tells the Ethiopians about living according to the will of God, including the distinction between clean and unclean foods. Then he tells everyone to bring their trumpets and to come to the Ark, to renew the kingdom of David. Although his father Zadok had already anointed David in Jerusalem, Azarias anoints him a second time in the presence of the Ethiopians, who celebrate with pipes and drums, singing, dancing and displaying their skill with horses and weapons. Afterwards, a banquet is held in the fortress, and David wears a raiment of fine gold. All this, we are told, occurred in the capital city, in Mount Makeda, in the House of Zion, when the Law was established for the first time by the king of Ethiopia.

After he has reigned for three months, David goes to war, accompanied by his mother Makeda and the Lady Zion. The Levites carry the Ark of the Law, together with other objects entrusted to them, as they used to march with Zion during the days of Moses and Aaron. The mighty warriors of Israel march on the right and the left of the Ark, before it and behind it, singing psalms as if they were the host of heaven rather than simply men created from dust. They destroy their enemies, including a city of vipers with the faces of men and the tails of asses attached to their bellies. The Ark exhausts the strength of their enemies and brings victory whenever David chooses to fight.

However romantic or extravagant we might find the story now, we are told that it was written to answer a serious question. The history of Solomon, the Queen of Sheba and the Ark of Zion is in fact a book within a book. It is provided with a prologue and an epilogue, both of which are written as a dialogue between St Gregory the Wonder Worker and a chorus of 318 Orthodox Fathers, the bishops who attended the Council of Nicaea in AD 325. The prologue claims that the story itself is preserved in a manuscript found in the Church of the Holy Wisdom by Domitius, who is said to have been patriarch of Constantinople, but whose name never appears in the patriarchal list. The story is told here in order to answer a question that had puzzled St Gregory, who is actually not Gregory the Wonder Worker but the Armenian saint Gregory the Illuminator. He had apparently been thrown into a cave because of his devotion to Christ, and he was persecuted for fifteen years. In the midst of his suffering, he began to think about the stupidity of the kings of Armenia, and to ask himself what the glory of kings was supposed to be. Was it based on military power, he wondered. Perhaps it depended on wealth, or on ruling other people. From these meditations, the reader is given a history of the world, beginning with Adam and including an account of how God revealed to both Abraham and Noah that in the generations to come he would send an Ark from heaven that would remain with their descendants.

The prologue describes the creation and the appearance of this Ark in thoroughly miraculous terms. It is said to resemble jasper, topaz, hyacinth and crystal. It catches the eye by force, and it astonishes and stupefies the mind of man. It was made by the mind of God and not by the hand of the artisan. God himself created it as a place for his glory to live. It is a spiritual thing filled with mercy, a heavenly thing filled with light, a thing of freedom and the house of God, who lives in heaven and moves on the earth. It lives among men and among angels – a city of salvation for men and a home for the Holy Spirit. We are told that the Ark contains not only the Tablets of the Law mentioned in the Hebrew Bible, but also the two other objects listed in the New Testament Epistle to the Hebrews: a vessel of gold containing a measure of the manna that came down from heaven, and the rod of Aaron that sprouted after it had become withered, even though no one watered it.

Furthermore, we learn that its creation was an explicitly Christian event, obviously quite different from anything one would find in the Hebrew Bible. The Ark is made by the Christian Trinity – Father, Son and Holy Spirit – to be the place of habitation for their Glory.

The bishops with whom Gregory is speaking confirm that the Ark was created before anything else. 'We understand perfectly that before every created thing, even the angels, before the heavens and the earth, before the pillars of heaven, and the abysses of the sea, he created the Ark of the Covenant.' They go on to describe how essential the Ark has been in the plan that God made to save the world from the consequences of the Fall. It is a prefiguration of the birth of the Redeemer from the womb of the Virgin Mary, God having lived in the Ark just as he lived in the womb of the Virgin before he appeared to the world in a body made from flesh. If the heavenly Zion had not come down and put on the flesh of Adam, they tell us, then God the Word would not have appeared, and salvation would have been impossible. The heavenly Zion should be understood as an image of Mary, the Mother of the Redeemer. The Law that God had written was placed in the Ark of the Covenant. God himself took up residence in the womb of Mary.

While he was in the pit, Gregory saw the future of the world and the end of history. He saw that the Ark of Zion would remain in Ethiopia until Christ appeared again and ruled the world from Mount Zion, when it would return to him. It would then be opened, and the testimony of the Tablets, the manna from the wilderness, the rod of Aaron and the spiritual Zion that came down from heaven would all condemn the Jews. By then, it would be too late for them to repent. They will be sentenced to eternal torment for having denied that Christ was the fulfilment of all the ancient prophecies.

As Gregory and the Orthodox Fathers confirm, the document found in the Church of the Holy Wisdom provides the answer to the question that the saint had asked himself in the pit. The glory of the kings of Ethiopia is to be found in the presence of the Ark of Zion, and their glory surpasses the glory of any other kings, including even the emperors of Byzantium.

There is a great deal that remains mysterious about *The Glory of Kings*, and our attempts to understand it have not been helped by the fact that so many scholars have relied on a translation published over seventy-five years ago by Sir Ernest Wallis Budge. Throughout his career, Budge worked at astonishing speed, and he was often criticized for being careless. With *The Glory of Kings*, the inconsistency of his translation means it is often impossible to understand what is being said about the Ark without consulting either the Ethiopic text published thirteen years earlier by Carl Bezold or the manuscripts themselves, and not everyone has done this.

The most tantalizing questions about the book are very basic. Who wrote it, when and why? After the final chapter, several of the manuscripts contain a colophon purporting to describe the origin of the book, but the colophon itself is mysterious. Parts of it are very difficult to believe, and much is left unsaid. If this book really is the Ethiopian national epic, which claims that the rule of the Ethiopian kings depends on the presence of the Ark of the Covenant, it is obviously essential to understand why it might have been compiled, or why the colophon might have been added. To do this, we need to begin at the ancient kingdom of Aksum, before the Arabian gods were abandoned for a new religion brought from Syria. Other records survive from these early years, and they tell us something very different.

CHAPTER 14

The Spice Road

On the walls of the great Temple of Deir el-Bahri, the oracle of the god Amun has survived for almost thirty-five centuries. 'A command was heard from the great throne,' it proclaims, 'an oracle of the god himself, that the ways of Punt should be searched out, that the highways to the terraces of incense should be penetrated.'

In ancient Egypt, and in the other empires of the Near East, the gods could not live without incense. Its fragrance was believed to nourish them, to call them down from heaven to live among men. The ritual of offering incense would encourage the gods to live within the images prepared for them, opening a door between heaven and earth. In one of the texts inscribed on the Pyramids at Saqqara, the power of incense is explained: 'A stairway to the sky is set up for me, so that I can ascend on it to the sky, and I ascend on the smoke of the great censing.'

Immense quantities of aromatic resins were required for the ancient cults, and these could be obtained only at great cost from peoples who lived at the edge of the world, in the Land of God. With his oracle, Amun was sending the queen of Egypt, a goddess herself, to secure the precious resins of frankincense and myrrh, to preserve the bond between gods and men. The incense was itself divine, it belonged to the gods and its presence on earth was proof that the gods still moved among men.

So the queen sent an expedition by land and by sea – five ships sailing on the Great Green, as the scribes of Egypt called the waters of the Red Sea. When they returned, they were loaded with incense and with the treasures and curiosities of a distant kingdom: gold, leopard skins, baboons, monkeys, even a giraffe. The ships were also loaded with incense trees in pots, the queen obviously hoping that she could offer her god his own land of Punt far to the north of the terraces, in Thebes itself.

In the inscriptions, the queen records her devotion. In answer to the divine command, she proclaims, 'I have led them on water and on land, and I have reached the terraces of incense.' The relief carved on the wall of the temple shows her offering incense to the god with her own hand. 'The best of the incense is upon all her limbs,' we are told, 'her fragrance is divine dew, her odour is mingled with Punt.'

Incense grew on both sides of the Red Sea, in Africa as well as in Arabia, and the animals carved on the temple wall are proof that the Egyptian Land of the God was found on the African shore. As the expedition had travelled by land and by sea, this would seem obvious enough, but there has been a long debate about exactly where Punt lay. Although the queen reports that, before her great expedition, incense had been brought to Egypt 'hand to hand', we know of several other expeditions to the incense kingdoms on the African side. The reign of Hatshepsut seems impossibly remote to us now, but almost a thousand years before her birth, an official of the pharaoh Pepi II travelled over-land to Tigray, the northern province of Ethiopia where the kingdom of Aksum would later arise, and he sent incense back to Egypt.

We know that incense was needed for the cult of the God of Israel, just as it was in Egypt and Babylon. When the Tabernacle was revealed at Mount Sinai, Moses was told that the Israelites would have to construct an altar of gold and acacia wood, and to place it before the veil by the Ark of the Covenant. Aaron was ordered to burn incense on it every morning and every evening, so that the fragrance would rise to heaven throughout the gen-erations. On the Day of Atonement, he was told, the high priest should enter the innermost sanctuary and approach the Ark of the Covenant, protected from the deadly force of the Ark by a cloud of incense. The ritual continued in the Temple that Solomon built in Jerusalem, in whose innermost sanctuary the Ark lay hidden from the gaze of the Israelites, except for the one day in the year on which one man would approach it. Even when the Second Temple was built and the Ark had disappeared, the high priest continued to enter the inner sanctuary with a cloud of incense.

The Second Book of Kings tells us that when the Queen of Sheba came to Jerusalem to test the wisdom of Solomon, she brought gifts with her – camels laden with spices, gold and precious stones. The latter two are conventional enough for any king or queen, but the spices are mentioned first. The word does not refer merely to pepper or cinnamon, valuable as these might have been. It refers to incense, and the trade in this rare commodity would have been the reason for her wealth. Without it, the gods would depart from men, and even the high priest of Israel would be unable to enter the sanctuary of the Ark. It would have to be bought at any price, and the Second Book of Chronicles assures us that the spices brought by the Queen of Sheba surpassed any others. It has even been suggested that incense rather than wisdom might have been the reason for the visit – that she arrived in Jerusalem hoping to encourage a lucrative trade between Sheba and Israel.

Neither of the accounts in the Hebrew Bible tells us where the kingdom of Sheba could be found, and this is frustrating if we are attempting to stēp between biblical and Ethiopian tradition with *The Glory of Kings* as a guide. No ships are mentioned in the Bible, and the Queen is said to have arrived with a caravan. Although she is clearly travelling by land, Jerusalem itself is inland, and a journey across land would have been essential at some point wherever Sheba lay. Elsewhere in the Bible, we learn that the ancestor of Sheba descended from both Shem and Abraham, which means that the people of Sheba would have been related to both Israelites and Africans. This claim lies at the heart of *The Glory of Kings*, but it still tells us little about where Sheba was thought to be.

Despite the conviction of *The Glory of Kings* that the Queen of Sheba was an Ethiopian queen named Makeda, it is often believed that Sheba must have been in Arabia. This is reasonable enough. There was a rich kingdom in South Arabia named Saba, which owed its wealth to the trade in frankincense and myrrh. When the angel Gabriel dictated the Quran to the Prophet Muhammad, as Muslims believe, he recalled the meeting between Solomon and the Queen of Sheba in one of the Surahs, and gave a clear indication where Sheba could be found in another.

In the twenty-seventh Surah, known as 'The Ant', we learn that the wisdom of Solomon allowed him to understand the speech of birds, and that he listened to the voices of the ants as they spoke to one another. One day, he noticed that the hoopoe was not with the other birds that had gathered about him, and he began to wonder about the sort of punishment he should inflict for such disobedience. The bird soon arrives, rather pleased with himself at knowing something that even Solomon does not know. He tells the king that he has been to Sheba, where he has seen a woman who possesses a wonderful throne and enormous wealth, but who worships the sun. It seems that Satan has been keeping her people from the true faith. Solomon is not sure whether he can believe everything that the hoopoe has told him, so he gives a letter to the bird and commands him to deliver it to the queen. When she receives it, she reads the letter to her council. Solomon has apparently told her not to resist him by force of arms. Instead, she should come to Jerusalem and surrender. The counsellors point out that Sheba has a splendid army and that the queen could fight if she chose. But she replies that kings can cause all sorts of problems. She sends Solomon a gift, in the hope that he might become less hostile. Unfortunately, Solomon is not impressed with what she sends, and he decides that it is time for war. As a first step, however, he asks which of his own counsellors will bring him the throne of the queen, before the people of Sheba come to him and surrender. One of the jinns promises to do so, and when the throne is delivered to the palace, Solomon disguises it in order to learn if the queen can recognize it when she arrives. She does recognize it, but when she enters the pavilion, she sees the polished floor and believes it to be water. To keep her clothes from being soaked, she raises her skirts and uncovers her legs. As soon as she sees her mistake, she realizes that she has been outwitted and surrenders with Solomon to the one true God, the Lord of the universe.

In the thirty-fourth Surah, entitled 'Sheba', the Quran provides a clear indication of where the kingdom would have been: 'For Sheba also there was a sign in their dwelling place, two gardens, one on the right and one on the left.' Because the people of Sheba turned away from God, he sent a flood to ruin them. In place of the two gardens that had nourished them, they had only bitter fruit and a few tamarisks.

The two gardens and the flood were believed by most of the

ancient commentators on the Quran to refer to the famous dam of Marib in South Arabia, which was a triumph of engineering in its day. When it collapsed in the sixth century AD, the region was devastated. The great masonry sluices can still be seen on either side of the ruins, on the left and on the right, as the Quran says. Water flowed along them to irrigate the gardens on both sides. For the Prophet, and for the angel who spoke to him, the disaster was still a vivid memory.

Arab tradition maintains that Marib was the capital of the Queen of Sheba, and the ruins of a vast temple that lie near the dam are still called by her name. For the Muslim scholars who wrote about the centuries before the revelation to Muhammad – the Time of Ignorance as they called it – the riches of Sheba and its queen were already part of a lost world. The ruins of the kingdoms in the south, of Sheba and its rival Himyar, had become a theme for poets.

> Himyar and its kings are dead, destroyed by Time:
> Duran by the Great Leveller laid waste.
> Around its courts the wolves and foxes howl,
> And owls dwell there as though it never was.

The reign of Solomon, however, would have ended almost a thousand years before the zenith of the kingdoms of the south. We have almost no idea how extensive the trade might have been when he was king in Jerusalem. Assyrian documents begin to mention Arabs in the ninth century BC, and it may be that a great empire to the north had become interested in them because of the riches passing along the caravan routes from the south to Gaza, and then to Egypt and the Levant. The Spice Road may have existed much earlier. Little evidence survives of the trade, and there has been almost no excavation of caravan cities along the route.

In Africa, the incense of Tigray had been known at a very early date. But could the Queen of Sheba have travelled from Tigray to Jerusalem by land? Hatshepsut may have sent five ships along the coast of Africa, but it was not easy to navigate the Red Sea by sail. The overland route between Tigray and Egypt was passable, but difficult, and the Nile is not navigable between Abyssinia and

Upper Egypt. If a queen from Tigray were going to Jerusalem, she would have to cross the Red Sea at some point anyway. Given the close ties that we know existed between Abyssinia and the kingdoms of South Arabia, an African queen might have chosen to cross immediately, and to take an established route north through caravan cities in the Hejaz.

But if we know that there was a kingdom of Sheba in Arabia, what can be said of Africa? The later prophecies included in the Book of Isaiah mention that Egyptians will come to Zion, along with Cushites and the tall Sebaites, and it would seem natural to assume that these verses refer to three African peoples. Josephus identified Seba with Meroe, a city on the White Nile and the Greek geographer Strabo claimed to know of two cities called Saba and Sabai on the African coast. In recent years, inscriptions have also been found in which the kings of the ancient Ethiopian kingdom called Diamat refer to Saba as lying within their own territory. Even the earliest of this evidence is still several centuries after the Bible tells us that Solomon reigned, but if Ethiopia and Eritrea stop fighting over their border, we may be able to learn a great deal more from excavation. The archaeology of the Horn of Africa has hardly begun.

One of the great mysteries of Ethiopian and Arabian history is whether the sophisticated civilization that arose on the African side of the Red Sea was the result of colonization from South Arabia. There is clearly a mixture of Semitic and Cushitic elements in Ethiopia. The language, the script, the architecture and the pagan religion of Aksum are all closely related to those of South Arabia. The question has become more volatile in recent years, and a suspicion has arisen that earlier scholars were simply unwilling to admit that a high civilization could have emerged from Africa, at least if it were possible to claim that it had been imported by colonists instead. The argument has also been made in the opposite direction, that South Arabia was blessed by the arrival of a sophisticated people from Ethiopia. In fact, the desire to see one side of the Red Sea as the parent and the other as merely a child may lead to confusion. The two areas seem to have been so closely linked that they are better seen as simply part of the same world. In later times, when the power of the Aksumite kings had spread to Arabia, they claimed the title of Saba along with their other dominions.

By then, at least, it would seem possible for a queen in Africa to have ruled a Sheba in Arabia.

Could the Queen of Sheba really have travelled from Ethiopia to Jerusalem and back, as *The Glory of Kings* claims, and could her son David have brought an Israelite Ark with him when he made the same journey? Aside from the absence of any contemporary evidence for either the queen or her son, the real problem is that the early history of Ethiopia is so different from the version offered in *The Glory of Kings*, and so different from what one would have expected if an Israelite Ark had been venerated in the vicinity of Aksum.

After the passing of Diamat and Saba, the kingdom of Aksum arose in the highlands of Tigray. While we know that the site was occupied by the first century BC, and probably even earlier, it soon became a regional power. Even though *The Glory of Kings* never mentions the name, it is here that Ethiopians themselves place the famous queen and the Ark brought by her son. When Francisco Alvares saw the city in the early years of the sixteenth century, he was shown two sarcophagi that were proclaimed to be the treasure chests of the Queen of Sheba, and he was informed that Aksum was 'the city, court, and residence of the Queen Saba, whose own name was Makeda'. Alvares described Aksum as 'situated at the head of a beautiful plain ... almost between two hills,' and the monuments of the ancient city are impressive enough for a famous queen, even if they were erected long after the reign of Solomon.

The *Book of Aksum* mentions fifty-eight stone monoliths, some standing and some fallen. Alvares described them as well, remarking that 'above this town there are many stones standing up, and others on the ground, very large and beautiful, and wrought with handsome designs'. The greatest of the stelae he thought was 'very straight and well worked, made with arcades below, as far as a head made like a half moon'. Two more he saw lying on the ground, 'very large and beautiful, with designs of large arcades, and ornaments of good size'.

The Aksumite stelae are the largest monolithic monuments in the ancient world, surpassing in height even the obelisks of Egypt. Although few people have heard of them, everyone who has seen them seems to have been astonished. 'A very magnificent work of art, formed of a single block of granite and measuring full sixty feet in height,' wrote the English traveller and painter Henry Salt at the end of the eighteenth century. 'The most admirable and perfect monument of its kind.' He thought the decoration bold and elegant, the hollow space running up the centre giving the massive object a lightness of form that had no rivals.

Why would they have been erected, however? Egyptologists who knew of them thought that, like the obelisks in Egypt, they might have been dedicated to the sun god. The stages and doors that were carved on the stelae would have depicted the nine heavens of the gods over whom the sun god ruled. The dedication might have been as they suggested, although now we know that the stelae mark the tombs of the Aksumite kings, and the sacrifices that would have been offered beneath them flowed down into the graves to honour the dead. Despite the history we are given in *The Glory of Kings*, the stelae have no part in the worship of the God of Israel. They were erected long after Solomon would have reigned, and the cult they served was pagan.

In Aksum itself, tradition has little to say of who might have raised these stelae or when, although demons have certainly been suspected. The history repeated along the streets of the city is rich and splendid, invoking the Queen of Sheba from the Old Testament, Queen Candace from the New Testament, the great dragon Arwe, King Romha who raised some of the stelae, Queen Gudit who destroyed some of the others, and dozens of other heroes and heroines. And yet another of the great achievements of the ancient kingdom has allowed a quite different history to be written. It has given us a source of contemporary evidence that does not depend on the inventions or the fallibility of scribes – a source that never mentions Solomon or the Ark of the Covenant.

The power and wealth of Aksum lay in the fact that caravan routes from the hinterland of Africa passed through it. Later accounts of the trade along the Red Sea record that ivory, tortoise shell, rhinoceros horn, hippopotamus hide, animal skins and slaves were transported through Aksum to foreign markets. In return, cloth, weapons, glassware and vessels of bronze and iron were brought into Africa. The ability to erect such immense and elegant stelae is a testimony to the resources possessed by the Aksumite kings, and the trade on which the kingdom relied was both extensive enough and sophisticated enough to support a gold coinage. This was extremely rare in the ancient world, and the coins of Aksum are not only unusual, but also unusually beautiful. They were struck in gold, silver and bronze, and depict the kings adorned with bracelets and magnificent high tiaras. Some coins were struck in a combination of gold and silver – a subtle technique that drew attention to the symbols they displayed. While the coins are fascinating as precious objects, they are also of immense importance as a historical record that has been deeply subversive, undermining the traditional histories of Ethiopian antiquity. They provide a list of kings that is absolutely unlike the lists preserved in the mythical history of Ethiopia. They do something else as well. They allow us to determine the point at which the kings of Aksum abandoned the ancient faith of Arabia, turning, as the Queen of Sheba announces in *The Glory of Kings*, from the worship of the sun to the God of Israel. Yet despite the claims of the epic, the Aksumite kings turn to the God of Israel as he revealed himself in the Christian Messiah.

The Aksumite king Ezana never appears in the traditional lists. He was forgotten in Ethiopia itself. The conversion was attributed to two mythical figures, Abreha and Asbeha, but in the coins of Ezana, who lived during the fourth century, we see the ancient disk and crescent of the gods of Arabia replaced by the Cross of Christ. The inscriptions once referred to him as the 'son of Mahrem', the ancient Aksumite god of war. Now they proclaim that he rules 'in the faith of God and the power of the Father, Son, and Holy Spirit'.

The story told by the coins is confirmed by a foreign and almost contemporary source, the Latin historian Rufinus. Toward the end of the fourth century, a few years after the events he describes, he claims that he met a man who had played a crucial role in the conversion. He is therefore providing an account that seems to be based on direct report, and his version was repeated by other historians in the following decades, including Socrates, Theodoret and Sozomenos.

The story that Rufinus preserves is a tale of adventure, disaster and great reward. It begins when the Syrian merchant Meropius decided to travel from Tyre to 'further India', taking two young relatives with him. The names of the boys were Frumentius and

Aedesius, and it was Aedesius to whom Rufinus claimed to have spoken.

On the voyage back from India, the ship on which the three are travelling stops for provisions, but they are horrified to discover that the treaties between Rome and the people of the port are no longer in force. Everyone on the ship is seized and killed. The boys escape death by chance, it seems. They had gone ashore and were captured while they were reading beneath a tree.

The men who have captured them take them to the king, who keeps them as slaves. While the boys were growing, the king observed that Frumentius was clever and capable, and eventually he appointed him as royal treasurer and secretary. Aedesius is described as 'loyal and honest of heart' but 'simple', and he was made royal cup-bearer – a position that was honourable, but hardly required the same abilities.

When the king died, his queen became regent for their young son. Although Frumentius and Aedesius were both given their freedom, the queen asked them to remain with her, to help her govern the country until her son was old enough to rule by himself. They agreed and Frumentius was given the position of minister.

At this time, Rufinus tells us, 'God stirred up his heart', so that Frumentius began to take an interest in the teachings of Christ. Merchants from Rome had been arriving in the country and were practising the faith, and Frumentius provided land and built churches for them. When the young king came of age, he tried to retain the services of Frumentius and Aedesius as his mother had done, but they were now keen to return to their own country. Aedesius set out for Tyre, where Rufinus would later meet him. Frumentius was keen to encourage the Christian faith at Aksum, and he travelled by way of Alexandria, so that he could tell the patriarch Athanasius about the new churches. He described 'many Christians already congregated, and the churches built on barbarian soil', and suggested that a bishop be appointed. Athanasius agreed, but then asked Frumentius if he could think of anyone else so clearly marked for the task by the spirit of God. The boy whose career began as slave, and who became a royal treasurer and minister, now finds himself consecrated as bishop of Aksum, and ordered back to the highlands of Tigray to supervise the growth of a new church in Ethiopia.

Although Rufinus is the source of almost everything we know about Frumentius, there is one very important addition. The name of Ezana may have disappeared from Ethiopian tradition, but Frumentius is remembered, and the story is confirmed by Athanasius himself, the most famous of all Eastern theologians. Athanasius was responsible for defeating the Arian heresy, in which Christ was said to be merely human and not divine. In his *Apologia*, he preserves a letter that the Roman emperor Constantius II wrote to the rulers of Aksum. It was evidently written about AD 356, and it reveals that the emperor had attempted to summon the Aksumite bishop Frumentius to explain his beliefs before the Arian patriarch of Alexandria. This was the hated George of Cappadocia, described by the historian Ammianus Marcellinus as a 'human snake'. George had been appointed in place of Athanasius, and the emperor was anxious to have his own man determine whether Frumentius was 'worthy to be considered a true bishop and to be ordained according to the law'. He evidently feared that Ethiopia was in the hands of clerics loyal to his enemy, Athanasius.

The consecration of a Syrian in Alexandria may be an apt symbol for the centuries to come. Ethiopia would remain indebted to both Egypt and Syria, but its kings and its clergy became even more fascinated by the ancient world of the Israelites, as they knew it from the Old Testament – a world to which *The Glory of Kings* maintained that the Christian empire owed its birth. But as we have seen with the account of early Israelite history presented in the Bible, the version of early Aksumite history presented in *The Glory of Kings* is quite different from the evidence we find elsewhere. With both Israel and Ethiopia, we have inherited myth as well as history, and it is not always easy to determine the point at which one touches the other.

The Glory of Kings is an attempt to explain a remote past, by people who had in effect lost their history. The discrepancy between the traditional king lists and the evidence of coins and inscriptions is proof of this. The history they write is largely imaginary, even though it does contain essential truths about the legacy that its authors had received from earlier centuries. The problem is not that the Bible contradicts *The Glory of Kings* by telling us that there was an Ark in the Temple at Jerusalem long after the death of Solomon. We have already seen that more than one Ark seems to have been envisaged by earlier sources within the biblical narrative, and *The Glory of Kings* itself tells us that the Jews built another Ark and put it in the Temple, even if it thoroughly disapproves of their doing so. The problem is simply that the traditional history of early Ethiopia and the history that we know from contemporary evidence are so very different. We have impressive remains of pagan Ethiopia, and we can identify the point at which pagan Ethiopia becomes Christian Ethiopia. We do not have any record of an ancient Ethiopian monarchy that followed the God of Israel or announced its adherence to Judaism at any point, although James Bruce and several Jesuit authorities did try to claim that the kingdom had embraced Judaism and then lapsed into pagan idolatry.

We also have no record of the Ark of the Covenant at this date. It is not only that the kings of Aksum fail to mention it in their inscriptions or on their coins, but that no one else does either. One visitor to Aksum might have been expected to do so. This was Kosmas Indikopleustes, the 'Indian Mariner', an Alexandrian merchant who wrote a *Christian Topography* in which he attempted to explain the structure of the universe. He was convinced that the Ark was an image of heaven and the Tabernacle an image of the visible world, and he writes of them both in terms that recall the mystical symbolism of Philo and Josephus. He was clearly fascinated by the Ark and the Tabernacle as keys to the mystery of the cosmos, and manuscripts of his *Topography* contain detailed illustrations to help his readers understand how they had been constructed. Even though he was in Aksum during the sixth century, and copied historical inscriptions for the Aksumite king of the day, he never mentions the Ark. He also believes that the Queen of Sheba was Arabian and not African.

It is often assumed that an ancient cult of the Ark is reflected in the dedication of the great church of Aksum to Mary of Zion, and in the fact that Ethiopian churches are built in imitation of the Temple of Solomon. However tantalizing these assumptions may seem, neither of them inspires confidence.

It is usually claimed that the 'cathedral' church of Aksum has been dedicated to Mary of Zion since antiquity, but few people seem to have looked at the evidence. It is simply taken for granted on the basis of Ethiopic texts such as the *Lives* of the saints or the

Book of Aksum, even though these were written more than a thousand years after the church is believed to have been founded. The dedication is not actually attested in any document of Aksumite date. Although it could be old, it does not appear in the records until many centuries later. Indeed, we lack any genuine information about the church of Mary of Zion during the whole of its existence until Alvares described it in 1520.

Ethiopian theologians did identify Zion with Mary. The Ark of the Covenant that contained the Law was seen as a forerunner of the Ark that held the New Law in the person of Christ. Yet whether such an identification existed in the early days of the Ethiopian Church remains unknown. No extant source actually names 'Zion' in Ethiopia at anything like such an early date, and no information survives about the dedication of any church in Aksum.

The earliest records of a dedication to 'Zion' that might have applied to a church at Aksum seem to date only from the medieval Solomonid dynasty, specifically to the reign of Amda Seyon, who came to the throne in 1312. At this time, 'Zion' was employed as a name for the kingdom, and the expression 'church of Zion' was included among the honorifics of the king in the Mamluk chancellery records. The designation might refer to the church of Mary of Zion, but it might also refer to the Ethiopian kingdom in general.

Even though *The Glory of Kings* describes the arrival of the Ark in Ethiopia, and even though the Ark was generally believed to dwell in the church of Mary of Zion, the book never refers to this church or to any seat of the Ark other than the mysterious 'Debra Makeda', where it was installed during the life of Makeda, the Queen of Sheba. If *The Glory of Kings* was compiled by the *nebura'ed* of Aksum – and we shall see that it probably was – this is extraordinary.

The churches of Ethiopia are so numerous that Jeronimo Lobo remarked that 'one can nowhere give a shout without it being heard at least at one church or monastery and very often at many of both'. These churches are often seen as an outward and visible sign of an ancient Judaic legacy in the country. They are thought to represent the Temple of Jerusalem, built in a Christian kingdom as a legacy of Israelite devotion. In particular, their division into three distinct areas is thought to imitate a similar division in the

Temple, an idea that seems to have originated with Job Ludolf in the late sixteenth century.

Those who have defined the supposed relationship of the round Ethiopian churches with the Temple have assigned to each of the three parts an equivalent in the Israelite model. The theory is that the form of the Israelite sanctuary was preferred to the basilica accepted by early Christians elsewhere because the Ethiopian cult was based on the Ark of the Covenant. But it is curious that the theory has been advanced about Ethiopian round churches; the Temple in Jerusalem is not described in the Bible as being round.

The round churches that are now thought to be so typically Ethiopian raise a number of questions. No Aksumite example is known. None is known from the time of the Zagwe, who rose to power in the twelfth century, and none can be dated with confidence even to the early years of the Solomonid dynasty who replaced them. The round church is almost certainly a late form of ecclesiastical structure in Ethiopia. An early record of one is preserved by Manoel de Almeida, who describes the round church of Amba Geshen built by the emperor Naod, who ruled from 1495 to 1508.

The most important reason for building round churches may have been that traditional houses in the central highlands of Ethiopia are usually round. This was the seat of power under the Solomonid emperors, and the new type of church seems to reflect the spread of Christianity into the regions where this style of domestic architecture was predominant. But this would not explain the interior structure of the church, and if one were to look for a model that satisfied Ethiopian religious aspirations when these round churches were built, there are two obvious candidates. Both are in Jerusalem, and both are octagonal structures in which a venerated stone is surrounded by two ambulatories: the church of the Holy Sepulchre and the Dome of the Rock.

Before the earliest of the round churches seems to have been built, the Solomonid emperors of Ethiopia were in regular communication with Jerusalem. Yigba Seyon even wrote and sent gifts to Ethiopian monks addressed 'to the city of Jerusalem, and to the tomb of the Messiah, my Lord'. Along with the Zagwe kings before them, they could not have failed to know the form of such a venerated tomb. They are known to have been keenly interested in the Holy City, and the emperor Yeshaq is said to have ordered a massacre of Muslims in 1423 when he learned that the Church of the Resurrection had been closed. The embassies of later emperors are also recorded, such as that of Eskender in 1481, which arrived with a decree from the sultan in Cairo permitting Ethiopians to enter the Holy Sepulchre for the ceremony of the holy fire. Ethiopians are known to have visited the convent of Mount Zion in the same year.

The *Rules of the Church* gives a detailed account of the symbolic meaning of almost every aspect of an Ethiopian church, and makes no explicit comparison between the church and the Temple in Jerusalem. It also never mentions the Ark of the Covenant in connection with the altar slab known as the *tabot*, even though this identification is commonly made. Instead, all the objects within the inner sanctuary of the church are associated with the death of Christ and his tomb. They recall the Holy Sepulchre rather than the Temple.

The Dome of the Rock is perhaps even more intriguing, and it is curious that it does not seem to have been noticed by those who claim that Ethiopian round churches are imitations of the Temple. The Dome has stood on the Temple Mount since AD 691, and before long Christian pilgrims who arrived from western Europe began to refer to it as the 'Temple of Solomon', even though the Bible told them that this Temple had been destroyed. By the eleventh century, not only was the Dome of the Rock often thought to be the Temple, but its octagonal shape was also described as being 'circular'. Until the fifteenth century, this curious tradition appears in accounts of pilgrims and visiting clergy, even though some of them at least were aware that the Dome had been built as a Muslim shrine. Eastern pilgrims also developed their particular term for the structure, calling it 'the Church of the Holy of Holies', in the belief that a secret room had been made under the rock, in which the rod of Aaron and the Tablets of the Law lay hidden among other relics once contained in the Ark. It would be ironic if an Ethiopian institution believed to be part of the legacy of Judaism and the cult of the Ark were in fact a copy of a Muslim building, which was itself based upon a Christian church. We would find ourselves in a web of symbols that led us in a circle.

If the claims made in *The Glory of Kings* seem to be later, the most important question is how much later. Our answer will depend on what we can discover about who might have written the book and why. It is a story that speaks of a people whom God has chosen, and a people whom he has rejected. Any decision about who these people might be, and any attempt to live by that decision, would be of immense political importance.

CHAPTER 15

The Aksumite Crusade

The Syrian priests had reached the Lakhmid camp at Ramla when the messenger arrived. Luck, it seems, was against the king who had written the letter. He was a Jew, and he had slaughtered the Christians who lived among the Jews of South Arabia. He was now writing to the Persian emperor and his Arab vassals, urging them to follow his example and kill anyone who shared the faith of their Roman enemies. But his letter to the Lakhmid king Mundhir III was not only delivered when the embassy of the Roman emperor was discussing terms of peace, it also fell into the hands of the imperial legate, the Syrian archbishop Simeon of Beth Arsham. The letters that he began to write when he heard the news of Christians having been martyred would destroy the Jewish state.

Simeon hoped that his letters would move the Patriarch of Alexandria to write to the Christian king of Ethiopia and urge him to send troops to Arabia to defend the faith. He also hoped that he could encourage Christians throughout the East to venerate the new Arabian martyrs. He succeeded in both his aims.

This was not just a question of religion. Arab tribes living along the frontier between the empires of Rome and Persia were involved in the struggle between the two great powers. They could be useful allies, and tribal disputes could serve as pretext for invasion, if any pretext were needed. By the early sixth century, two great confederations of tribes faced each other along the imperial marches. The Ghassanids moved through the deserts in the south and west, and the Lakhmids to the north and east of them. They had not merely adopted the politics of the imperial patrons. They were hostile to each other. Just as Rome and Persia used them, so they attempted to ensnare the great powers in their own struggles, exploiting the rivalry of their masters for their own ends.

Unlike the Ghassanids, who were Christian, the Lakhmids were pagan, although they eventually converted as their power waned in the sixth century. The accounts that survive of Mundhir, the Lakhmid king, can be confusing. He is said to have been an orthodox Christian who confounded the clergy sent by Severus of Antioch to convert him to the monophysite position. But he is also said to have been violently hostile to the Christian faith, sacrificing 400 Christian girls captured from a church or convent in Roman territory to the Arabian goddess al-Uzza.

The Jewish king had slaughtered the Christians at Najran, a caravan city built where the trade routes from South Arabia went their separate ways, one to Iraq and the other to the Mediterranean by way of the Hejaz. It had been built in a fertile valley, into which water flowed from the hills above it, and whose villages were surrounded with palms. Only ruins remain. Among the Christians of Najran, there were both Monophysites and Nestorians, each side convinced that its rival maintained heretical beliefs on the difficult question of how Christ could have been both human and divine. It seems that the Nestorians joined the Jews in massacring their Monophysite neighbours. When the Christians of Najran had been simply Nestorian, relations between Christians and Jews seem to have been amicable enough. Suspicion and hostility had grown dramatically as Monophysites became more numerous and more powerful. It would prove disastrous for Jewish interests that the Monophysites in Najran were in communion with the Syrian archbishop who read the letter in the camp at Ramla, with the Coptic Patriarch of Alexandria who would hear of it, and with the king of Aksum to whom the patriarch would write.

Simeon of Beth Arsham was not only a Monophysite archbishop, but also a highly effective apologist, a skilful publicist and a vigorous man of letters. To provoke as many authorities as he could, Simeon emphasized the role that the Jews of Tiberias had played in the events, drawing attention to their gravity in international terms. Tiberias was within the Roman empire, and given the history of Jewish rebellion against Rome, the matter could be presented as a serious threat. There may have been Jewish agents from other areas outside Roman control, such as Medina, but the most intriguing claim that Simeon makes is that the agents were 'Jewish priests' rather than rabbis.

Top left The 'Ark of Ishmael' photographed by Carl Raswan when he rode with the Ruwala bedouin, and included in his book *The Black Tents of Arabia*, published in 1935.

Top right The *mahmal*, which was still carried by the lead camel of the *haj* caravan in the early years of the twentieth century.

Above The 'Ark of Ishmael' leading the Ruwala through the desert, photographed by Carl Raswan.

Aksumite gold coins issued by Ezanas before and after his conversion to Christianity in the fourth century. At the top of the coin on the left is the pagan disk and crescent; at the top of the coin on the right is the Cross of Christ.

Title page of *Prester John of the Indies*, the first account of Ethiopia to be published in Europe, written by the Portuguese chaplain Francisco Alvares and printed at Lisbon in 1540.

Above The Church of St George, carved from the rock at Lalibela.

Moses receiving the Tablet of the Law, from an Ethiopian Octateuch of the late sixteenth century brought to the British Museum in 1868 from the imperial library of Tewodros II.

The Virgin Mary as a child brought to the Temple in Jerusalem, from a seventeenth-century manuscript of the *Miracles of Mary*. The Temple is depicted as a circular structure, reminiscent of Ethiopian round churches.

Christ grants the Covenant of Mercy to the Virgin, from a seventeenth-century manuscript of the *Miracles of Mary*.

David enters Jerusalem with the Ark of the Covenant hidden under brocade and carried on the head of a priest in the manner of a *tabot*, while his wife Michal looks down in horror.

An eighteenth-century manuscript painting of Moses receiving the Ark of Zion in the form of a *tabot*, which is then covered in brocade and carried on the head according to contemporary Ethiopian custom.

Engraving of a *tabot* with the inscription 'Ark of Zion', included by Hormuzd Rassam in his *Narrative of the British Mission to Theodore*, published in 1869.

An engraving of the Ethiopian emperor Yohannes IV, who requested that the British Museum return the manuscript of *The Glory of Kings* that had belonged to the emperor Tewodros II.

Facing page, above
The modern Chapel of the Tablet, next to the old Church of Mary of Zion at Aksum.

Facing page, below
The round church of Entoto Maryam, built in the nineteenth century above Addis Ababa.

Priests in procession at *Timqat*, carrying *tabotat* draped in brocade on their heads.

Below Dabtaras dancing at *Timqat*, holding prayer sticks and sistra.

In the letters that he wrote, Simeon provided a detailed account of the martyrdoms. They are disturbing to read even now. In fact, they may be more disturbing to read now than they were at the time. The persecutors are described as being driven by a sadism that is both ingenious and energetic, and the persecuted reveal a longing for death that seems suicidal. In his second letter, Simeon describes the burning of a church filled with Christians. Apparently, the Jews collected the bones of all the martyrs and carried them into the church, where they placed them in a pile. Then they brought in the priests, the deacons, the subdeacons, the readers and the sons and daughters of the covenant, as well as the laity, both men and women. The church was packed from wall to wall with people, some 2,000 according to the men who arrived from Najran. Having piled wood all around the outside of the church, they set light to it, burning the building and everyone inside it. There were a few women who had not been captured by the Jews. When they saw that the church was in flames, and realized that the Christians inside it were dying, they ran toward it calling out to one another that they should hurry to enjoy the sweet odour of the sacrifice. Then they rushed into the fire themselves and were burnt alive.

As well as being put to the torch, the martyrs at Najran were crushed, scalded with boiling oil, torn apart by animals and forced to drink the blood of their children. All this may have been expected by Syriac readers, who were accustomed to their heroes displaying a ferocious asceticism and a conviction that the body must be defeated at any price. The more appalling the tortures, the greater the victory for Christ.

The main source for the massacre is the *Book of the Himyarites*, which was discovered by chance when Axel Moberg was examining the binding of a liturgical manuscript in the early years of the twentieth century. It had been cut into pieces some 500 years before and used as stuffing for the cover. Only part of it survives, although we do have the table of contents. The entire book would have provided a full account of Christianity in Himyar, until the return of Kaleb to Aksum, and although the author is not known, it may have been written by Simeon himself.

The martyrdoms it describes are suitably appalling, but the book as a whole is fascinating, and the writing is vivid and dramatic. In the midst of a particularly harrowing description of the deaths of an elderly woman and her granddaughter, the author interrupts the narrative to tell his readers that men have just arrived from Najran, and have confirmed and explained the events that he is reporting, correcting one or two details. Nevertheless, the martyrdoms contain a compilation of conventional abuse directed by one side or the other against its enemies, and it is this that the modern reader may find more sickening than the atrocities, if only because we are aware of the depravities committed in our own time. When the Jewish king tries to persuade the elderly woman to escape death by admitting that Christ was simply a man, her granddaughter spits at him and tells him that she has done so because he has urged them all to spit on the Cross. She rejects him, and she rejects everyone who tells them to reject Christ. She then makes a wish that his mouth will be shut, and she denounces him as a Jew who has killed his Lord.

This accusation of deicide was enough for one distinguished Jewish scholar to regard the entire episode as the usual Christian attempt to provoke a slaughter of Jews by making them responsible for the worst crime imaginable. Certainly the charge was repeated in medieval and modern Europe as a sure way of inflaming hostility and violence, and it created a climate of hatred and bigotry that contributed to the horrors perpetrated under the Third Reich. In this case, however, even if the language of the letters of Simeon and the *Book of the Himyarites* seems to be conventional diatribe, and even if the letter attributed to the Jewish king is nothing more than a forgery, the inscriptions that the king himself erected indicate that he was proud of having destroyed churches and killed those whom he regarded as his enemies.

He would not seem to have provoked the conflict himself, however, and the worst of his outrages seems to have been committed in response to Christians burning a synagogue. As in most religious conflicts, it can be very difficult to regard one side or other as blameless. Hostility between Jews and Christians in South Arabia had certainly occurred in the previous century. The *Acts of the Martyr Azqir* survive in Ethiopic and describe how the saint met his death during the reign of Sharah-bil Yakkuf, the king of Saba, Raydan, Hadramawt and Yamanat, who is known to have been on the throne in 467.

There was a great deal more involved than merely the loathing that Jews and Christians felt for one another. As with the rivalry between the Ghassanids and the Lakhmids, the great empires were attempting to frustrate the ambitions of the enemy and advance their own interests. Rome was supporting Christians, and Persia was supporting Jews. Even though they had signed a truce early in the sixth century, they continued to intrigue in South Arabia through their agents. A Roman expedition occupied the Jewish trading colony on the island of Yotabe, and by about 520 Ethiopian troops were invading South Arabia. Even before the Jewish king Dhu Nuwas came to throne, it seems that the struggle had acquired a religious dimension. His father had begun to persecute Christians, probably because he saw them as agents for Ethiopian expansion.

When the Christian missionary Theophilus came to South Arabia in the fourth century, he found a great many Jews there. Legends preserved by the Jews of South Arabia claim that the religion had been introduced after the Queen of Sheba returned from visiting King Solomon in Jerusalem. Their union had produced a son, who was raised in South Arabia as a Jew. Solomon had sent Jews from Israel to supervise his education and training, and when they arrived, they built a fortress near Sana.

The Arab historian Ibn Ishaq also reports that missionary rabbis were brought to South Arabia by the last Tubba king of Yemen, Tiban Asad Abu Karib. He had led his armies against the Jews of Medina, but when two rabbis impressed him with their knowledge, he converted to Judaism and brought them to Himyar. His people had refused to allow the rabbis to enter the kingdom until they faced the local pagan priests in a series of trials by fire. Like the heroes of the Bible, the rabbis emerged from the flames unharmed.

Ibn Ishaq also tells us that the son of Tiban Asad Abu Karib was overthrown by Lakhnia Yanuf Dhu Shanatir, whose strategy to consolidate power depended on two tactics. He either killed the leaders of the great families, or he sodomized them, so that their shame would make them unfit for rule. Dhu Nuwas was evidently handsome enough for the latter to be attractive and Ibn Ishaq describes how he killed the king and secured the throne for himself.

The name 'Dhu Nuwas' seems to mean 'the Lord of the Curl' or something similar, and the coins and statues of the Himyarite kings depict them with long hair that falls in curls past their shoulders. In the inscriptions, however, his name appears as Yusuf Asar Yathar. His mother was Jewish, from Nisibis, which was an important centre of Jewish intellectual life and the location of the school of Judah Bar Bathyra. The city lay within the Persian sphere of influence, and both its Jewish legacy and its ties to Persia would be important in the career of the young king.

One day, Ibn Ishaq reports, the king sent for Dhu Nuwas, the son of Tiban Asad and brother of Hassan. He had been a little boy when Hassan was murdered, and had become a handsome young man who possessed both character and intelligence. When the messenger arrived, Dhu Nuwas understood what the king was planning, took a sharp knife and hid it under the sole of his foot. As soon as they were alone, he rushed at the king and stabbed him to death. He then cut off his head and put it in the window that overlooked the guards below. As he walked out, they asked him what had happened, and he told them to talk to the head in the window. They looked up, and when they saw the severed head of Lakhnia, they set off in pursuit of Dhu Nuwas. 'You must become king,' they told him, 'now that you have disposed of this revolting man.' So they made him king, and all the tribes of Himyar joined him. He was the last of the Yemeni kings. When he adopted Judaism, Himyar followed him.

This lurid account of the transfer of power may omit some of its political implications. The chronicle written by Zacharias of Mitylene records that Aksumite kings had the right to appoint the kings of Himyar. By claiming the throne himself, Dhu Nuwas may have been exerting a dangerous independence. When he interfered with Roman merchants, it seems, and began to slaughter Christians, the entire situation may have been too much for the Aksumite king to endure.

Political disturbance and civil unrest was bound to disrupt trade, and this may have been the reason that Dhu Nuwas himself seems to have borrowed large amounts of money from a Christian in Najran. Apparently, the loan did not solve his financial problems, and he was forced to ask for more. The booty of war could provide a source of revenue even if trade were collapsing, and his expedition against the Ethiopians who had settled in Zafar, Mukha and Najran may have been a way of meeting his debts as much as anything. While he burned their churches, he also seems to have carried off enormous amounts of loot.

As tensions rose between Jews and Christians, the synagogue at Najran was burned. Hayyan ibn Hayyan, a leading figure in the Monophysite community, was said to have instigated the attack. Dhu Nuwas now embarked on the persecution that led to his downfall. He had already imposed Judaism as a state religion in Himyar, meeting any resistance with force. The *Book of the Himyarites* reports that he swore oaths by the Ark of the Covenant and the Law of Moses, which suggests an Israelite warrior from the days of Joshua.

The Chronicle of Zacharias of Mitylene claims to have preserved the letter that Dhu Nuwas sent to Mundhir, the king of the Lakhmids.

> I became king over the whole country of the Himyarites, and I resolved to kill all Christians who confessed Christ unless they became Jews like us. And I killed two hundred and eighty men, the priests whom I found as well as the Ethiopians who were guarding the church. And I made their church into a synagogue for us. Then with a force of a hundred and twenty thousand men, I went to Najran, their royal city. When I had camped before it for some days and was not able to take it, I swore oaths to them, and their chiefs came out to me. But I thought it right not to keep my word to the Christians, who were my enemies. I arrested them, and made them bring their gold and their silver and their possessions. They brought these to me, and I took them. I also asked for Paul their bishop, and when they told me that he was dead, I did not believe them until they showed his grave. Then I dug up his bones and burned them, along with their church and their priests and everyone that tried to escape.

It may seem unlikely that the king would boast of breaking his word in this way, and one wonders if this part of the letter was written as Christian propaganda. Nevertheless, the general policy is supported by inscriptions that Dhu Nuwas erected. One found along the road to Najran describes him destroying the church and killing the Ethiopians in Zafar, the capital of Himyar.

News of these atrocities soon reached the Aksumite king. The *Book of the Himyarites* tells of a woman named Hammayya who fled to Ethiopia and informed the bishop and the king of what had occurred. Arab historians report that a Najranite named Daur Dhu Thalaban escaped the massacre and brought news of it to Kaleb, proving his veracity by showing the king a copy of the Gospel that had been damaged in the fire. He begged the king and the bishop to help the Christians of Arabia by sending an army against the Jewish king.

When the letter of Simeon of Beth Arsham reached Constantinople, the Roman emperor Justin I wrote to the patriarch of Alexandria, asking him to persuade Kaleb to organize an expedition to Arabia to avenge the martyrs. The patriarch wrote the letter and sent twelve priests to the court at Aksum with instructions that they should deliver it to the king. They found that he was already preparing his troops for an invasion. He was building 70 large ships at Adulis and 100 smaller ones. Eventually, he assembled a fleet of over 200 and before he sent it across the Red Sea toward Arabia, he asked for the blessing of Abba Pantelewon, one of the Nine Saints, who was living in a cave near Aksum. The saint promised that he would pray constantly for the king, who would return victorious.

When the expeditionary force arrived in Arabia, Kaleb succeeded in trapping Dhu Nuwas in an attack from two sides. According to Arab tradition, the Jewish king escaped his enemy in a dramatic gesture of defiance. 'When he saw the fate that had befallen him and his people, he turned to the sea and setting spurs to his horse, rode through the shallows until he reached the deep water.' Dhu Nuwas plunged into the waves of the Red Sea and was never seen again.

After his victory, Kaleb is said to have appointed the son of the martyr Arethas as chief of Najran and to have built three churches there, one dedicated to 'The Holy Martyrs and the Glorious Arethas'. Najran and its martyrs became the object of a cult that spread throughout the Christian world, as Simeon had hoped. Their deaths may be remembered in the Quran as well. The eighty-fifth Surah, known as 'The Mansion of the Stars', is usually thought to contain an echo of the martyrdoms. Ibn Hisham and al-Tabari tell us that the Jews of Yemen were the 'men of the trench'. Their victims are simply called 'the believers'.

The men of the trench were slain,
the fire stoked with fuel
when they sat above it
and were themselves witnesses of what they did to the believers.
They took revenge on them only because they believed in God ...

After Dhu Nuwas was defeated, Kaleb established Sumyafa Ashwa as viceroy in Himyar, but after four or five years he was deposed by Abreha, an Aksumite. The Greek historian Procopius describes Sumyafa as Himyarite by birth, and he says that Abreha had once been the slave of a Christian merchant at Adulis. Of the Ethiopian army, he writes, many of the slaves and all the other soldiers who were inclined to break the law had no intention of following the king. They stayed in Arabia with the aim of seizing the land of the Himyarites, which is extremely rich. Before long, they revolted against Esimiphaios, as he calls Sumyafa. They put him in prison and appointed another king for the Himyarites. The new king was Abramos, or Abreha.

The Arab historian al-Tabari agrees that Ethiopians who had remained in the Yemen rebelled against the authority of Aksum and its viceroy. Kaleb apparently attempted to restore Aksumite control by sending an army of 3,000 men under the command of one of his relatives. Unfortunately, the army defected, killing the leader and joining Abreha. Kaleb sent another expedition, but when Abreha defeated it, he was left to rule as he pleased.

Abreha used the titles 'king of Saba, Himyar, Hadramawt, Yamanat, and all their Arabs of the Coastal Plain and the Highlands', and as a Christian king of the Yemen, he built a new church at Sana. Muslim sources claim that he was attempting to create a rival sanctuary that would draw pilgrims from Mecca. At the time, it was a pagan shrine, in the hands of the Quraysh. When his plans were frustrated by the Quraysh – and some sources claim that they succeeded in defiling the church in Sana – he sent a punitive expedition against Mecca. His army included elephants, and in Islamic tradition, the expedition is believed to have been sent in the year that the Prophet was born. It is celebrated as the Year of the Elephant, and Surah 105 in the Quran, which is known as 'The Elephant', is usually believed to refer to this.

Did you not see how your Lord dealt with the Men of the Elephant?
Did he not bring their plans to nothing,
And send against them birds in flights
pelting them with stones of baked clay . . .

After his defeat, which the Quran describes as a miracle sent by God, the Jews in the Yemen took up arms again. The area has been called a cockpit for the rival religions in the East, and in the end, Kaleb had achieved little by his victory. He had created a vacuum of power that Aksum could not fill itself. The Persians were waiting and could not be kept out. They remained, until they faced the armies of the Prophet.

This is the only time in the long history of Judaism and Christianity that the two met as rival state religions. The victory of the Christian king over the Jewish king may now be almost forgotten, and both religions were to disappear from most of Arabia within a few years. Islam began as a revival of the original faith of Abraham, but the failure of Jews and Christians to recognize it as such meant that it became the third of the great Semitic religions. It expelled its rivals from the holy land in which the Prophet had been born. The victory of Kaleb was never forgotten in Ethiopia, however, and while many of the kings of Aksum whose names appear in the later lists are merely legendary, Kaleb has remained a historical king whose achievements really were the stuff of legend.

He is the only Ethiopian king to be mentioned in *The Glory of Kings*, and this has suggested that the great epic might actually have been written much earlier than its colophon would seem to suggest. Why would no other king be included, especially if it were written at a time when the Zagwe and the Solomonid dynasty that followed them had been fighting over the right to rule in the name of new Israel? If this were such a point of honour for later kings – the basis of their claim to rule – why would none of them have been mentioned in the epic itself, rather than merely in the colophon? Why were the Zagwe not denounced as usurpers, or the Solomonids praised as rightful kings?

It has also seemed odd that *The Glory of Kings* should be so obsessed with Jews, and with the superiority of Christianity over Judaism, and yet never mention Islam. In later centuries, Jews were not a threat in Ethiopia, but Muslims were. The empire of Rome is also described as a great power in the world, which it was during the reign of Kaleb but was certainly not by the time that *The Glory of Kings* is usually thought to have been written.

To provide an answer to these curiosities, one of the greatest authorities on ancient Arabia has suggested that the epic was largely written at the time when Judaism and Christianity were rivals in the region, and that it represents a battle that was itself epic between two kings who were determined to rule in the biblical image. Both had adopted the names of Israelite heroes. Kaleb may even have regarded South Arabia as a Promised Land, which should be his to rule because he claimed descent from the Queen of Sheba. Furthermore, he seems to have possessed a 'Solomon complex': to have become obsessed with building churches just as his ancestor had built the great Temple in Jerusalem. He is described as an imaginative and mystically inclined Crusader.

The suggestion is seductive, perhaps because it is imaginative and mystically inclined itself. It may not provide convincing answers, however. *The Glory of Kings* is presented as an antiquarian document, so it should not be expected to refer to later kings or later events. Whatever threat Islam presented in later centuries, Christianity has always needed to define itself against the Judaic traditions from which it emerged. Islam may seem to have been a much greater threat to Christian empires than Judaism was, and the conversion to Islam of Christians in conquered territories may have meant a dramatic reduction in the numbers of believers, but Judaism has usually been a much greater challenge to the Christian faith. Christians and Jews share a common scripture, which Christians and Muslims do not, and for this reason alone there is a profound sense of tension between the two rival interpretations. Beyond this, we shall see that the Solomonid emperors of Ethiopia were convinced that they were threatened by people called *ayhud*, or 'Jews'. With this in mind, the polemic in *The Glory of Kings* could easily reflect the anxieties of a later age.

The real problem with attempting to date *The Glory of Kings* to the sixth century is that we have so little evidence. Much of the argument is based on assuming that the traditions of Solomon and Sheba on which the epic relies were already current among

Ethiopians, and that the Ark of the Covenant was already believed to be preserved at Aksum. Yet there is no evidence for either of these assumptions. There is no reason to believe that the kings of Aksum had already begun to proclaim descent from Solomon and Sheba, and there is no reason to believe that they claimed the Ark was in Aksum. They may have, but we are facing an argument from silence. It would be difficult to prove that it is mistaken, but no easier to prove that it is correct.

It is intriguing, however, that anyone who believes that *The Glory of Kings* was written at such an early date has not also claimed that this was the very time in which Ethiopians begin to be fascinated by the Ark and by Israelite descent. Could it have arisen in the midst of the Crusade that Kaleb launched against the Jews of Arabia? This was certainly a religious war, and it was fought between two kings whose religions laid claim to the same ancient legacy. One of them is said to have sworn by the Ark of the Covenant and the Law of Moses. The other was fighting in the name of a saviour who came to fulfil that Law, and of whom the Ark was said to have been a prophecy or a prototype. Arab traditions certainly claim that the Ark was in Arabia, and that it passed to the Jurhum, a tribe who controlled the shrine at Najran. Is it possible that the Jewish king had gained control of the Ark? Had it again become a weapon in the battle to establish and secure a Jewish state? We are told that there were Jewish priests in Najran, who would be the most likely men to preserve a knowledge of its use, and who might have retained an interest in the Temple ritual that it would need. For them, it might have been a matter of professional responsibility and aspiration. Is it possible that Kaleb could have won it in battle, and that the imaginative and mystical theory already rejected is not quite imaginative and mystical enough?

If the Ark was to be brought from Ethiopia to Arabia, this was certainly the time at which Ethiopians were in Arabia in large numbers. After Abraha attempted to march on Mecca, it would only be a few years until the revelation of Islam. The political situation would soon change dramatically, the power of Aksum would decline until its kings began to move south, and the Dark Ages would begin from which the Zagwe would emerge, Abu Salih would claim that the Ark was in Ethiopia, and rival dynasties would fight to rule in the name of the kings of Israel.

The only other time in which Ethiopia and Arabia would be in such close contact occurred after the Prophet Muhammad found that the people of Mecca were generally opposed to the revelation he had received from God. As their hostility grew, and as his life in Mecca became more precarious, some of his first followers found refuge with the king of Aksum. The wife of the Prophet was among them. Of all the Christian kings to whom the Prophet sent letters informing them that God had spoken to him, the Ethiopian was the most favourable, and his reception of the refugees ensured that friendship existed for several generations between Ethiopian Christians and the new Muslim power to the north.

Still, there is no proclamation that the Ark had arrived. It would be nearly seven centuries before Abu Salih heard of it in Cairo. Yet the history of the Ark is a curious thing, and the Bible is often silent about it for what seems to be long periods of time. It may be that a Christian king, for whom the presence of God had been revealed in the person of Christ, did not attach the same importance to the Ark that we might expect. Perhaps the prophecy of Jeremiah had been fulfilled, and the Ark no longer came to mind. The silence is tantalizing, but it should not be discouraging. The Ark will reappear.

In South Arabia as well, it seems that dreams of an Ark remained alive across the centuries. A prophet named al-Mukhtar ibn Ali Ubayd al-Thaqafi is reported by the historian al-Himyari to have had an Ark, which he wrapped in brocade and carried on a grey mule. He claimed that the angel Gabriel had revealed a Quran to him as well as to the Prophet Muhammad. Together with his companions, he would walk around his Ark as if it were the Kaba, and they would proclaim that the Ark was with them, like the Ark of the People of Moses.

CHAPTER 16

The Ark of Lalibela

Francisco Alvares stood beside the mule he had ridden since the early morning, and looked about in astonishment. Even after fifteen years, when the Portuguese mission had returned to Lisbon and he published his account of the marvels he had seen in Ethiopia, this was the sight that would still seem beyond his powers of description. 'I weary of writing more about these buildings, because it seems to me that I shall not be believed if I write more,' he complained. 'Therefore I swear by God, in whose power I am, that all that I have written is the truth, and there is much more than I have written.'

He had arrived at the sacred city of Roha, now called Lalibela after the king who is believed to have founded it. The city was a complex of churches, 'the like of which and so many, cannot, as it appears to me, be found in the world, and they are churches entirely excavated in the rock, very well hewn'. The skill displayed by the masons was so great 'that neither a jeweller in silver, nor a worker of wax in wax, could do more'.

According to tradition, Lalibela had carved the city from the highlands of Lasta over three centuries before Alvares stepped ashore at Massawa in 1520, at a time when legends of a mysterious Ethiopian priest-king had begun to be told in the courts of Europe. The day before he arrived at Roha, Alvares had been shown the tomb of this 'Prester John' for which the princes of Europe had been searching, and a book that described his extraordinary status as both king and priest. 'They also say that this King was a mass priest for forty years,' Alvares reported. 'Among other miracles which they related of this King, and which they read to me in this book, is that when he wished to celebrate the angels served to him what was requisite, that is, bread and wine, and this was in those forty years that he was in retreat.'

The discoveries that Alvares made in the highlands of Lasta were the culmination of a long campaign to locate the lost Christians of the Orient, for Prester John had variously been thought to rule among the Turkish nomads and caravan cities of Central Asia, among the Christians of St Thomas in South India, and among the African kingdoms of Nubia and Ethiopia. He was first mentioned in the *History of Two Cities* by Otto of Freising, who had heard a rumour of him in 1145, during a conversation at Viterbo with Hugh, the bishop of Jabala in the Lebanon. Some twenty years later, a letter written in Latin and purporting to be from the king himself was circulated in Europe. 'Prester John,' it proclaimed, 'by the grace of God most powerful king over all Christian kings, to the Emperor of Rome and the King of France, our friends.' The letter announced that Prester John possessed the highest crown on earth along with gold, silver, precious stones and strong fortresses, cities, towns, castles and boroughs. He ruled over forty-two kings, all of them valiant and true Christians, and he had sworn an oath to conquer the Holy Sepulchre and the entire Promised Land.

The implications of the oath were of far greater interest to the princes of Europe than the descriptions of unicorns, phoenixes and other wonderful creatures who lived in the kingdom, or the rivers of precious stones, miraculous fountains, and robes woven by salamanders that could pass through flame as if through water. An ally who ruled beyond the Muslim powers of Egypt and the Levant and who could help to encircle the armies of the infidel might secure the prize for which Crusaders were struggling. The challenge was how to find him. He had been called 'Prester John of the Indies', but 'India' was a vague term that meant little more than 'the East', and there were believed to be Near, Middle and Far Indies, in any one of which his kingdom might lie. While European scholars and diplomats had accurate knowledge of some of these regions, precise information and fanciful speculation were usually combined and could not be distinguished.

When Ethiopia emerged as the most likely location, it was not European exploration that provided the first evidence for an African Prester John, but a mission from Ethiopia itself. In his *Supplement to the Chronicles*, published in Venice in 1483, Jacopo Filippo Foresti of Bergamo reports that an embassy from Prester John to the king of Spain had been delayed by contrary winds at

Genoa in 1306. The rector of St Mark, the cartographer Giovanni da Carignano, went to the harbour to question the delegates about their country, and although the map he produced was badly damaged, and then destroyed, maps drawn by later Genoese cartographers indicate that he had placed the kingdom along the upper Nile. The accuracy of his information was confirmed in 1438, when a genuine letter from 'John the emperor of the Ethiopians' was presented at the Council of Florence, and again in 1441 when Ethiopian monks arrived in Rome from Jerusalem.

European attempts to reach the kingdom of Prester John began in earnest in 1487, when the Portuguese king João II sent Pero da Covilhão to search beyond the lands of Islam. By then, even the poets of the Italian Renaissance had become fascinated by the idea of a remote Christian emperor, and Ariosto wrote in his epic *Orlando Furioso* that 'the Emperor of Ethiopia, wields the Cross instead of a sceptre'. He depicted the emperor living in a palace of jewels, and although his description contains the usual romantic elements, it is placed within a heroic struggle between Christians and Saracens. According to Ariosto, the Ethiopian emperor exacts tribute from the sultan of Egypt, who is terrified that his enemy might interrupt the flow of the Nile and destroy Cairo by famine. The princes of Europe would have been delighted to learn that this were true, and while modern scholars have debated whether the Portuguese mariners who began the Age of Discovery were looking for Prester John or for the spices of India, the two goals would in fact have had an identical military purpose.

Early in the fourteenth century, the Dominican Guillaume Adam wrote a treatise entitled *How to Exterminate the Saracens*, in which he proposed to destroy Muslim power in Egypt by placing warships at the southern entrance to the Red Sea and interrupting trade with India. Everything that was sold in Egyptian markets had been imported from India, including pepper, ginger and other spices, gold and precious stones, silks and rich textiles dyed with Indian colours. He described the trade routes of the Indian Ocean as if they were a human body, and were vulnerable for the same reasons. As food is transferred from the mouth to the throat, he suggested, and from the throat to the stomach, and from the stomach to the other parts of the body, precious goods have an outlet from the Indian Sea as if from the head, and they are dispersed through the Gulf of Aden as if through the throat. Then they pass to Egypt through the Red Sea, as if through the stomach, and on to the other countries of the world, as if to the other parts of the body. If the head were cut off, the stomach would wither away from lack of nourishment, and the other limbs would perish.

Ten years after João II sent Pero da Covilhão to search by land, the Portuguese sailed around the Cape of Africa into the Indian Ocean, and in 1507 Tristão da Cunha sent João Gomes to look again for the court of Prester John. The Portuguese desire for an alliance with the powerful enemy of the sultan of Egypt grew more urgent when they occupied Goa in 1510, and although they were struggling to defend their sea lanes from the Arabs, their king Manoel I grandly assumed the title 'Lord of the Conquest, Navigation and Commerce of Ethiopia, India, Arabia, and Persia'. In 1520, however, a Portuguese embassy led by Dom Rodrigo da Lima finally arrived in Ethiopia, where they learned that the first envoy, Pero da Covilhão, had succeeded in reaching the imperial court several years before, and was living happily with an Ethiopian wife and their children. He was regarded with favour by the emperor Lebna Dengel, who had granted him an estate, and the skill he had acquired in the Amharic language was placed at the service of his countrymen. Even so, the embassy was not a success. Lebna Dengel had recently defeated a Muslim incursion, and the holocaust of Ahmed Grañ, which could be resisted only with European allies and European weapons, had not yet begun. A treaty with Portugal did not seem to be a priority.

However, Francisco Alvares had been sent with the mission as chaplain, and his account of the country is of enormous importance for historians. It is not only the first description written by a European who had actually visited Ethiopia, but also the only description by a European of the Ethiopian empire in its medieval glory, before the ravages of Ahmed Grañ had destroyed the greater part of its ancient Christian culture, and before the Ethiopian request for military assistance against him brought Jesuit missionaries along with Portuguese soldiers. Even though the Ethiopian emperor Fasiladas would expel the Jesuits in 1632, the manuscripts and the icons made for his new capital of Gondar reveal the impact of Western European and Indian styles brought by the Jesuit mission. Gondar was a very different society from the medieval empire that Alvares had been privileged to see.

Even so, the rock churches of Roha were already part of a vanished order when Alvares saw them, and the kings whose capital they adorned had been overthrown. By 1520 the royal court was nomadic, the emperor visiting his provincial nobility and plundering their wealth to prevent their ambition becoming a threat to his own authority. The remarkable similarity between the churches of Lalibela and the ancient city of Aksum, supposedly built almost a thousand years before, suggests that Lalibela might be much older than the king with whom it is usually associated. Nevertheless, it was certainly used by the Zagwe as a religious and ceremonial capital near their seat of government at Adafa. Its abiding importance as a centre of pilgrimage can be judged in the Ethiopian proverb, 'He who does not make his way to the holy city of Roha is like a man who feels no desire to look upon the face of Our Lord and Saviour Jesus Christ.' But it was not just a site of dramatic beauty, or a shrine for religious devotion. It was a last desperate attempt in Ethiopian dynastic politics of the thirteenth century.

As one walks in the red earth, climbing towards the holy city of Lalibela, one can see nothing of the churches that so astonished the Portuguese chaplain Alvares almost five centuries ago. Among the stocks of yellow grass, beyond the walls of red stone, ancient and gnarled trees defy the appearance of exhaustion to send out a few leaves that turn towards the sun and offer shade to a boy and his goats. Beyond these few signs of life struggling in a harsh world, there is little to distinguish the scene from any other part of the highlands of Lasta.

Two or three houses further up the road are built of mud or rough stones, and are covered with sheets of corrugated tin. Small children run about and earnest young monks point the way, but there is still no sign of where the churches might be. The reason for their fame, however often it has been told, remains difficult to grasp until one actually stands among them. Lalibela does not rise to the sky on foundations built upon the earth. It lies within the rock.

Tradition describes the creation of the churches as miraculous, and so they appear. Even though some of the cuts are 40 or 50 feet deep, it is difficult to imagine picks and axes chipping away at the rock from above. The churches seem to rise from within the rock, as if the heart of the mountains had opened itself, forcing the city toward the sky as a witness to a truth in heaven. According to tradition, heaven is where they were revealed to the king in whose reign they are believed to have been made, and after whose name they are called. An angel carried Lalibela into the heavenly Jerusalem, where God showed him ten churches, each according to a different pattern, and commanded him to cut them from the rock in his own kingdom. This attempt to create a New Jerusalem is often thought to be part of an Ethiopian fascination with the legacy of the Israelites. There are certainly enough names at Lalibela to suggest a Second Jerusalem – Bethany, Golgotha, a Mount of Olives, a Mount of the Transfiguration, a River Jordan – but these are all names of sites holy to Christians. If Lalibela is a mystical topography, it belongs to the New Covenant rather than the Old. Above all, there seems to be no attempt to build a copy of the Temple in which the Ark of the Covenant once stood.

Cracks have begun to appear in some of the walls, and in places the churches are crumbling, returning quite literally to dust. Sometimes, drums and chanting echo deep within the rock, slower than a heartbeat, as if an ancient spirit endures to sing the praises of God in its own way, marking the passage of centuries – a voice speaking from a time before men had begun to worship on the mountain. In fact, some of the churches at Lalibela seem to have been made for creatures other than men. Doors and windows have been cut in the walls, some immensely tall and narrow, as if intended for angels, others so low that even the elderly nuns bow their heads as they pass through. When Lalibela began his great task, we are told, teams of angels worked beside the men of Lasta during the day, and continued through the night while the men slept.

One can still see the tombs of the saints, whose dust is believed to work miracles, but as one walks among the churches, one is more likely to encounter the living than the dead. Monks holding worn copies of the Psalms whisper the sacred verses in their meditation. Priests suddenly appear with the treasures of earlier and more splendid times, holding an open Gospel or a processional cross fashioned into a complex pattern of crosses within crosses, as if the simple fact of their revelation, the proof of their faith displayed before the eyes of visitors from a rich but less certain world, would induce a conviction that the ancient faith were still true.

At the great festivals, lines of priests and dabtaras dance on the rock above the churches. Only the rock and the sky and the holy men can be seen from below, and they appear to pass beyond the life of men, angelic forms between heaven and earth. They sing to the faithful below them, on the floor of the rock, and are answered in turn, the verses that pass between the sky and the earth repeating the words spoken between God and his creation.

The Zagwe who ruled from Lalibela were a new dynasty, although marriage to a princess from the previous line may have given them some claim to the throne. The hagiographies and the chronicles have preserved a number of fanciful tales about their rise to power, but we have no real knowledge of what occurred. We know only that, at some point before 1152, something occurred that the patriarch of Alexandria and his metropolitan in Ethiopia regarded as usurpation. Later Ethiopic legends hint that power changed hands because of a woman. It has even been suggested that this encouraged the editors of *The Glory of Kings* to regard women with suspicion, although the Bible has often been thought to provide enough reason itself.

The Zagwe were descended from the Agaw, the original inhabitants of the regions south of Aksum, who spoke a Cushitic language. They were, as the colophon of *The Glory of Kings* explains, not 'Israelites', and the accusation is made in the text as well. God had chosen the king of Ethiopia to be the only king over the Ark of the Law of the heavenly Zion. 'And as for those who reigned, who were not Israel, that was due to the transgression of the law and the commandment, at which God was not pleased.'

If God was annoyed at the Zagwe, he was not quick to display his anger. The Zagwe are generally supposed to have ruled in Ethiopia from about 1137 until 1270. While the Ethiopian records are thoroughly confused, and suggest anything between 133 years and over three centuries for the duration of the dynasty, the biographers of two of the patriarchs of Alexandria may offer some evidence to confirm these dates. In the meantime, the monarchy was in the hands of several Zagwe rulers, who were recognized as saints even when their enemies had become kings in their place.

Despite the contempt that the colophon of *The Glory of Kings* displays toward the Zagwe kings, it is actually during the reign of Lalibela that we first hear of the Ark of the Covenant in Ethiopia. It is recorded by an Armenian, Abu Salih, who lived in Egypt and wrote in Arabic during the late twelfth and early thirteenth centuries. Abu Salih not only refers to the Ark, but he also claims that the Zagwe were of thoroughly Israelite lineage, direct descendants of the house of Moses and Aaron.

It is not certain how Abu Salih acquired his knowledge of Ethiopia, which he calls 'Abyssinia' or 'India'. He could have met Abyssinian visitors to Egypt, or heard their stories from someone who had. Other details he could have acquired from Egyptian ecclesiastics who had learned something of the distant land to the south that lay under the jurisdiction of their patriarch. Some of his statements about Nubia and Abyssinia are confused and may have been little more than hearsay, distorted as they passed from person to person. Indeed, some might be no more than fantastical tales told by Nubians or Ethiopians anxious to make an impression in the magnificent capital of late Fatimid and Ayyubid Egypt. Nevertheless, there are reasons for taking what he has to say very seriously.

In the years when Abu Salih was writing, between 1200 and 1210, there was an unusual amount of diplomatic correspondence between Ethiopia and the patriarchate in Egypt. An unprecedented event was unfolding: the metropolitan of Abyssinia was about to be deposed and excommunicated. Messengers had been travelling between the capitals with letters for the patriarch John VI of Alexandria or for the king Lalibela in Ethiopia. The metropolitan in question, Michael of Fuwa, was actually living in Cairo at the time. He had fled there and had been given a house, where he waited uneasily while enquiries were made about his behaviour in Ethiopia. Abu Salih was fascinated by ecclesiastical affairs, and while he collected information for his book on the churches of Egypt and their dependencies in Nubia and Abyssinia, he would have been well placed to hear anything of interest.

Given the little we know of Ethiopia during the thirteenth century, the story of Michael of Fuwa is documented in extraordinary detail. At the beginning of the century, during the reign of the Ayyubid sultan al-Adil, the *History of the Patriarchs of Alexandria* records that the king of Ethiopia and Nubia sent messengers asking the sultan to put the question of a new metropolitan to the patriarch John VI. Tradition and protocol apparently required that a letter be delivered to the sultan, accompanied by splendid gifts. The letter would request that the sultan approach the patriarch for the consecration of a new metropolitan, and the messengers would usually remain in Egypt for about three months, while the patriarch sent to the remote monasteries of the Egyptian desert to find a suitable candidate.

When the patriarch John VI received the request, he began his search, but he could find no one suitable in either the monasteries or Cairo itself. He realized that the messengers were 'impatient from the length of their stay', presumably because they had been in Egypt for more than the usual three months. When he heard that they were preparing to complain to the sultan, he turned to the bishops in the hope of finding a candidate, even though this solution was highly irregular. The Coptic Church did not allow bishops to move from one see to another. Nevertheless, it was essential to find a metropolitan, and with the agreement of all the authorities concerned, the patriarch settled the appointment on Michael, the bishop of Fuwa.

The new metropolitan and the messengers departed for the south, and the *History* describes the lavish reception that awaited him. Lalibela himself rode three days out of the capital to greet him, accompanied by priests and bishops. When he arrived at the royal city, Michael entered it under a golden parasol decorated with jewels, and when he celebrated the liturgy, gold was scattered over him while censers were filled with aloe-wood and ambergris. At the House of the Metropolitan, ten priests served him and guarded the wealth of his church, as horses, mules and slaves were delivered to him. By happy coincidence, the rains fell again, and Michael was held in great respect. The king, we are told, was constantly riding to his house to visit him.

This state of grace lasted for only four years. In the fifth year, news reached Cairo that Michael was on his way back to Egypt. The reason for his return, he later claimed, was that the queen had forced him to consecrate her brother as bishop of the capital. Once he was consecrated, the new bishop began to go about under the umbrella of state, usurping the prerogatives of Michael, scheming against him and even plotting to kill him.

Michael insisted that this persecution was the reason why he had fled from Ethiopia. He had begun his journey with a large company of people, most of whom he had sent back. Even so, about a hundred continued with him on the way to Egypt, many of them perishing from the heat or the rapacity of local rulers. Nevertheless, Michael reached Egypt with a female slave, two male slaves and a civet cat. The patriarch provided lodgings for him and then wrote to the Ethiopian king, sending the letter with the priest Musa and one of his own attendants. A year later, the reply finally arrived. According to the king, Michael had killed one of the priests who guarded the church treasure, and the relatives of the dead man had tried to kill him in revenge. The king then described the extravagance that Michael had displayed – how he had built a vast house in the royal capital, with trees and water courses, known as 'the Castle'. It was whitewashed and contained long corridors, so that 'he who enters them becomes weary before he reaches their lowest part and their highest part'. Michael left the Castle only on Sundays, in high state, with 500 retainers, seated on a mule with the parasol held above him. He entered the sanctuary dressed in robes woven with gold and decorated with precious stones.

The messengers who delivered the letter made a formal request for a new metropolitan and brought with them the offerings decreed by custom. These consisted of a golden crown for the patriarch and gifts for the sultan, including an elephant, a lion, a giraffe and a zebra. The *History* records that the patriarch took all the Ethiopian gifts to the prince al-Kamil, the sultan himself being away from Cairo at the time. The prince admired the crown and remarked that had not realized Ethiopians could make such things. The messenger who had brought it replied that everyone knew the patriarch was too modest to wear a crown, but if he had, the emperor would have adorned it with jewels to rival the wealth of Egypt. When the messenger delivered the request for a new metropolitan, al-Kamil suggested that this could be arranged immediately. The messenger then delivered even more exaggerated praise of the Ethiopian king and his power, at which al-Kamil smiled. The patriarch, after some polite wrangling, was persuaded to take away his gifts, and he departed to arrange the new consecration.

The ceremony caused immense excitement. Everyone, it seemed, wanted to go to the church of al-Muallaqah to see it, and the price for the hire of donkeys at the Zuwailah Gate rose to three dirhams. The proceedings began with the deposition and excommunication of the old metropolitan 'on account of the misuse of his stewardship'. He 'descended from the church of al-Muallaqah with great shame, wailing and throwing dust on his head'. Then a monk chosen by the patriarch, whose name was Isaac, was consecrated metropolitan. Along with his elder brother Joseph, who was to go with him as a priest, he came from the monastery of St Anthony. The new consecration occurred on 7 March 1210.

This is all quite remarkable, if one considers that almost every aspect of Ethiopia at the time remains a mystery. The *History of the Patriarchs* even mentions Lalibela by name, with details about his family and his ancestry – something that appears in no other record of the ecclesiastical relations between Alexandria and Ethiopia. It is the only independent foreign confirmation of the existence of this great Ethiopian king, but its importance for the history of the Ark is even greater. Despite the difficulty we face in trying to understand the few documents that survive from this period, it shows that detailed and accurate information about Ethiopia would have been available in Cairo at the time when Abu Salih was writing. And it is this fact that makes his account so surprising.

Abu Salih reported on a number of Ethiopian relics. The king, he claimed, possessed the Throne of David, which was covered with golden crosses. He also possessed the Ark of the Covenant, of course, and Abu Salih describes it in some detail. This is immensely interesting, as the description seems to have little to do with the Arks reported in either the Hebrew Bible or *The Glory of Kings*. According to Abu Salih,

The Abyssinians possess the Ark of the Covenant, in which are the two tables of stone, inscribed by the finger of God with the commandments which he ordained for the children of Israel. The Ark of the Covenant is placed upon the altar, but is not so wide as the altar; it is as high as the knee of a man, and is overlaid with gold; and upon its lid there are crosses of gold; and there are five precious stones upon it, one at each of the four corners, and one in the middle. The liturgy is celebrated upon the Ark four times in the year, within the palace of the king; and a canopy is spread over it when it is taken out from its own church to the church which is in the palace of the king: namely on the feast of the great Nativity, on the feast of the glorious Baptism, on the feast of the holy Resurrection, and on the feast of the illuminating Cross. And the Ark is attended and carried by a large number of Israelites descended from the family of the prophet David, who are white and red, with blond hair. It is said that the Negus was white and red of complexion, with blond hair, and so are all his family to the present day; and it is said that he was of the family of Moses and Aaron, on account of the coming of Moses into Abyssinia. And Moses married the king's daughter.

While this may seem quite incredible, the detail that Abu Salih provides elevates it beyond some of his other claims – that the Nubians possessed the Ark of Noah, for example. Some of it is almost certainly legendary, but much of it would seem to be based on an accurate account of Ethiopian practice. It is all the more astonishing for being so unexpected. There are no earlier sources that might prepare us for what Abu Salih has to say.

The statement that Moses came to Abyssinia and married an Abyssinian princess is an echo of a story told by Josephus. It is found in midrashic literature as well, and it seems to have arisen as an explanation or an embellishment of the statement in the Book of Numbers that Moses had married an Ethiopian. Josephus reports that Egypt had been attacked by Ethiopian troops from Saba, and that Moses was sent as a general to drive them out. He attacked by land, rather than by the river, and drove the invaders back to their capital. As he fought below the walls of the city, an Ethiopian princess named Tharbis saw him and fell in love with him. She sent messengers to talk of marriage, and once he was victorious, he took the princess as his wife.

The claim that an Israelite elite in Ethiopia had white or red complexions and blond hair has led to bewilderment and con-troversy, even to the suggestion that Knights Templar were in Ethiopia at the time. It may have been based on a misunderstanding of the customary Ethiopian way of referring to themselves as 'red' people, in contrast to neighbouring 'black' people. This was an ancient form of distinguishing between races. It appears in the inscription of Ezana, where he differentiates the black Noba from the red Noba, and we find it even in the inscriptions of the pre-Aksumite rulers of Diamat and Saba. It can hardly have been true as far as Lalibela himself was concerned. His family derived from the Agaw and would have been black rather than 'white and red'. But his metropolitan, Michael of Fuwa, was described in the *History of the Patriarchs* as 'of cheerful countenance, tall of stature, with black eyes, brown in colour with redness, very handsome in appearance', and Abu Salih may be referring to the complexion of the metropolitan and his Egyptian attendants. They would have been expected to play a prominent role at these festivals, and as priests they could have been assigned to carry the *tabot*.

While it is also possible that the entire passage is a fantasy of the mysterious lands that lay to the south, the most plausible explanation would seem to lie within the pages of the Bible itself. In the Song of Solomon, the hero is depicted as having skin that is white and red, and his head is described as golden. If the priests in Ethiopia were believed to be descended from the house of David, it would be obvious that their appearance must resemble that of Solomon, the son of David. In the First Book of Samuel, David himself is described as having a red complexion. There is no need to assume that the report is evidence for Europeans having been in Ethiopia at the time.

The Ark that Abu Salih describes is apparently used during the liturgy in a way that recalls the *tabot*, the altar slab that is found in every Ethiopian church today. In fact, it is the *tabot* that is consecrated, rather than the church itself. Country people who worship in smaller churches throughout Ethiopia display an intense reverence and devotion to the *tabot*. For them, in the words of one modern Aksumite, 'it is virtually God himself'. It is believed to possess the power of the saint or angel to whom it is dedicated. It can heal and it can kill, and it is regarded as literally terrifying.

Most Christian Ethiopians have no doubt that the Ark of the Covenant is preserved in the church of Mary of Zion at Aksum, and that it also exists in every *tabot* in every church in Ethiopia. Yet the priests and the dabtaras, who are more learned in the ancient traditions of the church, express different opinions about these objects. There appears to be no codified and universally accepted account of precisely what a *tabot* is or what it represents. The *Rules of the Church*, which provide detailed accounts of the mystical significance of virtually every part of an Ethiopian church, never mention the Ark or the Tablet of Moses. Instead, the *tabot* is a symbol of the grave of Christ. The identification with the Ark of the Covenant, it seems, is not as absolute as most Ethiopians and most Western scholars assume.

One reason for the confusion about the *tabot* is the result of the symbolism that is often attached to the word. In the Ethiopic Old Testament the Ark of the Covenant is called a *tabot*, and the word is often used of the great relic in Aksum as well. Even when they speak of churches nowhere near Aksum, and especially when they are speaking in English, many Ethiopians will use the phrase 'the Ark of the Covenant' to refer to any one of thousands of *tabotat* in the country. On several occasions the Ark has been reported stolen, and while the theft of the Ark of the Covenant sounds extremely alarming, the phrase invariably means that a minor *tabot* has been taken. This may be a shocking crime in the eyes of any Christian Ethiopian, but it is scarcely on the same level as the plundering of the Shrine of the Tablet of Moses.

The use of the word *tabot* in the Old Testament creates a further problem. If the Ark of the Covenant is a *tabot*, then surely the altar slab ought not to be. The chest in which the slab is kept, known as the *manbara tabot*, would seem to correspond more accurately to an Ark, and the slab itself would be the equivalent of the Tablets. But symbolism tends to be fluid rather than precise. The *manbara tabot* is not usually seen as an Ark, while the *tabot* itself corresponds to both the Tablet and the Ark. For this reason, it can be called *sellat* as well as *tabot*. Foreign travellers and visiting clergy have often described the more logical version, even if it is mistaken.

The *tabot* is made of stone or a hard wood such as sycamore, although there are records of royal *tabotat* made of gold. They are square or rectangular in shape, small enough to be carried by a single priest, and often decorated with crosses or interwoven patterns. They often seem to be dedicated to more than one patron – God, Christ, Mary of Zion, or the Covenant of Mercy, or any of a host of saints, martyrs, and holy men – and are inscribed with their names. They are made by the members of the clergy, and are consecrated by the *abun*, the patriarch himself.

During the liturgy, the *tabot* is placed, always wrapped, on the *manbara tabot*, the chest in which it is stored. The paten and the chalice are then placed on the *tabot*, and the liturgy is celebrated over it. On festival days, such as *Timqat*, the *tabot* is taken out of the inner sanctuary of the church, wrapped in brocade or velvet 'like the mantle of Christ', and carried on the head of a priest in procession.

Although there is no evidence for the use of the *tabot* in Aksumite times, the Syrian Orthodox and Coptic churches both used wooden altar slabs or portable consecrated altars at an early date. It is still Coptic practice to set a consecrated altar board into the top of the altar. Known as the *maqt*, this is a rectangular panel placed in a special slot on the surface of the altar as a substitute reliquary. It is usually decorated with a cross, and in the four squares formed by the arms of the cross Greek letters form an abbreviation of the divine name: 'Jesus Christ Son of God'. While it only occupies a small area of the whole surface of the altar, the *maqt* is the most important element. The paten and the chalice will be placed on it when the liturgy is celebrated. If a properly consecrated altar is not available, the *maqt* itself can be used to celebrate the liturgy.

Whatever the Old Testament symbols or rituals have been applied to the *tabot* in Ethiopia, it would seem from these descriptions that the Coptic church does employ an object that could have been its ancestor. Unlike the Coptic or the Syrian altar tablets, the Ethiopian *tabot* was not essentially a portable altar, even though it is carried during ceremonial processions and hagiographies occasionally mention that monks who founded monasteries had *tabotat* in their baggage. A more important difference is that in the Coptic church, the *maqt* is not regarded as a symbol of the Ark. The Coptic church has its own 'ark', a wooden box known in Coptic as *thronos ente pipoterion*, or in Arabic as *kursi al-kas*, which contains the chalice in which the wine is mixed with water during the liturgy. It is placed in the middle of the altar, and a complex series of symbols is applied to it, including the throne of Christ, the Ark of Noah, the Ark of the Covenant, and the Virgin Mary.

Despite the common assumption that the *tabot* has always been central to the worship of the Ethiopian church, there is no evidence that it was known in Ethiopia during the Aksumite period. In the absence of any evidence, there is no reason to assume that Aksumite liturgical practice would have deviated from that of Alexandria. Variations in the Ethiopian church are likely to have been a later development, largely due to isolation.

Certainly by the time of the metropolitan Severus, who was installed during the patriarchate of Cyril II in the latter part of the eleventh century, there were serious differences in at least some of the observances of the Ethiopian church, grave enough for the metropolitan to write to his superior seeking his support in their suppression, 'forbidding them to observe the customs of the Old Testament, and mentioning to them the spiritual instructions from the holy books of the Old and New Testaments, and explaining in it what might support the correctness of his words to them.'

The outcome of his attempts to halt the 'Old Testament customs' is not known. These customs had arisen under previous bishops, who were indifferent to the peculiarities emerging in the Ethiopian church. No doubt they were to increase again under later bishops. In the case of Severus, his zeal seems to have provoked a reaction. He was accused of supporting the building of mosques in Ethiopia, under pressure from Egypt where the patriarch and the mother church were at risk from the Muslim authorities. Angry Ethiopians threatened to kill him, and the king arrested him. After that, any enthusiasm for reform by Egyptian metropolitans in Ethiopia seems to have been dampened, and whatever peculiarities had developed, or would develop in the future, remained more or less undisturbed.

It is more difficult to know whether *tabotat* were used under the Zagwe. The lives of the Zagwe saints were written at a later date, and could reflect the customs of later times. *Manbara tabot* do survive that are attributed or even dated to the reign of Lalibela, and while it may be overly suspicious to doubt them, these could have been inscribed later in honour of the royal saint.

It is intriguing that Abu Salih knew of Coptic altar boards, and although he records their use, he does not compare the Zagwe Ark with such objects. While *tabotat* are said to be Arks, was the Zagwe Ark a *tabot* similar to those we know today? This may seem a likely explanation, but Abu Salih does not tell us, and the Zagwe Ark may also have been something quite different.

Abu Salih tells us that the Ark of the Covenant was involved in the four great festivals of the year, when the liturgy was celebrated in the royal palace. From his description, these can be identified as: *Ledat*, the Ethiopian Christmas; *Timqat* or Epiphany; *Tensae* or Easter; and *Masqal*, the Feast of the Holy Cross. When the Ark was carried to the palace from the church in which it usually resided, it was apparently covered by a canopy, just as any *tabot* today is veiled from the laity by shimmering brocades when it is carried on the shoulders of the priests. Although Abu Salih refers to the royal palace and the palace church, he does not actually tell us where they were. Does his report connect the Ark with the church of Mary of Zion or the ancient capital of Aksum? The Zagwe apparently controlled at least part of the province of Tigray in which Aksum is located, but the city had ceased to be a capital long before. Beginning with al-Yaqubi, who wrote in the late ninth century, Arab geographers and historians tell us that the capital was Kubar rather than Aksum. In its detailed notes on Ethiopia, the *History of the Patriarchs* clearly regards the Zagwe city of Adefa as capital during the reign of Lalibela. It seems likely, therefore, that the lidded chest covered with crosses and precious stones, which Abu Salih identifies as the Ark of the Covenant, would have been lodged not in Aksum, and not in the church of Mary of Zion in the ancient capital, but in another church in another city. It is difficult to imagine the king allowing such a powerful sign of the mandate of heaven to be kept anywhere but in his own capital.

If we assume that the sacred relic would have been kept at the Zagwe capital, is it possible to determine the church in which it would have been placed? At Lalibela, of course, there are a number of splendid possibilities, but of the eleven churches we know today, it is possible that some of them were not intended to be churches. We know almost nothing of the early history of the city. Some of the churches may once have formed parts of royal or ecclesiastical palaces, and have become churches only later. Furthermore, the excavated churches or palaces are not the only possible sites at the city. A vast series of cuts in the rock has produced courts and galleries, terraces and tunnels, a maze of passageways leading up and down between the main structures, and there are also traces of massive construction blocks from buildings now vanished. One of the 'churches', then, might have been the splendid house of the metropolitan Michael, 'the Castle', with its interminable corridors. Another might have composed at least part of the royal palace.

Some of the galleries and balconies in the maze of passageways lead on to a splendid church whose entrances lie deep in an excavated court, and if one were going to suggest a candidate for a palace church, Beta Emmanuel might be the most likely. Indeed, it closely resembles what we know of the ancient palaces of Aksum. If the Ark that Abu Salih describes were once lodged in a church at Lalibela, one wonders if this church would have borne the same dedication to Mary as the church in which the Ark and the Tablets were later said to reside? If so, could the Ark at Lalibela have been kept at the church of Beta Maryam, and issued forth in procession to Beta Emmanuel on the four occasions in every year when it was required at the palace church? Neither Abu Salih nor any of the other medieval sources has told us.

The church that might have housed the Ark remains a mystery, but what of the Ark itself? Although at least one eminent scholar has remarked that the description by Abu Salih 'clearly shows the marked resemblance to the Old Testament Ark of the Covenant', one of the remarkable features of his Ark is that it is covered by a lid decorated with Crosses. Nothing else about the lid is at all similar to the account of the Ark given in the Book of Exodus, with which Abu Salih would certainly have been familiar. In particular, there is no reference to the cherubim, whose wings covered the Ark, making the throne from which God promised to speak to Moses. Even aside from this, the presence of Crosses clearly indicates that Abu Salih is describing an object created by Christians. Yet he seems convinced that it contains the Tablets of Moses, and this is perhaps the most intriguing part of his account. The next report that survives of the sacred object was written three centuries later by Francisco Alvares, the chaplain to the Portuguese mission who was the first European to describe the holy city of Lalibela. Yet the object he reports was no longer at Lalibela. It was at Aksum. And it was not the Ark of the Covenant that Abu Salih describes. In fact, it was not an Ark at all. It was a Tablet. The importance of Abu Salih as a witness may lie precisely in the fact that his Ark is so obviously not the Old Testament Ark of the Covenant, and that he is evidently not disturbed by the fact. The secret may lie in what it contains.

CHAPTER 17

A New Zion

Around the year 1270, the last of the Zagwe kings was finally trapped in the Church of St Qirqos. In desperation, he cried out for the saint to protect him, but his enemy, the Solomonid pretender Yekunno Amlak, shouted down his appeals for mercy. Calling upon the saint to deliver the Zagwe usurper into his hands, Yekunno Amlak killed the king in the church. The dynasty that had given Ethiopia the greatest of its royal saints had been overthrown, and the lineage of Solomon was restored to the throne – or so its proponents claimed.

While he was a boy, Yekunno Amlak had been given sanctuary at the great monastery of Daga Estifanos, which lay on an island in Lake Hayq and was named after the first Christian martyr, St Stephen. There he had been guided by the greatest of Ethiopian king makers, the abbot Iyasus Moa. Five centuries after the collapse of its power, it seems that the dead hand of Aksum was reaching out to seize the crown. The Solomonids insisted that they preserved the lineage of the ancient kings, descended from Solomon and the Queen of Sheba, and they would display an increasing devotion to Zion and to Mary as a New Ark of the Covenant. In the struggle to place them on the throne the abbots of the ancient monasteries played a decisive role.

The Solomonid claim may have been more a weapon to use against the kings of the Agaw than a statement of fact. Even though the Zagwe had their own claim to Israelite descent, at least according to Abu Salih, the weapon seems to have been effective. From the most ancient of the northern monasteries, Debra Damo, Iyasus Moa came south to establish a new centre of monastic power. He had been born into a powerful family, as had the abbot who had trained him, Abba Yohannes. This was no accident. The great Ethiopian monasteries offered little escape from the cares of the world. The wealth needed to support the monastic libraries and scriptoria that served as repositories of Christian faith and culture was based on a peculiar institution of land tenure known as *gült*. Under this system, the right to tax the produce of land rather than ownership of the land itself was granted to those in favour at the court. These rights could be revoked, and if *gült* provided a means for the emperor to control provincial leaders, it did so because its beneficiaries lived in constant fear of losing their privileges. They needed to defend them against ambitious rivals, and an abbot relied on the power that came from family alliances, and a knowledge of the Abyssinian establishment. He had responsibilities in the world of men, even though he was assumed to be outside it. He had acquired the status of a dead man, achieved by a frightening ascetic discipline.

The *Life of Iyasus Moa* describes the moment at which this transformation occurred. When he arrived at Debra Damo, he was consigned to hard labour in the mill. For seven years he suffered from hunger, thirst, and exhaustion. He was naked in the heat of the sun and in the bitter cold of night, fasting to the point of starvation, and devoting himself to prayers and vigils while others slept. Reminding him that a man who exhausts himself in this world will live forever, Abba Yohannes ordered him to carry heavy loads of wood to the monastery. Pushed beyond the limits of human suffering, the exhausted body collapsed in torment, and was suddenly filled with the power and strength of God. His old life had died, and he was born into another world.

Now that he was truly a monk, Iyasus Moa was ordered by the angel Gabriel to make his way south to Lake Hayq. He would be leaving Debra Damo for a site believed to have been sanctified three centuries earlier by the last of the Aksumite kings, Del Naod, who had built a church there. As a son of Debra Damo, a northern monastery that claimed to be part of the Aksumite *ancien regime*, Iyasus Moa had been led into the life of a monk by a northern abbot who had chosen power in the church rather than at the Zagwe court. On ground made holy by the last of the old kings, Iyasus Moa would fulfil his destiny as the spiritual father of Yekunno Amlak, and would restore what was claimed to be the old line of the Aksumite kings.

Hostility between the Zagwe and the old monasteries of the

north can be seen in the documents that record the allocation of *gült*. The Zagwe kings had ignored the ancient foundations, including Debra Damo. They withdrew their support and trans-ferred it to Debra Libanos of Shemazana, whose abbot had been born in Lasta, the Zagwe homeland. The dynasty was clearly intending to create a power base in the region under friendly clerics. Resistance in the northern provinces may have become difficult, and this would explain why Iyasus Moa set out for Lake Hayq.

After the victory of Yekunno Amlak and the foundation of the Solomonid dynasty, we begin to find traces of a more intense interest in Zion and other Israelite themes. Under Zara Yaqob in particular, who came to the throne in 1433, the Virgin Mary became the object of an imperial cult in which she not only seems to be elevated above Christ himself, but is explicitly identified with the Ark of the Covenant. But as in the times of the Zagwe, it is not always possible to know exactly when a tradition begins. Many of the royal chronicles or lives of the saints were written later than events that they purport to describe. So much of Ethiopian literature has been lost, and a great deal of what survived remains unread. And even when we do read it, we often struggle to under-stand exactly what the author is telling us. This is especially true of the role of Zion. Does the word refer to the Ark, to Aksum, to Ethiopia, to the Christian Church as a whole? Symbols of this sort often refer to more than one thing at a time, and while this can be attractive to theologians or mystics, it is often frustrating for later historians.

In 1312, the Solomonid emperor Amda Seyon certainly referred to Zion in his own regnal name, which means 'Pillar of Zion'. Mamluk chancery documents also record the title, and mention the 'Church of Zion' as well. In his chronicles we find a reference to 'the help of Zion the spouse of heaven and the glory of the whole world', while a Muslim cleric is reported as telling the king of Hadya that he should not 'go to the king of Zion'. Yet it is difficult to be sure exactly what Zion means at this time.

The most substantial evidence of the Solomonid fascination with Zion, and with the complex associations of Aksum, the Ark of the Covenant, Solomonic descent, and the Virgin Mary can be found a century after Amda Seyon, during the reign of Zara Yaqob. He not only promulgated a cult of Mary and described her as the Ark, but chose Aksum as the site of his coronation. In the *Book of Aksum*, we read that Zara Yaqob revived the ancient coronation ritual of the Aksumite kings. The city seems to have been more or less ignored by the Zagwe, but Zara Yaqob lived there for three years and seems to have been keenly interested in it. He passed laws that its people could not be forced to offer tribute or food when a king entered the city, and that certain ranks of official could not enter the precincts of 'our mother Zion, the cathedral of Aksum'.

The chronicle of his reign describes how the emperor went to Aksum 'to fulfil the law and the ceremony of tonsure according to the rites followed by his ancestors'. As he approached the city, all the people and the priests came out to meet him with demonstrations of great joy. The nobility of Tigray rode horses, and carried shields and spears, while women performed a dance that 'followed the ancient custom'. When Zara Yaqob entered the city, the governor of Tigray and the neburaed of Aksum stood on his right and his left. 'According to custom', we are told, they carried olive branches, which they waved. After he had entered the walls of the city, the king gave an order that gold should be brought, and he threw it onto the carpets that had been spread along his path. He did this, we are told, 'for the greatness of Zion'.

The chronicle was actually composed during the following century, in the reign of Lebna Dengel. Assuming that its report is accurate, it is still difficult to imagine how much of the ancient Aksumite ritual would have been recalled after more than six hundred years. Court ceremony is not always recorded, even in more recent times. When Queen Victoria died in 1901, much of the funeral ceremony had to be invented. She had reigned for so many decades that almost no courtiers survived who could recall the funeral of William IV. Nevertheless, it is intriguing that the governor of Tigray and the neburaed of Aksum are said to have held olive branches, which they waved as flywhisks. It seems that flywhisks are depicted on Aksumite coins, and on some of the finest examples it may still be possible to see branches with bunches of olives. Perhaps not everything had been forgotten.

It should not be surprising if Zara Yaqob was so anxious to restore or invent an ancient glory, especially one that involved dedication to the Virgin. He seems to have been intelligent, and educated, and he was born in unusual circumstances. His father, the emperor Dawit, had been devoted to the Virgin himself. When his enemies attempted to force him from throne, he went into retreat with his military adviser and the abbot of Debra Hayq Estifanos. For six days, the three men fasted and prayed together. On the seventh day, Mary appeared to Dawit, announcing that through her intercession a covenant had been made with the Holy Trinity. The Old Testament tells of a covenant that God made with the Israelite king David. Now Mary assured an Ethiopian king named after him that his family too will reign for generations.

Zara Yaqob was the son of Dawit by his third wife, and was apparently born through the intercession of the Virgin. While he was still in the womb, prayers to Mary were believed to have averted a miscarriage. He was convinced that he owed his life to her, and his devotion surpassed even that of his father. As a boy and a young man, his tutors included the famous scholar Abba Giyorgis of Sagla. At the age of thirty-five he ascended the throne, and within a year he had begun to write the *Epistle of Humanity*, setting the rules by which his people should live as Christians.

Dawit had been devoted to the Virgin as a matter of personal faith, but his son Zara Yaqob now decided that the entire nation should worship her with unprecedented intensity. Every church was required to have a *tabot* dedicated to Mary, and the people were required to prostrate themselves whenever her name was mentioned. Although anyone who refused would be excommunicated, the ferocity with which the cult was imposed aroused opposition despite the consequences.

The rite introduced by Zara Yaqob required that three episodes from the *Miracles of Mary* be read during the liturgy on Sundays, as well as on over thirty Marian feasts throughout the year. The reading was accompanied by hymns of praise, and a painted icon of Mary was censed. The most important of the feasts commemorated the Covenant of Mercy, which promised that everyone who kept the Marian feasts or even gave a drop of water in the name of the Virgin would be forgiven all their sins. One of the *Miracles of Mary*, which may have been written by Zara Yaqob or by one of his court clergy, describes how the covenant was granted. After the Ascension of Christ, Mary was lifted into heaven herself by the angels. The patriarchs of Israel all prostrated themselves before her. 'Glory be to God who created you for us,' they proclaimed. 'Flesh from our flesh and bone from our bone, through you we found salvation. You became the harbour of life from destruction, because the Son of God became incarnate through you.' Mary was brought to the throne of Christ, and a curtain of flame parted before her. Her divine son kissed her and placed her at his right hand. She could see David, the king of Israel, beneath the throne, and she was distressed when she looked at the place where the damned were tormented. She asked who would warn the living, and an angel told her not to fear, that God was with her and with those who believed in her. After she returned to earth, she recalled the terrible sight and devoted herself to praying for sinners. When he saw how his mother was moved by their sufferings, Christ appeared to her and asked what he could do. She suggested that he make a promise to her: anyone who built a church in her name, who clothed the naked, visited the sick, fed the hungry, gave water to the thirsty, comforted the grieving, copied holy books or chanted hymns should escape the punishments of Hell. To grant her request, Christ announced the Covenant of Mercy.

Although it was new, this Covenant of Mercy was believed to have been in force from the moment that Adam and Eve were expelled from the Paradise. God told Adam that He would be born from Mary and would redeem him. He also gave Mary to Moses as the Tablet of the Covenant, and called her Zion. She was the saviour of Israel, greater than all the prophets, apostles, saints, and martyrs, and the Covenant of Mercy was the greatest of all covenants. As well as the Ark, Mary was called the second Tabernacle, and the Holy of Holies in which the Ark of the Covenant had been placed.

In the *Revelation of the Miracle*, Zara Yaqob wrote that the prophets saw the Virgin Mary with her Son through a spiritual mirror in terms of images. Moses saw Mary at Mount Sinai in the tree that burned without being consumed by the fire. The tree was Mary, who carried the fire of Divinity within her body and was not burned by his heat. When God gave Moses the Tablet of the Law on which the Ten Commandments were written, and told him to make a golden Ark in which he could place the Tablet, the

Ark was the image of Mary, and the Tablet the image of her womb. The Ten Commandments written on the tablets were the image of her Son, who is the Word of the Father.

While it is easy to be impressed by the learning and energy that Zara Yaqob displayed, one may also be reminded of the Judaean king Josiah, who reformed the cult in Jerusalem and obliterated what he regarded as pagan abominations. Zara Yaqob was aware that his empire faced enemies inside its borders as well as outside. He displayed an intense hostility to what he believed to be sorcery and idolatry, including the use of magical prayers by Christians. 'If you see anyone sacrificing to Satan,' he wrote in the *Book of the Nativity*, 'kill him with a spear, or with a club, or with stones ...' He believed that God had placed him on the throne so that he could eliminate idolatry, and he was convinced that anyone found with magical prayers was guilty of the crime.

Just as the Deuteronomist claimed that the Israelites had been contaminated by mingling with the other peoples who lived in the Promised Land, Zara Yaqob was convinced that Ethiopian Christians had been contaminated by the pagan cults that surrounded them. Parish priests usually shared the life of the people they served, and maintained the faith by not demanding too much from converts who had been raised to believe in spirits inhabiting mountains, trees, rivers, and lakes. But the *Lives* of Ethiopian Saints are filled with dramatic accounts of stern holy men who took a more vigorous line, denouncing pagan cults and fighting with sorcerers and magicians. In his battle to defeat paganism in the provinces of Shawa and Amhara, Zara Yaqob employed holy men from the monastery of Debra Libanos. If he learned that people were returning to the old ways, sacrificing cows and sheep to serpent gods that lived in trees, he would arrange for churches to be built where the sacred trees had stood, and would send priests from Debra Libanos to serve in them.

In the *Book of Light* he placed a great emphasis on the responsibility of the clergy to teach. Every Saturday and Sunday, the people were required to come to church to be taught. If they lived too far away, a priest would be sent to them, and if there were not enough books, Zara Yaqob would build libraries. His devotion to learning may seem enlightened, but the system he imposed must have been a nightmare. Every Christian was required to have a confessor, and could not receive the sacrament without his approval. Pagan worship was abolished on pain of death, and anyone who sacrificed to pagan gods, consulted magicians or used magical prayers would be killed. Pagan priests were flogged, and their houses were destroyed. Christians were required to wear the sign of the Cross, which had to be displayed on weapons and on tools such as ploughs. As if that were not enough, the emperor decreed that every Christian should be branded on the forehead with the names of the Father, the Son, and the Holy Ghost. In Egypt, the Copts were tattooed on their hands with the Cross, and Zara Yaqob decided that Ethiopians should surpass them in devotion. He argued that branding was required by the Book of Revelation, and decreed that all his subjects should have the words 'I deny the devil' branded on the right arm, and 'I am the slave of Mary' on the left.

He was greatly disturbed when even these efforts were not sufficient to eradicate idolatry. The priests seemed to be powerless, and he suspected that Ethiopia was filled with magic and superstition, because there were no priests who taught the Word of God with sufficient vigour. Satan, he was convinced, had reduced the people of Ethiopia to slavery.

Despite the penalties imposed, there were some who resented the imperial cult and were determined to resist it. When the followers of the monk Estifanos refused to prostrate themselves before Zara Yaqob's icons of Mary, they were denounced as *ayhud* or Jews. They themselves denounced other groups as Jews, and there seems to have been a large number of dissidents all of whom were called Jews. Zara Yaqob fought rebels in Sallamt and Semien who 'became Jews, abandoning their Christianity'. When his son Galawdewos joined in a coup against him, and consulted pagan magicians and sorcerers it was said that 'he became a Jew, abandoning Christianity and denying Christ.' Ironically, in a kingdom that set out to imitate Judaic tradition and then denounced its enemies as Jews, it seems to have been thought possible to be pagan and Jewish at the same time.

The cult of Mary and its demands for icons led to some of the finest works of medieval Ethiopian painting, especially the panels produced by the court master Fere Seyon, 'the Fruit of Zion'. But the more we learn of the reign of Zara Yaqob, the more it suggests a people or at least a king gone mad. In this it may resemble the hysteria of medieval Europe. The legends of the Holy Grail are still inspiring, but they appeared along with an intense suspicion and persecution of Jews, and a hostility toward Muslims that induced the Crusaders to embark on a campaign of horrifying savagery. The paranoia of Zara Yaqob seems very similar. He inspired or imposed the most intense devotion to Mary and the Ark of the Covenant, and the consequences seem to have been appalling. Was Jeremiah's vision of the future preferable? Should the Ark have been forgotten, and should it have become irrelevant?

By one of the ironies of history, the Ethiopian establishment itself would soon be denounced as Jewish. The empire built by the warrior kings of the Solomonid dynasty would be threatened by Muslim tribes who had been supplied with firearms by the Ottoman Turks. When they turned to the Portuguese to defend them, Jesuit missionaries arrived who regarded the distinctive form of Orthodoxy practised in Ethiopia as a heresy of an especially vile sort.

Although Zara Yaqob is said to have revived the ancient coronation rites and to have taken a special interest in Aksum, very few of the medieval kings went there for their tonsuring. They would perform a brief ceremony of enthronement, and intend to be tonsured later, but events often overtook them. Most of their lives were spent on campaign, and few of them died from old age. Even though Baeda Maryam, the son of Zara Yaqob, was not crowned in the ancient city, it seems that he summoned Aksum to his coronation. His chronicle tells us that he commanded everyone with a part to play in the ritual to come to him, 'along with the inhabitants of the city'.

After the coronation of Zara Yaqob, the next emperor to be crowned at Aksum was Sarsa Dengel, in 1563. The ritual was celebrated with a magnificent display, and the chronicler provided a more detailed account of it. He begins by telling us that the emperor sent a message to the priests of Aksum, announcing that he was coming to celebrate the ceremonies of royalty before his mother Zion, the Ark of the God of Israel, as his fathers David and Solomon had done. When he arrived, he went to the church of Aksum, where the priests and deacons received him with the golden cross, the silver censer, and twelve parasols. They held curtains of silk, and of velvet, each in its own colour. Adorned with the vestments appropriate to their office, all the superiors of the monasteries of Shire and Tigray held crosses and censers, while they chanted the hymns of Yared. 'May you be blessed, O King of Israel!' they sang to him.

In front of the priests, the Daughters of Zion waited at the milestone to the east of the great church. The place was called 'Cutting the Cord', and the Daughters on either side of the road held a long cord between them. When the king arrived on his horse, two old women who stood with the Daughters raised their voices, and in a manner that the chronicle describes as arrogant and insolent, they demanded that the king tell them the name of his tribe and his family. 'I am the son of David,' he replied, 'the son of Solomon, the son of Ebna Hakim.' They questioned him again, and he told them, 'I am the son of Zara Yaqob, son of Baeda Maryam, son of Naod.' Once more they asked, and the king raised his hand, saying, 'I am Malak Sagad, son of King Wanag Sagad, son of Asnaf Sagad, son of Admas Sagad!' Having proclaimed his lineage, he raised his sword and cut the cord that the maidens held. The old women cried aloud, 'Truly, truly you are the king of Zion, the son of David, the son of Solomon!' Then the priests of Aksum began to chant on one side, while the Daughters of Zion sang with joy on the other. The king entered the court of the house of the heavenly Zion, casting a great quantity of gold on the ground, 'for the administration of the law'. Precious fabrics were draped over an ancient stone seat that was called the 'Throne of David'. The king sat upon it, and after the ritual tonsuring had been completed, he attended a liturgy and a banquet.

The Spanish Jesuit Pero Pais described the next coronation at Aksum, when Susneyos was crowned in 1606. He notes that sometimes the kings are crowned 'in the Garangaredaz church in the kingdom of Amhara'. Nevertheless, they believe it a greater honour to be crowned at Aksum, as this had been the seat of the queen of Sheba and of her son Menilek. In fact, they would rather delay the ceremony than perform it elsewhere.

Pais records a different form of the questions that had been put to Sarsa Dengel about his lineage. When Susneyos reached the place where the priests were waiting for him, two girls were holding a twisted rope by its ends. They asked the king who he was, and he replied that he was the king. The girls told him that he was not the king. He turned away and walked five or six steps, and then came back to them. The girls repeated the question, and asked whose king he was. He replied that he was the king of Israel, but the girls told him that he was not their king. He turned away again. When the girls asked him for a third time, he took hold of his sword and cut the rope, telling them that he was the king of Zion. The girls then proclaimed that he was in truth the king of Zion and should enter the city. All the people shouted, 'Long live the king of Zion!' and began to beat drums, blow trumpets, and fire their guns.

After the collapse of the Solomonid empire in the eighteenth century, Yohannes IV tried to revive the glory of Mary of Zion, including the coronation ceremonies at Aksum. He was the last Ethiopian ruler to be crowned at Mary of Zion in Aksum, and is said to have been devoted to the cult. His chronicle tells us that he often went to Aksum, 'to worship Zion, the temple of his fathers, the kings'. When he was ill, he 'put his hopes in his mother Zion'. His councillors prayed 'to God and to Our Lady Mary of Zion, the Ark of the Law', and when he was cured, 'the singers of Zion, and the others, men and women, the old and the young, glorified Our Lady of Zion, for he was called the King of Zion'.

The chronicle of Yohannes not only reports his coronation, it also explains the significance of the rituals. When the emperor is stopped by the Daughters of Zion holding their cord, their gestures indicate that his enemies may oppose him and wait for him like the thread of a spider. When he cuts the cord and offers gold to the people, it means that the emperor should overcome evil not with evil but with good deeds.

During the banquet after the coronation, one of the clergy retells what the Prophets and the Apostles have said about the name of Zion. The law will go forth from Zion. The trumpet will be blown in Zion. Because the king has come, Zion will rejoice. God has saved Zion, and delivered Zion from captivity. The Daughters of Zion should go forth and behold Yohannes, the King of Kings, and pray that God will send him the rod of power from Zion. Apparently a great many other themes were recited from the Old and the New Testaments, and Yohannes was delighted 'because he loved Zion with all his heart'.

Yohannes was not only devoted to Zion, he was devoted to the great epic of Zion, *The Glory of Kings*. The extent of his devotion to the book is revealed by one of the most dramatic episodes in the history of European imperialism. When the emperor Tewodros II was crowned in 1855, he wrote to Queen Victoria in the hope of furthering diplomatic relations between the Ethiopian and the British empires. Unfortunately, the Foreign Office failed to send a reply. After Tewodros read an insulting reference to his mother in a book written by the missionary Henry Stern, and then learned that the British consul had visited the Turkish pashas at Kasala and Matamma, he assumed that the British had begun to plot against him. He threw the consul and his secretary into prison, and had them chained and flogged.

When the news reached London, it produced an uproar. A letter from Queen Victoria was sent in the hands of Hormuzd Rassam, a Nestorian Christian who later achieved notoriety by suing Ernest Wallis Budge for libel, and after Rassam was put in chains as well, the government decided to send a military expedition under Sir Robert Napier. Twelve thousand British and Indian troops set out from Bombay and sailed across the Indian Ocean. Landing at Mulkotto, they marched four hundred miles across difficult terrain, hauling their artillery with elephants. Although Tewodros and his troops displayed remarkable courage, they were no match for European firepower. When the invaders stormed his fortress at Magdala, he shot himself.

As soon as the troops entered the palace, they began to loot the imperial treasury, including an immense number of manuscripts. Tewodros had intended to found a great church at Magdala, named 'the Saviour of the World' after venerable churches at Lalibela and Gondar. Imperial foundations of this sort were centres of scholarship as well as worship, and to provide it with the necessary library, the emperor had been collecting manuscripts by force from churches and monasteries throughout the country.

Despite the complaints of British troops, the loot from Magdala was retrieved by a prize-master, so that an auction could be held and the proceeds delivered more evenly. Napier may have reported that 'no booty was found at Magdala', but fifteen elephants and nearly two hundred mules were needed to carry the contents of the treasury away from the fortress to the plain of Dalanta where the auction was held. Because few of the officers realized how important the manuscripts were, the representative of the British Museum was 'in his full glory' and outbid almost everyone else, securing 359 books that he judged to be of special scientific interest. When the better part of the imperial library was delivered to the British Museum, it transformed Ethiopian studies in Europe.

Of all the manuscripts presented to the Museum, only one has been returned, and under extraordinary circumstances. The collection included a copy of *The Glory of Kings* written during the reign of Iyasu I, who had spoken to the Ark almost two centuries earlier. It had already been catalogued by William Wright, who later taught Budge at Cambridge, when a letter arrived from the new emperor Yohannes IV. The official translation from Amharic into English describes 'a book called Kivera Negust, containing the whole of the laws of Ethiopia and the names of the Shums (Chiefs) and Churches, and Provinces.' The translation also contains a sentence which was not in the Amharic original: 'I pray you will find out who has got this book and send it to me, for in my country my people will not obey my orders without it.'

Yohannes had cooperated with the Napier expedition, and the government in London was keen to maintain good relations with him. The Foreign Secretary appealed to the Trustees of the Museum, who were no doubt also moved by the desperate appeal in the translation of the letter. They took the extraordinary step of surrendering the property of the Museum. The manuscript was returned to Ethiopia, with a letter from Queen Victoria.

Yohannes carried the manuscript with him as he rode into battle against the Dervishes at Matamma, and when he died of bullet wounds, it was thought to have been lost. But it must have been saved by his confessor or by one of the monks in his entourage, because it was shown to the French envoy Hugues Le Roux in 1904. Le Roux had been extremely curious about the book, but had never been permitted to see it. Eventually, having performed an especially valuable service for the emperor Menelik, he was allowed to make a request. The emperor had assumed that Le Roux would want to hunt elephants, and was surprised when he asked to see the manuscript instead.

Le Roux later described their conversation: 'Menelik thought for a while. Finally he said, "I am of the opinion that a people defends itself not only with its weapons but also with its books. The one you speak of is the pride of this Kingdom. Beginning with me, the Emperor, right down to the poorest soldiers walking the roads, all Ethiopians will be happy that the book should be translated into the French language and brought to the knowledge of the friends we have in the world. Thus people will see clearly what links join us to the people of God, what treasures have been entrusted to our safe-keeping. People will understand better why God's help has never failed us against the enemies who attacked us." '

Even though the monks were alarmed at the suggestion of showing such a sacred object to a foreigner, Menelik insisted, and a week later Le Roux held it in his hand. Any doubts that he might have had were soon dispelled. On the title page he found an inscription: 'Or. 819, Presented by the Secretary of State for India, Aug. 1868'. Turning to the first page of text, he saw the stamp of the British Museum, with its lion and unicorn, and on the final folio the announcement: 'This volume was returned to the King of Ethiopia by order of the Trustees of the British Museum, Dec. 14th 1872, J. Winter Jones, Principal Librarian'.

Le Roux described his excitement when he realized that the volume had survived its extraordinary adventures. There was no longer any room for doubt, he wrote. The book that he held in his hand was the copy of the story of the Queen of Sheba that the emperors and priests of Ethiopia considered the most ancient of those that had been scattered in Abyssinian monasteries or had found their way into the libraries of Europe. This was the book that Tewodros had placed under his pillow before he killed himself. It was the book that the British troops had taken with them to London, and which a special embassy had returned to the emperor Yohannes. It was the book that Yohannes had with him in his tent on the day that he was killed by the Dervishes. Le Roux wrote that he found something thrilling in the touch of such a book, in which 'a people of dreams held, closely guarded, and as if in a precious receptacle, the delicious perfume of their most cherished traditions.' He believed that anyone for whom books were sacred things would understand the feelings he experienced at that moment.

How did a book of such importance that a kingdom could not be ruled without it come to be written? Had *The Glory of Kings* been part of the propaganda war between the Solomonids and the Zagwe? The colophon that appears in several of the manuscripts tells us that the book was translated into Arabic from Coptic in the days of Lalibela. It was apparently not translated into Ethiopic because the Zagwe were on the throne at the time, and they were not of Israel. If they had been of Israel, they would have translated it.

It is difficult to have complete confidence in the colophon. It also mentions that *The Glory of Kings* was copied by Abalez and Abalfarog. But Abalfarog is clearly the great Syrian polymath, Abu 'l-Faraj, who was also known as Bar Hebraeus, and in his accounts of the Ark of the Covenant we know that he saw its fate as very different from anything described in *The Glory of Kings*. There also seem to be no Coptic manuscripts of the book. The Coptic fragment that mentions Solomon and Sheba, which is often cited as evidence, displays no knowledge of *The Glory of Kings*. It is based on the Testament of Solomon.

While much of the colophon is misleading, some of it may be reliable, and may suggest that the book was compiled under circumstances very different from those usually assumed. If the book had been written to justify the claims of the Solomonid dynasty, it is surprising that there is not more specific mention of them. Instead, we are told of a translator named Yeshaq, and of the God-loving governor Yaibika Egzi. It is especially difficult to imagine anyone introducing the governor into the colophon if the information were not genuine. He led a rebellion against the Solomonid dynasty.

Yeshaq of Aksum, whose name is preserved as the translator of *The Glory of Kings*, lived at a critical moment. He introduces himself in the colophon with the modesty expected of a Christian scholar: 'your servant Yeshaq, the poor man.' It seems likely that he was neburaed of Aksum, holder of the highest office in the city. From the colophon we learn that he was alive when Yaibika-Egzi was governor of Intarta, a region in the northern part of Tigray. A document written in a sixteenth-century hand in the Golden

Gospel of Debra Libanos, but which seems to copy the text of an older land grant issued by Yaibika Egzi, mentions 'Yeshaq *neb-ura'ed* of Aksum' in a list of witnesses. It is quite likely that this is the same Yeshaq. The colophon describes an educated man, with access to the governor, and with a sense of deep responsibility for the heavenly Zion and for the glory of the King of Ethiopia. These would certainly be qualities appropriate to the greatest clerical office at Aksum.

Yaibika Egzi and his family formed a powerful local dynasty that virtually controlled Tigray throughout the early years when the Solomonid dynasty was consolidating its rule. Their rise can be seen in the titles and the other information preserved in the land grants of the Golden Gospel. While the successors of the Solomonid emperor Yekunno Amlak seem to have been occupied with maintaining their grip on the throne, the great northern governors used the opportunity to advance their own position. Early in the reign of Amda Seyon, Yaibika Egzi does not even bother to mention the emperor in one of the land grants in the Golden Gospel. It is this grant, with its suggestion of independence, that refers to Yeshaq the neburaed of Aksum.

Yaibika Egzi was later to mount an open rebellion against the emperor. In the *Life* of Abiya Egzi, we read that he tried to persuade the governor of Tamben to join him in revolt, but without success. The rulers of Intarta then misjudged the moment, with fatal consequences. The emperor Amda Seyon was more formidable than his predecessors. Having conquered Damot, Hadya, and Gojjam, he was able to crush a rebellion in northern Tigray. He marched on as far as the Red Sea, where he mounted an elephant and rode into the waters. This campaign meant the end of the Intarta dynasty, whose possessions were conquered and absorbed 'as far as the Cathedral of Aksum'. By 1322, there was no trace of them, and we have no idea of what happened to the neburaed Yeshaq.

The Russian scholar Sevir Chernetsov has recently suggested that the Intarta dynasty possessed an old Aksumite lineage, and if one evaluates the legitimate rights to the throne in the way they are set forth in *The Glory of Kings*, the claims of Yaibika Egzi seem to be stronger than those of Yekunno Amlak and his family. Furthermore, the Ark of Zion, the most important relic of the Christian kingdom, was in the possession of Yaibika Egzi. It was kept at the great church in Aksum, where one of his courtiers was neburaed. Yaibika Egzi may have been much more than a regional separatist or an unruly vassal. He may have aimed at the throne of the Christian kingdom itself. While the governor was planning his rebellion and searching for allies, the *nebura'ed* Yeshaq was compiling the ideological and moral justification: *The Glory of Kings*.

Could this be true? The colophon of Yeshaq never mentions the reigning emperor, Amda Seyon, by name. He may be evoked with his throne name, Gabra Masqal, in one chapter of the text itself, but that is all. Yet the governor Yaibika Egzi is mentioned, and in a flattering way. This implies that Yeshaq completed his work before the governor fell from power, and that he was serving the governor as he prepared it. Perhaps Yaibika Egzi really was descended from some ancient royal Ethiopian line. He was certainly a local Tigrayan ruler in succession to others of the same family, in an area that had never been firmly controlled by the new dynasty.

Under these circumstances, *The Glory of Kings* could have served Yaibika Egzi as well as it would serve Amda Seyon or his successors in the years to come. It may have become 'the Amharic national epic' only by default or by adoption. Since Amda Seyon won the battle between the Intarta dynasts and the Solomonid monarchy, he would have been able to exploit the work of Yeshaq and his colleagues. This may have been one of the reasons for the 'tribulation' to which the colophon refers. The resulting version of *The Glory of Kings* would have been harnessed to enhance the prestige of Amda Seyon and his dynasty, and of his own dream of a Zion in Africa.

The Glory of Kings still remains mysterious. If it really was the national epic, and if it was so important that the emperor Yohannes could not govern his country without a famous version of it, it is astonishing that so few copies of it are known. More manuscripts have survived in Ethiopic than in any other language of the Christian Orient. There are thousands of manuscripts of the New Testament. If *The Glory of Kings* was as important as the Bible or the Quran, why should only a handful of manuscripts exist?

CHAPTER 18

The Tablet of Moses

From the Chapel of the Tablet built by the emperor Haile Sellassie, the guardian can look across the precincts of the church of Mary of Zion, over the ruins and excavations of the ancient buildings. As we walked in the lengthening shadows of the afternoon, we saw him standing at the door of the Chapel, and then begin to descend the stairs. We called to him, and he walked over to us, a silver cross in one hand and a fly whisk in the other. When he stood before us, we bowed our heads to receive his blessing and kissed his cross through the railings.

The guardian had not held his post for long, and he was still a young man, dressed in a black cassock, with a white shamma wrapped about his shoulders. Waving his whisk at any insect that flew too near, he answered our questions about his duties within the hidden sanctuary of the Chapel. The guardian is not only a monk, but a virgin as well. He is not a priest. He is appointed for life, by the previous guardian. Despite his title, his life is dedicated to honouring the Tablet, rather than guarding it. After all, the Tablet was quite able to guard itself. The ritual he described involved offering incense and reciting Psalms in the presence of the Tablet of Moses. At times, he would walk around the Tablet, to honour it with the incense. These were the two rituals that he performed, and this had been the purpose of his life since his appointment as guardian. It would be his life until he died.

He also spoke of the miracle of the holy water, the *sebel* from the Chapel of the Tablet, describing how the water dripped from the arms of a cross kept within the Chapel. The water tastes of incense, and used to be given to the faithful within the gates of the Chapel, but the gates have remained closed since a popular book described the miraculous powers of the Ark of the Covenant six years ago.

To anyone familiar with Ethiopian history or with the sensational account written by the journalist Graham Hancock, it was remarkable that throughout the conversation, the guardian referred to the great relic as the Tablet of Moses, *sellata Muse*. He did not speak of the Ark of Zion or the Ark of the Covenant, or use any other phrase. He clearly believed his life was devoted to guarding a Tablet.

It was also intriguing that, despite his unique position, our conversation with the guardian was very like a conversation with any other Ethiopian monk, especially at Aksum. As he spoke of rituals that have been preserved across centuries, his thoughts were clearly directed toward eternity rather than the cares of today or tomorrow. His concerns were not those of the modern world, but once the perspective of monastic life has been accepted, it can seem consistent and reasonable. It is also very practical, and the guardian did not seem at all curious about his position, simply dedicated. A life devoted to the care of sacred relics or sacred rituals requires a practical temperament and discipline, after all. There are responsibilities to be met and duties to be performed. The guardian of the Tablet does not see his life in the way that a visitor excited by lurid speculations or a journalist might imagine. He does not seem to live in fear of the power of God, beyond the degree to which any monk or priest, or any other devout believer, might be said to live in fear of God. He does not tell stories of fire or pillars of cloud appearing in the sanctuary, and he does not seem alarmed that his life will be shortened by powerful rays emanating at the whim of a capricious but omnipotent deity. The experience of speaking to the guardian is nevertheless profoundly moving. He is a serious man, about a serious task, and his commitment to it and his belief in it are obvious. Rather than occult pyrotechnics, the mystery of the Chapel is the mystery of faith, and its power is the power of faith.

Although the guardian spoke of his duties in a practical way, the miraculous and the occult are often encountered in Ethiopia, and it is hardly surprising if one hears more extraordinary stories of the relic in the Chapel. The guardian never sees the Tablet. It is always veiled, but there are those at Aksum who insist that it shines with a mysterious light, and that it does inspire fear.

Those who speak of the sacred object in this way believe that it could not be removed against its will, but nevertheless, there is now a great anxiety about it in Aksum. While many of the clergy in Addis Ababa are familiar with foreign clergy and with foreign diplomats, journalists and scholars, Aksum has almost been a closed world. Even if the patriarch in Addis Ababa served as a parish priest in Manhattan and earned a doctorate from Princeton University, almost none of the Aksumite clergy is able to speak or read English, and none owns a computer. The immense publicity that erupted in 1992, when *The Sign and the Seal* was published, has left them anxious and confused.

They are concerned about what foreigners might try to do next, and rumours have begun to be printed that international spies and intelligence networks have decided to steal the Ark of the Covenant. Clergy who would have spoken openly about the great relic in Aksum are now nervous of doing so, and those who will speak to old friends are often anxious that their names remain private. When Graham Hancock wrote his book, he had not intended to disrupt the lives of the Aksumite clergy, but this has undoubtedly been the result. The great success of the book in addressing a readership who would otherwise know very little about Ethiopia, and whose interest in the relic at Aksum was part of a general curiosity about the lost wisdom of antiquity, has produced a kind of crisis.

Having spoken to the guardian and heard his account of the rituals and the object they honoured, it was important to speak to one of the dabtaras, who are revered and indeed feared for the extent of their learning. Their great erudition includes a knowledge of medicine and the related skill of magic. In Ethiopia, writing has often been regarded with suspicion, as something shameful and degrading, and yet too sacred to be allowed to spread beyond a small and highly educated class. The knowledge of its secrets gave access to magical powers, to the ability to perform evil as well as good. The dabtaras are known to prepare protective amulets and charms, or the magical texts required for divination. They can conjure spirits to perform marvels, invoking King Solomon and the saints. They can use their powers to prevent hailstorms.

The origin of the title *dabtara* is now obscure, but it recalls the Tabernacle in which the Ark of the Covenant was placed in the Priestly Code. In the Ethiopic translation of the Old Testament,

'Tabernacle' is translated as *dabtara orit* and at both Aksum and the royal court we know of *kahnata dabtara*, 'priests of the Tabernacle'. The phrase *dabtara martul*, 'Tabernacle of witness', was used to describe the church tent that accompanied the Solomonid emperor Amda Seyon on one of his campaigns. The sacred enclosure around the church of Mary of Zion was also called *dabtara* at the beginning of the century, at least according to the Deutsche Axum-Expedition. Although no one seems to know about this in Aksum today, it may be attested in the *Book of Aksum*, which refers to 'many ruined churches in the territory of the *dabtara*', and lists several of them, each with the description 'of the *dabtara*'.

There are also traditions that the name *dabtara* began to be used during the reign of Dagnajan, a king supposed to have ruled just before the advent of the Zagwe dynasty. The king is said to have taken a hundred and fifty priests from Aksum to Amhara. He had sixty *tabotat* that accompanied him onto the battlefield. As he kept these in tents known as *dabtara*, the name was applied to the priests who consecrated the sacraments.

We hoped to consult a dabtara who lived in one of the suburbs of Aksum, and after drinking Turkish coffee in the Garden of Ezana, we walked to see him in the cool air of the morning. He lived in a single room that stood by itself in a large garden surrounded by a wall. Although the room was plainly furnished, it was decorated with photographs of his family and printed illustrations of Christ and Our Lady Mary. From the other rooms, the women of his family came to bring incense and to make coffee: aunts, sisters, a wife and several daughters. As the dabtara sat down on his bed, we could smell the fragrance of the beans while they were tossed in a pan over the coals of the kitchen fire, followed by the tapping of the brass pestle as they were ground.

The dabtara was dressed in white robes, his shamma often covering the lower part of his face, while the shadow from his turban covered much of the rest. His eyes were keen, and his conversation revealed the learning and the acute intelligence that one might expect in one of the masters of ancient tradition. From time to time, he would reach beneath his bed to produce a copy of the Bible in Ge'ez, the classical language of Ethiopia. His learning might encompass many arcane or even occult matters, but the primary source of his knowledge of the greatest mysteries was clearly the Bible itself. In his hand he held a whisk, although the smoke of the incense drove the flies from his door as well as delighting his visitors.

He began by speaking of the coded writing that the dabtaras use to preserve their secrets, but insisted that its characters could not be revealed to anyone outside his room. He then wrote several lines of the script on a sheet of paper, and requested that anything written about the history of Aksum and the Ethiopian Church should be generous to the dabtaras. It would be easy, he said, to mock the ancient knowledge that the dabtaras preserved, or to scandalize or horrify those who had never been to Ethiopia and had no understanding of its traditions. He then spoke of the beginnings of the dabtaras. They were not priests, he reminded us, but they were wise men, as Solomon had been wise in the old days. They had knowledge of medicine and of magic. They could call the saints to perform miracles, and they could summon the spirits known as *zar*. He spoke of the ancient chants revealed to Yared by God, of the service the dabtaras offer the church by teaching the sacred music and dance, and of the rituals at the great festivals of Timqat and Hedar Seyon at which the *tabotat* are carried in procession. The priests, he told us, were descended from the Levites who arrived with the Tablet of Moses, and only the priests could carry a *tabot*.

No other church uses the *tabot* because only the Ethiopian Church has the Tablet of Moses. The Chapel of the Tablet contains what it says: the Tablet of Moses. The holy relic is the Tablet. God is in it. It is the only one in the world. The Bible tells us that the Law comes out of Zion. Therefore, the only law comes out of Aksum.

The *tabotat* are different from the Tablet. They belong to the New Covenant. They are Christian. Wine and bread are placed on the *tabot* during the liturgy. In the Bible, we read that the power of God entered Mary, and that Christ took flesh from Mary. The Cross on the *tabot* is like Christ himself. The bread and the wine of the sacrament are placed on the *tabot*. They are like the flesh and the blood of Christ. The priests then pray and sing, and the Holy Spirit descends for that moment upon it to perform the miracle.

Although the Old Testament spoke of animal sacrifice, the priests did not perform sacrifices when a new church was built and a *tabot* installed. Jesus himself was the final sacrifice, he said, and no other sacrifice is needed. Miracles often occur with the *tabotat*, but they must not be misunderstood. To help us understand the point, he told a parable about a man who was hungry and thirsty. When he was given a basket with some bread to eat, and a cup with water in it, was it the basket and the cup that satisfied his hunger and thirst, or was it the bread and the water within them? Wood or stone in themselves have no value, the dabtara said, but the power of God could act through them.

He spoke of the origins of the church of Mary of Zion and its *tabotat*. In the days of Frumentius, the first bishop of Ethiopia, there were three *tabotat* in the church. The ancient kings Abreha and Asbeha built twelve churches, each of which had a *tabot*. The dabtara was evidently referring to twelve chapels within the great church rather than twelve individual churches, because he went on to say that after the dreadful Queen Gudit destroyed the church, Anbassa Wudem rebuilt five churches. Still later, when the church of Mary of Zion was built again by Fasiladas after the invasion of the Grañ, the emperor built three churches.

Although many people believe that the sacred relic from the Chapel of the Tablet is carried in public at the great festival of *Timqat*, which celebrates the Baptism of Christ, the dabtara insisted that this was not the custom. Instead, the priests carry the *tabot* of Jesus from the church of Mary of Zion. His explanation of the custom was intriguing, but his next remarks were quite unexpected. The Tablet in the Chapel was unique, he told us, but it was not the only one. Another Tablet had been brought from Caesarea. According to tradition, Christ had given it to his disciples. It is unique, and it is the measure of all the *tabotat* in Ethiopia. Their size and their form follow it. Like the Tablet of Moses, he said, it is original, and it is known as the Tablet of Mary.

Both the guardian and the most learned dabtara we know in Aksum had stated that the Chapel of the Tablet contained exactly what its name suggested: the Tablet of Moses. Would the senior priest in Aksum, the neburaed, agree with them? And would he have anything to say about a second Tablet? In many ways, this was the most fascinating remark that the dabtara had made. In the Hebrew Bible, in the books of the rabbis who attempted to understand it, and in the reports of the Arab historians, the evidence would be easier to collate if there had been more than one Ark. Even though the editors of the Bible seem to have assumed that more than one Ark must mean more than one God, and found the idea quite unacceptable, this may not have been the assumption of earlier centuries. In Aksum, it seems, something of the ancient belief might still be glimpsed. The Tablet in the Chapel was unique, but there was another Tablet even so.

The title *neburaed* derives from the way in which it is conferred, by the laying on of hands. During the early years of the Solomonid dynasty, there were many of them in Ethiopia, especially as the abbots of great monasteries. Now, only the neburaed of Aksum remains. His predecessors were powerful men, controlling vast estates as fiefs, and possessing great privileges at court. They were allowed to sit in the presence of the emperor, while almost everyone else was forced to stand.

The present neburaed, the senior priest of Aksum, administers the religious life of the ancient city from an office in a simple row of rooms built of concrete, to the north of the Chapel of the Tablet. An old man with a thin white beard, the neburaed wore a shamma and a turban, and held a hand cross. His responsibilities weigh heavily on him. A formal appointment was required, and during the meeting he was constantly interrupted by deacons, who entered the office, approached him, bowed and kissed his hand, and then asked him about urgent business, or perhaps delivered a letter. His signature and his official stamp appeared on dozens of public notices, and bureaucracy and protocol are clearly demanding. When we entered the room, he appeared to be anxious, and throughout the conversation he weighed his answers carefully, as if he were conscious that a careless word might bring more publicity and more curious visitors to his ancient church, and make the burden of administering it even more onerous.

He spoke of the Tablet in the Chapel, of the Covenant of Mercy, of the importance to Ethiopia of Mary, and of the history of the church and the city, but he was often interrupted and distracted by the deacons and spoke only a few sentences on each topic. Nevertheless, he persevered and spoke of the identity of Our

Mother Zion. Under the Old Covenant, Zion was the holy city of Jerusalem, but under the New Covenant, it comprised every Christian. He then described the Tablet in the Chapel as the Tablet of the Law of the Covenant between Mary and Ethiopia. Despite the interruptions, his account of Aksumite tradition was fascinating. Like the guardian, he clearly believed that the sacred object in the Chapel was a Tablet. He also believed that the Tablet was the sign of a covenant, but he spoke not of the covenant between God and Israel made at Mount Sinai, but of the covenant between Mary and Ethiopia, the Covenant of Mercy, by which Christ allowed his Mother to save her Chosen People. Furthermore, the neburaed agreed with the dabtara that there was not only one original Tablet, but another as well. He repeated the tradition that it had been brought from Caesarea, where Christ had given it to his disciples. As the dabtara had said, this Tablet was unique and original, just as the Tablet of Moses was.

The conviction of the guardian, the dabtara and the neburaed that the Chapel of the Tablet did in fact contain the Tablet of Moses was in marked contrast with the emphasis that *The Glory of Kings* and many recent studies of Ethiopia have placed on the Ark of the Covenant. Yet there is evidence from earlier centuries that made the same claim, and which has largely been ignored.

From the reign of the Ethiopian emperor Yeshaq, between 1414 and 1429, we have evidence that seems to refer to the Tablets rather than the Ark. The cardinal Guillaume Fillastre added a map to the translation of Ptolemy's *Geography* produced by Giacomo Angelo, on which he recorded that in 1427 the 'Prester John' had sent two ambassadors from Ethiopia to Spain. They arrived in Valencia bearing a letter that the emperor had written to Alfonso V, the king of Aragon. The cardinal de Foix, legate of the Holy See, witnessed the audience with the king and later described it to Pope Martin V when Fillastre was present. From the reply that Alfonso prepared for Yeshaq, it appears that the Ethiopian emperor had employed the title 'Yeshaq, son of Dawit, possessor of the Tablets of the Law and of the Throne of David'.

The letter contained a proposal to arm the Aragonese fleet and to cement this alliance between Ethiopia and Aragon with a double marriage. Yeshaq would marry the Infanta Doña Juana, and the

Infante Don Pedro would marry an Ethiopian princess. This proposal seems to have been accepted, and two priests were sent to prepare lodgings for the princess in Ethiopia and to investigate the condition of the Ethiopian armies. Nothing further seems to be known about the adventure, except that letters from the king of Aragon to the Grand Master at Rhodes and to the king of Cyprus reveal that his agents were to travel through Jerusalem and then on to Egypt.

The claim made by Yeshaq mentions two of the objects that Abu Salih attributed to the Zagwe king: the Tablets of the Law and the Throne of David. The Ark of the Covenant seems to have been forgotten.

The account that Francisco Alvares wrote of his mission to Ethiopia survives in several versions. One of them, a copy made by the archbishop of Ragusa, Ludovico Beccadelli, includes some additional notes obtained from Ethiopian priests who were living in Rome. When Alvares mentions the thirteen tent churches that travelled with the nomadic imperial court, one of these notes explains that 'The Ethiopians say that the churches are twelve, as also are the tribes, and besides there is the church of the king, which contains the Tablets of the Law given to Moses.' Once again, the Tablets are mentioned in isolation.

In the Arabic records of the Muslim war against the Christian empire, known rather optimistically as *Futuh al-Habasha*, 'The Conquest of Abyssinia', we are told that the emperor Lebna Dengel marched to Aksum with his nobles and his troops. After they had assembled, the emperor ordered 'the great idol' to be brought from the church of Aksum. It was apparently a white stone encrusted with gold, and was so large that it could not be carried through the door of the church. A hole the size of the idol had to be opened, and 400 men were needed to carry it. They took the idol to the country of Shire, where it was stored in a fortress.

The statement that 400 men were needed to carry the idol suggests an object much larger than any of the other sources have reported, but if the description given by Arab Faqih is in any way correct, this immense stone object would seem to have been a tablet rather than a wooden box. In other words, the sources that lie behind the account would seem to have envisaged a Tablet rather than an Ark. The account was compiled at more or less the same time that Francisco Alvares wrote of an altar stone at Aksum that had been brought from Jerusalem, and it would seem to support the statements that Alvares recorded.

Yet another version of the story, which is more or less contemporary with that of Alvares, was published by Damião de Góis and then by Michael Geddes in his *Church History*. It is a translation of a document prepared by Saga Za-Ab, the ambassador of the emperor Lebna Dengel, when he arrived at Lisbon in 1527. Saga Za-Ab was a senior cleric, and he summarizes in a few pages the story of *The Glory of Kings* as 'the history of the said King David, which is a book about the bigness of St Paul's Epistles, and very pleasant to read'. He mentions the Ark and other details as they occur in *The Glory of Kings*, but he specifically states that only the Tablets of the Covenant were taken to Ethiopia: 'Azarias after having with great speed and secrecy got Tablets made in imitation of the Tablets of the Covenant of the Lord, did whilst he was offering sacrifice, with great dexterity steal the True Tablets of the Ark of the Covenant, and put his new ones in the place of them, none but God and himself being conscious to what he had done ...' Azarias eventually revealed to Menelik that 'he had brought the Tablets of the Covenant of the Lord along with him', and the young king went 'to the place where those Tablets were kept', dancing with joy in their presence. The Ark is never mentioned in these passages except as the original repository of the Tablets.

Astonishingly, we find ourselves with the testimony of a senior Ethiopian cleric who believed, around 1534, that only the Tablets of Moses had reached Ethiopia. Even at this late stage, therefore, when *The Glory of Kings* is supposed to have been for centuries the official account of national and dynastic identity, an Ethiopian bishop makes a claim that is quite different from the accepted view of Ethiopian history.

The Glory of Kings, as we know it from the published editions, is not the only version of the claim that the Ethiopian royal house descended from Solomon and the Queen of Sheba. The Portuguese traveller and historian João de Barros preserves a lengthy account of the tradition, in which he too refers to the Tablets of Moses rather than the Ark. According to the writings of the Abyssinian people, he tells us, the Queen of Sheba of Ethiopia had learned that

Solomon, the king of Judaea, had earned a great reputation for his power and his wisdom. In order to learn the truth about him, she sent an ambassador to Jerusalem, and when he returned and told her the things that he had seen and heard, she began to hope that she might acquire something of this wisdom even though she was an idolator herself. She left for Jerusalem with great pomp and display, sailing from the Red Sea port of Sabath, where a city has been named after her to mark the occasion. Having crossed the Red Sea to Arabia, she arrived at Jerusalem after a long journey in the desert. One of the first things that she saw was a kind of bridge built of wooden beams so that people might cross over the waters of a lake. Seized with the spirit of prophecy, she refused to walk on it, declaring that she could not place her feet on wood that had caused such suffering to the Saviour of the World. Later, when she was with Solomon, she asked him to have the beams removed.

Solomon received her with honour when she arrived, partly because of the quantities of gold, perfumes and precious stones that she had brought for the Temple and for the king to use in his palace. She stayed with him until she had been instructed in the law and had conceived a son by him. She gave birth on the way back to her kingdom, and when the boy had grown, she sent him to his father with a request. She asked that Solomon anoint him as King of Ethiopia before the Tabernacle of the Sanctuary, so that he could be her successor. She made this request despite the succession in her kingdom always having passed through the female line and not through the male. Apparently, this had been the custom of the pagans in the country.

The boy was called Meilech, and when he arrived at Jerusalem, he was received by his father with great tenderness. His request was granted, and when the time came for him to be anointed by the king, he changed his name to David, in memory of his grand-father. After he had been instructed in the Law of God, Solomon decided to send the boy back to his mother. From each of the twelve tribes of Israel, he gave him officials similar to those in his own household, and as head priest, he gave him Azaria, the son of Sadoch, who was the head priest in the Temple of Jerusalem. A few days before their departure, David asked that Azaria be allowed to enter the Holy of Holies to pray and offer sacrifice for the success of the journey, and while he was there, he stole the

Tablets of the Law. In their place, he put other Tablets that he had made for the purpose without telling David. After they had left Jerusalem and reached the borders of Ethiopia, he told him. Wanting to imitate his grandfather in his zeal for the honour of the Law of God, David went with great joy to the tent of Azaria, and taking the Tablets from the place where they were kept, he began to dance and to sing praises to God. Everyone who was with him joined in the dance and song, as soon as they saw the reason for his joy. When David returned to his mother, she entrusted the kingdom to him. Since that day, according to the Abyssinians, all their kings have been descended from him. No woman has reigned among them. Furthermore, all the officials who serve the kings are descended from the young men who arrived from Jerusalem with the new king.

In 1660, Balthasar Telles reported statements that the Roman Catholic patriarch of Ethiopia, Alfonso Mendes, had made five years earlier about a mysterious tablet at Aksum. It was supposed to be one of the Tablets of the Law, although it was said to be made of wood rather than of stone. Mendes himself was therefore unwilling to believe that it could really be one of the Tablets from Mount Sinai.

The Ethiopian historians, according to Mendes, tell a story that is widely believed among them. One of the Tablets of the Law is the altar stone of the church at Aksum, which in the past had been the capital of Ethiopia and the seat of the patriarchate. They say that it still survives, that it is a tablet and that it is made of very precious wood. But if it were one of the Tablets of the Law, which had been in the Ark of the Covenant, Mendes argued, it would not be of wood. The Tablets that God gave to Moses, both the first and the second pair, had been made of stone. It was a complete fiction that there were Tablets of wood in the Ark and that one of them was in Aksum.

Whatever Mendes had been told, earlier witnesses claim that the Tablet was indeed made of stone, and more recent witnesses who actually claim to have seen it have been in no doubt that it was stone. Is it possible that they were not shown the same object that earlier historians describe?

In the latter part of the eighteenth century, an Armenian merchant named Yohannes Tovmacean travelled to Ethiopia in the hope of selling jewels to the imperial family. In return for the gifts he presented to the empress Mentewab and her son Iyoas, he received nothing more than some animals and chickens, and a house in the palace compound furnished with a single small carpet. He was discouraged, but he remained in Ethiopia to supervise the state treasury. In 1764, while he was at Aksum with his companion Bijo, he claimed that he saw a stone kept in the church and was told that it was part of the Tablets that had been inscribed with the Ten Commandments.

There was also a large and ancient Abyssinian church, he writes, where a piece of the stone Tablet of the Ten Commandments carried by Moses was said to have been preserved. He claims that both he and Bijo were taken into the church and shown a closed altar said to contain this Tablet, but the priests did not open it. Bijo announced that he was a relative of the king, and when he insisted that they open it, they eventually agreed, although with a great deal of hesitation. They removed a parcel wrapped in cloth and began to unwrap it with some ceremony. Tovmacean saw a packet wrapped in another parcel of velvet, and apparently it was not until the priests had removed a hundred of these wrappings that they finally revealed a piece of stone with a few incomplete letters on it. Kneeling before the stone, they made the sign of the Cross, and kissed it. After this the stone was again wrapped and restored to the altar, which was then closed. 'This was a great relic,' Tovmacean reported, 'if it was indeed a piece of the tablet of the Ten Commandments which God gave to Moses.'

It seems that no claim was made to Tovmacean that this altar was in fact the Ark. He may have been shown a fragment of an old inscription, or possibly an old and broken *tabot*, which was specially venerated for some reason. It may really have been thought to be part of one of the Tablets of Moses. If the 'closed altar' were in the sanctuary, as seems most likely, the object may have been one of the *tabotat* used in the church at the time. But it seems very unlikely that the priests would have shown to a passing Armenian jeweller something that they had guarded for so long, and had protected even against emperors such as Susneyos. Neither his temporary rank as an imperial official nor the royal connections that his companion Bijo claimed to possess would have impressed the priests of Mary of Zion, who were capable of refusing an emperor himself. Tovmacean and Bijo were probably shown a local stone *tabot*. Whatever it was, however, he reports a tradition in which the emphasis is placed on a Tablet rather than on an Ark.

Another Armenian visitor, the Reverend Father Dimotheos Vartabet Sapritchian, came to Ethiopia a century later, during the reign of the emperor Tewodros. He was accompanying 'Sa Grandeur' the Archbishop Isaac de Kharpert of Jerusalem as legate from the Armenian patriarch of Jerusalem, and they were hoping to free the British prisoners held at Maqdala by the emperor. As part of such a delegation, Dimotheos was a cleric of undoubted position. He recorded that in May 1869 he was permitted to see the sacred object, the Tablet of the Ten Commandments, kept at the church of Mary of Zion.

Archbishop Isaac and his party were received with great respect by *dejazmatch* Kassa, the future emperor Yohannes IV. They went to the church to pray, and Dimotheos offers a brief description of the place and some of the Aksumite stelae nearby. Then he supplies a detailed account of his viewing the holy relic belonging to the church, with a great deal of quotation from his own speeches on the occasion. Dimotheos noted that the Abyssinians had very great veneration for a certain stone tablet, which was called the Tablet of the Ten Commandments. They believed that it was the same Tablet that God had given to the prophet Moses, and that it had been brought from Jerusalem during the reign of Minilik, the first king of Ethiopia. At the time of Jesus Christ, the Abyssinians said, a pious man called Ezekiel took the Tablet with him to Jerusalem. Presenting himself to Christ, he asked him for advice about the divine commandments written on the Tablet. Should they be accepted or not? Without opening his mouth, Jesus took the Tablet and wrote on the other side of it in letters of gold: 'Accept everything that is written here.' Since then the Tablet has been regarded as having been written by God himself.

Father Dimotheos was more than sceptical. The Abyssinians claim that this legend is found in their ancient books, he wrote, but it is contrary to the Holy Scriptures, in which it is expressly stated that the Tablet was placed in the Ark of the Covenant. He was indignant and outraged to see what he called 'a revolting lie' accepted as truth throughout the kingdom of Abyssinia. He was all the more keen to see the stone, so that he could tell everyone about the deception.

He had been told that the Tablet was in the Church of Aksum, placed in a precious coffer, and that no one could see it or touch it without being punished for their presumption. Apparently the emperor Tewodros had wanted to see it, but God did not judge him worthy.

Dimotheos and his party asked *dejazmatch* Kassa to order the priests to let them see the stone when they visited the church. They wished to venerate it, they said. The priests at Aksum must have puzzled as to how they should deal with the Armenians, and their prevarication annoyed Dimotheos. At first, they claimed that only the 'great Abounas' could grant the necessary permission. The new metropolitan was due to arrive soon, and their request could then be presented to him. Dimotheos launched into a speech, remarking that traditions should be respected, of course, but that theirs was simply astonishing. It prevented Christians from hon-ouring such a sacred object. Which was the more worthy of veneration, he asked, the Tablet or the Holy Cross? After some discussion, the priests agreed that the Holy Cross was the greater. Dimotheos then asked why, if the Cross was not hidden but exhibited everywhere, should anyone be prevented from touching and venerating this Tablet written by the hand of God himself? Dimotheos added that the secrecy and concealment surrounding this Tablet simply added to doubts about its authenticity: 'It would be better, then, that all were free to come and venerate it publicly, for then belief in its authenticity would be better armed, and it would attract greater respect.' After further lecturing the Aksumite priests on their failure to teach the Gospels to the adulterous, murdering, lying and hypocritical Ethiopians, while maintaining this much less important tradition, Dimotheos claims that they promised to consult together. They hoped, they said, 'that your request will be accepted, something which, until now, has never happened for anyone'.

The council was held. Perhaps from hearsay or even his own imagination, Dimotheos supplies an account of it. He describes how *dejazmatch* Kassa complained that 'the tablet of the Tabot of Moses' was losing its reputation through the refusal of the priests: 'It is a great blow for it, until now regarded among us as an object more worthy of respect than the Holy Cross itself, and to which, I dare to say, we render honours due only to the Divinity.' The priests decided to show the Tablet, and they came back to report this good news. But by now, Dimotheos had changed his tactics. He haughtily told them that as Christians they had faith enough. They did not need to see the object. Anyway, he added, they had with them a piece of the Holy Cross, worthy of all their respect and veneration: 'The laws engraved on your Tablet, we carry already inscribed at the bottom of our hearts.' At this, the dignitaries of Aksum retired in confusion. Dimotheos, with what veracity we will never know, states that when Kassa himself learned of the matter, he came and said, 'They are all ignorant, I ask you to excuse them, and to go to the church to see the Tabot of Moses.' And so Kassa, the 'Grand Prince', with all the great officers of his court and the clergy, went with them to the church.

When they arrived, Dimotheos reports, everyone went into the vestibule. They were then led by several of the clergy into the sacristy that had been built outside the church, to the left, at the end of a row of other rooms. Inside the sacristy, on the ground floor, there was a wooden attic that could be reached only by climbing a movable ladder. One of the priests climbed up it and then removed two planks from the ceiling to make room for the other priests, who followed him. Holding a censer in his hand, a deacon approached a coffer, and after he had censed it, he gave his censer to the visitors so that they could do the same. The coffer was a casket of Indian work. When it was opened, they saw the Tablet of the Ten Commandments.

They removed the Tablet so that they could examine it more closely. The stone was evidently pink marble of a type usually found in Egypt. It was quadrangular, 24 cm long by 22 cm wide, and only 3 cm thick. At the edges, it was decorated with engraved flowers. In the centre, there was a second quadrangular line in the form of a fine chain, and the space between the two frames contained the Ten Commandments, five on one side and five on the other. They were written, Dimotheos tells us, 'obliquely in Turkish fashion', and at the base of the Tablet, between the two frames, were three letters. He believed that they were some sort of date, which no one seemed able to read. As a final opinion of this great relic, Dimotheos wrote that the stone was nearly intact and showed no sign of age. He thought that it could be no earlier than the thirteenth or fourteenth century, but he did not reveal how he made his estimate.

The party then returned to *dejazmatch* Kassa, who was waiting for them in the vestibule of the church with his court and clergy. One of the clerics asked them what they had seen: 'Were not the ancient laws inscribed on the two sides of the mosaic Tablet, just as they are on the Tablet you have just seen?' The visitors replied that the commandments were inscribed on both sides of the Tablet, and Dimotheos remarked that the conversation went no further because the clergy feared that the truth would be discovered. The 'Grand Prince' at least was pleased with their reply, and he said: 'The suspicions which have occupied the spirits of some are now departed; they believed that the Ten Commandments were inscribed in the middle, now this Tablet is regarded by them as apocryphal.'

Dimotheos added that, in the presence of Kassa and the uneasy clergy, they did not wish to indicate 'that the stone which they guarded with them, in such great veneration, was not the true original, but those who know the Holy Scriptures need no proof to admit it'. He cites the biblical story that the divine laws were inscribed on two tablets, which were put into the Ark of the Covenant and then lost for ever. In addition, the original was written in Hebrew, not Ethiopic, and did not have a date on it. Dimotheos concluded that it was a forgery. The priests knew this, but employed it to impose upon the people, and had invented the 'traditional defence' of keeping it inaccessible from the laity.

Most probably, like Tovmacean a century earlier, Dimotheos was shown a typical stone *tabot*. Some of the examples in collections outside Ethiopia are decorated in a style very like his description. One intriguing point remains. The 'sacristy' that Dimotheos describes might perhaps have been the Chapel of the Tablet itself, if a separate chapel existed by that time. As he approached the church of Mary of Zion, walking 'to the left' would lead Dimotheos toward the north, and the end of 'a row of other rooms' would lead him to where the Chapel stood in 1906, beyond the small church of Mary Magdalene and the mausoleum of Tewoflos. Whatever he was shown, he may have been granted an extraordinary privilege. Even if the clergy decided that they could not reveal the sacred relic to him and decided to present a substitute, the story is another witness to the importance placed on the Tablet rather than on an Ark.

As all these accounts of the great relic at Aksum describe a Tablet rather than an Ark, it is intriguing that the Ethiopian church includes the Book of Jubilees in its canon of the Old Testament. Fragments of the Hebrew text have been discovered among the Dead Sea Scrolls, and passages have been preserved in Greek, Syriac, and Latin translations, but the entire book survives only in Ethiopia. Jubilees includes an alternative account of the revelation on Mount Sinai, in which Moses is given Tablets by an angel, but the Ark of the Covenant is never mentioned. It also tells us that when the Children of Israel enter the Promised Land, they will erect the Tabernacle of the Lord. It will contain an altar, but once again, there is no mention of an Ark.

CHAPTER 19

The Resurrection of Osiris

By October 1922, Howard Carter had become desperate. He had been digging in the Valley of the Kings for six years, but he had found almost nothing, and his friends were now anxious that he might be close to nervous collapse. 'After these barren years were we justified in going on with it?' he asked himself. 'We had worked for months at a stretch and found nothing, and only an excavator knows how depressing that can be; we had almost made up our minds that we were beaten...'

Nevertheless, he was determined to persevere for one final season, and even though his patron, the Earl of Carnarvon, had already decided to abandon the excavation, Carter persuaded him to reverse his decision and bear the cost one more time. On the first day of November, Carter had enrolled his workmen and was ready to begin. Cutting a trench towards the south from the north-east corner of the tomb of the pharaoh Rameses VI, he removed the huts built for labourers who had worked on the tomb 3,000 years earlier, and prepared to dig through the soil to the bedrock.

When he arrived for work on the morning of 4 November, he was surprised to see that his men had stopped and were waiting for him in silence. Something extraordinary must have happened, he thought, and he was soon greeted with the announcement that they had discovered a single step leading down into the earth. Fearful that the news was too good to be true, but desperate to believe that he had found an unopened tomb at last, he worked feverishly throughout the day and began again the following morning. As the steps emerged from the soil, Carter tormented himself by recalling all his previous disappointments. The tomb might never have been used. It might never have been completed. It might have been plundered by ancient grave robbers. But the excavation was gathering pace. Step followed step, and by sunset on the second day, Carter could see the upper part of a doorway, plastered and sealed.

Trembling with excitement, and with relief that his faith in the Valley of the Kings had been rewarded, Carter later wrote that it took all his self-control to keep from breaking down the door. 'Alone, save for my native workmen, I found myself, after years of comparatively unproductive labour, on the threshold of what might prove to be a magnificent discovery. Anything, literally anything, might lie beyond that passage.'

Even in his euphoria, he recalled that the cost of so many years of excavation had been met by his patron, and on the following morning he sent his famous telegram to England: 'At last have made wonderful discovery in Valley; a magnificent tomb with seals intact; re-covered same for your arrival; congratulations.'

Within three weeks, Carnarvon had made the journey by sea to Alexandria, and then up the Nile from Cairo to Luxor, where Carter was waiting. Accompanied by his daughter, Lady Evelyn Herbert, and by Carter's assistant, Arthur Callender, they opened the tomb in advance of the Egyptian inspectors. 'Slowly, desperately slowly,' Carter later wrote, 'it seemed to us as we watched, the remains of passage debris that encumbered the lower part of the doorway were removed.' Widening the hole a little, he inserted his candle and peered inside, his patron and his assistant standing anxiously beside him. He could see nothing at first. The candle flickered in the hot air that escaped from the chamber. As his eyes grew accustomed to the light, details of the room began to emerge from the mist: strange animals, statues and gold. For the moment, he was struck dumb with amazement. Eventually Carnarvon could endure the suspense no longer and asked if Carter could see anything. Carter struggled to find the words and could only say, 'Yes, wonderful things.'

As he peered into the antechamber of the tomb, Carter saw the great beds and the dismantled chariots, the thrones and boxes covered in gold, intricate alabaster vessels, furniture inlaid with ivory, faience, glass and semi-precious stones. Among the piles of objects on the floor of the antechamber, in front of the famous lion bed, was a chest unlike any other buried with the pharaoh, or any found elsewhere in Egypt. For the past seventy-five years, the treasures discovered with Tutankhamun have captured the imagination of the public, and the fascination with coffins of solid gold and all the other paraphernalia of the Egyptian dead is easy to understand. But in the excitement, this chest is often overlooked, and in many ways it is the most fascinating discovery of all. Of any object known to survive from antiquity, the chest is most like the biblical account of the Ark of the Covenant.

Standing on four legs capped with bronze, and rising to a gabled lid above a cornice with a gilded base, the chest is smaller than the Ark, but of almost identical proportions. Because of its size and its weight, the chest was provided with four poles so that it could be carried just as the Ark had been, by men who stood in front of it and behind it. Each pole can slide back and forth through bronze rings, which are attached to boards fixed underneath the box.

Both the gable lid and the box of the chest are built with a frame of ebony and recessed panels in a red wood thought to be cedar. Each panel has a border assembled from strips of ivory and polished ebony, laid alternately, and the ebony is covered with bands of hieroglyphic inscription, incised and filled with yellow paint. The words of the gods promise the king that his mouth, his eyes and his ears will be opened, and that his limbs will again be strong. Heaven will receive his soul, and earth his body, and he will be granted all kinds of sustenance. The gods assure the king that, in return for the offerings presented to them, he will enjoy the cool breeze, he will drink wine, and he will inhale the odour of incense. Like the sun-god, he will assume any form he chooses, he will live in the company of the gods in the boat of his father, Re, and he will be born again every day. He will live as long as the sun, and he will be granted all the other blessings given to a king when he is among the blessed dead.

Carved in the cedar panel at one end of the chest, within a rect-angular frame bearing the hieroglyphic sign for 'heaven', two figures stand facing each other: a god and a king. The inscription proclaims the god to be 'Onnophris, the great god, lord of the City of the Dead'. As a form of Osiris, god of death and resurrection, he wears a crown adorned with ostrich plumes and the *uraeus*, the royal serpent of Lower Egypt, and he is wrapped in the long white shroud of the mummified dead. The king who stands before him is Tutankhamun, and the hieroglyphic inscription indicates that, when the pharaoh performs the ritual before the god, he is dead himself.

The chest would have been carried in the funeral ceremony, when the long period set aside for mourning in silence had passed. The procession included priests who presided over the embalming of the body, and courtiers who carried the essential furniture for the tomb: thrones, beds, coffers with jewels and ritual garments, boxes with offerings, vases with unguents, and the four canopic urns containing the vital organs. Walking before the mummy, the priests poured libations of milk to ensure that the pharaoh would be reborn among the gods.

When they reached the Nile, the men and the women in the procession embarked on boats, which the priests directed along a route decreed by ancient liturgy – a pilgrimage to the holy cities of the Delta. Their first destination was the city of the west, Sais, which symbolized the earth in which the body would be buried. From Sais, they proceeded to Buto, in the north, whose famous canal suggested the waters of the primordial abyss and the waters that surround the child in the womb. In the east stood Mendes, whose name was written in hieroglyphics with the two pillars of Osiris, god of the dead, and signified the element of air. Farther south, at Heliopolis, they found the fourth element. Here was the city of the sun, where the creator of life appeared at dawn, his fire undimmed by the long journey across the waters of the night.

At each of the four cities, the priests stepped ashore, revealing objects from the chests carried by the courtiers, and leaving offerings by the river bank. When they reached the quay of the royal funerary temple, they sealed the boxes and chests that held the fabrics and the jewels they had displayed during the procession, and prepared for the final burial rites. Once the tomb was closed, they celebrated a banquet to symbolize the end of mourning, with songs and dances that evoked the act of creation and the ritual drunkenness of the goddess Hathor, as she watched over the dead and over the acts of love that would bring new life. The banquet would help the pharaoh, who was believed to share in its pleasures, to walk the path toward rebirth.

The chest left by the priests in the tomb of Tutankhamun when they sealed the entrance may be the only example that has survived, but even before its discovery we knew that such chests had been carried in Egyptian funeral processions. In 1893 the French director of the Egyptian Antiquities Service, Jacques de Morgan, discovered the mastaba tomb of the grand vizier Mereruka at Saqqara, the principal necropolis of the Old Kingdom capital at Memphis. Mereruka had served the pharaoh Teti at the beginning of the Sixth Dynasty, twelve dynasties and a thousand years before Tutankhamun. Long before the French archaeologist began his excavations, the Arab historian Abd al-Latif had described the ancient tombs as miraculous. 'The more you reflect on them,' he wrote, 'the more they increase your admiration; and the more you look at them, the more they enhance your wonderment.' The reliefs in the mastaba of Mereruka are certainly among the most brilliant ever carved by Egyptian artists. While they have become famous for their portraits of the family hunting among the reeds by the bank of the Nile, their depictions of birds and crocodiles and hippopotamuses, and their scenes of a pharaoh's daughter playing the harp for her husband and amusing herself among her dancing girls, they are also of immense importance as a witness to the ancient ritual. The funeral procession includes servants bearing offerings of oil and linen sent by the pharaoh, and many of them carry rectangular chests with gabled lids that rest on long poles at the front and the back. The artist was obviously depicting a type of chest almost identical to that discovered by Howard Carter in the tomb of Tutankhamun.

But if these chests resemble the Ark of the Covenant most closely in terms of appearance, they would seem to have been chests for ritual garments, and however important they were in the life of the dead, their status was rather different from the throne of God. There were other processions, however, and other shrines whose similarity to the cult of the Ark of the Covenant is more intriguing, especially as the Book of Exodus tells us that Moses was raised and educated at the Egyptian court, at the heart of the imperial cult.

Despite his brief reign and his death at the age of only sixteen or seventeen, Tutankhamun left an impressive relief on the walls of the Processional Colonnade at Luxor. The temple had been built earlier in the Eighteenth Dynasty by Amenhotep III as an arena for the Festival of Opet, and it looks toward the great temple of Karnak rather than toward the Nile. The festival was held during the second month of the Nile flood, and it involved a ceremonial procession in which the god Amun and his consort, the goddess Mut, accompanied by the god Khonsu, made their way from

Karnak to Luxor and back again. The progress of the Theban triad, as the divinities are named, was achieved through the transport of sacred barques belonging to each of the gods, and while the Festival of Opet became the most important celebration during the New Kingdom, the portable barques of the gods became the dominant element in Egyptian cult. The barques themselves were venerated as divine beings, temple inscriptions record how they bestowed their blessings on the pharaohs and, as in the biblical accounts of the Ark of the Covenant, they were believed to choose the path along which they would be carried, indicating their intentions to the priests in some mysterious manner.

On the western wall of the Processional Colonnade, the artists employed by Tutankhamun depicted the procession of the gods to Luxor, and on the eastern wall their return to Karnak. As the boat of the pharaoh escorts the sacred barges of the Theban triad, Tutankhamun can be seen pouring a libation over the flowers and the other offerings, and blessing them with incense. Priests from the temple carry the sacred barques at shoulder height and step aboard the river barges to make their way up the Nile toward Luxor. When Tutankhamun embarks on his own barge, he gives a signal for the flotilla to cast off, towed south against the current by boatmen on the river bank. With pennants floating in the cool air by the water, and musicians and singers to honour the gods, the banks of the Nile are crowded with people.

When the great barge of Amun ties up at Luxor, the reliefs show the ceremonial barque of the god carried in procession to the temple. The pharaoh stops to watch women dancing to the sistra, and then he enters the temple with the procession. While the most sacred of the rituals are performed within, crowds of people sing and dance in the streets outside, waiting to acclaim their king when he emerges from the sanctuary as a god.

The reliefs and the inscriptions on the walls of the temple at Luxor have preserved a clear and detailed account of the rites for which it was constructed, and even if some of the rituals are obscure or mysterious, we know far more about them than we do about the cult of the Ark in Jerusalem. Luxor was the most important shrine in Egypt dedicated to the cult of a living divine ruler. Its rituals involved a symbolic enactment of the divine conception and birth of the pharaoh, his acknowledgement by Amun-Re and recognition by the nine gods of the Ennead, his coronation and the proclamation of his *ka*-name. This renewal of divine kingship was achieved during the festival in which the sacred barques were carried in procession, and it was part of the great drama of the annual rebirth of Amun-Re himself. The triumph over chaos represented by the rebirth of a divine king ensured the rebirth of the god as well.

This dramatic event was achieved through the ritual of incense, whose mysteries served to identify the reigning pharaoh with his divine ancestors, and it was during this ritual that the king became a god. Tutankhamun walked into the Barque Sanctuary, but Amun-Re walked out, and the transformation is made explicit by the inscriptions on the walls. The name of the pharaoh suddenly changes into the name of the god.

Just as the offering of incense before the images of the gods could induce a god to take up residence in his statue, so too the performance of the ritual before the pharaoh induced the gods to live within him. In the vestibule before the sanctuary, the pharaoh experienced a series of transformations as he drew nearer and nearer to the god, his *ka* was renewed and, full of this force of divine life, he proceeded into the Barque Sanctuary. In the reliefs on the western wall, the pharaoh appears as a mortal king; on the eastern wall, as the living royal *ka*. In the words of Amenhotep III, who built it, the temple at Luxor was 'his place of justification, in which he is reborn; the palace from which he sets out in joy at the moment of his Appearance, his transformations visible to all'.

While the Festival of Opet was of enormous importance, it was not the only procession of sacred barques. From reliefs and inscriptions in the temple of Dendera, we know of the barque of Osiris, which played a prominent part in the Osiris mysteries. The barque of Amun-Re appears in the reliefs in the temple at Medinet Habu. The three barques of Amun, Mut and Khonsu that were carried at the Festival of Opet were also carried to Deir el-Bahri during the Festival of the Valley. The goddess Hathor journeyed every year in her barque to Edfu, and in the temple of Hathor at Dendera there were barques dedicated to Osiris, Sokaris, Isis, Nephthys, Horus and Hathor herself. In fact, the description of the mysteries of Osiris at Dendera records that as many as thirty-four barques were carried in the ceremonies, five of which were dedicated to Anubis, Isis, Nephthys, Horus and Thoth.

In the history provided by the Book of Exodus, Moses was raised at the Egyptian court by the daughter of pharaoh. The story, of course, is one of the most famous in the Bible. A new king had apparently come to the throne, who knew nothing of the loyal service that the Israelite patriarch Joseph had offered the kings who ruled before him. He suspected that a flourishing Israelite community might turn against him if Egypt were ever attacked, making a common cause with his enemies. He decided to rule them with a heavy hand, but as he grew more oppressive, the prosperity of the Hebrews grew more obvious. After he tried to exhaust them through a programme of forced labour, he decided to exterminate them by ordering the midwives to kill any male child at birth. After the midwives disobeyed the order, because they feared God, he issued a proclamation that his people should throw any son born to the Hebrews into the Nile.

When Moses was born, his mother hid him, but by the time he was three months old, she realized that she could conceal a growing child no longer. She placed him in a basket of bulrushes sealed with bitumen and pitch, and took it down to the river, while his sister hid and waited to see what would happen. When the daughter of pharaoh come to the river to bathe, she found the child and, realizing that it was one of the Hebrews, she decided to find a Hebrew nursemaid to care for it. Fortunately, his own mother was chosen for the task, and after Moses had grown, he was brought to the palace and raised as the son of the pharaoh's daughter.

The name 'Moses' has long been known to be of Egyptian origin, despite the Hebrew etymology provided for it in the Bible. If he had been raised in privileged circumstances among the Egyptian elite, close to the court and the elaborate rituals that surrounded the divine pharaoh, is it possible that the religion Moses presented to the people of Israel as he led them in the wilderness was of Egyptian origin? Is it possible that the Ark was not only similar in appearance to the chest from the tomb of Tutankhamun, but similar in function to the Egyptian processional shrines?

The curious position of Moses, who stands on both sides of the great divide between Egypt and Israel, has tantalized scholars for generations. The question became even more intriguing during the twentieth century, after the discovery and translation of the inscriptions left by the heretical pharaoh Akhenaten, who ruled in the Eighteenth Dynasty and may have been the father of Tut-ankhamun. He overturned Egyptian religion and promulgated a cult of the god Aten, the single creative force in the universe. The famous *Hymn of Akenaten* has been seen as the basis of Psalm 104, and while the Egyptian origin of the Psalm is not as obvious as that of the famous passages in the Book of Proverbs, it is true that the *Hymn* is very different from conventional Egyptian religion. Could Moses have been the founder of a monotheistic religion that followed a pattern already laid down in Egypt?

The suggestion was startling when it was first made, as it appears to contradict everything that the Bible tells us about Egypt and Israel. Egypt is simply a land of idolatry. It stands for everything that Israel is meant to reject when the Chosen People depart for the Promised Land. When the God of Israel reveals himself on Mount Sinai, and Moses descends to find that the Children of Israel have made a Golden Calf, the Hebrew text says very little about the idol. Modern scholars have suggested that the incident is a veiled denunciation of the later cult established at Dan and Bethel by the Israelite king Jeroboam as an alternative to the Temple at Jerusalem, but the Aramaic translation in the Jerusalem Targum tells us explicitly that the idol is an image of the Apis Bull. This was an incarnation of the Egyptian god Osiris, and its cult was of immense antiquity. The appearance of the Apis Bull is recorded as early as the First Dynasty. It was also of immense importance. In 1851 Auguste Mariette discovered the Serapeum at Saqqara, and found twenty-eight huge sarcophagi which held the mummified bodies of every incarnation of the Apis Bull from the reign of Rameses II to the Twenty-sixth Dynasty. The Bible presents the Golden Calf as an absolute horror and abomination. It was a violation of the covenant between God and his Chosen People. The story became part of the liturgy of the Day of Atone-ment, reminding Israel of the sin committed at Sinai in the hope that God might turn aside from his wrath, renew the covenant and allow life to continue for another year.

What do other ancient records tell us about Moses and his education as an Egyptian? No evidence has been found in Egyptian papyri or inscriptions about either the life of Moses or the events of the Exodus. Aside from the Bible itself, the earliest account of the Exodus that survives was written by Hecataeus of Abdera in the fourth century BC. He describes Egypt as suffering from a plague. The Egyptians interpret this as a punishment sent by the gods, who are angry that foreigners have been allowed into Egypt and have brought foreign rites and customs with them. The only solution, apparently, is to expel the strangers. Under Kadmos and Danaos, some of them set out for Greece. Others follow Moses to Palestine. In a dramatic departure from Egyptian orthodoxy, Moses instructs his followers that they should never make images or worship them. He tells them that God does not possess a human form. In fact, God is the heaven that surrounds the earth. He is the lord of everything, and he cannot be depicted in images.

Hecataeus is not the only ancient historian to write in these terms, and although they share a number of themes, the differences between them suggest that they were relying on more than one source, none of which has survived. For anyone who has read only the biblical account, the effect is quite disconcerting, as if the Bible were being seen through a looking-glass. The Israelites were not a Chosen People who fled Egyptian slavery to seek a Promised Land. They were an unclean people who were expelled from the holy land of Egypt because they were not fit to live in it. The most extravagant example of this stance was adopted by the Egyptian priest Manetho, who wrote what is clearly an Egyptian refusal to accept the terms in which the Bible described Egypt and its religion.

When the Egyptian king wanted to see the gods, Manetho claims, he was told that he would be able to see them only if he drove all the lepers out of his kingdom. In obedience to these instructions, the king sent the lepers to work in the quarries of the eastern desert. While they were labouring among the rocks, they chose a priest from Heliopolis as a leader, who issued a set of instructions. They must not worship the gods, spare any of their sacred animals, abstain from other forbidden food or associate with other people. With help from the Hyksos, they rebelled against the king, who fled to Ethiopia. Their leader took the name Moses and launched a reign of terror in which everything holy was violated. Temples were laid waste, the images of the gods were destroyed and sacred animals were roasted on fires. After thirteen years of this horror, the Egyptian king was able to return and drive the lepers out of his country.

While the Bible claims that Moses imposed a religion that

required its adherents to turn from the wickedness of Egypt and embrace righteousness, Manetho inverted the Hebrew scripture, claiming that Moses turned from the righteousness of Egypt and embraced wickedness. But not all the ancient sources place Egypt and Israel in such absolute opposition. Apion, a Greek grammarian born at the oasis of El Kargeh, believed that Moses was an Egyptian priest from Heliopolis, who taught an Egyptian sun cult to the Jews. Pompeius Trogus, a Celt from Narbonne who wrote in Latin during the reign of Augustus, reported that Moses established a cult in Egypt. After he went to Jerusalem, he established an Egyptian cult there as well. He could do this because he 'secretly took the sacred objects of the Egyptians' – objects that the Egyptians had been attempting to recover by force when they were destroyed in a storm. These remarks suggest that whatever sources the historian was using assumed that the Ark of the Covenant was not simply like an Egyptian shrine, it actually was an Egyptian shrine. Even though it is not mentioned by name, it is the sacred object around which the Israelite cult was based in the Bible, and it is described in terms that suggest it would have been worth sending an army to recover it.

Perhaps the boldest statement about Moses as an Egyptian appears in the treatise *On the Jews*, written in the second century BC by Artipanos, himself a Jew. If Manetho was writing to contradict the Bible, Artipanos seems to have been writing to contradict Manetho, and despite his Jewish origin, his account of Moses is quite independent of the Bible. Although Moses was a Jew, he was the founder of Egyptian religion and civilization. He invented the hieroglyphic script, wrote the sacred texts and proclaimed a religion, dividing Egypt into thirty-five nomes and assigning a deity, sacred objects, images and even animals that should be worshipped in each of them. Instead of Moses being an Egyptian priest who establishes the religion of the Jews, he is a Jew who establishes the religion of the Egyptians.

The distinction between Egyptian and Israelite religion involved two different views of time, and two quite different answers to the question of where the power of God was located. One was determined by the cycle of the seasons, especially the annual pattern of death and rebirth through the flooding of the Nile. In the other, the rhythms of nature were subordinate to a God outside history who revealed himself in a succession of saving acts: choosing a people, delivering them from bondage, making a covenant with them, and leading them into a promised land. This is a linear process in historical time. The Ark of the Covenant is clearly depicted as part of the saving acts of God. It is revealed at Mount Sinai and is constructed according to an original in heaven. It contains the Tablets of the Law that set out the regulations of the covenant God has made, and it leads the Chosen People into the Promised Land, destroying their enemies as it goes. It displays a power outside the natural world, which threatens the natural order. To avoid death, strict precautions must be taken before one even approaches it, let alone touches it.

Yet once the Ark is placed in the Temple, it becomes part of a system by which not only the covenant with Israel is maintained and renewed, but the natural harmony of the world as well. The Ark can bring life as well as death, and even in the Bible this can be seen when David places it in the house of Obededom after Uzzah is killed, while he considers whether he can safely bring it into Jerusalem. The cosmic nature of the Temple is indicated in the Bible, but in later Jewish accounts it is made more explicit and more elaborate.

The order and harmony of creation was celebrated at the New Year Festival, when the Ark was carried in procession. This was the most important festival at the Temple, the festival of the manifestation of God, of the enthronement of God. Of the three great Jewish festivals, Josephus saw it as 'by far the greatest and the holiest', and it seems at one time to have included a dramatic celebration of the kingship of God, in which the Ark was carried out into the streets of Jerusalem and brought back to the Temple in triumph. The procession repeated the triumphal journey of God through the heavens, and crowds of worshippers saw and heard the revelation of the saving power of God. When the Ark was returned to the Temple, God once again sat on his throne in Zion.

On the basis of the Book of Psalms, scholars have argued that an annual festival existed at a very early date in which the Ark was carried to the Temple Mount with great ceremony. Their theories have been criticized because there is no explicit mention of such a festival in the Hebrew Bible, and because they relied on the testimony of a wide range of cults practised in different places at different times. This was the result of a belief that religion could be studied scientifically, that it passed through similar stages of development in every culture according to laws that could be recovered through historical research. A massive edifice of world religion was assembled on this basis, the evidence 'all marching into line and all marking in time', with elements added from a variety of sources and differences neglected in order to emphasize similarities. Nevertheless, whatever the excesses of the Scandinavian Patternists or the Myth and Ritual school, the Psalms do seem to preserve liturgical songs from such a festival. Unfortunately, they do not tell us the exact time at which it was celebrated. It may even have been a complex of holy days that eventually became the Jewish New Year, the Day of Atonement and the Week of Booths.

These days occurred in the autumn, a time in which the people of Palestine longed for rain. Without rain, after the dry months of the summer, the crops of the coming year would never grow. At the festival, God was revealed as overpowering the forces of chaos that threatened life, establishing order and harmony in the universe throughout his reign as king. The day on which God becomes king over the earth and executes judgement on his enemies is described by the prophet Zechariah, who proclaims that its blessings will be revealed as water:

And on that day living waters shall flow out from Jerusalem ... and the Lord shall become king over all the earth.

And if any of the families of the earth do not go up to Jerusalem to worship the King, the Lord of Hosts, there will be no rain upon them.

In the triumphal procession described in Psalm 68, musicians and princes accompany the Ark and recite the saving acts of God throughout history. During the march through the wilderness, and during the revelation at Mount Sinai, water is the sign of the presence of God and of his power: 'the heavens poured down rain, at the presence of God ... Rain in abundance, O God, you shed abroad; you restored your heritage as it languished.' In the vision of Ezekiel as well, which occurs in the Temple at New Year, during the Feast of Tabernacles, water flows from the door of the Temple out toward the East. Water from the sanctuary of the Temple brings life and fertility to the world.

During the time of the Second Temple, when the Ark was no longer kept in the Temple, we know that there was a ritual for rain associated with the Feast of Tabernacles. It is described in the Mishnah as a time of great rejoicing – a carnival atmosphere in which men danced with burning torches, and the Levites played instruments through the night. The priests led a procession through the Eastern Gate, the Water Gate, to Siloam, where they filled two golden flagons with water. When the procession returned, the water was received at the Temple with the words of the prophet Isaiah: 'With joy you will draw water from the wells of salvation.' At dawn, a priest climbed to the great altar and offered two libations, of water and wine, which flowed beneath the altar on the western side, the direction from which rain clouds would appear. The water and the wine flowed down to Kidron and from there, it was believed, to the River Jordan.

The great Jewish festivals were all kept in the new religion that emerged from Judaism after the death of Jesus Christ, and the Feast of Tabernacles at which the Ark had once been carried became Epiphany. Among the Western churches, Epiphany is now celebrated as a feast commemorating the appearance of the infant Christ to the Three Wise Men, the magi who had come to worship him from the Orient. In the East, however, the festival still retains its original purpose. It celebrates the revelation of Christ as God when he was baptized in the Jordan by his cousin John the Baptist, when the voice of God acknowledged him, and the Holy Spirit appeared above him in the form of a dove.

In Alexandria and throughout Egypt, Epiphany not only commemorated the baptism of Christ. As the ancient autumn festival at Jerusalem had done, it marked the beginning of the New Year as well. Christian Egyptians followed the ancient practice of dividing the year into three seasons: flood, sowing and harvest. The dates were slightly different, and the Christian calendar placed the beginning of the season of harvests on 6 January. In the fourth century, Epiphanius wrote that Egyptians believed the date to mark the birth of Christ, as well as the performance of his first miracle at Cana thirty years later, where he changed water into wine. He added that many Egyptians drew water from the Nile on this day, believing that the water changed to wine. The origin of this belief is to be found in the cult of the flood of the Nile, which rises in June and falls in July. When it begins, the water turns red with the soil of Ethiopia and Nubia. The dramatic change in colour was thought to be a miracle performed by the gods.

For thousands of years, Egyptians had been convinced that, every time the Nile flooded, it repeated the steps by which the world had been created. When the primeval water began to recede on the first day, a lotus bloomed in the shallows, and the sun god emerged from its flower. As the water receded still further, the first land appeared, on which the sun god could rest. Every summer, the fields and marshes of the Nile valley would return to this primeval water as the river rose with the summer rain from Ethiopia and the Sudan. Every autumn, as the flood waters drained into the Mediterranean, fields would appear above the waters, covered with a new layer of rich soil.

The floodwaters were venerated as a god, Hapy, 'the flood', imagined as a man with pendulous breasts who bore the produce of the earth after the flood. His bounty was seen as the gift of the god Osiris, king of the land of the dead, and god of resurrection. Osiris had been killed by his brother Set, the god of chaos and evil. Although the body of the dead Osiris sank into the waters of the Nile, it was restored to life by the goddess Isis, his sister and his wife, and the death and resurrection of the god were seen in the seasons of flood and harvest that governed the life of Egypt. In the Pyramid texts of the Fifth Dynasty, Osiris was identified with the fertilizing power of the 'new water' of the Nile flood, while descriptions of the gods mourning for Osiris were part of the Coffin Texts during the Middle Kingdom.

> Hail, you are Osiris, the great on the riverbanks, at whose wish Hapy emerges from his cavern...
> Hail, you are the maker of grain, he who gives life to the gods with the water of his limbs, and bread to every land with the water that takes form under him.

In the *Book of the Dead*, the Nile is said to appear by the command of Osiris: 'making all cultivated lands green by your arrival, great source of things that bloom, sap of crops and herbs, lord of millions of years'.

Even before Alexander the Great conquered Egypt, Greek writers and philosophers had been fascinated by the Nile. Plutarch called it 'the effusion of Osiris', and new versions of the Osiris myth made the ancient cult more compatible with Greek tradition. From the cult of the Apis Bull as an incarnation of Osiris, a new god began to be worshipped – an Egyptian version of the Greek god Dionysus named Sarapis. Rituals were established that linked Osiris-Sarapis with the flooding of the river, and the Hellenistic myth spread to the old cults of Osiris at Abydos. New temples were built, the most famous at Philae, which was believed to be the last resting place of the god. In the festival of the flood, libations of wine were poured into the river, celebrating the reddening of its waters with the silt carried down from the highlands of Nubia and Ethiopia. In the Ptolemaic temple at Philae, a tomb effigy depicted the dead Osiris with his penis erect. Even from beyond the grave, the god was clearly able to generate life.

The Greek historian Herodotus reported that the rise of the Nile was accompanied by rituals and festivals. Prayers and vigils were held throughout the night and were lit by torches. There were processions from the sanctuary to the riverbank, in which worshippers carried a statue of the Nile and a vessel for the sacred water, or held palm branches or reeds. When they reached the river, the priests recited prayers and threw offerings into the water along with papyri of the *Hymn to the Flood*, in which the gods asked the Nile to flood generously. When the clergy returned to the temple to offer thanks for the flood, the people continued to celebrate beside the river.

Muslim historians such as al-Masudi in the tenth century describe celebrations very similar to the accounts of Greek and Latin authors, or Egyptian documents of the Ptolemaic, Roman or Byzantine periods. Masudi believed that nothing in Egypt was as beautiful. Egyptian Christians kept a vigil throughout the night by the light of thousands of lamps and torches, everyone carrying vessels of gold or silver. Monks and priests walked in procession behind the Cross, while they recited prayers.

But why would the Christian festival have been held in January, and not when the Nile was actually in flood? In January, the river is actually at its lowest level. The reason seems to be that the ancient Egyptians had employed a solar calendar that consisted of twelve months. Each month contained thirty days, with an additional five intercalated days, but no allowance was made for the additional quarter day of the astronomical year. Over the centuries, the festivals set by the calendar advanced through the real solar year – a phenomenon known as the Sothic cycle. Eventually, the festival of the Nile had been observed on a wide range of dates between June and January, according to papyrus and inscriptional records. A papyrus from Oxyrhinchus records that in the second century AD, the festival of the Nile was being held in the month of Tybi, which began on 27 December and finished on 25 January.

Egyptian Christians would have fixed the commemoration of the Baptism of Christ on 11 Tybi to place the pagan celebrations in a new context. This occurred with a great many pagan festivals as Christianity was carried into new territories. The flooding of the Nile was now the gift of the Christian God, its waters having been sanctified by the baptism of Christ.

The Ethiopian Church was under the authority of the older church in Egypt until 1959, and it is hardly surprising that the festival of Epiphany is observed in Ethiopia with great enthusiasm. At Aksum, and indeed in any village or town of Christian Ethiopia, this is the most important day on which the *tabotat* are carried in procession. As it commemorates the baptism of Christ, it obviously requires a *Timqata bahr*, a 'Water of Baptism'. The new church dedicated to Aregawi, the eldest of the Nine Saints, stands beside the Bath of the Queen of Sheba, as the great Mai Shum reservoir is known. This is the destination of the *tabotat*, which are carried there with full pomp and ceremony.

A universal fast of nine hours is prescribed on several days of the year, including the day before Christmas and the day before *Timqat*. After they have fasted, the priests remove the *tabotat* of each church from the innermost sanctuary known as the *maqdas*, and wrap them in brocade or velvet cloth 'like the mantle of Christ'. As they leave the church, each *tabot* is carried on the head of a priest in procession to a meeting place beside a stream, a pond or a lake. There are often several *tabotat* arriving from different churches, and the lavishly embroidered velvets or brocades in which they are wrapped hang in folds around the faces of the priests who carry them. These bearers, and the priests and deacons who walk beside them, are shaded by ceremonial parasols, tasselled and decorated with silver stars and suns in the image of the dome of heaven. Some of the clergy carry processional crosses on long wooden poles, cast from bronze or silver and worked into elaborate patterns, symbols of the brass serpent that Moses carried on a pole in the Book of Numbers. In the brilliant light of the sun, the silver and tinsel decorations of the parasols, the heavy priestly crowns and the richly coloured robes of the clergy all evoke the splendours of Paradise, a world transfigured and restored to the glory it lost in the Fall. With mounting excitement as well as reverence, the eyes of the faithful gaze upon the *tabotat* as they are carried high over the heads of the clergy in the centre of the procession.

Despite its immense importance in proclaiming the victory of Christ over the powers of darkness, *Timqat* is not just a solemn ritual. It is a celebration in which the streets are filled with townsfolk and pilgrims dressed in brilliant white shammas, happy to be meeting their friends on such a holy day, and to talk and to watch their children as well as chant the praises of their God. A tall *kabaro* drum is carried at the head of the procession, while the priests and *dabtara* sing in honour of the Baptism of Christ. The people near them shout in joy, as the procession moves past the great stelae that honour the dead kings of Aksum toward the water.

At one time, the *tabotat* of Aksum may have included the Ark of the Covenant itself. In modern times, however, the holy object never leaves its sanctuary, and the *tabotat* of the churches are led by the *tabot* of Mary, which always takes precedence over those of the other saints. When the procession reaches the church of Aregawi, the *tabotat* are installed in the innermost sanctuary, while a tent is pitched in front of the church. Inside the tent, throughout the cold night of highland Tigray, the assembled choirs perform the sacred chants and prayers of Epiphany. Any other men or women whose devotion has given them strength will keep the vigil as well.

Throughout the night, the singing is led by the dabtara, whose vast knowledge of the sacred chant evokes respect and even fear. Robed and turbaned, they move in time to the chant, sometimes dancing in a series of shuffling steps known as *aqwaqwam*. In one hand, each dabtara holds a sistrum, the ancient rattle used in the cults of the Egyptian goddesses Hathor and Isis. In the other, they wave long prayer sticks known as *maqwamia*. These are often equipped with a metal head in a double volute, rather like an Ionic capital, on which the men can lean during the long services of the night. As the sistra are inclined, to right and left in unison, metal discs slide on to each other with a sort of whispering clash, marking the slow rhythm of the chant.

The singing and dancing performed by the Ethiopian dabtaras used to seem scandalous to foreigners. When Vasilii Posniakov, the messenger of the Russian tsar Ivan the Terrible, came to Jerusalem in 1558 to see the patriarch, he was horrified at the behaviour of Ethiopians in the Church of the Holy Sepulchre. He was quite unable to understand a form of worship that was ostensibly Christian, and yet so different from his own. He thought that they were heretics, of course, but he also suspected that they were mad. Complaining that they walked around the Holy Sepulchre beating on four large drums, jumping about and dancing like clowns, he was astonished that God should tolerate something that he himself could barely endure. Devilry he called it.

The Ethiopians, of course, had their own explanation. The ceremonial dance of the dabtaras brings to life the passage in the Second Book of Samuel, when King David danced for joy before the Ark of the Covenant as it entered Jerusalem. According to *The Glory of Kings*, the same dance was performed beside the Nile by his grandson, Bayna-Lekhem, when he learned that the Ark itself was with him on the way to Ethiopia. He jumped up and skipped like a lamb, like a kid that has been fed the milk of its mother, just as his grandfather David had danced before the Ark of the Law of God. He beat the ground with his feet, shouting aloud in his joy.

The morning after the vigil, on the day of Epiphany itself, the culmination of *Timqat* is reached when the people and the clergy approach the water. As the water is blessed, the odour of frankincense floats across it. The priests scatter the water over the people, but many of the boys and men throw themselves into it, splashing each other and many of the crowd as well.

In the past, this aspect of *Timqat* aroused the same sort of disapproval among European visitors, especially clergy, as the dabtaras in the Holy Sepulchre. Although it celebrates the baptism of Christ, the Jesuits and other Europeans who came to Ethiopia in the sixteenth century saw the festival as an annual baptism, a repetition every year of a holy rite that should occur only once in the life of each Christian. Along with circumcision, the celebration of the Saturday sabbath, and married priests, this was an Ethiopian tradition they could not reconcile with their own view of the faith. Francisco Alvares described at length the *Timqat* ceremony that he witnessed at the church of Makana Sellassie. As a Catholic priest, he believed that an annual or even a second baptism would be heresy. He was convinced that 'it is their custom to be baptized every year, as that was the day on which Christ was baptized'. The same belief is repeated by others, including Lobo a century later, who confirmed that 'they repeat baptism every year'. It was evidently difficult for them to understand that the ceremony of *Timqata Kristos*, the Baptism of Christ, was performed as a commemoration and did not constitute an annual baptism.

Alvares was also shocked that Ethiopians would tolerate nakedness when both men and women were present. He claimed to have seen the imperial chaplain standing in the water of *Timqat* as naked as the day his mother bore him. There had been a sharp frost, and he was also quite dead with cold. Those who were to be baptized walked down the steps into the water with their backs to the emperor, but when they climbed the steps, both the men and the women were completely exposed to his gaze.

The Ethiopian *Synaxarion*, which describes the festivals of the church calendar, should have made the Ethiopian doctrine about *Timqat* clear enough. It explains the day as a great festival among all Christian peoples, on which they cleanse themselves with holy water in imitation of the Baptism of Christ. During this festival, they are granted remission of all their sins, provided that they continue in the purity that they receive. Nevertheless, the Ethiopians themselves seem to have made their position even more difficult to understand, perhaps because of the difficulty of translating Ge'ez or Amharic into Latin or Portuguese. Two ambassadors were sent from Ethiopia to Europe in the early sixteenth century: Matthew the Armenian in 1513 and Saga Za-Ab in 1524. Both discussed the matter. Comments by Matthew were included in the *Embassy to the Great Emperor of the Indians* by Damião de Góis, and unfortunately the Latin text does employ the word 'rebaptize'. This will not have helped. In his *Confession*, the emperor Galawdewos merely states that 'we believe in one baptism, for the remission of sins'. Not surprisingly, perhaps, Roman Catholic writers continued to believe that the festival represented a renewal of baptism rather than a commemoration.

The Scottish traveller James Bruce was not a man to tolerate Roman pronouncements on matters of doctrine, and he dealt with the matter roundly. He had read the Jesuit authorities on Ethiopia, and he devoted several pages to proving that they 'shewed great ignorance and malevolence, which they helped with falsehood and invention', especially about the question of rebaptism. He describes the *Timqat* ceremony he saw at Adwa, finding it performed decently enough, although afterwards 'two or three hundred boys, calling themselves deacons', plunged into the water, muddying it and throwing it around, and the 'great solemnity' of Saga Za-Ab eventually 'turned into a riot'. Bruce also witnessed the ceremony later in the presence of the emperor at Qaha, in Gondar. In a frontal assault on Jesuitical pretensions, Bruce cited many points against the account that Alvares had written of *Timqat*. These ranged from a denial that the king, the queen and the metropolitan could have been naked, to a disquisition about the weather. Alvares had claimed that it was freezing, and after considering whether or not oil and salt had been added to the water – essential ingredients for baptism in the Eastern churches – Bruce sarcastically suggested that the salt 'might have contributed to cooling the water, that had frozen under the rays of a burning sun'. Bruce was adamant that 'no baptism, or any thing like baptism, is meant by the ceremony; that man is no more baptized by keeping the anniversary of our Saviour's baptism, than he is crucified by keeping His crucifixion'.

If the festival was as disturbing to the Jesuits as other supposedly Jewish customs to which Ethiopian Christians were devoted, how did the various participants in the debate think that it had arisen? Bruce mentions that the emperor Lebna Dengel had declared to Alvares that the 'present ceremony was lately invented by a grandfather of mine, in favour of such as have turned Moors, and are desirous again of becoming Christians'. Alvares does record the conversation, noting that Moors and Jews were involved. It may be that the latter were schismatic Christians denounced as *ayhud*, and the word 'grandfather' may have referred to someone more distant than Alvares implies. We know that the emperor Zara Yaqob prepared a special pool for *Timqat*, only to see it demolished by 'pagan saboteurs', and the chronicle of the war conducted by Amda Seyon in 1329 mentions that the king celebrated at Bahela 'the feast of Epifanya, that is the Baptism of Christ (*Timqat*), which He instituted for the remission of sins'. Even further back, and beyond any reigning dynastic 'grandfather' of Lebna Dengel, Abu Salih describes the 'Ark of the Covenant' making one of its four annual appearances at *Timqat* while the Zagwe were still on the throne.

If *Timqat* really had been instituted for returning apostates, the Roman Catholic objections would seem to be reasonable. The ritual really would have constituted a second baptism into the Church. As it is, the story is difficult to reconcile with the fact that its celebration is mentioned before the grandfather of Lebna Dengel. What no one seems to have realized is that the *Timqat* was simply the Ethiopian form of a festival observed throughout the Christian East. Especially as it had arisen in Egypt, it would have been extraordinary if the Ethiopian Church had not celebrated the festival at a very early date. Given the isolation of Ethiopia and the unique nature of its Church, it would also have been extraordinary if the festival had not been celebrated in a way that seemed exotic to foreigners.

It is easy to sneer at the romantic accounts of *Timqat* written during the nineteenth and twentieth centuries, at writers who have felt themselves to be carried back to the pages of the Old Testament, who heard the echoes of the ancient Egyptian mysteries. Philologists and historians were meant to pursue an objective truth and to speak in a detached and dispassionate voice. Even now, when a more personal involvement is encouraged by social scientists, or at least admitted to be inevitable, when an identification with people whose history and culture have been totally different is seen as a necessary part of understanding what they are doing, enthusiasm for the great festivals of Christianity is still often thought to be unseemly. The Ethiopian Church was part of an imperial system that imposed its will on neighbouring peoples, and imperialism, it must be remembered, is something to be denounced.

Even if those who saw the festival in earlier generations were more enthusiastic than objective, it would seem unfair to accuse them of overstating the emotional elevation of the festival, or its profound resonance in the heart of anyone raised as either a Jew or a Christian. *Timqat* is unique. In Ethiopia, the ancient ritual procession of the Ark from the Temple in Jerusalem has been reunited with a new faith whose God claimed that he would destroy the Temple and raise it again in three days. The ancient cosmic victory of God over the waters of chaos and the monsters of the deep, which was proclaimed in the Psalms, is repeated in the baptism of Christ, in his passage through water and his triumph on the other side of death. The festival is a bridge across a division that has provoked mistrust and hatred for almost 2,000 years. Even more than that, *Timqat* retraces the steps from the ancient revelation on Mount Sinai to the still more ancient faith of the dying and rising god whose body sank beneath the waters of the Nile. The festival of Epiphany that was celebrated in Egypt not only venerates the baptism of Christ as a proclamation of death and resurrection of the Christian God; it also remembers the death and resurrection of the Egyptian god Osiris in the floodwaters of the Nile. When Aaron made the Golden Calf, the ancient cult of Osiris in the form of the Apis Bull seemed to threaten the covenant with the God of Israel. Now the two faiths that stood as enemies in the Book of Exodus are brought together in the greatest ritual of the African Church.

The pattern of ancient Myth and Ritual that proved so controversial earlier this century may not be easy to find at the source of the Egyptian, Hebrew, Mesopotamian or even Christian cults. But it does appear in the early centuries of the Christian era, and in Ethiopia its truth is proclaimed in dramatic terms. Even so, the Ethiopian view is perhaps more inspiring, as well as more intriguing, than anything the scholars had imagined. The Mosaic distinction has been a source of pain for 2,000 years. It may seem ironic that a nation in which war and tyranny have produced such terrible suffering in recent decades should be said to have healed this ancient wound. This is a land where the Christian empire of the north is increasingly seen as having imposed a harsh rule on its neighbours for centuries, from which thousands of Ethiopians who claimed a Jewish heritage fled to Israel. Its own wounds are scarcely healed. And yet this is what *Timqat* proclaims.

CHAPTER 20

The Lost Tribes

War and famine had been the only news from Ethiopia, it seemed. The emperor who claimed descent from King Solomon and the Queen of Sheba had been overthrown in 1974. He had been held prisoner and then died in mysterious circumstances, probably murdered. The Red Terror had consumed thousands, war was raging in the north, and appalling scenes of starvation and death had been broadcast to the world. In the midst of these horrors, a dramatic escape occurred. Negotiations between the government of Israel and Ethiopian dictator Mengistu Haile Maryam had brought thousands of Falasha to the Promised Land. Black Jews, believed by many to be a Lost Tribe of Israel, were flown out in two dramatic airlifts, Operation Moses and Operation Solomon. A new Exodus had once again brought Jews out of Africa.

The Falasha, or *Beta Esrael* as they called themselves, 'the House of Israel', were often seen as part of an ancient Jewish legacy in Ethiopia. Along with customs preserved by Ethiopian Christians, including circumcision, dietary laws, the Saturday sabbath and the *tabotat* that symbolized the Ark of the Covenant, they were thought to have survived from the days of the Aksumite kings.

But once they were in Israel, questions began to be asked about how Jewish the Falasha really were. Decisions were of immediate religious importance. How were the Falasha to be accepted into the Jewish state? They might have believed that they were Jews, but how authentic was their tradition? Did some ritual of conversion need to be performed before they were recognized to be truly Jewish?

The question was also of historical interest. Especially through the work of scholars such as Kay Kaufman Shelemay and Steven Kaplan, it began to be realized that the Falasha were in fact of Christian rather than Jewish origin. They were one faction of an

Ethiopian battle to create a New Israel in Africa. The conclusion was highly controversial, and as the colour of the Falasha aroused prejudice among some Israelis, especially when large numbers of immigrants began to arrive from the Soviet Union, the suggestion that the Falasha were not really Jewish enough to be Israelis could cause great offence and great anger. Nevertheless, the conclusion seemed difficult to dispute.

For centuries, travellers and scholars had been fascinated by the impression that life in Ethiopia seemed to follow the ancient patterns of the Old Testament, and that the sorts of Judaic belief or practice found in Ethiopia were too extensive and too deeply rooted to have arisen simply through an imitation of the Bible. There must have been some ancient Judaic presence in Ethiopia to account for them, and the traditions about the Ark of the Covenant were believed to be connected to this legacy.

One of the curious aspects of this belief was the fact that it was accepted with almost no reference to Aksumite history. And although Ethiopians seem to have been fascinated by Judaic or Old Testament themes in later centuries, there is no evidence of this during the Aksumite kingdom. There may be explanations for why evidence does not survive, but its absence should have aroused suspicion that the Old Testament themes were part of a later and not an earlier Ethiopia.

Another curiosity is that, while the devotion to these themes was thought to exceed what might have emerged from an enthusiastic reading of the Old Testament, almost no one bothered to look at what emerged from an enthusiastic reading of the Old Testament in other countries. In fact, a great deal could emerge from it, and the fascination with the Ark, the Temple, Mosaic Law and Zion on some occasions rivals or even surpasses what one finds in Ethiopia. As a Presbyterian minister recently wrote about his childhood, 'I still find it somewhat difficult to decide if a Scots Presbyterian is an Old Testament Christian, with a stress on the Law and the Psalms, or a New Testament Jew, who attends his synagogue – as Jesus' custom was – on the sabbath day.'

The immense attraction of the Old Covenant within the New Covenant often appears at moments of extreme crisis. As the armies of Islam swept across the ancient empires of Rome and Persia during the seventh and eighth centuries, the crisis became spiritual as well as military. If the Christian empire was in retreat before the armies of a prophet from the deserts of Arabia, God must have decided that something was very seriously wrong. In the territories they conquered, Muslims displayed a marked hostility to images of Christ and the Christian saints. This became obvious when the caliphate issued coins without any image, only with quotations from the Quran. Just as the Judaean king Josiah began to realize with horror, as he read the Book of the Law discovered in the Temple of Jerusalem, that his kingdom was living in violation of the covenant made with God, so the Byzantine establishment began to suspect that this might be the point at which a dreadful sin had been committed. The armies of Byzantium marched into battle with images of the saints. The armies of Islam did not. Victory belonged to Islam. Could Byzantium have defied the Second Commandment that Moses had written on the Tablet and placed in the Ark of the Covenant? Were its icons the images forbidden by God when he spoke to Moses? Was this why God had turned against them?

The suspicion plunged the Byzantine empire into chaos. It is known as the Iconoclastic Controversy, but it was no mere academic debate. Images were removed from public display and destroyed. Crowds fought to save them. Churches were stripped of their icons. It was, in effect, a civil war.

Of those who continued to defend the veneration of images, the greatest champions were St Theodore, who lived in the monastery of Stoudios in Constantinople, and St John of Damascus, who had served at the court of the caliphs. As they assembled their arguments and prepared a defence that finally secured the veneration of images and retained one of the distinctive traits of the Eastern Church, they looked to the Ark of the Covenant to provide the essential proof. God may have forbidden graven images when he delivered his Ten Commandments to Moses. Despite this prohibition, he not only permitted, he even commanded that Moses make images of the cherubim on the very Ark in which the commandments were placed.

St John of Damascus was keen to explore the reason why God might have instructed images that were carved by the hands of men to be placed above an object of such sanctity. He argued that it was obvious that no one could really make an image of God.

He was simply beyond representation. On the other hand, the created world could not be worshipped and adored in place of God, as if it were actually God itself. The cherubim were part of the created world and were subject to its limitations. Especially as they were depicted prostrate in adoration before the divine throne, it was legitimate to depict them. In fact, it was all the more fitting that an image of the heavenly servants should appear above the image of the divine mysteries, by which he meant the Ark, the staff of Aaron and the mercy seat, all of which were made by hand.

To make the same point, St Theodore relied on a quotation from Theodore of Antioch. We should tell any heretic who argues that we should not venerate images of the saints that have been made by hand, or who denounces these images as idols, that the cherubim, the mercy seat, the Ark, the rod of Aaron and the Tablet that the prophet Moses made were venerated even though they had all been made by hand.

The Ark could be used to argue in a completely different direction, however, and as the Western Church attempted to make sense of the passions in the East, it did so. In fact, the Ark appears to have been part of a general fascination with the Old Testament among the Frankish clergy.

When Pippin became king of the Franks, the clergy turned to the Bible as a guide to what they should do. The Old Testament described the anointing of the kings of Israel by priests and prophets, so in 751 the Frankish clergy anointed Pippin. They looked on the history recorded in the Bible as a prototype of Frankish history. The destiny of the Franks, they believed, would be realized in becoming a New Israel.

Some fifty years later, in the region of Soissons, the hands of a priest began to be anointed at his ordination. This was an invention in imitation of the Old Testament model. It had never been employed at Rome. Charlemagne tried to discourage it, but the Frankish clergy produced more and more complicated rituals of anointing based on the Old Testament model, and in the tenth century, they succeeded in passing these to Rome itself.

In 793, Theodulph, the future bishop of Orleans, was commissioned to prepare a detailed reply to the Acts of the Iconodule Council of Nicaea held in 787. The treatise he wrote was a detailed rebuttal of both Eastern positions: of those who venerated icons and of those who believed them to be idols. It was read before Charlemagne, and the manuscript still contains the record of his approval.

Once again, the Ark of the Covenant played a central role. Theodulph saw God as a remote king, separated from the creatures that he had made by an immense distance. The abyss between God and man was bridged only by his will. There was no unbroken chain of symbols that joined the visible and the invisible worlds, by which man might ascend to God. It was through his commandments that God revealed himself, and his greatest gift to the human race was the Law. Although there were few visible signs on which any of us could rely, the greatest of these was the Ark of the Covenant, in which the Law had been preserved.

The Ark was unique, according to Theodulph. 'Shimmering,' he described it, 'with so many awe-inspiring and incomparable mysteries.' When Bezalel made it he relied not on his own imagination, but on the will of God. He was filled with the Spirit of God as he fashioned the Ark from wood and gold. As a work of art, the Ark was free from the arbitrary nature of icons created through the imagination of men. The painted images produced in the workshops of the imperial capital Constantinople could not be compared to the Ark of the Covenant, which had been created by the mind of God himself.

When Theodulph built his own chapel at St Germigny-des-Prés, he placed an image of the Ark of the Covenant in the mosaic apse, above the altar. A Byzantine church would normally have contained a mosaic of Christ and the saints, as the revelation of God in human form. The iconoclasts would have preferred simply the outline of a Cross, one of which survives in the Church of St Irene in Constantinople – a simple image that conveyed the essential truth of Christian doctrine without recourse to human form. For Theodulph, however, it was the Ark that conveyed the presence of God and the essential elements of the faith.

The Ark was depicted again in France at the royal abbey of St Denis, in the midst of the ambitious programme of the Abbot Suger, who launched the Gothic style in the twelfth century. Suger was an extraordinary man, a poet, theologian and patron of the arts. He has been called the father of the French monarchy, and he left a rare account of his intentions in building the abbey, clearly indebted to the Platonic mysticism of which St Denis himself was believed to be a distinguished exponent. The abbey was built as a new Mount Zion, the joy of the whole earth, and it displayed a royal mysticism of kings who ruled as heirs of the line of David. In one of the chapels, a tall window of stained glass urges us, in the words of Suger himself, to make the ascent from the material to the immaterial. It includes the Ark of the Covenant surmounted by a Cross. The Ark is the foundation of the Christian altar, and Suger provides a verse by way of explanation: 'On the Ark of the Covenant the altar is established with the Cross of Christ; Here Life wishes to die under a greater covenant.' The Ark is surrounded by the four cherubim that appeared in the vision of Ezekiel, and again in the Revelation of St John.

Although the history of the Old Testament could be immensely attractive to peoples who had lived outside or on the margins of the Roman empire and its classical traditions, the Mosaic Law that Theodulph admired so much began to be studied with a new interest during the Renaissance, at the very time that classical sources were being discovered again. After the Reformation, a serious debate began in Europe about whether the Mosaic Law was still in effect. Martin Luther did not see Old Testament legislation as binding on Christians, and Calvin more or less agreed with him. But when Piscator wrote a commentary on Exodus in the early years of the seventeenth century, he claimed that many of the Mosaic laws were still in force.

A few years later, English radicals known as Fifth Monarchists took up arms to attain this goal. They hoped to see the Kingdom of God on earth, and they were hoping not for a return to Paradise, but for the establishment of the godly monarchy proclaimed in the Book of Daniel. In this Kingdom, the predestined elect would rule under Mosaic Law.

Among English Puritans, and among those who left for New England, adherence to the laws of the Old Testament could take extreme forms. The *Laws and Liberties of Massachusetts*, published in 1648, lists fifteen crimes for which capital punishment should be imposed, each of which can be matched in the Mosaic Law.

This interest in Mosaic Law was often part of an interest in reviving the covenants of the Old Testament. The English translator William Tyndale, whose work formed the basis of the King James Version of the Bible, believed that Mosaic Law was still in force in the most literal sense, and towards the end of his life he became fascinated by covenant as well. In 1537, Calvin and his followers marked their triumph in Geneva by a civic ceremony in which the citizens swore that they would obey the Ten Commandments along with the laws of the city. Calvin, it seems, was intent on making the city a covenanted community. In 1591, George Gifford proclaimed that 'God hath put his covenant of mercy in England since the nation of England did profess Jesus Christ and were all sealed with the seal of the covenant.' Covenants based on the Old Testament can be found in the Mayflower Compact sworn by the Pilgrim Fathers who landed at Plymouth Rock in their own Promised Land of Massachusetts, in the Scottish National Covenant of 1638, and in the Solemn League and Covenant proclaimed between England and Scotland in 1643. Scotland and England, it was decided, should be understood as Israel and Judah, a northern and a southern kingdom that had originally been one people and had become separated through history.

The English fascination with covenants and with the Old Testament in general became more intense during the English Revolution. Unlike the French or the Russian Revolutions, it had no precedents, and as men and women faced the political situation after 1640, they searched for some sort of guide to help them understand it. The Bible had been available in English for a century. If its prophecies could be understood, readers felt, they should be able to understand their destiny. This belief was often held by men and women who had received little education, and the middle years of the seventeenth century were the time of the 'mechanik preacher', the self-educated layman who interpreted the Bible according to his own inspiration. John Bunyan, who is still famous for writing *Pilgrim's Progress*, was one of these preachers. But the belief was not confined to such people. John Milton, Isaac Newton and men of the highest intellect and most sophisticated education would have agreed.

The Holy Scriptures were believed to be a history of past deeds, naturally enough. Beyond that, they were believed to be a guide to future events, and even to the political disputes of the present day. The Book of Revelation and the Old Testament prophets were believed to give the history of Parliament during the most difficult years of the Revolution.

The belief that the Bible, and especially the Old Testament, provided a key to the desperate times in which the English found themselves led to the sorts of proclamation that we might have expected in Ethiopia. England was equated with Zion, and the English were believed to be a Chosen People, the heirs of the Israelites in the Old Testament. Their struggles were simply the struggles of the Israelites repeated after thousands of years. In 1645 Richard Byfield announced to the House of Commons: 'The nation of England at this day is God's Sion.' Preaching to the Parliamentary soldiers at the beginning of the civil war, William Bridge told them, 'You are now coming out of Egypt (for the Romish superstition and that party is called Egypt, Sodom, Babylon) ... to the Promised Land.' In 1653, John Rogers described Oliver Cromwell as a second Moses, 'that great deliverer of his people ... out of the house of Egypt'.

The followers of John Wycliffe attacked images in churches and wished to replace them with the Ten Commandments in English on church walls. This became a common Anglican practice, and most of the whitewashing of walls was conducted by Elizabethan bishops rather than Puritan vandals, whatever we may like to believe now.

A similar conviction that one could live an Old Testament life had begun to appear in Germany. Anabaptists gathered at Munster in 1534, under the guidance of Thomas Müntzer, who taught a doctrine of Inner Light similar to that adopted a century later by the Quakers in England. His followers were originally hoping to recover the perfection of Adam before the Fall, but their ideals soon changed from Paradise to the Israel of David, Solomon and the Maccabees. The Anabaptists were to be warrior saints in a New Israel. Evil must be destroyed by force of arms, and Müntzer saw himself as Gideon, leading the people into battle.

A century after the Anabaptists at Munster had been crushed by the authorities, more ambitious attempts to apply the Old Testament as a standard of life focused on England. After Martin Bucer had visited England from Germany, he published his thoughts on the English Reformation in 1550, under the title

THE ARK OF THE COVENANT

Concerning the Kingdom of Christ. He described the kings of
England as the Old Testament kings David, Solomon, Ahaz,
Hezekiah and Josiah. The Ten Commandments, he claimed, should
be the basis of civil law as well as Church law. Old Testament
regulations imposing the death penalty for blasphemy and other
crimes were still to be obeyed. Bucer often repeated statutes listed
in Deuteronomy, and insisted that the Old Testament Sabbath
should be observed on the Christian Sunday.

At the coronation of Edward VI, Archbishop Cranmer described
the young ruler as a new Josiah. Like the reforming king of the
Old Testament, he would destroy idolatry and the tyranny of the
papacy. The imagery continued under his successors. In the reign
of Elizabeth, reforming kings of the Old Testament were cited as
models for the Christian monarch, their concern for the Levites
and the priests cited as an invitation for the queen to care for the
clergy.

One of the most extended descriptions of Elizabeth as an Old
Testament monarch was published after her death by the Puritan
William Leigh. David was the least and last of his father's house,
he observed, just as Elizabeth was in her father's house. David had
been persecuted from his youth, and so was Elizabeth. Saul was a
king and hostile to David, while Mary was a queen and hostile to
Elizabeth. David was an exile at Engeddi, while Elizabeth was
imprisoned at Woodstock. Doeg denounced David to Saul, and
Gardiner denounced Elizabeth to Mary. David declared himself
innocent to Saul, as Elizabeth did to Mary. Saul in his spirit of
fury decided to have David killed as he played his harp. Winchester
in his spirit of popery decided to have Elizabeth murdered as she
prayed. David was pitied by Achish, the king of Gath, who was a
stranger to him and an enemy of his religion. Elizabeth was pitied
by Philip of Spain, who was a friend to her, but an enemy of her
religion. As part of the equation of Elizabeth with David, Leigh
refers to the Ark of the Covenant: 'David brought the Ark into his
City by the hands of the Levites. So doth Queen Elizabeth the
Religion of her Christ, into the bowels of all her kingdoms, by a
beautiful ministry.'

As if the example of David were not enough, Leigh also com-
pares her to Joshua, while England is identified with Israel: 'For
so good a God, so gracious a Prince, so great plenty ... If all God's

blessings, both heavenly and earthly, is not for Moab, Ammon or Mount Seir, but for the hill of God's holiness, Israel, England, and Mount Zion.' He then constructs an even more elaborate comparison between Elizabeth and Hezekiah, identifying the popish enemies of England with Sennacherib, the king of Assyria, and with Ammon, Gebal and Edom, the 'Romish Edomites'. With the help of God, Jerusalem and England under the leadership of Hezekiah and Elizabeth will defeat them.

This sort of Old Testament imagery was not confined to Puritans. The established Church was even more enthusiastic, having found it especially helpful as a way of proving that Henry VIII was entitled to lead the English Church away from Rome. They constantly demonstrated the supremacy of the Crown over the Church by referring to the way in which the Old Testament kings had supported the Temple in Jerusalem and the purity of belief in God. Bishop Jewel mentions David, Solomon and the reforming kings as monarchs who established the limits to be observed by priests within their realm, while the first volume of John Overall's *Convocation Book* relied on the Old Testament to demonstrate the right of the divinely appointed prince to rule.

The famous theologian and preacher Lancelot Andrewes used the Old Testament for the same purpose, including the texts on which he chose to speak at the commemoration of the Gunpowder Plot. He refers to David's concern for the Ark and Solomon's building of the Temple as examples of the right and duty of kings to bring about change in the religious sphere.

The English were especially keen to apply Old Testament Sabbath laws to Sunday. A devotion to the Christian Sabbath can be found in Europe as well, but in England the regulations were applied with rigour and over a long period of time. This was especially popular in the eighteenth century, and the Lord's Day Observance Act, which was passed in 1781, is still a force in public life over two centuries later.

Although the Restoration of 1660 brought an end to some of the more extravagant claims of living in the midst of biblical revelation, they did not disappear from English life, but survived with a special vigour in Dissident circles. One of the most famous of English prophets, Joanna Southcott, was born in 1750, and when she began to hear voices, she joined a Wesleyan congregation.

She was expelled after she announced that divine providence was working through her, but she began to write her prophecies and was brought to London by William Sharp, an engraver who was a friend of the poet and artist William Blake. In 1794, the Spirit commanded her to seal up her writing in a large box, which would be opened after 120 years. Known as 'Joanna Southcott's Box' or 'The Ark of the New Covenant', it was made of oak and sealed with copper nails, bolts and rope. It was intended to be opened in the presence of twenty-four bishops, and after the time stipulated by the prophet had elapsed, her followers attempted to encourage a sufficient number of bishops to assemble, but without any success. Even now, the Panacea Society claims to preserve the Ark and still advertises in the national press. Apparently, the secrets we need to prepare for the coming of the Messiah are kept in the Ark, and disorder and crime will continue to multiply in England until the bishops accept their responsibility and assemble to open it.

The Reformation and the English Revolution were in full spate as the English began to emigrate to the colonies of the New World, many to pursue explicitly religious aims. The Puritans of New England clearly saw their lives in terms of the Old Testament. They had made a dangerous journey over the ocean after leaving their homeland to escape religious persecution, and they struggled with nature and with the Indians in the New World. This was compared to the Exodus, the flight from Egypt to escape slavery, the journey through the wilderness, the fight with the serpent in the wilderness, and so on. The results could be disastrous. Adopting the same view of the covenant as the Judaean king Josiah, Puritans insisted that the native peoples abandon their traditional culture and embrace Puritan standards, otherwise God would threaten the entire community with destruction.

In the New World, Israelite speculation continued to grow, becoming more detailed and more comprehensive. In 1740, three members of a Zionitic brotherhood in Vermont were consecrated as priests and admitted to the ancient Order of Melchizedek. They wore priestly dress with special breastplates when performing baptisms.

This sort of enthusiasm was not confined to sectarian eccentrics, however. In 1776, Benjamin Franklin proposed that the Great Seal of the United States should depict Moses with his rod lifted and the Egyptian army drowning in the Red Sea. Egypt was clearly the British empire, the Red Sea was the Atlantic, and George III was the wicked pharaoh. Thomas Jefferson proposed a different design that drew on the symbols of the same Exodus: the Israelites marching through the wilderness under the pillars of cloud and fire that God had sent to guide them, rising above the Tabernacle and the Ark of the Covenant. As if this were not enough, it was also debated that Hebrew should be considered as the ideal language for the new Chosen People of America.

The rigours of this second Exodus were no less terrifying than the first. In 1777, a preacher in New Haven compared the colonists with the Israelites as they began to complain about the trials they faced in the wilderness.

> How soon does our faith fail us, and we begin to murmur against Moses and Aaron and wish ourselves back again in Egypt where we had some comforts of life, which we are now deprived of? – not considering that ... in any deliverance there are great troubles and afflictions ...

In 1789, a preacher named Nathanial Wood began addressing small meetings from which a sect known as the New Israelites arose. They claimed literal descent from the Lost Tribes of Israel and began to work on a Temple. They also began to search for gold, 'to pave the streets of the New Jerusalem'.

In 1823, Ethan Smith published a book entitled *View of the Hebrews, or the Tribes of Israel* in America. Rumours had begun to circulate of mysterious discoveries – treasure discovered in the ground that suggested the American Indians might be the Lost Tribes of Israel. It was in the midst of this sort of speculation that Joseph Smith claimed to have discovered golden tablets in the ground containing the Book of Mormon. The Church of the Latter-day Saints that he founded set itself the goal of building a new Zion in America, and would become the most successful religion to appear since Islam. By 1832, the Saints had begun to describe themselves as the literal descendants of the ancient Israelites, and Joseph Smith himself declared that 'the whole of America is Zion itself from north to south'.

As part of their plans to build a new Zion, the Latter-day Saints restored the Old Testament priesthoods of Aaron and Melchizedek. When they began to prepare their plans for a Temple, they turned to the accounts of the Temple of Solomon that could be found among Freemasons. Many of the early converts to the new Church were Freemasons, and Mormonism was described as 'the true Masonry'. According to its own traditions, Freemasonry is as old as the Temple of Solomon, although records are difficult to locate before the initiation of Elias Ashmole in 1646. Each Masonic lodge is a recreation of the Temple of Solomon, and Masonic records would have provided the Saints with an immense amount of information about the Temple and its significance.

The Temple had been a subject of intense interest among European men of learning, and a serious debate had arisen about how it should be understood. The discussion involved idealists and historians, the latter basing their views more closely on the Old Testament and seeing the Temple as a more modest structure than the great repository of cosmic knowledge imagined by their rivals.

Isaac Newton wrote an account of the Temple of Solomon to explain the vision in the heavenly Temple that St John the Divine reported in the Book of Revelation. To interpret the prophecy, to decipher its coded messages, Newton believed that it was essential to understand the Temple in all its detail.

Newton saw the entire world as the Temple of God. A natural philosopher was therefore a kind of priest. He also saw religious ritual in cosmic terms. The processions of Egyptian priests revealed that the science of the stars lay at the heart of their theology. The priests of the Hebrews circled the fire as they approached the altar, lighting seven lamps that represented the planets in their motion around the sun.

Newton was convinced that the Greeks and Romans had fallen into the Egyptian error of worshipping the stars and planets as if they were gods in their own right. The Israelites had not been corrupted to the same degree, the prophets having called them back to the true faith. Ancient Israelite architecture was therefore of immense interest to him, as the most reliable representation of the cosmos.

In believing this, he was part of a wide movement after the Reformation to reconstruct the true Temple, relying largely on the vision of Ezekiel. As the vision of the prophet would have been divinely inspired, it would follow the true pattern in heaven. Architects in particular had become fascinated by the idea of a sixth architectural order, which embraced the others and expressed more clearly the harmonies of the universe. They believed that it had been directly inspired by God when he instructed Solomon to build the Temple. Their hope lay in the conviction that true beauty did not belong to the world of the senses. Following late antique philosophers such as Macrobius, Boethius and St Augustine, they embarked on a comprehensive attempt to reconstruct the Temple on cosmological and aesthetic principles. Like Philo, they were attempting to reconcile Plato and the Bible, the legacy of Greek philosophy and Hebrew prophecy.

Those who embarked on the quest discussed the Temple in terms of the numerical ratios of divine harmony, convinced that the intervals of the musical scale as the Pythagoreans described them are represented in the Temple. It was a microcosm of creation, which demonstrated the harmony of the stars and planets. As in the account that Philo gave of the Ark of the Covenant, the symbolic significance of the Temple was far greater than the reality of its construction.

The most ambitious attempt was that of Villalpando, who attempted to prove that the Temple of Solomon was identical with the Temple of Ezekiel. He also claimed that the Temple of Solomon would have been identical with the Temple of Herod, as there could have been only one Temple. This meant that he had to argue away the evidence of Josephus and devise an ingenious compromise between the various descriptions in the Bible – a task that was all the more complicated because Ezekiel used two systems of measurement. The larger produced a Temple that was thirty-six times the size of the smaller.

Before he turned to the Temple, Villalpando considered the Tabernacle. He produced a diagram to show how the twelve tribes of Israel were arrayed about the Ark of the Covenant in the form of a square, facing the four cardinal points of the compass. Within this square, he envisaged another square consisting of the four camps of the Levites, grouped around the tent in which the Ark was guarded.

As the Temple was based on the Tabernacle, Villalpando assumed that it must have possessed twelve bastions along its perimeter, corresponding to the twelve tribes of Israel. Four inner bastions corresponded to the camps of the Levites. These he believed to be symbols of the sublunar world of the four elements, while the twelve outer bastions were the signs of the zodiac.

He also believed that the Temple was related to the human body as a microcosm – a model of the universe. The body is circumscribed by the four humours, just as the Temple possessed four inner bastions. Villalpando followed the principle of Vitruvius that a building should reflect the proportions of the human body. In its humanity, however, he saw the Temple as cosmological, and he claimed that when Juan de Herrera first saw his drawings, he exclaimed that he had seen the hand of God in the form of architecture.

Villalpando was a mystic and an enthusiast of the ancient Egyptian wisdom that Renaissance scholars believed had been preserved in the writings of Hermes Trismegistus. His work was attacked even before it was published by those who believed that textual criticism and sound exegesis rather than mystical speculation about cosmic harmony should provide the basis for reliable reconstruction.

Villalpando was also criticized for ignoring the Jewish sources, although if one did consult them, the complications could become almost insurmountable. Another version of the Temple was produced by Perrault, who was commissioned to reconstruct it on the basis of the description given by Moses Maimonides. The illustrations that Perrault prepared were to accompany a translation of the *Mishneh Torah* into Latin. The result was very different from the reconstruction of Villalpando, and although he too was often criticized, and did not have as great an impact, Perrault left a remarkable legacy nonetheless. He was at work as an architect on the chapel that Louis XIV had commissioned for Versailles. The revised plan that he produced for the chapel in 1698 employs the same elements that can be seen on his lateral elevation of the Temple.

An even more explicit attempt to recreate the Temple had already been undertaken when Philip II commissioned a vast monastery and mausoleum in the plains of Castille known as *El Escorial*, 'The Slagheap'. It was described as 'another Temple of Solomon whom our patron and founder sought to imitate in this work'.

Not only was the Escorial intended to be a recreation of the Temple, but Philip himself was compared to King Solomon. In the dedication to a Spanish edition of Vitruvius, the author explained that the virtues of the ancient king had come to life again: 'To whom should a book on architecture be dedicated but to this second Solomon and prince of architects? To him they owe their present knowledge and the restoration of their art after it had lain for many centuries forgotten, debased, and even treated as an object of disdain.' In case there was any doubt about how closely the two kings should be identified, an illustration of King Solomon published by Plantin depicts the king with the features of Philip.

The Escorial was not intended to be a precise reconstruction. Its correspondence was of a symbolic nature, although some explicit parallels were described at the time it was built. Its division into convent, palace and church was said to recall the divisions of the Temple. The library of the Escorial was decorated with frescos, and along the western wall under 'Arithmetica' the Queen of Sheba is depicted as she questions King Solomon. In every other painting in the library, the inscription is in Latin. Only here is it in Hebrew, and it records a passage from the Wisdom of Solomon: 'All things by measure and number and weight.' As Solomon speaks to the queen, he points at a board on which Pythagorean numerology is represented.

The Masonic fascination with a mystical Egypt and with the Temple of Solomon has been enormously fertile. At its heart lies a dream that we shall see again – a conviction that the abyss between Egypt and Israel, one denounced as idolatry and the other revered as the true faith, might be bridged. Freemasonry had a great impact on the politics and culture of the eighteenth century in both Europe and America, but its legacy has acquired a new popular currency, and in a way that would have seemed inconceivable a few decades ago. Once again, there has been a sense of living in times of revelation drawn from the Bible. But now, it is not merely a biblicism that resembles the beliefs of medieval Ethiopian, it is a biblicism that proclaims itself to be Ethiopian. Our story, it seems, has come full circle.

In the nineteenth century, educated blacks in the New World had begun to take pride in Herodotus having described the Egyptians as a people with dark skin and hair like wool – as black, in other words. If the greatest civilization of antiquity had been black, then the assumption that the white race was superior to the black was surely false. On this basis, black Freemasons began to claim that Freemasonry was a black invention, the first Mason having been Egyptian and therefore black. When Marcus Garvey formed his United Negro Improvement Association, he had already been a Mason himself for some time, and he based his new organization on Masonic lines. Along with an interest in Egyptian antiquity, there was also a great enthusiasm for Ethiopia among black writers and intellectuals at the time. In 1930, when Ras Tafari became the emperor Haile Selassie I, Garvey sent a telegram to Addis Ababa: 'Greetings from Ethiopians of Western World.' He also described the coronation as a fulfilment of biblical prophecy, of a prince coming out of Egypt, and of Ethiopia stretching out her hands to God.

Those who lived through it had tried to explain the English Revolution in terms of the Bible, because it was the most easily available and the most authoritative of books. For those who now attempted to explain the oppressed condition of blacks in the New World, the Bible was also a source of inspiration. They were living as an oppressed people, like the Jews who had been chosen by God, but who suffered in Egypt and then in Babylon. The term 'Ethiopian' had long been applied to people of dark skin, regardless of where they came from. Aside from Egypt, Ethiopia was the African country mentioned in the Bible, and it was often described in glowing terms. Not only did the Ethiopians stretch out their hands to God, but the treasurer of Candace, 'queen of the Ethiopians', is the first Christian convert mentioned in the Acts of the Apostles.

The translation that Ernest Wallis Budge had made of *The Glory of Kings* was available by the time that Haile Selassie was crowned and it provided an authority of some antiquity, if any more were needed, of two essential truths. Haile Selassie was descended from King Solomon, and Ethiopia was the real Zion. If both these were true, then despite what *The Glory of Kings* might say on the subject, surely Israelites must be black. White Jews were merely impostors. In circles that began to revere Haile Selassie as God incarnate, *The Glory of Kings* began to be seen as the authentic voice of biblical revelation. Even though no copy existed in Europe when the English translators of the Bible set to work under the patronage of James I, there is now a conviction among Rastafarians that the king himself ordered *The Glory of Kings* be to be excised from the translation, so that the superiority of the white race would not be challenged by Holy Scripture.

Beliefs of this sort have been given global prominence through the work of Jamaican musicians, whose influence has been out of all proportion to the small population of the island. Bob Marley is only one of the most famous heroes of Jamaican music. Much of modern popular music sold throughout the world is derivative of Jamaican innovation and is touched in some way by Rastafarian conviction of a New Zion, in which a black Israel will be delivered from the oppression of Babylon, where the Ark of the Covenant is a vessel in which the princes, priests and warriors of Israel have found sanctuary.

Temples built again in Europe and America, covenants, sabbaths and claims of Israelite descent, an Exodus in England or the New World, David and Hezekiah sitting on a throne in London ... these were not simply literary conceits. They were believed to be real. England had really entered into a covenant with God. America really was the new Zion. All this is merely a selection. It could be multiplied from dozens of other sources, from the imperial court of Byzantium to the cotton plantations of the Confederate States. They all confirm the generative power of the biblical narrative. Even the most literal claims to Israelite descent arise from the pages of the Bible and need little other encouragement.

One might describe this as a Judaic substratum, but it is based entirely on the sacred scripture, and although one should never forget the extent to which Christian interpreters of the Old Testament have depended on superior Jewish scholarship, it is not based on direct contact with Jews. The diversity and the intensity with which claims to Israelite identity have been made throughout the Christian world means that one should be very careful before claiming that the Old Testament nature of Ethiopian Orthodoxy depends on a Jewish presence in Ethiopia. It would be difficult to imagine that there were never Jews in Ethiopia, especially as the Jewish presence in South Arabia had been so obvious, but the Bible itself provides a sufficient explanation for the nature of the Ethiopian Church.

This is not simply a digression into the curiosities of European or American history. It has been claimed that the cult of the Ark of the Covenant in Ethiopia is part of the legacy of ancient Judaism. Yet the first reports of the Ark of the Covenant during the dynasty of the Zagwe do not describe a Jewish object. If the description is accurate, it is a Christian object. Elsewhere an intense interest in the legacy of ancient Israel was based on a Christian reading of the Old Testament rather than the activity of people who were themselves Jews. If the same were true of Ethiopia, then Ethiopian claims about the Ark become easier to understand.

CHAPTER 21

The Dust of Its Hiding Place

When Villalpando and his critics argued about which of the elaborate and magnificent reconstructions of the Temple might be true, they were arguing about whether they should be mystics or historians. If they were trying to recover the details of its construction in the Bible or the ancient Jewish sources, should they rely on vision and inspiration, or on scepticism and a careful attention to detail? Their disagreement was largely about how they should look at the evidence of earlier ages, however, and not about what the evidence itself might be. Even if they were to choose history and turn their backs on mysticism, they might find that the evidence itself had been compiled to convey a mystical rather than a historical truth. It might reveal very little to the rigorous testing of a historian.

The problem they faced four centuries ago is still a problem for us today. While the history of scholarship can be a dull business – too dull even for many scholars – we need to know something about it if we hope to make a serious enquiry of the ancient evidence. Without any knowledge of who might have made the same attempt in earlier centuries, of why they might have done so, of the obstacles they might have faced, and of what they might have believed they discovered, we could find ourselves walking in the dark, condemned to repeat the errors of earlier times.

In the past two or three centuries, we have become increasingly concerned with a kind of truth and fact that emerged in the scientific and technological revolution, and we have begun to assume that religious truths should be true in the same sense. We then reject them if we discover that they are not, or we insist that they must be true whatever the sceptics might say – either because their assertions are mistaken, or simply because the word of God does not lie.

335

When we look for the Ark of the Covenant, however, we are searching through ancient and medieval texts of varying degrees of sanctity. Some are Holy Scripture to at least one of the great religions, while others are the chronicles of kings or the records of European clergy. Nevertheless, the evidence that we have is largely preserved in books, or it is based upon books. It is literary evidence, and while we are often tempted to believe that there is a world of hard fact behind the text, which we can recover if we are sufficiently persistent or ingenious, this may not always be the case.

When the emperor Iyasu enters the sanctuary at Aksum and commands the priests to bring the Ark of the Covenant to him, the chronicle reports the events that follow as a miracle. The Ark is sealed with seven locks, and the priests open these one after the other. They only succeed with six, however. The seventh cannot be moved, and when they finally decide to carry the Ark unopened into the presence of the emperor, the Ark releases the seventh seal and reveals itself to Iyasu of its own will.

In the Revelation of John, the visionary sees the fiery throne of the chariot surrounded by the cherubim who adorned the mercy seat of the Ark of the Covenant, and whose wings spread over the Ark in the inner sanctuary of the Temple where it was placed at the order of King Solomon. A mysterious figure sits on the throne, holding in his right hand a scroll that has been sealed with seven seals. With a loud voice, an angel asks if anyone is worthy to break the seals and open the scroll. No one in heaven or on earth or under the earth is able to open it, or to see what is written inside it, and the visionary weeps that no one should be found worthy. Then one of the elders tells him not to weep: 'The Lion of the Tribe of Judah, the Root of David, has conquered. He can open the scroll and its seven seals.'

By the time that Iyasu came to the throne of Ethiopia, the emperors were not only proclaiming descent from King Solomon and the house of David, they had begun to style themselves, 'Conquering Lion of the Tribe of Judah'. The chronicle is therefore applying to the great king whose achievements it is honouring the immense stature of the Lamb of God in the Book of Revelation, the one chosen to open all the seals and reveal the astonishing secrets of the Last Days. If it seems extravagant to compare the emperor to Christ himself, it should be remembered that they were believed to be relatives, both descended from the same house of David. It should also be remembered that chroniclers could be required to read their work before a discerning and keenly interested audience: the son and successor of the dead emperor.

If the account of Iyasu meeting the Ark of the Covenant is so clearly dependent on the Book of Revelation and its vision of the sealed scroll, and if it was so obviously written to glorify the dead emperor, is none of it to be believed? Is it all simply a pious fraud?

It is not the only example, of course. We have already seen that Abu Salih described the Ark of Lalibela as carried by men whose skin was white and red and whose hair was golden. The description has given rise to fanciful theories about Crusaders in the highlands of Lasta, but the remarks are perfectly reasonable if one has read the description of Solomon in the Song of Songs. The Ethiopian royal house claims descent from the house of David, and the ancestors of the priests came with the son of Solomon from Jerusalem. It would be quite obvious to a medieval author that they should resemble the account of Solomon given in the Bible.

The description of Iyasu meeting the Ark may have been written with the Book of Revelation in mind, but that does not mean that the emperor did not enter the sanctuary to see the Ark, and it does not mean that the great relic was not delivered to him. We have too many other records from both earlier and later centuries to believe that the sanctuary was empty when the emperor waited for the Ark.

The clergy at Aksum now tell us that the sanctuary contains the Tablet of Moses. They speak specifically of a tablet, using the word *sellat*, rather than the general word *tabot*, which could be applied to either a Tablet or the Ark in which it might have been kept. Could this really be the Tablet of Moses that was once kept within the Temple of Solomon in Jerusalem? The possibility may seem too fantastic to contemplate, but it should not be dismissed as impossible simply because it would be astonishing. The Black Stone and the Station of Abraham in Mecca demonstrate that it is quite possible for sacred stones to survive in a holy city near the Red Sea for at least fourteen centuries. In fact, we have no idea how long these stones have been venerated at the Kaba. The Bible naturally associates the Tablets of Moses with Moses himself, but

Islamic tradition associates the stones at Mecca with Abraham and even with Adam, whose antiquity obviously surpasses that of Moses or anyone else. It would obviously be difficult to argue that one were older than the other on the basis of these traditions alone.

We can also imagine a route by which the Tablets of Moses might have reached Aksum. Despite earlier claims, this is unlikely to have been through Egypt. The Nile is not navigable through Nubia and south into Ethiopia, and the overland route is possible but very difficult. There is also no evidence that the Ark was carried by way of Egypt. But there is evidence that it came to Arabia, that the Ark was saved from Jerusalem and passed into the hands of the Jurhum, who controlled the sanctuaries at both Mecca and Najran. And the massacre at Najran, as we know, provoked the Crusade led into Arabia by the Aksumite king Kaleb.

Is the Arabian evidence really credible, however? It would seem to be no less credible than the evidence of the biblical accounts of the Ark. The real challenge of the evidence may not be the accounts of the Arab historians so much as the biblical text itself. The authors and the editors who wrote and preserved the relevant passages were trying to make sense of an object that was already ancient by the time they were writing, and which had disappeared from Jerusalem by the time that the Bible existed as we know it today. It would seem to have survived from an ancient and mythic time – a time when the Bible tells us that God spoke to Moses in a way that he no longer speaks to anyone. It was already a relic from a different age, in which God moved in the world in a manner that no one alive had ever seen. And what is more, no one writing in the later age had ever seen the Ark. There are suggestions in the Psalms that it was carried in procession, but Josiah appears to have put an end to these. Otherwise, the Ark seems to have remained in the sanctuary of the Temple and to have been visited only by the high priest on a single day of the year, the Day of Atonement. Even then, he covered the Ark with a cloud of incense.

If the later authors were trying to understand the Ark themselves, they also seem to preserve doubts its about the authenticity, or at least to raise the question in an interesting way. Moses destroys the first Tablets, which the author of Exodus tells us were written with the finger of God. The prophet then writes the laws himself on a second set of Tablets. Does this suggest that the contents of the Ark in Jerusalem were not genuine? Is the statement part of factional struggle between the priests at Jerusalem who controlled the Ark and those from other shrines who did not? Or does it suggest that any copy of the heavenly original should be seen as genuine? If the original were in heaven, then any material form would be a copy. One copy would be no more original than another copy. The real Ark and the real Tablets would be the immaterial prototypes.

In the days when scholars were more inclined to provide rational explanations for the miracles in the Bible than they are today, suggestions were made about the Tablets of Moses. Could the Ark of the Covenant have contained a meteorite, whose appearance in fire from the sky would have seemed to be a miraculous revelation from heaven? Could the Ark have contained an ancient idol, once part of a pagan cult, but then brought into the worship of the God of Israel, a legacy of the years in the wilderness? Could the ancient idol itself have been a meteorite? These might seem to be curious suggestions, although the use of stone pillars that were later despised by the reforming king Josiah would suggest that distinctions between the Israelite cult and paganism were not as strict as some biblical authors would have liked their readers to assume. The evidence of the sacred stones at Mecca may help us to understand the process. Muslims insist that there is only one God, and they make the assertion with no less vigour than Jews. They are also no less hostile to idolatry. Yet we have seen that ancient pagan stones can survive in the Islamic cult at Mecca even today, and can even be thought to be signs of the covenant between the one true God and the human race that he created. Josiah might have found the idea disturbing, and there were clearly Muslims who regarded the Black Stone with suspicion, but if Islam could countenance a transformation of this sort, there is no reason why Judaism could not.

If the great relic at Aksum is a Tablet, however, it may seem odd that Ethiopians have referred so often to the Ark of the Covenant. Could the Ark itself ever have come to Ethiopia? Even the authors of the Hebrew Bible seem to have left evidence in the text that the Ark was replaced, or at least that more than one of them had been made. Would this make the possibility any less remote? It is certainly unlikely that a wooden box could have survived outside the peculiar conditions of an Egyptian tomb. Wandering in the desert, battles, capture, processions, incense, blood – all these would have weakened it, and the climate of Ethiopia would not have been conducive to an ancient wooden box surviving if it ever reached the highlands of Tigray. The Ethiopian accounts also describe what seem to be different boxes, and the earliest report, that of Abu Salih, is already describing an Ark that is clearly Christian. If his account is accurate, the Ark of Lalibela is a Christian Ark. Whatever Abu Salih believed that it contained, the Ark itself was decorated with crosses and is very different from anything that could be imagined in the pages of the Hebrew Bible or as part of a Judaic cult. On the basis of his account, one would assume that the Ark itself was not the essential part of the Ethiopian relic. The essential part would therefore be the Tablet.

But if the relic is a Tablet, why is it so often said to be the Ark? The accounts that we have from Ethiopia indicate that the Tablet was kept within a box. It would therefore be perfectly reasonable to refer to the Tablet and the box that held it as the Ark. The fact that the word *tabot* is also used to describe a stone altar tablet as well as the chest in which the tablet is kept must also have contributed to the identification of Tablet and Ark. A stone tablet can be called a *tabot*, and the Ark is also called *tabot*. It is not always clear which of them an Ethiopic text or an Ethiopian speaker may have in mind.

Beyond this choice of words, the great advantage of religious symbols is that they are fluid and protean, and can be applied to more than one object in a way that would break the rules of a stricter logic. In the writings of Zara Yaqob, we have seen that the same symbols used to describe the Ark can be used to describe the Tablet. And *The Glory of Kings* speaks of the Ark as if it were really the Tabernacle. These three – Tablet, Ark, Tabernacle – existed one within the other, yet the distinctions between them are not entirely clear. All of them are signs of the presence of God. In some mysterious way, they are the same thing. Once again, the Arabian evidence may help us to understand how this is possible. The Black Stone is not a chest. It is a stone. Yet it is still said to contain the record of the covenant between God and man. In other words, a stone tablet can be both a Tablet and an Ark.

But why would the Tablet be described in the singular? The Hebrew Bible refers to two tablets of stone on Mount Sinai. Why would there be only one in Aksum? A simple explanation would be that only one of the two had survived, but it is also noticeable that Francisco Alvares refers to the relic as an altar stone from Zion. Could it have been an altar stone of great antiquity that began to be called the Ark of the Covenant at a later date, when Ethiopian Christians became increasingly fascinated with the Old Testament, or when they came under pressure from Jesuit missionaries to explain the number of Old Testament customs that they preserved? Although the Tabernacle and the Temple were provided with objects that were specifically called altars and were distinct from the Ark, it is certainly true that on the Day of Atonement the cover of the Ark was sprinkled with blood in the manner we might expect of an altar. And given that the sacrifice of Christ, according to the account of the Tabernacle in the Epistle to the Hebrews, replaced the ritual of the Day of Atonement, it would be quite reasonable for the Tablet of Moses and the altar stone to be identified.

If the great relic were an altar stone, could it still be an Ark? The answer may seem to defy logic, but it would nevertheless appear that it could. We have already seen that sacred stones can be given new forms of sanctity, and it is important to remember that *The Glory of Kings*, other Ethiopic sources, European reports and the testimony of the clergy at Aksum do not describe an Ark that is employed with the cultic regulations of the Old Testament. At least, the Priestly Code is not applied to the relic at Aksum, even though it is readily available in the Ethiopic translation of the Old Testament. This is reasonable enough. Even if it does display a number of Old Testament customs, the Ethiopian Orthodox Church is Christian rather than Jewish. But it is important to remember that this is an object that is described in New Testament terms. It is said to be Mary, the Mother of Christ, and the earliest account of it refers to the crosses that adorn it. It is therefore, strictly speaking, a New Testament rather than an Old Testament Ark. In terms of its religious symbolism, it is younger than the Ark of the Old Testament. Given its involvement in rituals that step back in time beyond the division between Egypt and Israel, it is also in a curious way older than the Ark of the Old Testament.

If one takes the Old Testament, the New Testament and *The Glory of Kings* seriously, they all regard the Ark as a copy of a heavenly original. Certainly we have seen that it is possible to replace the Tablets with others that are still believed to be authentic. If the original is in heaven, then a copy is still a copy. It is not the earthly object in which authenticity resides. Given the statement about replacement of Tablets, and the likelihood that the Arks in the Old Testament were duplicated or replaced, it is difficult to see why the Ark in Aksum would have to be any less authentic than those described in the Bible.

Is it possible that the Tablets of Moses did reach Ethiopia, but were replaced with a later stone? It is possible, although the Ethiopian chronicles and the clergy at Aksum would deny that it occurred. James Bruce certainly maintained that the great relic had been destroyed when the armies of Ahmed Grañ captured Aksum, although he was not the sort of man to write that the Ark had been in Ethiopia anyway. The emperor Takla Haymanot II apparently claimed that the Grañ had destroyed it, but Muslim tradition insists that it was saved. The Jesuits claim to have destroyed the box, but it seems that the Tablet itself was saved before they could seize it. Would this really make any difference to the authenticity of the relic? Not, it seems, if we take Exodus seriously. It is also important to remember that the Ark was a kind of portable Temple, and it was certainly possible to rebuild the Temple. The Second Temple may have been built after the Temple of Solomon had been destroyed, but it was the Temple nonetheless. *The Glory of Kings* also tells us that David made a new Ark when he brought the Ark up to Jerusalem, but this did not mean that it was no longer the original Ark.

In recent years, people throughout the world have become fascinated by the Ark at Aksum, and there has been increasing pressure on the priests at Aksum to allow their relic to be examined. Given what we know of the descriptions of the Ark in the Hebrew Bible, of the sacred stones at Mecca, and of the early accounts of the Ethiopian Ark, is there any reason for the Ethiopian Orthodox Church to alter its tradition and examine the relic in the Shrine of the Tablet? There would seem to be little point in it. Descriptions of the Black Stone show that a superficial examination may reveal almost nothing about an ancient stone that has been handled much, and anything more would surely be unacceptable to the Aksumite clergy who have guarded it for centuries, as well as to millions of the faithful for whom they have guarded it. We should also remember that supposedly definitive examinations are not always as conclusive as we assume they are going to be. In the years that have passed since the radio-carbon dating of the Shroud of Turin, it has begun to emerge that there may have been phenomena that influenced the result, that were not understood at the time and are only beginning to be understood now. Technology is always developing, and there is no reason to assume that what we possess at any given point will be final and definitive.

It is also true that the announcement of the dating of the Shroud did not cause those who believed in its authenticity to abandon their belief. And if the result of the test had been different, it is doubtful that many people would have decided that Christianity were suddenly true. In this sense, the question of origin may be interesting, but fundamentally trivial. After all, it is true that the relic of the Shroud is not an essential tenet of Roman Catholic belief, and that the relic at Aksum is not essential to Orthodoxy. Solomonic descent may have been central to the position of the royal house, but the key doctrines surrounding the nature of Christ and the efficacy of his Death and Resurrection – doctrines that the Ethiopians share with other churches such as the Copts, the Syrian Orthodox and the Armenians – are not affected by what is believed about the relic at Aksum.

How then should we understand the mystery? Of all the attempts at explaining the Ark of the Covenant, the Alexandrian philosopher Philo is among the earliest to survive. His account of it was thoroughly mystical. Even though we rely on the histories of Josephus to understand the circumstances surrounding the final destruction of the Temple in the first century AD, and even though he was a priest in Jerusalem himself, he shared the mystical explanation that the Alexandrian philosophers had proposed. As a historical curiosity, the Ark would seem to be almost pointless. It is only if it offers an answer to the human predicament, a means by which we can escape from the constraints of birth and death and of time itself, that it would seem to have any real purpose. This is what Philo would have maintained, at any rate. For this, we need to return to Aksum.

The Tents of Israel

In the streets of Aksum, it can be difficult now to remember that this is a holy city in which heaven and earth are believed to meet. The ancient metropolis may have survived the years of civil war, and new boulevards stretch away to the south, but war has been threatening once again, and if one stands in the dust among the poor houses near the great church of Mary of Zion, one sees little more than a shadow of the glorious kingdom of antiquity. Even the shrine in which the Ark of God is guarded by its Keeper can seem a disappointment, erected only thirty-five years ago and decorated with the sort of cheap ceramic tiles that one might expect in a local hotel or restaurant. But the ways of God are not the ways of man, the prophet Samuel was told, and He does not choose as men choose.

It is one thing to sit in a library at Oxford or Harvard surrounded by printed books on Ethiopia, a monument to five centuries of scholarship in which the chronicles and hagiographies of a remote empire have been preserved and analysed in the clear light of Semitic philology. It is quite another thing to find oneself in the presence of the living tradition at Aksum, for however tired and broken the city may seem, like the rod of Aaron it stands as witness to miraculous life called forth by the presence of the Ark. We may be confused or discouraged as we try to follow the path left by the ancient prophets, priests and philosophers, but many people would say that at Aksum one can feel closer to the presence of the Ark than anywhere else, even on the Temple Mount. Whatever the rabbis believed had been hidden in the rock beneath the Temple of Solomon, the power of the Ark is still visible in Ethiopia, its presence drawing hundreds of thousands of pilgrims to the great festivals held in its honour.

The most difficult challenge for those of us who live in the modern world is not so much to recover facts that may have been forgotten or objects that may have been lost, but to see those facts or those objects in something like they way they would have been seen in ancient or medieval times. Our attempt to follow Yehudah ha-Levi in the footsteps of the Ark is obviously hindered by the centuries that stand between us and the accounts of the Ark in the Bible. And as if that were not problem enough, even by the time that the Bible begins to be corroborated through the evidence of other ancient Near Eastern records, the era of the Ark at Jerusalem has passed. The reforming king Josiah is decreeing that the sacred processions would carry the Ark no longer. The prophet Jeremiah is calling the Ark an irrelevance. Ezekiel never sees it in his heavenly Temple. None of the books preserved in the Hebrew Bible records its fate.

By the time that the biblical accounts of the Ark seem to have been compiled, the forty days when Moses might have stood on Mount Sinai would already have been as distant as the Zagwe and the Ark of Abu Salih are for us now. Most scholars have become very sceptical about the biblical descriptions of the Ark, but even without the apparatus of critical scholarship, a simple reading of the Bible suggests that there are very different accounts of it. One of the mysteries of the Ark begins as soon as it is made.

Perhaps we should be looking for what the Ark would do, if it were at Aksum, rather than hoping to catch a glimpse of it by forcing the Guardian to uncover it and then trying to identify it by its appearance. In the Hebrew Bible, the Presence of God in the Ark stands at the centre of the cult and defends Israel against its enemies. Even the rabbis argued over whether the same Ark performed both these tasks, but both were clearly believed to be essential. Even so, the power of the Ark does not seem to be absolute. At least, it is not employed without condition, and the Bible reports several occasions in the history of Israel when the wickedness of the Chosen People would cause the Ark to desert them. The faithful at Aksum would see the ancient miracles repeated in their own history. When the rest of Africa was overwhelmed by European armies during the imperialist adventure, Ethiopia remained free, and its church survived, flourishing in a way that has seemed impossible for the Copts and the Syrians to whom it owed so much. It is hardly surprising that the Orthodox should see their endurance as the New Israel as proof that the promise of the Ark is true, that the miracle of its presence has ensured the survival of both nation and Church. As in the Old Testament, of course, this protection was never absolute. There have been invasions and civil wars, and the imperial house no longer rules in Addis Ababa, but the singularity of Ethiopian history remains. Whatever we choose to think about it, the fact cannot be denied. Or so they would say at Aksum.

Many of us in the West have believed that the time of miracles has passed. Especially during the Reformation, we began to read the Bible for its plain sense, its historical sense. This seemed to offer a way of returning to original purity, of departing from old and corrupt medieval ways. In doing so, we applied standards of evidence to the text that it may never have been written to answer. Modern men were reading an ancient book and asking modern questions of it. We are still wrestling with the Bible, in this sense, attempting to apply rules to it that we have applied elsewhere, and we still find it difficult to decide what sort of history the Bible is trying to tell us.

At the end of the second millennium, we find ourselves in the midst of dramatic and bewildering change, as our ancestors did during the Reformation and the Enlightenment. The sharp distinctions with which we have been living are beginning to seem less absolute, as if the boundaries between science, philosophy, religion and mysticism were becoming fluid or were even disappearing. Our future seems likely to bear a startling resemblance to our past – a Platonic or Pythagorean world of digital information, in which the intangible and intellectual are more real than any material form.

The holy men of the Syrian tradition, whose mystical treatises have been read by Ethiopian monks and hermits for centuries, were strange creatures. They were not even thought to be men. They had passed beyond the limits of human existence and now stood between earth and heaven. They were alive, and yet they had already died. They lived in the body, and yet they had discarded it. They were themselves, and yet something else at the same time. They could pass through the gates of existence into a world that was simply beyond existence, where the distinctions we normally employ became meaningless.

The men who carried the Arks in Ethiopia aspired to these ideals. The greatest among them lived with the angels, and yet the empires of the world seemed to rise or fall at their command. Should we see the mystery of the Ark at Aksum in terms of this peculiar world, with its paradox and contradiction? Some of the difficulty we encounter in trying to make sense of the Ark arises from its fundamental nature. It is protean, elusive and subtle. It was made from wood and held two pieces of stone, and yet it is said to be alive. It was on earth, and yet it was in heaven at the same time. It was filled with life, and yet it seemed more often to bring death. God was within it, and yet he was still outside it. It was made on Sinai, and yet it was created before the entire universe. It revealed the Creator of everything, and yet it seemed to vanish into nothing.

In Ethiopia, this tension is perhaps even more explicit. *The Glory of Kings* describes an Ark that is Jewish and yet Christian; it belongs to the Old Covenant as well as the New. It is a wooden box, and yet it is also a woman. Even Abu Salih describes an object that was made by Moses and is nevertheless decorated with the Cross of Christ. And in Ethiopia today, there are thousands of Arks, even though the Ark is unique.

If the Ark is supposed to pass from heaven to earth, from God to man, it would hardly be surprising if it were simply beyond our understanding. Philo certainly saw it as a mystery, something given material form as a way of taking us out of ourselves and back to God. Long after it had disappeared, Philo spoke of it as if it still existed.

In the Psalms we find a witness to the ancient processions of the Ark. Several generations of scholars have struggled to understand exactly how or when the Psalms would have been recited, but it seems difficult to deny that they were sung in the presence of the Ark as it was carried out of the Temple in Jerusalem. They repeated the ancient mythology of Zion, in which God defeated the powers of chaos that lived in the waters of the Abyss. Whatever may lie under the Temple Mount, it is at Aksum that the Ark retains its ancient ceremonial office. Of all the Arks that emerge from the confusion of the earliest records, the Ark at Aksum is the one that is still active. If the Arks had the power to choose where they would go, this is the Ark that has chosen to remain among the

Children of the Covenant, as an abiding witness to an ancient truth.

Ritual and sacrament are believed to dissolve the boundaries of conventional time and space. At Aksum, and throughout Ethiopia, this is the reason that the Ark is carried in procession on the great festivals such as *Timqat*. As a recreation of the Baptism of Christ, *Timqat* summons the ancient victories of God over the waters of chaos and death: Creation, Flood, Exodus, Conquest, Mount Zion on which the Temple once stood. The faithful are present simultaneously at the victories of God in history and outside it, participants in the cosmic victory of Zion, in the triumph of order and harmony throughout the universe. This is not a rational process, of course. The Ark is not a rational thing. But this is why *Timqat* is celebrated nevertheless.

Several years ago, His Holiness Abuna Paulos remarked to us that when he returned to Ethiopia after serving as a parish priest in New York, he began to realize that the affluent lives we led in North American and Europe had been purchased at a heavy price. We were comfortable, perhaps, but our eyes were closing and our ears were growing dull. Ethiopia might be poor, at least as the West would see it, but its people had laid up treasures of a spiritual kind that the West would need. Many of us are inclined to agree that wealth stands in the way of spiritual life, although the question is rarely simple. The Ark, the Tabernacle and the Temple all required precious metals and costly fabrics, and if the Israelite prophets denounced the extravagance of the cult, the priests might have agreed with Philo, or with the abbot Suger who built St Denis. The opulence of his abbey was precisely the vehicle by which the human soul could rise above its material confinement.

We have also seen that the Ark itself is never a simple thing. It embodies political as well as mystical aspirations, and its legacy in Ethiopia would seem to be no less vexed than its legacy elsewhere. It is often said quite seriously that powerful symbols have a life of their own, independent of those who believe them. This may seem to be especially true of the Ark, which returns from the shadows even after it has been forgotten. But we may also have the power to make our own choice about what a symbol will mean to us. The Ark could be a palladium behind which the faithful march against their enemies, to secure a purity of belief or a purity of race. But so much of the history of the Ark suggests something different. It is made when Israel turns away from Egypt, but the Temple that Solomon built for it was said to lead Israel back its old master. David brings the Ark to Jerusalem as a symbol of a new united Israel, but David himself is not pure Israelite and the cult of Zion is deeply indebted to old ways of Canaan. *The Glory of Kings* speaks of a people who are chosen in place of other peoples, but who are themselves a mixture of peoples. The great festival of *Timqat* recalls the faith of Egypt, of Israel, and of the New Covenant of Christ. Whatever it might have seemed to some of those who wrote about it, the Ark need not be a narrow tribal talisman, bringing life to a chosen few and death to the rest. It may also tell us, as the Fourth Evangelist wrote, that in our father's house there are many mansions.

But if that is what we choose the Ark to mean, is it really at Aksum? From the beginning, it seems, it has been difficult to know if the Ark should be understood in historical or mystical terms. All that we know of its creation suggests a shrine of remote antiquity that survived into a historical age. In this respect, the role of the Ark at Aksum today, where it continues to be part of a powerful myth of cosmic rebirth, seems no different from the biblical accounts. To deny this may mean that we ask the wrong questions about it.

After the English Revolution, dreams of Israel remained especially strong among Dissenters, whose faith and imagination were nourished by visions of revelation on the holy mountain, tabernacles and pillars of cloud in the wilderness, chariots of fire, engraved tablets, and angels around the Ark of God. Two hundred years ago, an English visionary raised in this tradition, who had seen the gates of the Heavenly Jerusalem open before him in the streets of London, dismissed the arrogance of the intellect and proclaimed an eternal truth that stood behind the hard facts of science.

> The atoms of Democritus
> And Newton's particles of light
> Are sands upon the Red Sea shore,
> Where Israel's tents do shine so bright.

These are the words of William Blake, but they may reveal the secret of Aksum as well. Whatever the confusion in which we struggle as we try to find our place within the material world, the testimony of the Ark is no less real. God may move among us just as he did in the days of David and Solomon, and the complaint of Sir Fulke Greville that 'all now rests in the heart' may have been no less true in antiquity. For those who can see them, the tents of Israel shine bright at Aksum.

Select Bibliography

Primary Sources

A. d'Abbadie and P. Paulitschke, *Futûḥ el-Hábacha, des conquêtes faites en Abyssinie au XVIe siècle par l'Imam Muhammad Aḥmad dit Gragne*, Paris, 1898.

Abu Salih, *The Churches and Monasteries of Egypt and Some Neighbouring Countries*, ed. and tr. B.T.A. Evetts, annot. A. J. Butler, Oxford, 1895.

C. Bezold, ed. and tr., *Kebra Nagast: Die Herrlichkeit der Könige*, Abhandlungen der Philosophisch-Philologischen Klasse der Königlich Bayerischen Akademie der Wissenschaften 23, Munich, 1909.

E.A.W. Budge, *The Queen of Sheba and Her Only Son Menyelek*, London, 1922.

E.A.W. Budge, *The Book of the Saints of the Ethiopian Church: The Ethiopic Synaxarium*, 4 vols., Cambridge, 1928.

J. Charlesworth, ed., *Old Testament Pseudepigrapha*, 2 vols., Garden City, N.Y., 1983-7.

C. Conti Rossini, ed. and tr., *Acta Sancti Yārēd et Sancti Pantaleonis, Vitae Sanctorum Antiquorum*, Corpus Scriptorum Christianorum Orientalium, Script. aeth., ser. 2, vol. 17, Leipzig, 1904.

C. Conti Rossini, ed. and tr., *Historia regis Sarṣa Dengel (Malak Sagad)*, Corpus Scriptorum Christianorum Orientalium, Script. aeth., ser. 2, vol. 3, Leipzig, 1907.

C. Conti Rossini, ed. and tr., *Documenta ad illustrandam historiam: I. Liber Axumae*, Corpus Scriptorum Christianorum Orientalium, Script. aeth., ser. 2, vol. 8, Leipzig, 1909-10.

C. Conti Rossini and L. Ricci, *Il Libro della Luce del Negus Zar'a Ya'qob (Maṣḥafa Berhān)*, Corpus Scriptorum Christianorum Orientalium, Script. aeth. 47-8 and 51-2, Louvain, 1964-5.

F. H. Coulson et al., ed. and tr., *Philo*, 12 vols., Cambridge, Mass., 1929-62.

H. Danby, *The Mishnah: Translated from the Hebrew with Introduction and Brief Explanatory Notes*, Oxford, 1933.

I. Epstein, ed., *The Babylonian Talmud: Translated into English with Notes*, 35 vols., London, 1935–52.

H. Freedman and M. Simon, eds., *Midrash Rabbah: Translated into English*, 10 vols., London, 1939.

Getatchew Haile, ed. and tr., *The Mariology of Emperor Zär'a Ya'əqob of Ethiopia*, Orientalia Christiana Analecta 242, Rome, 1992.

I. Guidi, ed. and tr., *Annales Iohannis I, Iyāsu I, et Bakāffā*, Corpus Scriptorum Christianorum Orientalium, Script. aeth., ser. 2, vol. 5, Leipzig, 1903.

Al-Hasan ibn Ahmad al-Hamdani, *Kitab al-Iklil*, Book 8, ed. and tr. N. A. Faris, Princeton, 1940.

G.W.B. Huntingford, ed. and tr., *The Glorious Victories of 'Āmda Ṣeyon, King of Ethiopia*, Oxford, 1965.

Kosmas Indikopleustes, *La topographie chrétienne*, ed. and tr. W. Wolska-Conus, Sources chrétiennes 141, 159, 197, Paris, 1968–74.

S. Kur, ed. and tr., *Actes de Iyasus Mo'a, abbé du couvent de St-Etienne de Ḥayq*, Corpus Scriptorum Christianorum Orientalium, Script. aeth. 49 and 50, Louvain, 1965.

A. Moberg, ed. and tr., *The Book of the Himyarites: Fragments of a Hitherto Unknown Syriac Work*, Lund, 1924.

J. Neusner, ed., *The Talmud of the Land of Israel*, 35 vols., Chicago, 1982–94.

F. M. Esteves Pereira, *Chronica de Susenyos, rei de Ethiopia*, 2 vols., Lisbon, 1892–1900.

J. Perruchon, *Les chroniques de Zar'a Yâ'eqôb et de Ba'eda Mâryâm, rois d'Ethiopie de 1434 à 1478*, Paris, 1893.

H. Spurling and M. Simon, *The Zohar*, 5 vols., London, 1931–4.

H. St J. Thackeray et al., ed. and tr., *Josephus*, 2 vols., Cambridge, Mass., 1926–65.

W. G. Waddell, ed. and tr., *Manetho*, Cambridge, Mass., 1940.

Secondary Sources

P. Ackroyd, *Exile and Restoration*, London, 1968.

A. Ahlström, 'The Travels of the Ark: A Religio-Political Composition', *Journal of Near Eastern Studies* 43, 1984, 141–9.

M. de Almeida, *Some Records of Ethiopia, 1593–1646, Being Extracts from the History of High Ethiopia or Abassia*, ed. C. F. Beckingham and G.W.B. Huntingford, London, 1954.

F. Alvares, *The Prester John of the Indies: A True Relation of the Lands of the Prester John*, rev. and ed. C. F. Beckingham and G.W.B. Huntingford, 2 vols. Cambridge, 1961.

W. R. Arnold, *Ephod and Ark*, Harvard Theological Studies 3, Cambridge, Mass., 1917.

J. Assmann, *Moses the Egyptian: The Memory of Egypt in Western Monotheism*, Cambridge, Mass., 1997.

M. Barradas, *Tractatus Tres Historico-Geographici*, tr. E. Filleul and ed. Richard Pankhurst, Wiesbaden, 1996.

J. de Barros, *Asia de João de Barros: Terceira Decada*, Lisbon, 1563.

J. Blenkinsopp, 'Kiriath-jearim and the Ark', *Journal of Biblical Literature* 88, 1969, 143–56.

J. Bruce, *Travels to Discover the Source of the Nile*, 5 vols., London, 1790.

K. Budde, 'Ephod und Lade', *Zeitschrift für die alttestamentliche Wissenschaft* 39, 1921, 1–42.

T. Busink, *Der Tempel von Jerusalem. Von Salomo bis Herodes*, 2 vols., Leiden, 1970–80.

J. Buxtorf, *Historia Arcae Foederis*, in B. Ugolini, *Thesaurus Antiquitatum Sacrarum*, Venice, 1744ff.

A. F. Campbell, *The Ark Narrative (1 Sam 4–6; 2 Sam 6)*, Society of Biblical Literature Dissertation Series 16, Missoula, 1975.

A. F. Campbell, 'Yahweh and the Ark', *Journal of Biblical Literature* 98, 1979, 31–43.

E. Cerulli, *Il Libro Etiopico dei Miracoli di Maria e le sue fonti nelle letterature del medio evo latino*, Rome, 1943.

B. S. Childs, *The Book of Exodus*, London, 1974.

R. E. Clements, *God and Temple*, Oxford, 1965.

R. J. Clifford, *The Cosmic Mountain in Canaan and the Old Testament*, Harvard Semitic Monographs 4, Cambridge, Mass., 1972.

S.J.D. Cohen, *From the Maccabees to the Mishnah*, Philadelphia, 1987.

N. Cohn, *The Pursuit of the Millennium: Revolutionary Millenarians and Mystical Anarchists of the Middle Ages*, rev. ed., London, 1970.

N. Cohn, *Cosmos, Chaos and the World to Come: The Ancient Roots of Apocalyptic Faith*, New Haven and London, 1993.

M. Cramer, *Das Christlich-Koptische Ägypten Einst und Heute*, Wiesbaden, 1959.

P. Crone and M. Cook, *Hagarism: The Making of the Islamic World*, Cambridge, 1977.

F. M. Cross, *Canaanite Myth and Hebrew Epic*, Cambridge, Mass., 1973.

F. M. Cross, 'The Priestly Tabernacle in the Light of Recent Research', in A.

Biran, ed., *Temples and High Places in Biblical Times*, Jerusalem, 1981, 70–90.

G. H. Davies, 'The Ark in the Psalms', in F. F. Bruce, ed., *Promise and Fufilment: Essays Presented to Professor S. H. Hooke*, Edinburgh, 1963, 51–61.

G. H. Davies, 'The Ark of the Covenant', *Annual of the Swedish Theological Institute* 5, 1967, 30–47.

P. R. Davies, 'The History of the Ark in the Books of Samuel', *Journal of Northwest Semitic Languages* 5, 1977, 9–18.

P. R. Davies, *In Search of 'Ancient Israel'*, *Journal for the Study of the Old Testament Supplement Series* 148, Sheffield, 1992.

M. Dibelius, *Die Lade Jahwes*, Göttingen, 1906.

R. P. Dimothéos (Sapritchian), *Deux ans de séjour en Abyssinie*, Jerusalem, 1871.

J. Doresse, *In the Land of the Queen of Sheba: Ancient and Modern Ethiopia*, London, 1959.

J. A. Eaton, *Kingship and the Psalms*, London, 1976.

J. A. Eaton, *Festal Drama in Deutero-Isaiah*, London, 1979.

O. Eissfeldt, 'Lade und Stierbild', *Zeitschrift für die alttestamentliche Wissenschaft* 58, 1940–1, 190–215.

I. Engnell, *Studies in Divine Kingship in the Ancient Near East*, Oxford, 1967.

A. Erman, 'Bruchstücke koptischer Volkslitteratur', *Abhandlungen der Königliche Preussischer Akademie der Wissenschaften zu Berlin*, 1897, 3–64, esp. 24–6.

T. E. Fretheim, 'The Ark in Deuteronomy', *Catholic Biblical Quarterly* 30, 1968, 1–14.

R. E. Friedman, 'The Tabernacle in the Temple', *Biblical Archaeologist* 43, 1980, 241–8.

M. Geddes, *The Church History of Ethiopia*, London, 1696.

G. Gerster, *Churches in Rock: Early Christian Ark in Ethiopia*, London, 1970.

D. de Goís, *Fides, Religio, Mores que Aethiopium sub Imperio Preciosi Ioannis . . .*, Louvain, 1540.

D. de Goís, *Legatio magni Indorum Imperatoris Prebyteri Iohannis, ad Emanuelem Lusitaniae Regem, Anno Domini MDXIII*, Dordrecht, 1618.

M. Griaule, 'Règles de l'Eglise (Documents éthiopiens)', *Journal asiatique* 221, 1932, 1–42.

R. Grierson, ed., *African Zion: The Sacred Art of Ethiopia,* New Haven and London, 1993.

J. Gutman, 'The History of the Ark', *Zeitschrift für die alttestamentliche Wissenschaft* 87, 1971, 22–30.

G. Hancock, *The Sign and the Seal*, London, 1992.

J. M. Hanssens and A. Raes, 'Une collection de tâbots au Musée Chrétien de la Bibliothèque Vaticane', *Orientalia Cristiana Periodica* 17, 1951, 435–50.

M. Haran, 'The Ark and the Cherubim', *Israel Exploration Journal* 9, 1959, 30–8, 89–94.

M. Haran, 'Otfe, Mahmal and Kubbe' [in Hebrew], in A. Biram et al., eds., *D. Neiger Memorial Volume*, Jerusalem, 1959, 215–21.

M. Haran, 'The Nature of the "Ohel Mo'edh" in Pentateuchal Sources', *Journal of Semitic Studies* 5, 1960, 50–65.

M. Haran, 'The Disappearance of the Ark', *Israel Exploration Journal* 13, 1963, 46–58.

M. Haran, 'The Priestly Image of the Tabernacle', *Hebrew Union College Annual* 36, 1965, 191–226.

M. Haran, 'The Divine Presence in the Israelite Cult and the Cultic Institutions', *Biblica* 50, 1969, 251–67.

M. Haran, *Temples and Temple-Service in Ancient Israel*, Oxford, 1978.

R. Hartmann, 'Zelt und Lade', *Zeitschrift für die alttestamentliche Wissenschaft* 37, 1917–18, 209–44.

G. R. Hawting, 'The Disappearance and Rediscovery of Zamzam and the "Well of the Ka'ba"', *Bulletin of the School of Oriental and African Studies* 43, 1980, 44–54.

G. R. Hawting, 'The Origins of the Islamic Sanctuary at Mecca', in G.H.A. Juynboll, ed., *Studies on the First Century of Islam*, Carbondale, Illinois, 1982, 25–47.

M. E. Heldman, The Marian Icons of the Painter Frē Ṣeyon: A Study in Fifteenth-Century Ark, Patronage, and Spirituality, *Orientalia Biblica et Christiana* 6, Wiesbaden, 1994.

C. Hill, *The World Turned Upside Down: Radical Ideas during the English Revolution*, London, 1972.

C. Hill, *The English Bible and the Seventeenth-Century Revolution*, London, 1993.

C. Hill, *Intellectual Origins of the English Revolution*, rev. ed., Oxford, 1997.

D. R. Hillers, 'Ritual Procession of the Ark and Psalm 132', *Catholic Biblical Quarterly* 30, 1968, 48–55.

J. K. Hoffmeier, *Israel in Egypt*, New York, 1997.

S. H. Hooke, ed., *Myth and Ritual: The Myth and Ritual of the Hebrews in Relation to the Culture Pattern of the Ancient Near East*, London, 1933.

S. H. Hooke, ed., *The Labyrinth: Further Studies in the Relation between Myth and Ritual in the Ancient World*, London, 1935.

S. H. Hooke, ed., *Myth, Ritual, and Kingship: Essays on the Theory and Practice of Kingship in the Ancient Near East and in Israel*, Oxford, 1958.

D. A. Hubbard, *The Literary Sources of the* Kebra Nagast, unpublished doctoral thesis, University of St. Andrews, 1956.

G.W.B. Huntingford, *The Land Charters of Northern Ethiopia*, Addis Ababa, 1965.

C. Snouck Hurgronje, *Mekka*, 2 vols., The Hague, 1888–9.

W. H. Irvine, 'Le sanctuaire central israelite avant l'établissement de la monarchie', *Revue biblique* 72, 1965, 161–84.

A. R. Johnson, *Sacral Kingship in the Ancient Near East*, Cardiff, 1967.

S. Kaplan, *The Monastic Holy Man and the Christianization of Early Solomonic Ethiopia*, Wiesbaden, 1984.

S. Kaplan, ' "Falasha" Religion: Ancient Judaism or Evolving Tradition? A Review Article', *Jewish Quarterly Review* 79.1, 1988, 49–65.

S. Kaplan, *The Beta Israel (Falasha) in Ethiopia*, New York, 1992.

Kefyalew Merahi, *The Covenant of Holy Mary Zion with Ethiopia*, Addis Ababa, 1997.

O.H.E. Khs-Burmester, *The Egyptian or Coptic Church*, Cairo, 1967.

K. Kitchen, 'Punt and How to Get There', *Orientalia* 40, 1971, 184–207.

C. R. Koester, *The Dwelling of God: The Tabernacle in the Old Testament, Intertestamental Jewish Literature, and the New Testament*, Catholic Biblical Quarterly Monograph Series 22, Washington DC, 1989.

C. H. Krinsky, 'Representations of the Temple of Jerusalem before 1500', *Journal of the Warburg and Courtauld Institutes* 33, 1970, 1–19.

H. Lazarus-Yafeh, *Intertwined Worlds: Medieval Islam and Bible Criticism*, Princeton, 1992.

J. D. Levenson, *Sinai and Zion*, San Francisco, 1987.

E. Littmann et al., *Deutsche Aksum-Expedition*, 4 vols., Berlin, 1913.

J. Lobo, *The Itinerário of Jerónimo Lobo*, tr. D. M. Lockhart, London, 1984.

L. Lozzi, *La confessione di Claudio, re d'Etiopia (1540–1559)*, Palermo, n.d.

W. McKane, 'The Earlier History of the Ark of the Covenant', *Transactions of the Glasgow University Oriental Society* 21, 1965–6, 68–76.

W. McKane, *Jeremiah*, vol. 1, Edinburgh, 1986.

A. Mendes, 'Carta di ill. et rev. D. Alfonso Mendes patriarcha de Ethiopia pera o padre Balthazar Telles . . .', in B. Tellez, *Historia geral de Ethiopia a alta*, Coimbra, 1660.

P. D. Miller and J.J.M. Roberts, *The Hand of the Lord: A Reassessment of the 'Ark Narrative' of I Samuel*, Baltimore, 1977.

U. Monneret de Villard, *Aksum*, Rome, 1938.

J. Morgenstern, 'The Ark, the Ephod, and the "Tent of Meeting"', *Hebrew Union College Annual* 17, 1942–3, 153–265; 18, 1943–4, 1–52.

S. Mowinckel, *The Psalms in Israel's Worship*, 2 vols., Oxford, 1962.

S. C. Munro-Hay, *Excavations at Aksum*, London, 1989.

S. C. Munro-Hay, *Aksum: An African Civilisation of Late Antiquity*, Edinburgh, 1991.

S. C. Munro-Hay, *Ethiopia and Alexandria: The Metropolitan Episcopacy of Ethiopia*, Warsaw and Wiesbaden, 1997.

S. C. Munro-Hay and B. Juel-Jensen, *Aksumite Coinage*, London, 1996.

N. S. Murrell et al., eds., *Chanting Down Babylon: The Rastafari Reader*, Philadelphia, 1998.

A. Musil, *The Manners and Customs of the Rwala Bedouins*, New York, 1928.

E. Naville, *The Temple of Deir el Bahari*, 3 vols., London, 1895–1908.

V. Nersessian and R. Pankhurst, 'The Visit to Ethiopia of Yohannes T'ovmacean, an Armenian Jeweller, in 1764–66', *Journal of Ethiopian Studies* 15, 1982, 79–104.

G. D. Newby, *A History of the Jews of Arabia*, Columbia, South Carolina, 1988.

E. Nielsen, 'Some Reflections on the History of the Ark', *Supplement to Vetus Testamentum* 7, 1960, 61–74.

P. Pais, *Historia da Ethiopia*, 3 vols., Porto, 1945–6.

F. E. Peters, *The Hajj*, Princeton, 1994.

F. E. Peters, *Mecca*, Princeton, 1994.

J. R. Porter, 'The Interpretation of 2 Samuel VI and Psalm CXXXII', *Journal of Theological Studies* 5, 1954, 161–73.

F. Praetorius, *Fabula de Regina Sabaea apud Aethiopes*, inaugural dissertation, Halle, n.d. (=1870).

V. Rabe, 'The Identity of the Priestly Tabernacle', *Journal of Near Eastern Studies* 25, 1966, 132–4.

G. von Rad, 'The Tent and the Ark', in *The Problem of the Hexateuch and Other Essays*, London, 1966, 103–24.

H. Rassam, *Narrative of the British Mission to Theodore, King of Abyssinia*, 2 vols., London, 1869.

C. Raswan, *The Black Tents of Arabia*, London, 1935.

D. B. Redford, *Egypt, Canaan, and Israel in Ancient Times*, Princeton, 1992.

W. Reimpell, 'Der Ursprung der Lade Jahwes', *Orientalistische Literaturzeitung* 19, 1916, 326–31.

H. Graf Reventlow, *The Authority of the Bible and the Rise of the Modern World*, London, 1984.

J.J.M. Roberts, 'The Hand of Yahweh', *Vetus Testamentum* 21, 1971, 244–51.

J.J.M. Roberts, 'The Davidic Origin of the Zion Tradition', *Journal of Biblical Literature* 92, 1973, 329–44.

M. Rodinson, review of E. Ullendorff, The Ethiopians . . ., *Bibliotheca Orientalis* 21, 1964, 239–41.

M. Rodinson, 'Sur la question des "influences juives" en Ethiopie', *Journal of Semitic Studies* 9, 1964, 11–19.

S. Rubenson, 'The Lion of the Tribe of Judah: Christian Symbol and/or Imperial Title', *Journal of Ethiopian Studies* 3.2, 75–85.

U. Rubin, 'The Ka'ba: Aspects of Its Ritual, Functions, and Position in Pre-Islamic and Early Islamic Times', *Jerusalem Studies in Arabic and Islam* 8, 1986, 97–131.

H. Salt, *A Voyage to Abyssinia and Travel into the Interior of that Country, Executed under the Orders of the British Government, in the Years 1809 and 1810*, London, 1814.

G. Scholem, *Jewish Gnosticism, Merkabah Mysticism and the Talmudic Tradition*, New York, 1960.

E. C. Selwyn, 'The Feast of Tabernacles, Epiphany and Baptism', *Journal of Theological Studies* 13, 1912, 225–49.

C. L. Seow, 'The Designation of the Ark in Priestly Theology', *Hebrew Annual Review* 8, 1985, 185–98.

C. L. Seow, *Myth, Drama, and the Politics of David's Dance*, Harvard Semitic Monographs 44, Atlanta, 1989.

I. Shahid, 'The Book of the Himyarites: Authorship and Authenticity', *Le Muséon* 76, 1963, 349–62.

I. Shahid, 'Byzanto-Arabica: The Conference of Ramla, A.D. 524', *Journal of Near Eastern Studies* 23, 1964, 114–31.

I. Shahid, *The Martyrs of Najran*, Subsidia Hagiographica 49, Brussels, 1971.

I. Shahid, 'The *Kebra Nagast* in the Light of Recent Research', *Le Muséon* 89, 1976, 133–78.

K. Kaufman Shelemay, *Music, Ritual, and Falasha History*, East Lansing, Michigan, 1989.

K. Kaufman Shelemay, 'The Musician and Transmission of Religious Tradition: The Multiple Roles of the Ethiopian Däbtära', *Journal of Religion in Africa* 22, 1992, 242–60.

Taddesse Tamrat, 'Some Notes on the Fifteenth Century Stephanite "Heresy" in the Ethiopian Church', *Rassegna di studi etiopici* 22, 1966, 103–15.

Taddesse Tamrat, 'The Abbots of Däbrä Hayq 1248–1535', *Journal of Ethiopian Studies* 8.1, 1970, 87–117.

Taddesse Tamrat, *Church and State in Ethiopia 1270–1527*, Oxford, 1972.

Taddesse Tamrat, 'Ethiopia, the Red Sea and the Horn', in R. Oliver, ed., *The Cambridge History of Africa*, vol. 3, 1977, 98–182.

B. Telles, *The Travels of the Jesuits in Ethiopia*, London, 1710.

K. van der Toorn and C. Houtman, 'David and the Ark', *Journal of Biblical Literature* 113, 1994, 209–31.

J. S. Trimingham, *Christianity among the Arabs in Pre-Islamic Times*, London, 1979.

N. H. Tur-Sinai, 'The Ark of God at Beit Shemesh (1 Sam. VI) and Pereş 'Uzza (2 Sam. VI; 1 Chron. XIII)', *Vetus Testamentum* 1, 1951, 275–86.

T. L. Thompson, *The Bible in History: How Writers Create a Past*, London, 1999.

E. Ullendorff, 'Candace (Acts VIII. 27) and the Queen of Sheba', *New Testament Studies* 2, 1965–6, 53–6.

E. Ullendorff, *Ethiopia and the Bible*, London, 1968.

E. Ullendorff, *The Ethiopians*, 3rd ed., London, 1973.

C. H. Walker, *The Abyssinian at Home*, London, 1933.

J. Van Seeters, *In Search of History: Historiography in the Ancient World and the Origins of Biblical History*, New Haven and London, 1983.

J. Van Seeters, *The Life of Moses: The Yahwist as Historian in Exodus–Numbers*, Louisville, Kentucky, 1994.

R. de Vaux, 'Les Chérubins et l'arche d'alliance, les sphinx gardiens et les trônes divins dans l'ancien orient', in *Bible et Orient*, Paris, 1967, 231–59.

M. Walzer, *Exodus and Revolution*, New York, 1984.

J. Wellhausen, *Die Composition des Hexateuchs und der historischen Bücher des Alten Testaments*, 3rd ed., Berlin, 1899.

A. J. Wensinck, *The Ideas of the Western Semites concerning the Navel of the Earth*, Verhandelingen der Koninklijke Akademie van Wetenschappen te Amsterdam, n.s. 17.1, Amsterdam, 1916.

K. W. Whitelam, *The Invention of Ancient Israel*, London, 1996.

Y. Yadin, *The Temple Scroll*, London, 1985.

Index

Aaron, brother of Moses 15, 22, 39, 46, 49–50
  rod of 50, 110, 114, 115, 138, 208–9, 225, 319, 345
  sons killed by Presence 49, 141
Abraham, patriarch 6, 18, 100, 154
Abreha (Abramos), king of Himyar 235
  expedition to Mecca 235–6, 238
Abu Salih, chronicler 238, 239, 252, 256, 258, 283, 314, 337
  Ark of Lalibela ('Ark of the Covenant') 250–2, 256, 257, 340
  Coptic altar boards 255
Aisha, wife of the Prophet 186–7, 190
Akhenaten, heretical Egyptian pharaoh 300–1
akitu festival 97
Aksum 1–3, 5–7, 10, 29, 42, 53, 193, 217
  altar stone from Jerusalem 284
  church dedicated to Mary of Zion 193, 222–3, 268, 275, 345
  Ark appears at *Timqat* festival 314
  Ark of the Covenant 222, 223, 252–3, 282–4, 292, 310, 342
  Chapel of the Tablet 275, 279, 280, 282, 291
  great idol 283–4
  guardian of the Tablet 275–7
  Tablet of Covenant of Mercy 282
  Tablet of Mary (from Caesarea) 280, 282, 310
  Tablet of Moses 275, 279, 280, 282, 286, 337

  Tablet of Ten Commandments 288–91
  tabotat 280, 287–8, 291, 310
  coinage 219
  conversion to Christianity 219, 222
  coronation rites revived by Solomonids 261, 266–8
  cultural interchange with South Arabia 216–17
  dabtara 277, 278–81, 310–11, 312
  coded writing 279
  origin of title 277–8
  singing and dancing 310, 311
  expedition against Dhu Nuwas 234–5
  Kaleb, king of 229, 234–5, 236, 338
  neburaed of 223, 261, 272–4, 280–2
  similarities with rock churches of Lalibela 244
  stelae 217–18, 288, 310
Ali ibn Abi Talib 186–7, 190
Alvares, Francisco 217, 223, 240, 243, 244, 257, 283–4, 341
  on festival of *Timqat* 312–14
Amda Seyon, emperor 260, 273, 274, 278, 314
Arab shrines *see mahmal; markab*
Ark of the Covenant (Ark of Zion) 8, 10, 20–3, 81
  abbey of St Denis 320–1
  absent from lists of Temple goods 109, 111
  alternatives 7, 8, 29, 35, 105, 339
  at Ashdod, Gath and Ekron 56
  at Beth-shemesh 57
  at Gibeon 52

361

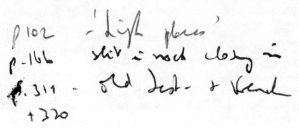